Congress Oversees the United States Intelligence Community

Congress Oversees the United States Intelligence Community, 1947–1989

Frank J. Smist, Jr.

The University of Tennessee Press

KNOXVILLE

Library of Congress Cataloging in Publication Data

Smist, Frank John, 1951–
    Congress oversees the United States intelligence community,
1947–1989   /   Frank J. Smist, Jr.
        p.   cm.
    Revision of author's thesis (Ph. D.)—University of Oklahoma,
1988.
    Includes bibliographical references.
    ISBN 0-87049-649-2 (cloth : alk. paper) :
    ISBN 0-87049-651-4 (pbk. : alk. paper)
    1. Intelligence service—United States.   2. Legislative oversight—
United States.   3. United States—Politics and government—1945–
I. Title.
JK468.I6S53   1990
327.1′273—dc20   89-70511   CIP

To my mother, Victoria Smist,
and my wife, Shirley,
with love and appreciation.
This book would not have been possible
without your love, support, and
encouragement.

Contents

List of Tables   ix

Preface   xi

1   Congress and Intelligence: An Overview, 1776–1989   1

2   Investigative and Institutional Oversight Combined:
    The Church Senate Committee, 1975–76   25

3   Institutional Oversight Triumphant: The Inouye, Bayh,
    and Goldwater Senate Select Committees, 1976–84   82

4   Investigative Oversight Triumphant: The Nedzi and Pike
    House Committees, 1975–76   134

5   The Reemergence of Institutional Oversight in the House:
    The Boland Committee, 1977–84   214

6   Congress and Intelligence, 1985–89: A Look Back
    and a Look Ahead   252

Notes   283

Bibliography   309

Interviews   315

Index   327

Tables

1. Two Models of Congressional Oversight: Institutional versus Investigative   20
2. Membership of Church Committee (1975–76)   29
3. Membership of Inouye Committee (1976)   86
4. Membership of Bayh Committee I (1977–78)   87
5. Membership of Bayh Committee II (1979–80)   88
6. Membership of Goldwater Committee I (1981–82)   89
7. Membership of Goldwater Committee II (1983–84)   90
8. Membership of Nedzi Committee (1975)   137
9. Membership of Pike Committee 1975–76)   138
10. Membership of Boland Committee I (1977–78)   218
11. Membership of Boland Committee II (1979–80)   219
12. Membership of Boland Committee III (1981–82)   220
13. Membership of Boland Committee IV (1983–84)   221

Preface

The publication of this book marks the completion of a journey that began over ten years ago. In August 1979 I began a year's study as a University Fellow at Georgetown University. It was my good fortune to fall under the influence of two exceptional teachers and scholars, James Lengle and Ray Cline. From Lengle I became fascinated with the U.S. Congress as a political institution. From Cline I learned about the U.S. intelligence community and its importance to national security.

A year later I began doctoral studies at the University of Oklahoma as one of the first four Carl Albert Fellows. Under the direction of Ronald Peters, Gary Copeland, and Steve Ballard my studies focused upon congressional committees, oversight, and the U.S. intelligence community. For my doctoral dissertation I decided to examine how the Congress conducted oversight of the U.S. intelligence community from 1947, when the CIA was created, through 1984.

In the fall of 1982 I became the first Carl Albert Fellow to participate in the Congressional Fellows Program sponsored by the American Political Science Association. Fellows work on Capitol Hill for a full year dividing their time equally between the House and Senate. My first assignment was with the chairman of the House Democratic Caucus, the late Representative Gillis W. Long of Louisiana. Then, on the Senate side, I worked with the Senate Republican Steering Committee.

My year in the Congressional Fellows Program was one of the most exciting times in my life. I accompanied Mr. Long on a district trip to Louisiana. I was also the guest of the Canadian government in Ottawa for a week in April 1983 when I was invited to observe how a parliamentary system differs from our own. Every week brought each of us in the program new insights into how our government really works.

The highlight of my Washington experience was the field research for my doctoral dissertation. My doctoral committee had given me a target of thirty interviews; I did more than five hundred. When I began I sought to interview chairmen, members, and staffers from the intelligence oversight committees as well as members of the executive branch and intelligence community. I particularly sought out individuals from the Central Intelligence Agency, Federal Bureau of Investigation, and National Security Agency. In addition I sought out members of the press and groups particularly interested in this area.

Fortunately, when I began my research, most of the key individuals were still alive and were willing to be interviewed. Political scientists can never attain the objectivity that can be found in the laboratories of natural scientists or the calculations of mathematicians, but they must attempt to attain such objectivity. In the intelligence area there is considerable controversy. I sought to listen to all sides of issues and attempted to let the burden of the evidence shape my final assessments.

The information I received from my interviewees is a critical component of this book. I taped interviews with David Aaron, Harold Brown, Frank Carlucci, and William Colby. For the rest I took detailed notes which I typed up within twenty-four hours and returned to the interview subject. My shortest interview was fifteen minutes while my longest was six hours. I did most of my interviews in person but did several over the telephone. I interviewed most of my sources more than once.

In the bibliography I have included a partial list of interviewees. Many requested that I not quote them directly in the text and some requested that I not include their names in the bibliography. I have honored these requests. For future scholars I have donated all my papers to the Carl Albert Congressional Research and Studies Center on the University of Oklahoma's Norman campus. Included in this collection are the four interview tapes, the more than two thousand pages of typed interview notes, and the public source material I collected. I have also given the center a copy of this book with all of the confidential interview sources identified. I am grateful to archivist John M. Caldwell for all his assistance.

Many individuals gave graciously and generously of their time and themselves while I wrote my doctoral dissertation and later adapted and expanded it into this book. I am grateful to Carol Orr, director of the University of Tennessee Press, and Cynthia Maude-Gembler, acquisitions editor. I especially appreciate the work of Stan Ivester, manuscript editor at the Press, whose excellent copyediting improved the manuscript and whose sense of humor made my own work much easier.

The Carl Albert Congressional Research and Studies Center was a great place to study. I am especially grateful for all the support and encouragement I received from the director, Ron Peters. Gary Copeland was both an outstanding teacher and a good friend. I am also glad I was associated with former Carl Albert Fellows Matt Moen, Ron Grimes, Mike Sharp, and Doc Syers.

To Chattar Samra, Velma Foree, and especially to Gary and Joanna Storm, thanks for your support and love.

I also am especially grateful to six of my interviewees for giving so generously of themselves to help educate me: David Boren, John Elliff, Lee Hamilton, the late Bryce Harlow, Bobby Inman, and Walter Pforzheimer.

Loch Johnson and Fred Kaiser read the entire manuscript and offered helpful advice that I have tried to incorporate. I also received valuable support and encouragement from Brint Hilliard, Jeanetta Horne, Tom Dowdy, Paul Rutledge, Clark Jolley, Scott Weaver, and Mrs. John W. Raley.

My research assistant Brad Lovelace was invaluable. My typist Paula Thompson was patient and extremely efficient. Finally, Brent Thompson was super in his encouragement and in helping me get both the dissertation and the book manuscripts in on time.

On April 20, 1989, I accepted appointment as the first director of global studies at Rockhurst College in Kansas City, Missouri. Chuck Moran and Tom Trebon are two colleagues I value highly and whose friendship I truly treasure. M. Kay Dellinger, my administrative assistant, and Jeff Lodermeier have helped ease my workload at the Global Studies Center.

At Rockhurst College I am delighted to work under President Thomas J. Savage, S.J. Not only has he taught me that the sun "rises in the East and sets in Wyoming," but he represents the very best in Jesuit education, living out in his own life the Jesuit ideals of wonder, freedom, and commitment.

Others at Rockhurst to whom I am endebted for their assistance and encouragement include Sister Michaela M. Zahner, Sister Gertrude Patch, Joan Caulfield, Dan Petree, Tom Audley, Larry Padberg, Fern Gregory, Sister Rosemary Flanigan, and Bob Jacobi.

Finally, family members whose love and support I will treasure until the day I die include my brother Michael, Mary and Walter Stachowicz, Mary and Gwinn McCormick, and Gwen and Dick Wilburn.

Of course, I myself accept full responsibility for any errors of fact or judgment.

**Congress Oversees
the United States
Intelligence Community**

1 Congress and Intelligence:
An Overview, 1776–1989

Congress and Intelligence: 1776–1947

When the Founding Fathers wrote the United States Constitution at Philadelphia in the summer of 1787 they devised a system of government characterized by the separation of powers and by checks and balances. The Founders were very concerned with the problem of governmental tyranny, which they defined as the concentration of all executive, legislative, and judicial power in the same hands. To prevent this from occurring, the Founders, as James Madison observes in *Federalist Paper* 51, sought to give to each of the branches "the necessary constitutional means and personal motives to resist encroachments of the others." [1] The Founders sought to have ambition counteract ambition. Concerning foreign policy, the Founders gave the president the power to appoint ambassadors and negotiate treaties but required that the president also seek the "advice and consent" of the Senate. In *Federalist Paper* 64, John Jay observed that, with respect to treaty making, "perfect secrecy and immediate dispatch are sometimes requisite." [2] Jay also noted that under the system devised by the Founders the president "will be able to manage the business of intelligence in such a manner as prudence may suggest." [3]

Throughout American history, intelligence has had an important role to play in foreign policy. From the time of the American revolution until World War II, intelligence entities were developed during times of war and then reduced in size and influence after the conflict ended. In fact, during the American Revolution, General George Washington himself became our first great spymaster. Discussing the role of intelligence, Washington wrote to Colonel Elias Dayton on July 26, 1777:

> The necessity of procuring good intelligence is apparent & need not be further urged. All that remains for me to add, is that you keep the whole matter as secret as possible. For upon Secrecy, Success depends in most

> Enterprizes of the kind, and for want of it, they are generally defeated, however well planned & promising a favourable issue.[4]

During the American Revolution, the Continental Congress itself ran intelligence operations through its Secret Committee which devised and approved covert actions, and its Committee of Secret Correspondence which dealt with secret agents.[5]

Prior to World War II, intelligence was an issue primarily during wartime. There are few examples of intelligence issues during peacetime. For example, in his first message to the Congress in 1789, President Washington asked for and received authority to create a Foreign Intercourse Fund. A portion of the monies appropriated to this fund were accounted for solely on the certificate of the president and were used for secret activities. The Congress codified this legislation in 1810.[6] In 1847, when Congress sought to learn how funds appropriated under this area were being spent, President Polk sent a letter to the House claiming, in effect, executive privilege, and the Congress did not seek to pursue the matter further.[7] Up until World War II, the United States created military intelligence units only during major conflicts such as the Civil War and World War I. After hostilities ended, most of these units were downgraded and deemphasized.

Yet all this was to change radically as a result of the Japanese attack on Pearl Harbor on December 7, 1941. This attack caught the American naval and army forces there by surprise. Prior to this attack, American intelligence had broken the Japanese diplomatic cipher and had intercepted and deciphered messages that gave clear and definite indications that the Japanese intended to attack Pearl Harbor. Unfortunately, because of the fragmented nature of American intelligence, key Japanese messages were not decrypted in a timely fashion, and the most important intelligence information was disseminated slowly to key policy makers in Washington and never disseminated to the military commanders in Hawaii. Consequently, Pearl Harbor is best described as an "intelligence failure."[8]

Following World War II, key policy makers in both the executive and legislative branches were determined that the mistakes and problems that had led to the intelligence failure at Pearl Harbor would not be repeated. In 1947 Congress considered legislation creating a central intelligence agency and unifying the military services. Clark Clifford, who helped draft this legislation for President Truman, recalled Truman's directions to him:

> Truman said: "We have two great lessons from World War II. One was we could never again be without a permanent operating intelligence agency. The different branches of the government received volumes of information

that would come in daily. No central location was there where all the information could be centered, collated, and studied. If we had such an operation, we could have very well had the naval base prepared at Pearl Harbor. The information was never centralized and studied. Second was that we could never go through another war with the Navy Department and the War Department as separate operations in competition one with the other. If the army or navy had given as much time to defeating the enemy as they gave to fighting each other, the war could have been ended a good deal sooner." [9]

Congress therefore passed the National Security Act of 1947, creating not only the Central Intelligence Agency but the National Security Council and unifying the military services under the leadership of the secretary of defense and Joint Chiefs of Staff. It also created a separate air force. On September 18, 1947, the CIA formally came into existence. The director of central intelligence was to have access to all intelligence relating to national security and was to coordinate this information for the president. The CIA itself was to be both a central coordinator and central evaluator of intelligence information.

With the creation of the CIA a major new chapter was beginning in the history of American intelligence. After 1947 attempts continued to be made to coordinate American intelligence. At the same time intelligence entities proliferated.

On November 4, 1952, the National Security Agency, responsible to the secretary of defense, was established by presidential directive. On August 1, 1961, the Defense Intelligence Agency (DIA) was established by Defense Department directive. The National Security Agency is concerned with cryptography and code-breaking while the Defense Intelligence Agency coordinates intelligence for the Pentagon. Other major components of the intelligence community include the Federal Bureau of Investigation, the Department of State, the Department of Energy, the Department of the Treasury, the Drug Enforcement Administration, Army Intelligence, Navy Intelligence, Marine Corps Intelligence, and Air Force Intelligence.

While the Central Intelligence Agency is responsible for intelligence activities outside the United States, the Federal Bureau of Investigation is responsible for such activities conducted within the United States. The Department of State collects information from American diplomats overseas while the Department of Treasury collects economic information. The Energy Department collects information about nuclear programs as well as oil and other energy matters. The director of central intelligence (DCI), who also serves as director of the CIA, is supposed to direct the overall U.S. intelligence effort. However, the DCI's leadership is frequently challenged by the secretary of defense, who controls more than 80 percent of all intelligence expenditures. As a result, despite advances made in centralizing intelligence, the American intelligence community frequently resembles a collection of independent fiefdoms and baronies. Tension, competition, and division are inherent in such a system.

Congress and Intelligence: 1947–89

With the passage of the National Security Act of 1947 the Congress itself now had a new intelligence role. From 1947 until 1974 the executive branch dominated intelligence policy. Congress still had a significant role in that the legislative branch appropriated funds for the intelligence community. However, for the most part, the Congress was willing to defer to executive-branch leadership. The activities of the intelligence community were overseen by a few senior members of the Armed Services and Appropriations committees in each chamber and, virtually all of this oversight was conducted behind closed doors.

This interbranch cooperation on intelligence was due to two factors. First, executive and legislative branch members were sensitive to the need for a strong and effective intelligence community in light of the Pearl Harbor disaster. Second, there was agreement that the Soviet Union posed a grave danger to the United States and that only a policy of long-term, patient but firm and vigilant containment could protect the U.S. national security. [10]

Institutional Oversight Triumphant: 1947–74.
Following the creation of the CIA in 1947 intelligence oversight responsibility was entrusted by both the Senate and the House to their respective Armed Services and Appropriations committees. Each of these committees set up special intelligence subcommittees. The subcommittees were comprised of the full-committee chairman and the ranking minority party member along with two or three other committee members considered to be responsible and trustworthy.

As Lawrence R. Houston, general counsel of the CIA at this time, noted: "Security was impeccable. We never had the slightest breach." [11] The members put aside all partisan differences in their intelligence oversight activity. Staff was kept to a bare minimum. Subcommittee meetings were unannounced to shield the meetings from any public or press attention. Intelligence officials were not told the room in which a meeting would be held until an hour before it was scheduled. Before these meetings began, security officials swept the room for "bugs." However, no listening devices were ever discovered. Nothing was put in writing and no records were kept about these meetings. There was little input into the subcommittees from the public, press, or clientele groups. The subcommittees met only with the director of central intelligence or other high-ranking intelligence officials.

In conducting oversight hearings the subcommittees usually began by having the director of central intelligence give a quick overview of the world and current hotspots. The hearings frequently took on the appearance of an "insider's newspaper." [12] Within the intelligence community a standing rule was adopted that no question asked by members of the Armed Services and Appropriations subcommittees would go unanswered. However, the members frequently asked no questions. A former CIA legislative counsel at this time observed: "We allowed Congress to set the pace. We briefed in whatever detail they wanted. But one of the problems was you couldn't get Congress to get interested." [13] As Clark Clifford noted: "Congress chose not to be involved and preferred to be uninformed." [14]

Usually the subcommittees met only two or three times a year. And, although the subcommittees did not seek to learn much about U.S. intelligence activity, they were still interested in and supportive of what was happening in this area. The disposition of the subcommittee members was to leave the matter up to the executive branch. The president was the commander in chief and the chief formulator of foreign policy, and the Congress preferred to defer to executive leadership in intelligence matters. [15] When the CIA overthrew the governments of Iran in 1953 and Guatemala in 1954 the subcommittees were very supportive. In fact they were briefed by Director Dulles about the 1953 overthrow of Prime Minister Mossadegh of Iran only after it had occurred. Yet the committees supported this action strongly and, instead of being upset about not having been informed in advance, were only surprised about "how very cheaply" the ouster had been accomplished. [16] As former Congressman Robert F. Ellsworth observed:

> When you think back to the old days, it was a different world and a different perception of us and our role in the world. The political zeitgeist of the time was that the CIA was wonderful. In politics, anybody who wanted to make trouble for the CIA was seen to be a screwball and not to be countenanced. [17]

This was the attitude that permeated the intelligence oversight subcommittees.

Throughout the entire 1947–74 period, Senate oversight of intelligence kept in the hands of the Armed Services and Appropriations committees. These two committees were dominated by members who firmly endorsed both U.S. intelligence and executive leadership in foreign affairs. Key senators on these committees included Styles

Bridges, Harry Byrd, Leverett Saltonstall, and later Stuart Symington and John Stennis.[18] Yet there was one individual and one alone in the United States Senate to pioneer in intelligence oversight and call all the shots: Senator Richard Russell. For Russell, the Senate was his life. Given the accolade "Mr. Senate" Richard Russell was a man of great talent and ability who had no hobbies, no wife, and no family. His life revolved around the Senate and in intelligence matters he dominated his colleagues regardless of what formal position he occupied in the body.[19] He served in the Senate from 1933 until 1971 and in that time became the dominant leader in both intelligence oversight and the workings of the Senate itself.

For a time Russell chaired both the Armed Services and Appropriations CIA subcommittees. Other key overseers and intelligence community supporters such as Carl Hayden, Leverett Saltonstall, and Margaret Chase Smith also had joint subcommittee memberships. During this period, there were two major challenges to Senator Russell's position on intelligence oversight. The response to these challenges by his colleagues demonstrated their trust in Russell.

Beginning in 1953 Senator Mike Mansfield pushed for the creation of a joint Senate-House CIA committee to oversee intelligence. The proposal (S. Con. Res. 2) was fully reported by the Rules Committee on February 23, 1956. In a letter to Chairman Theodore Francis Green of January 16, 1956, Russell stated his opposition to S. Con. Res. 2 in these terms:

> It is difficult for me to foresee that increased staff scrutiny of CIA operations would result in either substantial savings or a significant increase in available intelligence information. . . . If there is one agency of the government in which we must take some matters on faith, without a constant examination of its methods and sources, I believe this agency is the CIA.[20]

On April 11, 1956, the Mansfield resolution was defeated by a vote of fifty-nine to twenty-seven on the Senate floor.

Later, on July 14, 1966, Russell was challenged a second time. Senator J.W. Fulbright had introduced S. Res. 283 which would have set up a Senate Committee on Intelligence Operations composed of nine members from the Appropriations, Armed Services, and Foreign Relations committees. Once again Russell won, this time in a vote of sixty-one to twenty-eight. Following his victory Russell invited Foreign Relations Committee Chairman Fulbright and Senators Burke B. Hickenlooper and Mike Mansfield to sit in on his subcommittee hearings. Fulbright and his Foreign Relations colleagues actually attended a few of these meetings but found:

> They would never reveal anything of significance. They would never tell us how much money was being spent, where it was in the budget, or what

they were doing with it. There was no stenographic record kept and the oversight was neither thorough-going nor effective. All this was basically a device to silence the critics in the Senate.[21]

And it was an effective device at that.

Senator Richard Russell was a very successful practitioner of what I define as "institutional oversight." That is, he was a strong believer in intelligence and executive leadership in foreign affairs. Russell also used his position in the Senate to protect those he was overseeing. For example, in February 1967, the press disclosed that the CIA had secretly funded the National Students Association. In response to the uproar Senator Russell called a closed-door meeting of the CIA subcommittees with Director of Central Intelligence Richard Helms. After the meeting, Senator Russell let slip "accidentally" that he had known and approved of this funding from the very beginning. Following Russell's defense of the CIA, the story quickly disappeared.[22] This was the manner in which institutional oversight was implemented in the United States Senate in the Russell Era.

From the late 1940s through the mid-1970s, the House Armed Services Committee also practiced institutional oversight. The chairmen who dominated the committee included Carl Vinson (1949–53, 1955–65), L. Mendel Rivers (1965–71), and F. Edward Hebert (1971–75). All were strong advocates for the intelligence community and presidential leadership in foreign affairs.

Carl Vinson was a domineering chairman. He assigned numbers and not names to the Armed Services subcommittees so that they would know they controlled no particular turf. Vinson assigned all bills to subcommittees, and staff were not permanently assigned so that he could reposition them as he wished. As chairman, Vinson was a complete autocrat. While Lyndon Johnson was a member of the committee, he asked Vinson during a public hearing: "Mr. Chairman, when can I ask a question?" Chairman Vinson replied: "You just have. Sit down." And Lyndon Johnson sat down.[23]

With respect to intelligence oversight, Vinson was a strong supporter of those he was overseeing. He believed there was no need to dig too deep into methods and operations. Intelligence oversight was conducted by an executive committee of five senior members with a three-to-two party ratio. There was one staff member. No records were kept of committee meetings, and members had a great amount of trust in the intelligence community. This was more a "stay in touch" committee rather than a "vigorous oversight" operation. The members were concerned about needless congressional "meddling" with intelligence.[24]

A similar attitude prevailed under the chairmanship of L. Mendel Rivers, during whose time the oversight process was formalized.

However, meetings were unannounced, and no transcript was kept of them. According to the principal staffer at the time, the intelligence-community people did a good job in answering questions but "only if we asked the right questions." All that survived the oversight meetings was the personal memories of the participants. The relationship between the intelligence overseers and their counterparts in the intelligence community was punctuated by a good amount of trust.[25] The House Armed Services Committee functioned as proponents and supporters of those they were overseeing. The House Appropriations Committee also had an important role in intelligence oversight. As set forth in Richard Fenno's *The Power of the Purse*, the House Appropriations Committee was a firm defender of the House's prerogative to cut executive budget requests. Yet, with respect to intelligence, the Appropriations Committee did not function in accord with the model Fenno sets forth in his work. Under Chairman Clarence Cannon intelligence oversight was done by a special five-member subcommittee personally selected by the chairman. As later–House Appropriations Chairman George H. Mahon recalled, "Mr. Cannon totally dominated the subcommittee" and used oversight hearings as opportunities to swap war stories with Allen Dulles, the director of central intelligence.[26] The oversight was conducted in an extremely loose way. The members thought they should not really know these things. The intelligence community must be trusted and not pressed on anything. Funding requests were almost automatically approved, and the subcommittee had only one or two meetings a year with the DCI. It was a very rare occasion when a budget hearing would go to a second day.[27]

A similar situation initially prevailed during the chairmanship of George H. Mahon. Members were very carefully selected for the CIA subcommittee. All "headline hunters" and those considered "irresponsible" were automatically excluded.[28] Although the budget was reviewed in more detail, Appropriations staff had to go to CIA headquarters to see files and documents, and no material or notes could be taken from the CIA. Intelligence officials would periodically bring classified materials with them to Capitol Hill to be used at closed-door hearings. However, because there was no place to store classified material, none of this material could be left when these hearings were over. Although at times some attention was given to the budgets of the Defense Intelligence Agency, the National Security Agency, and the military services, the overall exercise of oversight on intelligence budgets was terribly weak and ineffective.[29] Intelligence was the only area where House Appropriations was an advocate and proponent of increased spending rather than an avid budget cutter.

All four committees—the House and Senate committees on Appropriations and Armed Services—were practitioners of institutional oversight. All were strong supporters and advocates of the very intelligence community they were overseeing. The intelligence community, in turn, was extremely responsive to the demands of the overseers. For example, when the chairman of the Senate Appropriations Committee wanted film of his foreign travels developed, the CIA was happy to oblige.[30] Likewise, when a ranking Republican member of the House Appropriations Committee, Congressman Gerald R. Ford, expressed a desire to meet a real live Soviet defector, the CIA was quick to arrange such a meeting.[31] But, in terms of asking the hard questions as to the merits and costs of specific programs and activities, these committees rarely got involved.

In the closed-door oversight conducted by these committees, secrets did not leak. In fact, when one senior member of the Appropriations Committee told a staffer seeking a job with the intelligence community about material discussed in a classified briefing, the member was disciplined by his colleagues and was never allowed to again sit on a classified intelligence appropriations hearing.[32] Yet the advocacy oversight practiced by these committees was to hurt the intelligence community in the years ahead. Intelligence professionals excused this failure by explaining that Congress was too busy. However, the lack of vigorous and critical oversight gave the intelligence professionals a freedom of action that they freely used to their advantage. As former CIA General Counsel Lawrence R. Houston ruefully observed: "Congress was too busy. But it was our fault too. Throughout the late 1950s and 1960s, we became a little too cocky about what we could do. Administrations developed a habit of looking to us to handle the tough ones.[33] Unfortunately for the intelligence community the failure of the Congress to do no more than advocacy oversight led the CIA and the other intelligence agencies to engage in activities that would be both carefully and publicly examined in the years ahead by congressional committees with a very different oversight mindset.

Congress and Intelligence: 1975–89
In 1975 a major change occurred in the way Congress dealt with the U.S. intelligence community. In the aftermath of Vietnam and Watergate considerable distrust of the executive branch existed within the Congress. On December 22, 1974, the *New York Times* published a front-page article by Seymour Hersh charging that the CIA, in direct violation of its charter, had "conducted a massive, illegal domestic intelligence operation during the Nixon Administration against the antiwar movement and other dissident groups in the United States." [34] On January 14, 1975, President Ford appointed a commission headed

by Vice-President Nelson Rockefeller to investigate the Hersh charges. In the past the Congress had been content to defer to executive-branch leadership in this area. Now, it was not.

On January 27, 1975, the United States Senate appointed a select investigative committee under the leadership of Senator Frank Church to investigate charges of illegal and improper intelligence-community activities. The committee was also given a mandate to recommend to the Senate how to correct any deficiencies it found. The Senate Select Committee to Study Governmental Operations with Respect to Intelligence Activities was in existence for fifteen months. The Church committee conducted an exhaustive investigation. In public the committee conducted twenty-one days of hearings. Besides an interim report on assassination plots, the committee released six final reports and seven volumes of hearings. It made 183 recommendations to the Senate on how to improve foreign and military intelligence and how to protect the rights of Americans. In carrying out its Senate mandate, the Church committee had conducted one of the most sweeping and intensive investigations in the history of the Senate.

Like the Senate, the House also created a select investigative committee to examine the intelligence community. On February 19, 1975, a House Select Intelligence Committee of ten members was created under the chairmanship of Representative Lucien Nedzi. However, unlike the Senate inquiry, the Nedzi committee's investigation never got off the ground. First the committee was unable to agree on a staff director. Then the committee's Democrats revolted when they learned that Chairman Nedzi, a Democrat himself, had done nothing when he had learned of intelligence abuses while serving as the principal intelligence overseer on the House Armed Services Committee. The Nedzi committee self-destructed.

On July 17, 1975, the House created a second select intelligence committee, this time with thirteen members under the chairmanship of Representative Otis Pike. The Pike committee also had a mandate to investigate abuses and make recommendations. Altogether the Pike committee conducted twenty-eight days of public hearings. Like its predecessor, the Pike committee was racked by internal dissension. At the same time open warfare broke out between the committee and the executive branch. On January 29, 1976, the House repudiated the Pike committee when it voted 246 to 124 to suppress the committee's final report. Later, when a draft copy of the committee's final report was leaked to the press, the House voted 269 to 119 on February 19, 1976, to conduct an official investigation into the leaking. All thirteen members of the Pike committee and thirty-two staff members were compelled to testify under oath about the leaking of the report. The intelligence investigators of the Pike committee had themselves become the subject of a hard and searching examination.

Following the intelligence investigations of 1975 to 1976, the Senate and House created permanent select intelligence committees. On May 19, 1976, the Senate voted seventy-two to twenty-two to create a permanent intelligence committee. There was a natural progression from the Church committee to the Senate's permanent select intelligence committee. However, the situation was entirely different in the House of Representatives where not until July 1977 was a permanent select intelligence committee created. This new House committee went out of its way to disassociate itself from the Nedzi and Pike committees. In the history of the Congress there has never before been a permanent select committee. Both permanent committees are similar to standing committees in that they have the authority to recommend legislation. However, the fact that both are select committees places the appointment of members solely in the hands of the party leaders. This phenomenon represents a reversal of the trend toward subcommittee decentralization that characterized reform efforts in both houses during the 1970s.

From 1976 to 1984 the permanent Senate Select Committee on Intelligence had three different chairmen. Senator Daniel Inouye (1976–77) and Senator Birch Bayh (1977–80) were both Democrats while Senator Barry Goldwater (1981–84) was a Republican. The Senate committee continued the work begun by the Church committee and considered legislative proposals, such as a charter for the intelligence agencies and protection of Americans' rights as citizens, that were made by the Church committee in its final reports. The permanent committee also set in place oversight structures to examine intelligence budget requests and covert action proposals by the president. For the first time an annual intelligence authorization bill was put into place so that the Congress both authorized and appropriated money for the intelligence community.

From 1977 to 1984 the House Permanent Select Committee on Intelligence was chaired by Representative Edward Boland, a Democrat from Massachusetts. The House committee represented a clear break from the work begun by the Nedzi and Pike committees. Under the leadership of Chairman Boland, the House committee sought to prove that it, unlike its predecessors, could be trusted with classified information. Like the Senate committee, the House committee established structures to oversee both the budget of the intelligence community and covert action proposals.

This book examines the interaction of the executive and legislative branches in the area of intelligence policy. It suggests that the congressional committee is the appropriate institution to study in order to understand congressional intelligence oversight. The work of the oversight committees will be examined in two distinct time periods: 1975 to 1976 and 1976 to 1984. A concluding chapter will examine developments in this area from 1985 to 1989.

Theoretical Problems

One of the most significant tasks entrusted to the legislative branch by the Founding Fathers is the responsibility of the Congress to oversee the activities of the executive branch. There are three questions for oversight to address. First, is the executive branch obeying the law and conducting activities in accord with the mandates provided by the United States Constitution and legislation passed by the Congress? Second, are there any abuses that have arisen or any deficiencies that have been uncovered that need to be corrected? Finally, in the light of both time and events, how can the performance of a function of government deemed essential and entrusted to the executive branch be both improved and strengthened? When they engage in oversight activity, congressional overseers address these primary questions.

In conducting oversight Congress is engaging in an activity essential to the conduct and survival of representative democracy in the United States. Integral to the system of government created by the Founding Fathers are the concepts of authorization and accountability. Congress authorizes executive-branch activity when it passes legislation, approves agency budgets, and confirms executive appointments. Through its conduct of oversight, the Congress also demands accountability from the executive. As the Congress has evolved as an institution, both the Senate and the House of Representatives have chosen to entrust oversight responsibility to specific congressional committees. Usually the committees engaging in oversight activity are assisted in their efforts by input from other members of Congress, constituents, clientele groups, and the press. In addition, most oversight activity takes place in public and is accessible and visible to all who have an interest. Consequently the congressional committees that engage in oversight activity are agents of both their parent chamber and the general citizenry.

However, in the intelligence area, there are some special conditions that radically alter the manner in which oversight is conducted. The key factor that distinguishes intelligence oversight from other types of oversight is the inherent secrecy permeating this entire policy area. For congressional overseers outside the intelligence area, high public visibility is a common and normal characteristic of congressional oversight. These overseers and the press and the public have access to considerable information about most activities being examined. A relationship develops in which there is interplay between the overseers and both the press and the public. However, due primarily to the sensitivity of the subject matter, the congressional oversight of intelligence takes place for the most part behind closed doors.

As a result, some problems and issues have arisen with respect to congressional oversight of intelligence that touch upon fundamental questions of democratic theory. Since 1947 a consensus has existed within both the executive and legislative branches that intelligence is of vital importance to the national interest of the United States. Like other public policy areas, intelligence is characterized by a separation of powers between the branches. Although intelligence is an area of critical importance to the executive branch, the Congress retains a vital oversight role that includes elements of authorization and accountability, wherein the most critical problem arises. How is the Congress to conduct oversight in a policy area deemed of great importance by both the executive and legislative branches but characterized by legitimate needs for secrecy and security that exist in few other policy areas?

On the one hand, if Congress conducts oversight that is too public, then the danger exists that the oversight process itself could harm or gravely damage public policy in a vital area. On the other hand, if the inherent secrecy of the policy area, the lack of input from the press and public, and excessive congressional concerns about maintaining security lead to an oversight that is truncated and ineffective, then the necessary oversight required to permit the system of separation of powers and checks and balances to function will not occur. Consequently, congressional overseers in the intelligence area must walk a fine line to avoid conducting oversight that will either irreparably damage a vital governmental function or be so weak that it is meaningless.

In the entire period from 1947 to 1989 the Congress has struggled to find a path that avoids both these pitfalls. As a result, the examination of how this struggle has unfolded will be a central focus of this book. The struggle itself has serious implications for the democratic theory at the very core of representative democracy in the United States.

This book is a study of congressional oversight of the United States intelligence community from the creation of the CIA in 1947 through

1989. It builds upon the work already done by political scientists on congressional committees, oversight, and the relationship between Congress and the executive branch in the intelligence area.

In order to understand and address the theoretical problems and issues in this study, it is necessary to have a detailed understanding of how congressional oversight of the intelligence community evolved in both the Senate and House. The time period considered is characterized by a transition from old to new approaches. In an examination of this transition the issues at stake become readily apparent as the Congress seeks to exercise intelligence oversight in the context of generally increasing its assertiveness and supremacy.

A careful qualitative study of the Senate and House investigating committees and their respective progeny provides insight and understanding of the various forces and issues that have come to shape and influence executive-congressional relations in this area. Such research is by necessity qualitative, requiring interviews with participants in the oversight process. In assessing the comments of the participants, differing views and interpretations of events will emerge. To resolve these differences, a careful and objective weighing of the evidence is the only way the material can be approached.

I used three sources of information in this research. First, I examined the public record, including the Church committee's seven volumes of hearings and seven volumes of reports as well as the Pike committee's four volumes of hearings and two volumes of committee proceedings. Although the Pike committee's final report was suppressed by the House of Representatives, a purloined copy was published in the *Village Voice* in special supplements on February 16 and 23, 1976, and by Spokesman Books in 1977. Similarly, I examined the published hearings and reports of the permanent intelligence oversight committees plus relevant issues of the *Congressional Record* and articles in the *New York Times* and *Washington Post*.

Second, I conducted extensive interviews. Altogether I conducted more than five hundred interviews with members of the Senate and House, congressional staff members, executive branch officials, members of the U.S. intelligence community, journalists, political scientists, and outside observers. Of special significance were interviews with Chairmen Stennis, Church, Inouye, Bayh, Boren, Nedzi, Pike, and Hamilton. I also interviewed key staff members of the oversight committees. In addition, I interviewed Richard Helms, William Colby, and Stansfield Turner, three directors of central intelligence, along with a considerable number of other executive-branch officials who dealt with and were affected by these committees. Moreover, I interviewed Seymour Hersh, whose stories in the *New York Times* led directly to the creation of the investigative committees, along with Philip Taubman and George Lardner, Jr., who covered this area for the *New York Times* and *Washington Post* respectively.

Third, I examined the scholarly research on intelligence oversight. Although this particular area has not been the focus of a great amount of research, two works merit special attention. The best book to date has been written by Loch Johnson, who served as Senator Church's personal designee on the Senate committee. His book *A Season of Inquiry* is a political scientist's personal memoir of the Church committee. It provides a valuable insider's perspective.[35] In addition I examined the recent work of Bob Woodward in *Veil: The Secret Wars of the CIA 1981–1987,*[36] an investigative reporter's highly critical assessment of congressional intelligence oversight.

Congressional Committees: The Fenno Model

I have employed a committee model that builds upon earlier committee research, especially the work of Richard Fenno. In *The Power of the Purse,*[37] Fenno studies the Appropriations committees of both the House and the Senate. Fenno conceives of the congressional committee as a distinct political system. As such it has certain identifiable and interdependent internal parts, it exists in and relates to an external environment, and it tends to stabilize its internal and external relationships over time. Internally the committee as a political system is concerned with its parent chamber, the other legislative chamber, executive agencies, and clientele groups. At this level the key problem for the committee is adapting to the demands of the other political actors. This view of the committee as a political system is indebted to the work of David Easton.[38]

According to Fenno the committee researcher seeks information in order to explain and predict committee behavior. Fenno believes there are three basic materials of description: (1) normative expectations of the various participants, (2) perceptions, attitudes, and images of the participants, and (3) the behavior of participants. Fenno also contrasts goal expectations (*what* others think the committee should do) with maintenance expectations (*how* others think the committee should do it). For Fenno, an in-depth examination of the House and Senate Appropriations committees and their place in the appropriations process is justified for the information it will yield. Even more importantly, such an approach will enable the political scientist to explain and possibly predict committee behavior.[39]

In *Congressmen in Committees* Fenno employs an analytical framework that builds upon the base he established in *The Power of the Purse,* an intensive study of the House Appropriations Committee. Fenno expands his analysis to consider six House committees: Appropriations, Ways and Means, Interior, Post Office, Education and Labor, and Foreign Affairs. He begins by assuming that congressional committees are an integral component of the legislative process and that they differ in important respects. House committees differ in terms of: (1) influence in congressional decision making, (2) autonomy, (3) success on the chamber floor, (4) control exercised by the chairman, and (5) domination by the executive branch. As a result, the comparative analysis of House committees is a subject worthy of study.

For Fenno there are five key variables that shape committee behavior. The independent variables are member goals and environmental constraints. These help to shape the intervening variable which Fenno terms "strategic premises" or decision rules. At the end of this process are the two dependent variables: the decision-making process itself and the decisions that result from this process. In *Congressmen in Committees* Fenno identifies significant differences in the independent variables that affect committee decision processes. For example, with respect to member goals, House members seek: (1) reelection, (2) influence within the House, and (3) good public policy. Regarding environmental constraints, Fenno delineates different degrees of pressure brought on committees by: (1) the parent chamber, (2) the executive branch, (3) clientele groups, and (4) members of the two major political parties. Differences in member goals and environmental constraints are found by Fenno to be characteristic of the committees he examines.[40]

Fenno divides House committees into two types. The first type has a House orientation in decision rules, an autonomous decision-making process, emphasis on committee expertise, success on the House floor, group identity, and more member/nonmember satisfaction. Examples of such committees include Ways and Means, Appropriations, and Interior. On the other hand, the second type has an extra-House orientation in decision rules, a permeable decision-making process, deemphasis on committee expertise, a lack of success on the House floor, weak group identity, and more nonmember/member satisfaction. Examples of such committees include Education and Labor, Foreign Affairs, Post Office, and all of the Senate committees.[41]

Fenno proposes further committee research building upon the framework he has established:

> We do not know enough to speak confidently of committees whose members we have not interviewed and whose performance we have not exam-

ined. Descriptive studies of congressional committees seem destined to continue. And for good reason. The bulk of congressional decisions will continue to be made by committees. We dare to hope that political scientists interested in other committees will find in this study an invitation to take its variables and categories and try them on for size.[42]

In *The Politics of Finance* John Manley, who continued the work of Fenno in his own study of the House Ways and Means Committee, quotes K. C. Wheare:

> The student of committees has to make a choice. Either he can try to hack his way through the jungle on foot or he can try to get a bird's eye view of the terrain from the air. If he chooses the first alternative, the most he can hope for is to clear a portion of his territory; if he chooses the second, the most he can hope for is to produce a rough sketch-map of the whole area.[43]

Both Manley and Fenno have chosen to clear a portion of congressional territory occupied by a single committee. The research I conducted as the basis for this book has been done in a similar fashion.

Intelligence Oversight Committees: The Internal and External Environments

Fenno has examined both the structure and function of particular committees. In carrying out their legislative responsibilities, oversight has been a peripheral and not the dominant concern of the work of these committees. For the committees I am going to examine in this book, oversight is why they exist. Consequently Fenno's work is useful in examining the structure of intelligence oversight committees but less helpful in understanding how these committees have functioned.

Using Fenno's structural model I view the Senate and House intelligence oversight committees as independent political systems. The dependent variables are the decision-making process adopted by each of the committees and the decisions that resulted from that process. The independent variables are the internal and external factors that shaped and influenced member and ultimately committee behavior. Questions I addressed in my research included: "What are the goals of members on these committees?" "What are the environmental constraints that affect the intelligence committees?" "How important and influential are the parent chamber, the executive branch, clientele groups, the press, and partisan considerations?" "What are the 'strategic premises' or decision rules that shape or determine member and committee behavior?" The search for answers to these questions suggests that the work of Fenno can be applied to research on the congressional committees that have conducted intelligence oversight.

But I found that there are several characteristics of intelligence oversight committees that appear to be unique. First, the committees are concerned with the secret function of government. Most of the work of these committees from 1947 to 1989 took place behind closed doors, with the notable exception of the 1975 to 1976 investigating committees, which were unique in the amount of work they conducted in public. Second, beginning with the Church and Nedzi committees, both chambers have chosen to entrust intelligence oversight to select committees. Very little research has been done on select committees. For example, in Keefe's and Ogul's *American Legislative Process* select committees are dismissed as of little significance and merit only two paragraphs.[44] In *Congressional Committees,* William L. Morrow observes that, in the past, select committees have provided useful information for Congress and the general public and have allowed the seniority system to be circumvented.[45]

The only other work of significance on select committees was done by V. Stanley Vardys, who found that House select committees functioned as educational institutions for both the House and the public and that they provided forums and service centers for interest groups that had inadequate access to regular standing committees.[46] Yet the select intelligence committees were a different kind of select committee from those previously examined by political scientists. The permanent Senate and House select intelligence committees (created in 1976 and 1977) were virtually standing committees. The only difference between them and true standing committees was the rotation of members (an eight-year limit in the Senate and a six-year limit in the House) and the fact that members were chosen directly by the party leaders and not through the normal party caucus procedures. Even with respect to the investigating committees of 1975 to 1976, the term "select committee" was not really appropriate. The debates on the floor and the interviews I conducted suggest that it was the widespread expectation in both chambers that the investigating committees would be incorporated in permanent successor committees. This occurred in the Senate but not in the House because the Pike committee was repudiated as a renegade by its parent chamber. As a result, despite both chambers having used select committees in this area, the committees created were a new and unique variation on the select committee model.

Third, with respect to the external environment, there are characteristics unique to the intelligence area. Because the committees created since early 1975 have all been select committees, party leaders have had a significant impact due to their responsibility for selecting the members. The party leaders also set the ratio of majority to minority party seats. The executive branch has had a special influence over the intelligence committees because of the secrecy involved. The executive branch, as gatekeeper, has controlled access to classified and sensitive information. And there has been a relative absence of input from clientele groups. Finally, the press has exerted significant external influence on these committees. The print media, especially the *New York Times* and the *Washington Post,* have framed the issues and played a crucial role as agenda setters for these committees.

Intelligence Oversight Committees: Two Oversight Models

All of the intelligence committees created since 1975 have been intended specifically to exercise oversight as their primary function. In the past four decades a considerable body of literature has been developed that is concerned with oversight and the way it is exercised by the Congress. A number of political scientists have done case studies of specific committees.[47] Recent work by Ogul and Aberbach includes lists of variables that facilitate oversight. For example, Ogul has identified twelve elements of what he calls an "oversight-maximizing syndrome."[48] However, all of these studies look at oversight as a secondary function of a committee. For the intelligence committees to be examined here, oversight is primary. In this respect these committees are unique creatures of the Congress. They combine the structural characteristics to be found on other committees with the primary function of doing oversight. As a result, Fenno's model, which he used to study committees whose primary purpose was not oversight, is not totally applicable to a study of intelligence oversight committees whose primary purpose is oversight. While his model is useful in understanding the structure of intelligence oversight committees, it is not very useful in understanding how these committees function in carrying out their oversight responsibilities. The intelligence oversight committees are unique committees worthy of further study.

For congressional intelligence overseers there are two distinct oversight models they can choose to adopt. It is important to note that, as I have used it in this book, the term "model" does not have the very formal sense found in some social science literature. Although the term will be used to describe the investigative and institutional oversight approaches, "model" as I have employed it throughout this study signifies more of an outlook, perspective, or attitude that characterizes the mindset and actions of the two different views of intelligence oversight.

The models developed here are unique. I have found nothing in the

Table 1.   Two Models of Congressional Oversight: Institutional versus Investigative

	Institutional Attitudes	*Investigative Attitudes*
Toward staff	Seeks Washington insiders: academics and national security careerists to understand institutions and processes.	Seeks outsiders: aggressive investigators and lawyers to unearth wrongdoing and deficiencies.
Toward parent chamber	Seeks to retain maximum approval and support. Responsible and responsive.	Seeks to educate members as well as press and public of need for corrective action. Aggressive, in danger of becoming renegade.
Toward executive branch	Deferential: tends to accept without question any information from executive. Seeks a partnership and common ground with minimum of conflict and controversy. Tends to become advocate for those it oversees; becomes co-opted or "educated." Wants to prove trustworthiness.	Suspicious: does not trust executive to provide unbiased information. Uses critics, GAO, outside consultants in adversarial relationship. Searches constantly for failures and abuses; enjoys seeing executive branch officials squirm. Greatest fear is becoming co-opted.
Toward press	Suspicious: sees press as sensationalistic; wants to maintain low visibility. Prefers closed-door private hearings; sees no role for press.	Views press as ally, communication vehicle to educate other members and public. Stages dramatic, sensational hearings to call attention to abuses.

scholarly literature that approaches oversight from this perspective. I developed these models while evaluating the conflicting views of oversight that emerged during the course of interviews I conducted with members and staff on the Church and Pike committees in early 1983. In subsequent interviews, I found this institutional-investigative distinction extremely helpful in understanding intelligence oversight for the entire 1947–89 period. I believe these models constitute a significant advance in oversight research. Scholars, intelligence overseers, those subject to intelligence oversight, and the general public should find them expecially useful as explanatory tools. Future scholars might also explore the possibility of applying these models to oversight conducted outside the intelligence area.

In examining the work of congressional intelligence overseers, I believe that the two models contribute significantly to an understanding of how these committees function. The models delineated here are based on an examination of the literature on oversight and on an analysis of the data collected in the course of research on the intelligence committees.

Table 1 shows the attitudes characteristic of members of Congress who practice institutional and investigative oversight. The four attitudinal relationships examined in Table 1 are the four most critical relationships in intelligence oversight. First, staff have an extremely important role in all oversight activity. Because of the enormous and varied demands on the time of members of Congress, much of the preparation for and conduct of oversight is of necessity delegated to staff. Second, the most essential relationship for all congressional committees is with their parent chamber. Committees are representatives of their parent chambers authorized to do their work and held accountable for their actions by the parent chamber. Third, the executive-branch relationship is extremely important. Intelligence oversight committees are examining work performed by the executive branch while the executive branch has control over committee access to evidence and witnesses. Fourth, the press, although not as important in the intelligence area as in other more public policy areas, exercises considerable influence in stimulating investigative activity. Moreover, congressional overseers may choose to use the press as a means of communication to educate their colleagues and the public about issues of concern.

The "Institutional Oversight" Model
The "institutional oversight" model sees oversight as a cooperative relationship between the legislative and executive branches. The oversight conducted is dominated by an attempt to understand institutions, focusing on their functioning, processes, and procedures. Both the legislative and executive-branch officials in this model see oversight as a way to strengthen and improve a function that both agree is necessary and proper. Oversight is viewed as not just policing for the sake of policing but as a means to see if the executive branch is: (1) in accord with the law, (2) achieving what it is supposed to be achieving, and (3) identifying areas that need to be strengthened or improved.

The practitioners of institutional oversight eschew conflict, controversy, and sensational publicity. Although oversight by its very nature tends to be adversarial, the practitioners of institutional oversight prefer to view oversight as supportive. They describe the relationship between their committee and the executive-branch officials and functions that they oversee in terms of mutual support: "lawyer-client," "parent-child," "a marriage with some rough spots at times," and "a partnership." Executive-branch officials come to view such oversight vehicles as "a secure forum where we can make our needs known and obtain relief." In addition, this kind of oversight is viewed by many in the executive branch as giving the intelligence community "more credibility."

For those who practice this type of oversight, there is an ever-present danger that they will be co-opted. Because practitioners of institutional oversight tend to seek consensus they frequently don't want to cause ripples or stir up criticism. In fact these overseers at times adopt the mindset of those they are overseeing. Members and staff on such committees see themselves as "careful" and "responsible." Frequently the staff members come from the intelligence community and return to it after their period of service in the Congress ends. Moreover, at times, an insider mindset develops where the members and staff see themselves as "clean" while outsiders are "unclean." Senator Church described this phenomenon in these terms: "It is a very heady experience to be behind the door when secrets are revealed. You are part of the elite group which knows what is going on. It is, to put it quite simply in one word: intoxicating." [49]

The "Investigative Oversight" Model
The "investigative oversight" model views oversight as involving an adversarial relationship between the legislative and executive branches. The oversight conducted is dominated by aggressive investigative activity. There is a constant searching for failures and abuses. Findings are revealed in dramatic hearings open to the press and the public. Conflict and controversy are frequently present. The key objective of such oversight is education, making both the Congress and the public aware of abuses, problems, and deficiencies.

Those who conduct investigative oversight tend to be characterized by a prosecutorial outlook. While the institutional model tends to be staffed by scholars, lawyers are the ideal staffers for investigative committees. Also, unlike the institutional overseers, investigative overseers go out of their way to prevent themselves from being co-opted. As one practitioner of this type of oversight noted: "You need guts, brains, and a willingness to deal with controversy. You never show any deference to anyone in the intelligence community." [50] At times the relationship between the legislative and executive branches is characterized by antagonism and animosity. Commenting upon the investigative overseers who visited CIA headquarters during the investigations of 1975 to 1976, one intelligence official who worked closely in coordinating their requests described them in these terms: "They were obnoxious. There was the atmosphere of drawn battle. They were continually trying to find evidence of wrongdoing or coverup."[51] Such a relationship was a far cry from the harmonious interbranch relations maintained in the institutional oversight model.

There are two other aspects that distinguish the investigative from the institutional model. First, many of the institutional staffers tend to be national security careerists. This means they tend to circulate among the congressional oversight committee, the intelligence community, and academia. A type of network mentality develops. At the same time, investigative staffers rarely, if ever, become national security careerists. The last thing these people would ever do is take a job within the intelligence community. Second, practitioners of the investigative oversight model frequently seek outside help. For example, during the investigations of 1975 to 1976, investigative overseers enlisted the assistance of the General Accounting Office and actively sought and obtained the testimony of intelligence-community critics and outsiders such as Samuel Adams (an ex-CIA employee who charged that General Westmoreland had engaged in a coverup in Vietnam) and Admiral Elmo R. Zumwalt, Jr. Practitioners of institutional oversight shuddered at the very thought of such tactics.

From 1947 to 1989 both the institutional and investigative models were utilized by the committees conducting intelligence oversight. As has already been noted, the oversight conducted by the Armed Services and Appropriations committees in both chambers from 1947 to 1974 was institutional. The Nedzi committee also attempted to conduct institutional oversight. The Pike committee adopted investigative oversight while the Church committee used both models. The permanent intelligence committees have increasingly implemented institutional oversight.

The intelligence oversight committees of the Congress are performing a service of great significance to the national security of the United States. The failure of both the executive and legislative branches to properly oversee intelligence prior to the Japanese attack on Pearl Harbor contributed to that intelligence failure. The congressional overseers in this area today are charged with a most important function. Nuclear weapons that can destroy the United States are less than thirty minutes away. An intelligence failure today along the lines of what occurred at Pearl Harbor could endanger the very existence of the

United States. In national security both the executive and legislative branches have important and at times conflicting responsibilities. The struggle of the Congress to achieve equality with the president in the intelligence area since 1947 illustrates a classic dilemma of American democracy that goes back to the very origins of the Republic. Moreover, intelligence overseers have to balance the government's legitimate interests in secrecy with the people's right to know what is going on in their government and how government funds are being expended. As former CIA Director Allen Dulles noted in his book *The Craft of Intelligence:* "It is necessary that both those on the inside—the workers in intelligence—and the public should come to share in the conviction that intelligence operations can help mightily to protect the nation." [52] The committees that conduct intelligence oversight are in a real sense ombudsmen; they are duly delegated representatives of both the Congress and the American people in this essential area. How well they do their work can have a significant impact upon the effectiveness of U.S. intelligence.

2 Investigative and Institutional Oversight Combined: The Church Senate Committee, 1975–76

In the aftermath of Watergate and the resignation of President Nixon in August 1974 serious questions were raised in the U.S. Senate about the propriety of activities of the U.S. intelligence community and the adequacy of Senate oversight in this area. On December 9 and 10, 1974, Senator Edmund Muskie chaired meetings of the Senate Government Operations Subcommittee on Intergovernmental Relations which examined proposals to strengthen congressional oversight of the nation's intelligence activities. At these hearings Senator Charles Mathias (R., Maryland) spoke strongly in favor of S. Res. 419, which he had co-sponsored with Senate Majority Leader Mike Mansfield (D., Montana). S. Res. 419 called for the establishment of an investigative committee to conduct a comprehensive inquiry of U.S. intelligence activities and to recommend how to improve Senate oversight. According to Mathias:

> It is quite clear that our foreign and our domestic intelligence agencies, including agencies that are so highly valued as the CIA and the FBI as well as other departments and agencies, have in the course of their activities violated the constitutional guarantees of citizens and have operated outside of normal constitutional processes. . . . there is an urgent need to determine exactly what our intelligence needs now are and how they can most effectively function under firm constitutional guidelines, providing for rigorous oversight and for accountability.[1]

At the same time Senator Howard Baker (R., Tennessee) argued for the passage of S. 4019 to create a joint Senate-House committee for legislative and oversight activity over the CIA, FBI, NSA, and DIA. Baker was especially critical of the existing oversight mechanisms:

> I believe it is clear that, as a whole, Congress possesses minimal information regarding the programs, goals, and extent of the federal intelligence community, that the current mode of congressional oversight of intelligence-gathering activities is inadequate, and that the ability of Congress to

participate with the president in the formulation of defense and foreign policies is significantly impaired as a result of this lack of information and oversight.[2]

Such sentiments represented a growing concern in the Senate in December 1974.

As noted earlier, on December 22, 1974, the *New York Times* published a front-page article by Seymour Hersh charging that the CIA, in direct violation of its charter, had "conducted a massive, illegal domestic intelligence operation during the Nixon administration against the antiwar movement and other dissident groups in the United States." Hersh reported that the CIA had maintained files on ten thousand American citizens and had engaged in break-ins, wiretapping, and the surreptitious inspection of mail. In some cases the abuses had begun in the 1950s.[3] Hersh's story was based on access he had been given to what Director of Central Intelligence William Colby named the "Family Jewels." The Family Jewels, compiled by Colby while James Schlesinger was director of central intelligence, consisted of 693 pages of possible violations of the law or questionable activities undertaken by the intelligence community. According to Colby the Family Jewels included: (1) Operation CHAOS, directed against the anti–Vietnam War movement, (2) surveillance and bugging of American journalists to trace security leaks, (3) CIA connections with the Watergate conspirators and the Nixon White House "plumbers," (4) the CIA's mail intercept program, (5) experiments with mind-control drugs, (6) CIA cooperation with police departments and other government agencies, and (7) assassination attempts. In December 1974 Colby himself was the director of central intelligence. In that capacity he had met with Hersh and confirmed those parts of the Family Jewels to which Hersh had been given access prior to the *New York Times* story of December 22, 1974.[4]

The Hersh story provoked an immediate reaction in both the executive and legislative branches. On December 23, 1974, Henry Kissinger, at the behest of President Ford, directed DCI Colby to report to the president the substance of the allegations contained in the Hersh newspaper article. On December 24 James Angleton, the head of the CIA's counterintelligence staff and director of the CIA's mail-intercept program, resigned from the agency. In late December, Colby reported to President Ford about the Family Jewels. According to Philip Buchen, counsel to the president, Ford wanted to create a commission, patterned after the Warren commission, to investigate the allegations against the intelligence community. Following President Kennedy's assassination in 1963 President Johnson had appointed an investigative committee headed by Chief Justice Earl Warren and including members of Congress. No separate Senate or House investigations of the

Kennedy assassination were held at that time. In December 1974 President Ford sought to create a joint commission from the executive and legislative branches to investigate the allegations against the intelligence community. However, as Buchen observed, "the times of LBJ were gone." This time the two houses of Congress would conduct their own investigations. The leadership in both houses turned aside Ford's offer of an interbranch commission. On January 4, 1975, Ford appointed a seven-member executive-branch commission headed by Vice-President Nelson Rockefeller to look into the charges of illegal domestic CIA activities. As Buchen observed, the Congress "simply disregarded the fact that there was a Rockefeller commission." [5]

For the United States Senate the Hersh article was the spark that led directly to the creation of a special Senate investigating committee. On January 15, 1975, DCI Colby testified before the Senate Appropriations Intelligence Operations Subcommittee. During the course of his closed-door testimony, Colby showed Chairman John L. McClellan and the other members an unclassified forty-five page report that confirmed much of what Seymour Hersh had already written about CIA domestic spying. Without consulting the White House, Colby agreed to McClellan's request to make the report public.[6] Two days later Senator Mathias, speaking for himself and Senators Mansfield, Muskie, and Baker, introduced S. Res. 19. Building upon the resolution that he and Mansfield had introduced the previous October, Mathias once against proposed the formation of a select committee to study all aspects of U.S. intelligence activities.

On January 20, 1975, the Senate's Democrats caucused and voted forty-five to seven to set up a bipartisan select committee to examine the U.S. intelligence community. Senator John Stennis, the principal overseer of the intelligence community on the Armed Services Committee, strongly and passionately spoke out against this proposal. However, within the caucus, Stennis was opposed by Senators Frank Church, Stuart Symington, Walter Huddleston, and Alan Cranston.[7] With the defection of moderates like John Pastore, a member of the McClellan subcommittee who was very upset by the material Colby had disclosed, Senator Stennis realized that his attempts to prevent the formation of a select committee were hopeless. In its own analysis of the caucus vote, the *New York Times* reported: "This is really the first time that John Stennis has gone to the mat and gotten decisively trounced." The *Times* observed that many senators and senior aides left the caucus talking about "the end of an era." [8]

On January 21 Senator Pastore introduced S. Res. 21, which flowed directly from the Senate Democratic Caucus vote of the day before. It called for the formation of an eleven-member select committee to investigate whether any "illegal, improper, or unethical" activities had been undertaken by any individuals or agencies in the U.S. intelligence community. Arguing in support of S. Res. 21 on the floor of the Senate, Pastore said he did not want a "witch hunt" conducted.[9] However, he noted that "I am afraid we will do irreparable harm to the security and survival of the country unless we do this." While stating that the intelligence agencies were "absolutely necessary for our security and our survival," [10] Pastore was equally concerned that the American people might lose their "confidence" in these agencies.[11] The Senate agreed. On January 27, 1975, S. Res. 21 was passed by a vote of eighty-two to four.

With the adoption of S. Res. 21 the Senate had made a dramatic change in the way it exercised intelligence oversight. Prior to the passage of this resolution, oversight was conducted by a few senior members of the Armed Services and Appropriations committees. As has already been noted, the oversight subcommittees met infrequently, held few formal sessions, and told the Senate and the public little. Now, however, the Select Intelligence Committee had been established by the Senate to perform a two-fold task: (1) to investigate charges of abuses, and (2) to propose legislative remedies to correct any abuses or deficiencies it might find.

Under the leadership of its chairman, Senator Frank Church of Idaho, the Select Intelligence Committee launched what turned out to be a fifteen-month investigation. The committee had 11 members (6 Democrats and 5 Republicans) and, at its peak, 150 staff members. Altogether the committee conducted over eight hundred interviews of individuals, held 126 full-committee meetings, held 40 subcommittee meetings, held 250 executive hearings, conducted twenty-one days of public hearings, amassed 110,000 pages of documentation, released to the public fourteen volumes of hearings and reports, and made 183 recommendations to the Senate. For the first time in American history, public hearings were conducted into the innermost workings of U.S. intelligence. Agency directors and personnel were compelled to testify under the glare of television lights.

Recruitment of Committee Members

Because the investigative committee created by S. Res. 21 was a select committee, members were appointed by the president of the Senate upon the recommendation of the majority and minority leaders. Unlike members of standing committees, who are chosen in the party caucuses, members of the Select Intelligence Committee were to be picked directly by the party leaders. The leaders were technically free

Table 2.   Membership of Church Committee (1975-76)

Member	Age	Years in Senate	1974 ADA Rating	1974 NSI Rating
Church	51	18	83	0
Phil Hart	63	16	100	0
Mondale	47	11	100	0
Huddleston	49	2	55	22
Morgan	50	0	—	—
Gary Hart	38	0	—	—
Democratic average	49.7	7.8	84.5	5.5
Tower	50	14	5	100
Baker	50	8	16	100
Goldwater	66	18	6	100
Mathias	53	6	90	11
Schweicker	49	6	85	33
Republican average	53.6	10.4	40.4	69.0
Committee average	51.5	9.0	60.0	61.0

Source: *Alamanac of American Politics 1976.*

to pick whoever they wanted. In addition, service on the select committee did not affect membership on standing committees. In effect, appointment was an additional committee assignment cost-free in its effect on standing committee assignments. The majority leader appointed six members to the select committee while the minority leader appointed five. The majority leader selected the chairman while the minority leader selected the vice-chairman.

For the Democrats, Majority Leader Mike Mansfield had a distinct philosophy about how committee appointments should be made, reflecting how he viewed the Senate as a political institution. For Mansfield the Senate was a body of one hundred equals. As former Mansfield aide Charles Ferris observed: "Mansfield was anti-elitist. He believed that there should not be super senators. The notion that there were giants in the Senate assumed there were pygmies." [12]

For the Select Intelligence Committee, Mansfield sought to appoint a cross-section of Senate Democrats. As Staff Director William Miller observed, "Mansfield was anxious to have a spread of youth and age." In making his selections Mansfield took into consideration prior interest and involvement in intelligence issues as well as whether members requested appointment to the select committee.[13]

Initially Mansfield designated Senator Philip Hart of Michigan to be chairman. In his sixteen years in the Senate the sixty-three-year old Hart had compiled a consistently liberal voting record. In fact in 1974 Hart received a 100 percent rating from the Americans for Democratic Action.[14] As a member of the Judiciary Committee, Hart had been a stern and vigorous defender of the rights of Americans. But, above all, Hart had earned the respect of his peers. He was viewed as a man of courage and integrity and had been called "the conscience of the Senate."[15] However, because he was seriously ill with cancer, Hart was unable to assume the chairmanship. Eventually Hart did become a Democratic member of the select committee but, because of his ill health, he was unable to participate fully.[16]

When Hart was unable to accept the chairmanship Mansfield turned to Senator Frank Church of Idaho. Church, the third-ranking Democrat on the Foreign Relations Committee, had in 1972 served as chairman of the Subcommittee on Multinational Corporations. Church's subcommittee had investigated the involvement of ITT and other multinational corporations in Chile and examined links between ITT and the CIA. In addition, in the Democratic Caucus of January 20, 1975, which considered S. Res. 21, Church had argued strongly for the creation of the Select Intelligence Committee. As Church himself recalled his appointment as chairman of the new committee: "I was chosen by Mansfield. I talked with him before the decision was made. I had no input on the choice of the other Democrats appointed to the select committee."[17]

Besides Church and Hart, Mansfield also appointed Mondale of Minnesota, Huddleston of Kentucky, Morgan of North Carolina, and Gary Hart of Colorado. Walter Mondale, the protégé of Hubert Humphrey, was at that time one of the leading liberals in the Senate. A former attorney general of Minnesota, Mondale was especially interested in domestic intelligence abuses. Like Church, Walter Huddleston had argued strongly in the Democratic Caucus for the creation of the Select Intelligence Committee. In addition, Huddleston was a member of the Appropriations Committee. Finally, both Robert Morgan and Gary Hart were appointed to the select committee even though they were both first-year members of the Senate. Each had requested assignment.[18] Morgan, like Mondale, had served as attorney general of his home state and was especially interested in domestic intelligence. Gary Hart, who had served in 1972 as the campaign manager for George McGovern's presidential campaign, was a new member of the Armed Services Committee.

The Democratic members of the select committee were a cross-section of liberal and moderate Senate Democrats. An examination of the past voting records of these members (Table 2) shows that on the 1974 ADA (Americans for Democratic Action) index, Philip Hart and Mondale had 100 percent ratings while Church was rated 83 percent. On the more conservative National Security Index (NSI), all three of these members rated 0 percent. In contrast, Huddleston had an ADA rating of 55 percent and an NSI rating of 22 percent. Although Morgan and Gary Hart had no previous Senate votes, Morgan was perceived as a moderate while Gary Hart was seen as being further to the left. As Staff Director William Miller observed, Huddleston and Morgan were from the "middle" of the party.[19]

In representation of standing committees, the Select Intelligence Committee contained members from the principal committees that dealt with the intelligence community: Appropriations, Armed Services, Foreign Relations, and Judiciary. However, with the exception of Church who ranked third on the Foreign Relations Committee and Philip Hart who ranked third on the Judiciary Committee, all of the other Democratic members ranked very low in seniority on the key oversight committees. Huddleston, for example, was ranked last among Democrats on Appropriations, and Gary Hart was next to last on Armed Services. Neither Mondale nor Morgan were on any of the four principal standing committees. Significantly, Mansfield did not appoint to the select committee any of the senior Democrats such as John Stennis, Stuart Symington, or John McClellan who had been the Senate's key intelligence overseers. On the Armed Services Intelligence Subcommittee there were four Democratic members. None of the four—Stennis, Symington, Howard Cannon, and Thomas McIntyre—was appointed to the Select Intelligence Committee. This was due both to Mansfield's deliberate choice and the fact that these members had no desire to sit on a committee that would be investigating their own past oversight efforts. As a result the Democratic members of the select committee represented a clean break with the past.

On the Republican side, Minority Leader Hugh Scott made the appointments for his party. Scott received letters requesting this assignment from Bob Dole, Paul Laxalt, Charles Mathias, Richard Schweiker, and Lowell Weicker.[20] In the end Scott included Mathias and Schweiker in his list of appointments. Unlike Mansfield, who had failed to appoint any of the old Senate overseers and supporters of the intelligence community, Scott appointed both staunch defenders and steadfast critics to serve on the select committee. Unlike Mansfield, Scott was caught in the middle between intelligence critics and the Ford administration which wanted the Republican leader in the Senate to protect its interests.

Scott named John Tower of Texas as vice-chairman. In addition Scott appointed Goldwater of Arizona, Baker of Tennessee, Mathias of Maryland, and Schweicker of Pennsylvania. Both Tower and Goldwater were members of the Armed Services Committee and staunch defenders of the intelligence community. Also appointed was Howard Baker, who had served as vice-chairman of the Senate Select Committee on Presidential Campaign Activities (the Senate Watergate Committee). On that committee Baker himself had focused attention on the CIA's involvement in Watergate. Baker was a member of both the Foreign Relations Committee and the Joint Committee on Atomic Energy. Moreover, he had cosponsored resolutions in 1974 and 1975 calling for a restructuring of Senate intelligence oversight. The final two Republican members were Charles Mathias and Richard Schweicker. Mathias, a member of the Appropriations and Judiciary committees, had cosponsored with Majority Leader Mansfield resolutions to create an intelligence investigating committee. Mathias was deeply disturbed by reports of intelligence-agency abuses. Finally, Richard Schweicker, a member of the Appropriations Committee, had been involved in intelligence oversight in both the House and Senate for ten years. Like Mathias, Schweicker saw a definite need to investigate alleged abuses.

The 1974 voting ratings of the five Republicans on the select committee show a definite contrast. Three senators—Tower, Goldwater, and Baker—have 100 percent scores on the NSI index and very low ADA scores. The other two Republicans—Mathias and Schweicker—have low NSI scores and high ADA scores. The Select Intelligence Committee as a whole, therefore, had five decidedly liberal members, three markedly conservative members, and one moderate. (See Table 2.)

As for committee assignments the Republican members of the select committee represented the four key standing committees. Mathias and Schweicker were both members of the Appropriations Committee, ranking eighth and ninth respectively. Goldwater and Tower were both members of the Armed Services Committee, ranking second and third. In addition Goldwater, the ranking Republican on the Armed Services Intelligence Subcommittee, was the only member of that subcommittee from either party to serve on the select committee. Baker was the seventh-ranking Republican on the Foreign Relations Committee. And Mathias was the fifth-ranking Republican on the Judiciary Committee.

In discussing how members were recruited for the select committee, Hugh Scott noted that "the members were picked by Senator Mansfield and myself." [21] The choices certainly reflected this bipartisan process. As Mansfield observed on the day the Church committee members were officially announced:

> The select committee is equipped with a bipartisan membership. The senators . . . selected for service on this committee are no different than the rest of us. They are not tied with a blue ribbon or a white or pink ribbon. There is no higher or lower order of patriotism in the Senate. There are no first- or second-class senators. Those who will serve are men of competence, understanding, and decency. They will do the job which the circumstances and the Senate require of them. [22]

Commenting upon those selections, Mitchell Rogovin, who served as special counsel to Director of Central Intelligence Colby, observed: "The makeup of the committee members was of the highest order. You couldn't have asked for better people." [23]

Members of the Church committee differed in age, years in the Senate, ideology, and attitudes towards the intelligence community. In a real sense they reflected the diversity of the Senate itself.

Service on the Select Intelligence Committee had some definite costs for each of the members. The most important was time. As Michael Madigan, counsel to Senator Baker, observed:

> It [service on the Select Intelligence Committee] has no political benefit. In fact, it is a vast political detriment. The time it takes up. You get no benefits from serving on the intelligence committee. There are no pork-barrel benefits to be obtained and no state issues involved. [24]

While not offering much in terms of benefits, service on the select committee also carried definite political risks. For example, during his 1980 reelection campaign, Senator Church's conduct as chairman of the select committee was attacked by his opponent and was one of the factors in his defeat. Nevertheless the committee was a highly attractive assignment. As one select committee task force leader commented: "It [member participation] was incredible. Most of the time, there was a consuming and emotional involvement on the part of the committee members." [25]

Supporting this assessment another senior select committee staff member noted: "There was terrific attendance and very careful preparation." [26] Such statements show that, despite its costs and risks, the Select Intelligence Committee was attractive to Senate members.

Why was the select committee attractive? First, it followed in the tradition of other Senate investigating committees. In the 1950s an investigative committee propelled Estes Kefauver's career to the national level. For each of the members of the Select Intelligence Committee, the Senate Watergate Committee and the attention and fame that had come to its members were very recent memories. As one senior select committee staff member observed:

> Right before this we had the Watergate hearings. Sam Ervin became a national hero. Ervin even got to do American Express commercials. Howard Baker became majority leader after his Watergate exposure. Sam Dash also became well known. The Church committee provided all of the members with the opportunity to get out of the pack in the Senate. This committee provided an opportunity for political visibility.[27]

Moreover, the work of the committee was extremely significant for national security. Following the Senate Democratic Caucus vote in support of the creation of the select committee, Senator Church commented: "We're talking about a thorough investigation of the entire intelligence community as it works inside and outside the United States. This has never been undertaken before."[28] In discussing why Senator Baker spent so much time in intelligence oversight, Madigan observed: "Baker thinks it is a very crucial and important area."[29] That such an investigation had never been done before further enhanced the attractiveness of membership.

Another attractive feature of membership was the knowledge that could be gained. As one senior select committee staff member noted: "There is nothing particularly beneficial from service on such a committee. For the most part, the only attraction is being in the know. That is the only thing going for it: basic interest in the subject and curiosity."[30] Senator Church agreed, calling access to such privileged information "intoxicating."[31]

In addition, all the members who were on intelligence-related standing committees could use information from the select committee in their other assignments. For example Gary Hart made use of the knowledge he gained on the select committee in his work on the Armed Services Committee, to which he was a newcomer. Also, for a senator like Walter Mondale who had no other committee assignments related to intelligence, membership on the select committee provided entry into foreign affairs and intelligence.

A final benefit came from the manner of selection itself. The members were picked directly by the majority and minority leaders. As Senator Scott observed, both he and Senator Mansfield were looking for members who were "responsible" and "trustworthy." Thus selection was a sign of the respect in which the member was held by his party leader, a special mark of prestige within the Senate.

The Church committee was, in short, an attractive committee. Besides the opportunity to conduct a historically significant investigation, service on the committee provided members with information available to no one else. Moreover, the prospect of national attention meant that the personal goals of members outside the Senate could be furthered. In sum, service on the Committee held the promise of advancing both the public policy as well as personal goals of the members.

Leadership of the Chairman

As chairman of the select committee, Senator Frank Church found himself in charge of the most sweeping congressional investigation of intelligence since the creation of the modern American intelligence system in 1947. Church was well aware of the importance of the work of the committee:

> I think it had to be one of the most important congressional investigations in our time. It is important because there is no more pernicious threat to a free society than a secret police which is operating beyond the law. Reports in the press suggested that the intelligence agencies were operating in violation of the law. If these abuses had not been uncovered and had the agencies gone unchecked, we might well have seen a secret police develop in the United States. Once that begins, the Constitution itself is in very real danger. [32]

At the same time, Church was also cognizant of the dangers: "The committee had a tortuous course to follow. We were in a minefield through which we wandered for eighteen months. I do think we avoided the major mistakes that undermined and destroyed the House committee." [33] In his capacity as chairman, Frank Church's philosophy of leadership and his own legislative style were to strongly influence the work of the committee.

When he became chairman of the select committee, Frank Church had already completed eighteen years in the Senate, during which he had built a reputation as a loner. Christopher Lydon of the *New York Times* described Church as "a conscientious and independent student of policy, a wide reader and effective writer . . . a somewhat vain and distant man even with his fellow senators, an orator whose eloquence sometimes has more performance value than persuasion in it." [34] These traits can be seen clearly in Church's actions as chairman. He did not seek to rigidly impose his own beliefs or understanding of the issues on the other members. His outlook was summed up by Frederick A. O. Schwarz, Jr., chief counsel of the committee: "His philosophy was that they are grownups. They will make up their minds on the merits." [35] At times Schwarz himself was disappointed that Church was not more active in lobbying or "working on" other members of the committee.[36] Such activist leadership was simply not consistent with Church's philosophy or legislative style.

Although Church did not seek to shape members' beliefs, he did work actively to foster consensus. He was very much aware of the sensitivity of the committee's assignment and of the committee's internal tensions and divisions. Throughout the committee's history the members frequently met behind closed doors with Church as the key person seeking to foster unity. As Church noted:

> A very sensitive assignment had been given to the committee. The possible political repercussions were obvious. There was a certain amount of tension within the committee. We were able to overcome the problems as they arose by talking them through. The committee dealt with problems as they came along.[37]

In seeking to make consensus a reality Church also worked to maintain the support of Vice-Chairman Tower. Church himself described Tower's role: "Considering his antipathy towards the investigation, he worked. He was not obstructive. He didn't make my life miserable. In fact, he was very supportive. I respected him highly."[38] Church worked continuously to keep Tower on board. A senior staff member who closely observed this relationship commented: "Church did a very good job. His first good job was to get John Tower as his vice-chairman. There was the understanding that they'd all do it together. Everybody stayed together."[39]

At times Church could have won committee decisions on the basis of either partisan or ideological lines. However, he deliberately chose not to do so. As Nicholas Horrock of the *New York Times* commented: "He [Church] probably could have bludgeoned his committee to positions on certain issues, for quite often he had the votes to do so either on party lines or ideology. But in most cases he chose compromise, and compromise was his style."[40] Church's consensus leadership was one of his most valuable contributions.

Besides encouraging unity and consensus, Church also exercised leadership by picking the two key staff members, Staff Director William Miller and Chief Counsel Frederick A. O. Schwarz, Jr. As one senior staff member observed: "Church was responsible for hiring Bill Miller and Fritz Schwarz. This made the committee strong on two fronts with the staff. The staff is everything in these things. The staff is the base. . . . On the House side, the staff was not as good."[41]

Miller and Schwarz brought two competing oversight philosophies to their key positions. Miller was an institutional insider, Schwarz a hard-nosed investigator and outsider. Discussing the differences between these two, a task force leader on the select committee asserted:

Bill Miller was the quintessential Washington insider. He was a true embodiment of the type of institutional commitment to the Senate that could be seen in his work for Mansfield, Cooper, Case, and Mathias. Miller was a true master of consensus politics as practiced by the Senate as an institution. Bill had far more of an interest in understanding institutional processes and long-term trends. He was interested in the role of intelligence and made an attempt to get beyond the immediate issue and put it into perspective. Fritz Schwarz was a brilliant litigating lawyer. He was an advocate. Fritz was an investigator trying to get to the bottom of the matter to find out what happened.[42]

Ironically Church's own philosophy is reflected in both of these men. Like Miller, Church had made a major commitment to understanding how institutions work and how government functions, a commitment illustrated by his Foreign Relations Committee work on seeking to understand how the United States became involved in Vietnam. At the same time Church's work also had aspects of the Schwarz mentality as can be seen in his investigation of ITT and Chile as chairman of the Subcommittee on Multinational Corporations. The *New York Times* called that investigation "the most promising current version of the old Kefauver phenomenon."[43] In their radically different approaches to the work of the select committee, Miller and Schwarz reflected the two sides of Frank Church.

As might be expected, throughout the existence of the Select Intelligence Committee there was enormous tension between Miller and Schwarz. Church was quite aware of the philosophical differences between these two key staffers and the resulting friction within the committee:

> They did complement each other. The only problem was that they turned out, because they were so different, to split the committee apart. The result was a dual-headed investigation. That was the way we finally handled it. To avoid a serious internal upheaval, Miller turned his focus to covert activity in the international field. He presided over that end. Schwarz took on the CIA and FBI illegal activities that occurred in the United States. That way we tried to avoid the combustion that these two stirred up in the committee. I myself directed them into these particular paths. You have to remember we were subject to incredible pressures. To do the job that was given us, I felt that it was necessary that we avoid internal fighting.[44]

Hiring Miller and Schwarz and later directing them into complementary areas were two of Church's most significant acts of leadership.

Another area in which Church exercised a key role was in maintaining security. As Church commented:

> Security was important. I realized from the outset that there were great pressures in this city to stop the investigation. Anything that happened that

might discredit the committee would be used to undermine the investigation. So the preventing of leaks of sensitive information affecting the national security was of top priority.[45]

Church did not merely discuss security in principle, he took specific actions. He noted: "There was strict surveillance of documents going in and going out, a process of accounting for them. Members had to sign for documents. The secured auditorium in the Dirksen Building was specially prepared for the committee's work."[46] According to Church this emphasis on security had the desired effect: "Remember, this was a fifteen-month investigation of the CIA, FBI, NSA, DIA, and IRS. There was not one single leak affecting the national security."[47]

Notwithstanding, I discovered that there were two disclosures of information that, although they did not affect the national security, did have an impact on the committee. First, a Church committee staff member discussed some confidential material with a dinner companion at a Washington restaurant. An intelligence officer overhead the conversation, and the matter was brought to Senator Church who promptly fired the staffer.[48] Second, prior to the release of the committee's assassinations report, both Democratic and Republican members leaked to the press information about President Kennedy's relationship with Judith Campbell Exner. The Republicans in particular were delighted to have something to use to tarnish the late president's reputation while the Democrats tried to defend it.[49]

As Church noted, these particular leaks were "politically motivated" and "did not affect the national security."[50] With respect to security, Church believed, "the members themselves showed the discipline that I felt we had to display if a permanent intelligence committee was to be created."[51] The committee was not only laying foundations for a permanent oversight committee but avoiding an area where the House Select Intelligence Committee stumbled badly. As chairman, Church had a significant role in setting the atmosphere for the committee's investigation, selecting and directing the staff, and maintaining essential security.

Yet there was one action Church took that had an adverse impact on the committee, his decision to run for president in 1976. One task force leader of the select committee observed: "The greatest downside for Church was the fact that he ran for president. By doing this, he allowed people to discredit things as being motivated by his presidential hopes."[52] Church himself noted:

I did not enter the presidential race until the investigations of the committee were concluded and all that remained was the final report. The active substantive work was done. Then I got into the race. It was a long gamble when I got in. I tried hard to respect the responsibility I had taken on by staying out of the presidential race until the investigation was completed. From then on, I was in the race.[53]

Ironically, actions taken by Church as chairman to advance the work of the committee actually hurt his presidential efforts. Staff Director Miller noted: "He devoted his entire energy to the problem of dealing with the intelligence agencies. As a result, he gave up the presidency."[54] Chief Counsel Schwarz agreed with Miller, adding:

He didn't make any wrong decisions because he was interested in running for president. Certain actions he took with respect to the committee actually hurt his presidential candidacy: (1) He stuck with it. He was torn with anguish. He told me and Miller to "get it done." He also told us to do a good job. (2) He made the decision not to hold certain of our hearings in public. The best example is assassinations. He held them in private. To charge that Church used the committee to run for president is unfair.[55]

In *A Season of Inquiry* political scientist Loch Johnson, who served as Senator Church's designee on the select committee, discusses the constant pressure put on staffers by advisors working on the Church presidential campaign to find material and opportunities to promote Church's campaign.[56] For example Johnson quotes a Church presidential campaigner who wanted Johnson to be more helpful: "Exposure, Johnson, exposure! That's the name of the game."[57] As a result Church's own actions were unfairly viewed as being solely motivated by his presidential ambitions.

Commenting upon Church's conduct as chairman, one senior select committee staff member observed:

Any of the big Democrats would have acted in a similar manner. Politicians are not going to run an investigation in secret. Church always had as his style not to do too much in the Senate but to do a lot in the press. It would have been better to be a member of the club than to be focused on the press.[58]

A key aide to Chief Counsel Schwarz agreed and added:

Of course Church was trying to use it [the committee] for his advantage. That's the nature of politics. You can't have the Senate involved in anything and not have politics. Politics can't not be involved. Church went pretty far in using it for a vehicle for publicity. He milked it for every bit of dramatic publicity.[59]

Because the committee had the task of investigating abuses and proposing reforms it had an important educational task to perform for both the Senate and the country. Publicity was an important tool in this effort. Unfortunately Church's presidential ambitions permitted critics to charge that the chairman was using the committee as a vehicle to further his own political interests.

These ambitions were a divisive force on the committee. On the Republican side, a top aide to Senator Tower repeatedly commented that, as a select committee staff member, "I worked for the Church for President Committee." [60] Joseph Di Genova, another top Republican staffer, commented in even stronger terms: "My whole vision of him [Church] is blurred by his drive for recognition, publicity, his obvious ambitions for higher office. The committee was used to boost those ambitions. I didn't have much respect for Church as a truly dispassionate and neutral chairman." [61]

Criticism of Church was not limited to Republicans. David Aaron, a key aide to Senator Mondale and a select committee task force leader, observed:

> Any chairman of that committee would have been faced with the problem of trying to run a sober, responsible investigation and yet needing to generate enough political interest so that the agencies would pay attention to them and not fluff them off and say no. There are those who think Frank Church went overboard in this respect. I will tell you I thought he went overboard at times in that respect. I think that it is a mistake to put the chairmanship in the hands of somebody who is running for president and to have ambitions there. That was true for Church. [62]

Similar criticism was expressed by a senior staff member who served as both a task force leader on the select committee and later as staff director for Senator Church on the Foreign Relations Committee:

> In the early stages, he [Church] hoped that the committee would provide a takeoff for his presidential campaign. He had visions of rising like Truman and Kefauver. Instead, he got his ass shot off. He then really receded. It is really only when Church goes off to become a serious presidential candidate that serious work at the committee got started. [63]

Ironically, Philip Hart, Mansfield's first choice for chairman, had no presidential aspirations. Church did, and they hurt his chairmanship.

Yet the record does not support the critics' contention that the select committee was merely an extension of the Church presidential campaign. Church was effective as chairman, and the committee's successful completion of its investigation was due in no small part to his leadership.

Unfortunately for the Senate committee, Church's presidential ambitions inspired other members to have similar thoughts. As Loch Johnson observed, "Visions of the White House danced in the heads of other committee members, too." [64] Nevertheless, despite the problems caused by his presidential campaigning, Church's chairmanship was successful overall.

Internal Relations

The members of the select committee shared the view that their task was to conduct a fair and thorough investigation. Their norms were unity and bipartisanship. How these principles were implemented was described by a counsel on the committee: "Everything was done by consensus. A vote was a rare exception. Most things were done with the consent of the group. Church kept Tower informed of everything." [65] This view was supported by the recollections of Joseph Dennin, another select committee counsel:

> The key to understanding the Church committee was the constant compromising, the desire to find what the common denominator was that would bring all the members aboard. It was necessary to get the approval of all the members of the committee. There was a constant toning down to get a report that all eleven senators would say they could support. [66]

This pursuit of consensus dominated the internal relations of the committee.

In the aftermath of Watergate, Senate Democrats could have attempted to make intelligence a partisan political issue. Frederick A. O. Schwarz, Jr., chief counsel of the select committee, discussed how this could have been done and what the consequences would have been:

> This could have easily been made into a Nixon's bad-guy type of committee. But there would have been a heavy price for doing this, a political price. The committee would not have retained Republican cooperation and support. And it would have resulted in no credible recommendations for reform. The importance of the full factual record would have been lost. These problems have been deep and sustained since FDR. It is not just one bad person. [67]

The select committee's restraint on partisanship was attested to by Howard Liebengood, a close aide to Senator Baker on both the Watergate committee and the Church committee:

> This [Church committee] was really not a partisan committee in contrast to the Senate Watergate Committee. By and large, the Church committee was nonpartisan in staff relations and in the thrust of the leadership. In the days of the Senate Watergate Committee, the majority staff did everything in secret. The Senate Watergate Committee was brutally partisan. There was not much communication between the majority and minority. By way of contrast, on the Church committee, Republicans and Democrats worked hand in hand on projects together. [68]

There were several factors to foster consensus. The movement to create a select committee had been bipartisan. In the hearings conducted by the Senate Government Operations Subcommittee on Intergovernmental Relations in early December 1974 Republicans such as Howard Baker and Charles Mathias were just as concerned about intelligence abuses and deficiencies as Democrats such as Mike Mansfield and Edmund Muskie. This bipartisan spirit influenced the creation of the select committee. In S. Res. 21, establishing the committee, the majority party was given only one seat more than the minority. Such a ratio encouraged majority-minority cooperation. In addition the vice-chairman was more than just the ranking minority member. In S. Res. 21 the vice-chairman was authorized to preside over meetings in the absence of the chairman and to discharge other duties the chairman assigned him. Both Church and Tower made this partnership work, in sharp contrast to the concurrent experience in the House.

Also facilitating consensus was the desire of each of the members to protect the legitimate interests of the legislative branch. Despite their tremendous ideological differences, the members shared a desire to maintain the constitutional prerogatives of the Senate. As a senior staff member observed:

> Church and Tower were opposite types but there was a higher interest that both supported. They stayed together and did not break up on this on partisan lines. The larger interest was the assertion of legislative-branch authority. Tower stuck up for the Senate in negotiations with the executive branch and the White House. Tower was the vice-chairman, and he acted like one.[69]

The Select Intelligence Committee was originally given a mandate to conduct a nine-month investigation. However, after the Ford administration turned over to the committee all of the Rockefeller commission materials on assassinations, the time given the committee to complete its work was extended to fifteen months. There were three distinct parts of the inquiry: (1) January to July 1975 for committee organization and the assassinations inquiry, (2) August to December 1975 to prepare for and conduct public hearings, and (3) December 1975 to April 1976 to prepare and release final reports. In each of these periods the committee had to make decisions and resolve disagreements.

During the January to July 1975 period the committee resolved three key issues: (1) hiring the staff, (2) focusing its investigative efforts, and (3) deciding to conduct an assassinations inquiry. The only major internal disagreement that surfaced publicly during this stage was whether to hold private or public assassinations hearings. Senator Baker had argued strongly for public hearings. As he later observed:

> I had hoped for public hearings on this subject, carefully sanitized to avoid the disclosure of properly classified information and the identification of

"sources and methods." It seems to me that without a record clearly supporting a conclusion of presidential responsibility, or the absence of it, that a public examination of the witnesses was more important than would otherwise be the case.[70]

However, the other members would not agree, and Baker acquiesced: "The committee determined not to hold public hearings and I abide by that decision."[71]

During the August to December 1975 period the first open splits occurred. Member interest and participation was very high during twenty-one days of public hearings. Two of the hearings provoked an open split. First, on October 29 and November 26, the committee conducted hearings on the National Security Agency. Because of the sensitivity of the NSA's work Tower, Goldwater, and Baker opposed public hearings. Second, on December 4 and 5, the committee publicly discussed U.S. covert actions in Chile. Again Tower and Goldwater opposed public hearings. Note that in both cases those opposed did not object to hearings, only public hearings. Finally, on November 20, the committee released an interim report on assassinations. Although all members signed the report, Tower and Goldwater expressed their dissatisfaction publicly. As Goldwater remarked: "My chief concern is the diplomatic damage this document may do to our country. It is difficult to predict the reactions of our friends and enemies abroad, but I believe it will be generally unfavorable to our interests."[72] Despite these internal divisions, however, a solid and bipartisan majority remained intact.

In the final period, from December 1975 to April 1976, the committee's major task was to write up final reports and make recommendations to the Senate and the country. To accomplish this they divided into two subcommittees. The Foreign and Military Subcommittee, chaired by Senator Huddleston, included Gary Hart, Mathias, and Goldwater. The Domestic Subcommittee, chaired by Senator Mondale, included Phil Hart, Morgan, Baker, and Schweicker. Huddleston and Mondale now became the real chairmen of the select committee because Church was increasingly occupied by campaign activities as he pursued his quest for the Democratic presidential nomination. In addition, a dramatic change in the public mood occurred during this final period due to the assassination of the CIA's station chief in Athens and the unauthorized leaking of the House Select Intelligence Committee's final report. Illustrating the committee's reaction to this change in public mood, Committee Chief Counsel Frederick A. O. Schwarz, Jr. believed that, had the assassinations report been debated after these two events, it probably would not have been publicly released.[73]

When the committee's final reports were released, Tower and Goldwater objected to all three of them, so all were released by nine-to-two votes. Both Tower and Goldwater had two major objections: (1) the material included in the reports was too sensitive, and (2) many of the changes proposed were too restrictive and were unsupported by the committee's work. Ironically, although they voted in support of the final reports, Mondale, Phil Hart, and Gary Hart issued a written dissent claiming that too much material had been left out due to security concerns. As recounted in Loch Johnson's *A Season of Inquiry,* such divisions were present from the very beginning, and this is not surprising considering the wide range of opinion reflected in the members. It is also not surprising that the committee interests, which encouraged members to keep differences below the surface for the sake of a successful investigation, would be superseded by a public surfacing of differences as members now sought to shape the forthcoming public debate and Senate decisions. What is remarkable is that the committee still retained a solid bipartisan majority supporting the final reports.

In fact, in the entire life of the Church committee, there was only one vote of six-to-five. One of the most hotly debated issues was whether the intelligence budget should be disclosed to the public. On the final day of the committee's existence, the members voted six to five to urge the Senate to disclose this figure. However, as DCI Colby recalled: "At the end, the committee voted that the budget should be opened, but they've never done it. That's so wonderful a congressional action. You vote to do it, and then you just don't happen to get around to doing it. So everybody's happy. It's great." [74] The select committee's six-to-five vote was an expression of principle. Practically speaking, it had no impact. This action symbolizes the way the committee was run. Until an overwhelming majority was assembled nothing decisive or irrevocable would be undertaken.

Senator Church commented on the pressures the members faced: "We didn't satisfy those who wanted the CIA blown out of the water and the intelligence agencies dismantled or the perennial protectors of intelligence." [75] Despite such pressures the members stayed together, and for two reasons.

First, as has already been noted, the leadership of Frank Church and the partnership he formed with Vice-Chairman John Tower were critical. On the role of Church and Tower in fostering consensus, Chief Counsel Schwarz observed:

> Church gets a lot of credit for that decision [to work closely with the Republicans on a nonpartisan basis]. It was a very wise decision. Also credit John Tower. He is not my ideological cup of tea but, on the Church committee, he was 98 percent supportive of the choices we made. It was basically a sound and cooperative relationship. [76]

Second, there were three members who were especially important in building and maintaining consensus: Philip Hart, Howard Baker, and Charles Mathias. Despite his advanced cancer, Philip Hart, in the words of Staff Director Miller, "devoted considerable time and energy and provided guidance." [77] He truly served as the conscience of the select committee. On the Republican side, Baker and Mathias were the key members keeping the committee together. As one task force leader observed, "In the end, bipartisanship was due to Mathias and Baker." This same staff leader noted: "The Senate as an institution fosters consensus politics. This is the Senate at its best." [78] In the way that internal relations were maintained, the Select Intelligence Committee is a case study in consensus politics.

Committee Staff

In conducting its investigation, the Select Intelligence Committee relied to a considerable extent on its staff. Staff members were critical in preparing both the hearings and the reports. The two key staff members were Staff Director William Miller and Chief Counsel Frederick A. O. Schwarz, Jr. Both were hired by Committee Chairman Frank Church and differed greatly on the direction they believed the inquiries should go.

Initially William Miller was asked by Senate Majority Leader Mike Mansfield to become staff director. Philip Hart, who was originally supposed to have been chairman of the select committee, also asked Miller to assume this post. Miller agreed to become staff director and was hired after unanimous approval by the committee members. Miller had a distinct view of how the staff should be recruited and how they should function:

> The initial impetus was to do everything by agreement. There was the idea of a unified staff. The initial design was that every member had to be approved by the committee as a whole. We would avoid having partisan divisions. The first duty was to the committee. We sought people who were knowledgeable by direct experience. You need people with experience. I wanted a number from the intelligence community. Loyalty to the Constitution was the key. To discover the truth, I wanted a mix of experience: (1) practitioners, (2) bright young historians, and (3) investigators. In every case we wanted those with experience to problems. Traditionally you seek lawyers to do the inquiry and the staff work. We needed a spread of the disciplines. [79]

Before joining the committee Miller himself had extensive Washington experience as a foreign service officer, aide to Senator Cooper, and staff director of the Emergency and Delegated Powers Committee. Senators Church and Mathias were cochairmen of this committee, and Philip Hart was a member. Miller called the Senate a "straightforward, reflective body." [80] In Miller, Church was hiring a Washington insider to serve as staff director.

Frederick A. O. Schwarz, Jr., joined the committee as chief counsel. He was hired by Church after having been recommended by John Doar and Burke Marshall, who both had close ties to the Kennedys. Unlike Miller, before joining the committee, Schwarz "didn't know any of the senators." [81] In fact he came to the committee directly from the New York law firm of Cravath, Swaine, and Moore. Joseph Dennin, a counsel on the select committee, described Cravath as

> one of the most competitive law firms in America. I don't know anyplace where people are more driven, where they are driven to succeed at any cost. That is the thought that prevails. At Cravath the attitude was let's get it done and win even if it takes twenty-four-hour days and seven-day weeks. [82]

Consequently it was not surprising that Schwarz had differences with Miller. As Schwarz himself observed:

> Bill Miller and I had a difference of approach. Bill's approach favored seeking out the wisdom and advice of the great experts. Bill wanted to press for wise advice from the sage people of experience. My view, and the view which ultimately prevailed, was that you had to build answers through detailed presentations of the facts. Identify the wrongdoing. Make sure it was checked. Develop facts, draw general lessons, propose reforms. I wanted to press for exposure. [83]

Unfortunately the differences between Miller and Schwarz produced a considerable amount of tension between them. One staff member described the result as "combustion." But, ironically, the differences turned out to be beneficial. As Select Committee Counsel Frederick Baron observed:

> It helped the committee greatly. Either approach [Miller's or Schwarz's] to the exclusion of the other would not have fulfilled the committee's mandate. They were two very capable people. Clearly, Fritz Schwarz's investigative case studies attracted the attention of the country. It was a rare achievement that the Church committee was able to focus the attention of the entire nation on intelligence oversight. Bill Miller made a great contribution with the intelligence case studies. The final product was a series of legislative recommendations which were bolstered by the work done by both sides of the committee's staff. [84]

Such thoughts were seconded by James Dick, also a committee counsel: "They were diametrically opposed to each other. They each had to carve out their own turf areas. The soft-spoken Bill Miller versus

Fritz the litigator. A Mutt and Jeff routine. It worked to the advantage of the Church committee to have both types." [85]

Originally the committee was divided into four task forces: (1) Command and Control, (2) Foreign Intelligence, (3) Domestic Intelligence, and (4) Defense Intelligence. Each task force had a leader plus three to five professional staff members. The leaders were, respectively, David Aaron, William Bader, John Elliff, and Alton Quanbeck. When the Ford administration turned over assassinations data to the committee, a fifth task force was created ad hoc under the direction of Miller and Schwarz. Altogether, nineteen professional staff members worked on the Assassinations Task Force. In addition each committee member was allotted a "designee." As described by Counsel Joseph Dennin, designees were created to meet a special need:

> The material that was being handled was very sensitive. Everybody realized that senators don't do anything all by themselves. Senators turn to their office staff or AA [Administrative Assistant] for help. To avoid that, each senator was allowed to put a person on the staff who could be cleared and be his designee, be responsible to him alone. There was believed to be more prestige attached to being a designee. [86]

There was a hierarchy of staff members. The first tier consisted of the staff director and chief counsel. Second came the task force leaders and designees. Third were the professional staff members. The fourth level consisted of the research staff and other support personnel.

Miller and Schwarz did most of the hiring. There was no dearth of applicants. As one designee observed:

> This seemed to me a good example of very good people being attracted to something new. Anytime a new thing is started up, all kinds of bright, ambitious people come out of the woodwork. You do not find the same thing happening with an existing entity. The glamour has faded. Also, they can only hire one person at a time. We had fifty openings. You could hire the best around. [87]

Both Miller and Schwarz used the attractiveness of the committee to hire a cross-section of the best people available. As Counsel Joseph Di Genova observed: "This was a very diverse group. We had Ph.D. types, former ambassadors, military people, CIA types, and historians." [88] For staff members the work was challenging and exciting. Counsel Joseph Dennin commented: "There was a sense of sitting with the 'best and the brightest.' There you'd go daily, and you could meet and listen to and make small talk with people like Bundy and Sorensen." [89] Counsel James Dick added: "This was an exciting time for me. Here I was just two years out of law school, and I was giving a warning about his Miranda rights to [former Attorney General] Katzenbach." [90]

Typical was Counsel David Bushong's remark: "This [my work on the select committee] was the peak experience of my life. I've never topped it. The only thing that ever came close was managing Nancy Kassenbaum's campaign for the Senate for three months." [91]

Ideally both Miller and Schwarz had hoped to have a unified and bipartisan staff. However, in practice, there were both partisan and ideological differences among the staff members. As recounted by one senior staffer, Chief Counsel Schwarz quickly encountered just this problem shorty after he joined the committee: "Fritz [Schwarz] went to Goldwater's designee, Charles Lombard, and told him: 'This is your part.' He responded: 'Fritz, I'm not here to work for you. I'm here to spy on you.' As a result Fritz realized his resources were drastically reduced." [92] The adversarial process kept both sides honest.

Despite their differences there were forces uniting the staff. One was the committee's office in the Dirksen Building. Counsel Joseph Di Genova commented: "There was an interesting spirit. All of us were crammed into Dirksen G-308. It was physically secure but it was like being in a World War II bunker." [93] Staffer Peter Fenn had similar recollections:

> It was like a rat's maze. The Democrats and Republicans were together. You could hear telephone conversations. For example, there was Charles Kirbow [Tower's designee]. Charlie would go to the pay phone outside to make his calls so nobody could hear him. We'd all go out and wave to Charlie in the phone booth. One time we came back from a meeting with NSA on getting documents. Charlie was on the phone to these same NSA people and said: "If you give this material to the committee, your head is caught up your ass." We looked over the partition and waved to Charlie. For a secret, secret committee, in terms of attitude, agenda, we were all right there, all available. The space turned out to be very enhancing. It brought us all together. The work environment was extraordinarily intense. At a minimum, it was twelve-hour days. [94]

Although staff members were not polygraphed, an issue of real concern to the members and senior staffers was maintaining security. Only one security problem resulted in the dismissal of a staff member. Among the materials given to the committee by the intelligence community was a February 23, 1973, CIA memo that discussed a meeting held with Senator Henry Jackson to talk about upcoming hearings to be conducted by Church on ITT cooperation with the CIA. The memo stated, in part: "Comment: Senator Jackson was extremely helpful throughout 23 February on the issue of the agency's problems with the Church committee" [95] This document and other relevant materials were examined by a professional staff member on the committee. What happened was described by a close aide to Church:

The committee found some documents. [This staffer] was talking to some folks at a restaurant. He mentioned this and an intelligence-community person was at the next table. He overheard and the community complained. [This staffer] was fired not for disclosing sensitive information about a CIA operation but rather for the disclosure of information on Senator Jackson that gave the impression that Jackson was in the pocket of the CIA on Track II on Chile.[96]

Discussing the staffer's dismissal, a political scientist then on the staff observed: "He was fired for showing classified information to someone outside the committee. There was great sensitivity that anything like that would discredit the committee."[97] The seriousness with which this particular disclosure was met was typical. As Staff Director Miller commented:

We didn't use polygraphs. Our view of polygraphs was that of the majority of the Senate at that time. This view was best expressed by Senator Sam Ervin of North Carolina, who often stated that polygraphing was "twentieth-century witchcraft." We believed that the legislative branch should give clearance to the staffers. We took the FBI and its background check as our agent. There were a few staffers ousted as a result of the FBI check. The reason was suitability and pressure, not disloyalty. We chose the auditorium in the Dirksen Building because we could get everyone involved in the same place. There was one door. There was a unified file system. That side worked pretty well.[98]

The good security record was an important sign to both the Senate and the executive branch that the committee could be trusted with sensitive information.

Commenting on the staffing of the Warren commission, Howard Willens noted: "We made a mistake by hiring generalist big shots to head each of the different panels. We should have had forty legal lawyer-drones who would have just chewed through the evidence and come up with a report."[99] Unlike the Warren commission, the Select Committee on Intelligence possessed both "big shot" generalists and legal "drones." In large measure this was due to the differences in philosophy and approach of Miller and Schwarz and the diverse staff they hired. One Republican designee observed: "Accidentally, maybe Church knew what he was doing when he hired both Miller and Schwarz."[100] Maybe he did.

The Committee and the Senate

The most important institutional relationship for the committee was with its parent chamber, the Senate. As Task Force Leader John Elliff commented, "The committee maintained the confidence of the Senate every step of the way." [101] The committee's very creation signified a revolution in intelligence oversight. The relationship between the Senate and its committee demonstrates how both functioned as political institutions.

On January 20, 1975, the Senate Democratic Caucus voted forty-five to seven in support of a resolution calling for the creation of a bipartisan select intelligence investigating committee. On January 27, 1975, the Senate itself created the Select Intelligence Committee when it passed S. Res. 21 by a vote of eighty-two to four. S. Res. 21 directed the new committee to

> conduct an investigation and study of the extent, if any, to which illegal, improper, or unethical activities were engaged in by any agency or by any persons, acting either individually or in combination with others, in carrying out any intelligence or surveillance activities by or on behalf of any agency of the federal government. [102]

During the floor debate surrounding the passage of S. Res. 21, Senate Majority Leader Mike Mansfield clearly defined the Senate's expectations:

> The select committee's task is precise. Neither witch hunt nor whitewash will be here conducted; and there will be no wholesale dismantling of our intelligence community. What we hope to obtain is a full and objective analysis of the role of intelligence-gathering in a free society today measured against current laws, practices, and policies in the intelligence community. It is a task that is long overdue.
>
> It used to be fashionable, Mr. President, for members of Congress to say that insofar as the intelligence agencies were concerned, the less they knew about such questions, the better. Well, in my judgment, it is about time that attitude went out of fashion. It is time for the Senate to take the trouble and, yes, the risks of knowing more rather than less. We have a duty, individually, and collectively, to know what legislation enacted by Congress and paid for by appropriations of the people's money has spawned in practice in the name of the United States. The Congress needs to recognize, to accept and to discharge with care its coequal responsibility with the presidency in these matters.
>
> The committee has been equipped with full authority to study, to hold hearings and to investigate all activities—foreign and domestic—of the intelligence agencies of the federal government. In the pursuit of that mandate, I have every confidence that the committee will act with discretion, with restraint and with a high sense of national responsibility. The Senate is entrusting this committee with its deepest confidence. [103]

Mansfield clearly set forth the Senate's mandate to the select committee, and eighty-one other senators voted with him. The era of Richard Russell's "institutional oversight" had been dramatically ended and repudiated.

Unlike standing committees, the select committee introduced no legislation in the Senate. Therefore there is no legislative record to show how well the committee fulfilled the Senate's mandate. Nevertheless there are five key decisions in which the Senate exercised accountability and approved the committee's work. The first two were the votes in the Democratic Caucus and on the Senate floor that led directly to the creation of the select committee. By votes of forty-five to seven and eighty-two to four respectively the Senate demonstrated its overwhelming support.

Originally the Senate had given the committee nine months to complete its work. However, after the Ford administration turned over its assassinations data, the members decided to conduct a major investigation into this area. As a result the committee had to ask for an extension of its life. Interestingly enough, the House Select Intelligence Committee was confronted with a similar problem, but its request for an extension was rejected by the House. However, in the Senate, the request was approved by unanimous consent. This third decision demonstrated that the select committee retained the overwhelming confidence of the Senate.

After the committee completed its study of assassinations an interim report was prepared entitled *Alleged Assassination Plots Involving Foreign Leaders*. Under the provisions of S. Res. 21 the committee could have simply released the report. However, President Ford asked the committee to delete twelve names from it. DCI Colby charged in a press conference that publication with the names could put those individual's lives in danger. In the background was the incessant public wrangling between the administration and the House Select Intelligence Committee over that committee's alleged leaking of sensitive information. The Senate's select committee decided to bring its assassinations report and the issues surrounding public release to the Senate floor.

The Senate's decision on November 20, 1975, concerning the public release of the report constitutes the fourth key decision. According to Task Force Leader John Elliff, the Senate's consideration of the report was its "most dramatic" illustration of support:

Under S. Res. 21 the committee could release the report itself. Under S. Res. 400 [which created the permanent intelligence committee which succeeded the select committee], if the executive branch objects the committee goes to the Senate. When the report was completed, the president said I want you to take the names out. S. Res. 21 didn't require this but the committee went to the Senate anyway. You see here the committee respecting the prerogatives of the Senate. This was due to smarts in the judgment of Bill Miller, Mathias, Phil Hart, Baker, and Church. There was a secret Senate session. The committee laid out the issues. Because the executive was objecting to the release of the assassinations report, the committee went to the floor of the Senate to give the Senate the opportunity not to publish this report. The committee got an absence of disapproval. The committee released the report with names. If we were going to maintain the trust and respect of the Senate, the committee had to do this.[104]

Unlike the three previous decisions, no formal vote was taken by the Senate on publishing the assassinations report.

Why was no vote taken? In the *Washington Post* George Lardner reported: "Chairman Frank Church (D-Idaho) and his colleagues were reportedly advised by Senator Alan Cranston (D-Calif.) that the outcome might be a close vote that would not stand out as ringing support of the report's public release."[105] Similar sentiments were reported by David Rosenbaum in the *New York Times*:

> Administration supporters, who opposed the release of the document, had pressed in debate for a vote because they thought that a narrow margin favoring release would reduce the report's impact. The Democrats apparently agreed with this opinion and decided to block a vote. As a result, at the end of the four hour secret Senate session, the matter was tossed back to the Senate intelligence committee which voted to make it public.[106]

Commenting after the Senate's decision not to take a vote, Senator Robert Byrd of Virginia, the Senate Democratic Whip, declared that he had objected to a vote because: "The Senate had delegated to the committee the responsibility for making a report, and a vote today would have been demeaning to the committee."[107] Select committee members John Tower and Barry Goldwater were extremely upset by the public release of the report but the force of their arguments was lessened when the other Republican members on the committee supported the release. The select committee thereby retained majority support in the Senate.

Finally, the fifth decision of the Senate regarding the select committee occurred after the committee had gone out of existence. One of the committee's principal recommendations was that a permanent Senate intelligence oversight committee should be established. On May 19, 1976, the Senate voted seventy-two to twenty-two in favor of S. Res. 400, creating just such a committee. Tower and Goldwater voted against the resolution. But fellow Republicans Howard Baker, Charles Mathias, and Richard Schweicker supported S. Res. 400, and the revolution in intelligence oversight continued. By the time the fifth decision had been reached there had been erosion in the overwhelming support the select committee had initially commanded. However, the committee still retained a majority and, more importantly, a solid bipartisan majority. This experience demonstrates the Senate's ability to exercise policy guidance and accountability over a select committee as well as how a Senate committee was able to maintain strong chamber support over an extended period.

The Committee and the House

Meanwhile a parallel investigation was being conducted on the other end of Capitol Hill by the House Select Intelligence Committee, the Pike committee. There was some contact between Senate Select Intelligence Committee staffers and House Judiciary Committee staffers. But almost all of the Senate committee's contact with the House was limited to contacts between the two select intelligence committees. And even here contact was minimal. Because the Senate committee was an investigative and not a legislative committee there were no conference meetings between the Church and Pike committees. As Senator Church observed: "There is a tradition of two independent houses. There was liaison with Pike for the purpose of avoiding duplication. I tried to avoid duplication. There was plenty to investigate." [108] Summarizing the contacts, Chief Counsel Schwarz commented: "There were two or three meetings between Church and Pike and Miller and myself in Church's hideaway office. Interestingly enough, Pike came without staff people. At these meetings, we agreed on a few things the other [committee] would cover. There were a few steps in the direction of cooperation." [109]

The investigation conducted by the Church committee was a bipartisan effort, and Church kept Vice-Chairman Tower and the rest of the committee fully briefed. Both Miller and Schwarz were powerful figures with major roles in the investigation even though they were staffers. Pike had no such bipartisan effort. He basically was the House committee. As Loch Johnson notes, Pike's staff director, in comparison with Miller and Schwarz, was "young" and "inexperienced." [110] These meetings reflect the deep chasm between the Senate and House investigating committees.

Even though there was little contact between the Senate and House committees there were strong feelings of antipathy between them. Chief Counsel Schwarz described the House committee as being populated by "ideologues": "We were practical about information. They were ideological. The Pike committee staffers had vague unsupported ideological views. They had the feeling: 'What can we learn from anybody else?' They alone possessed virtue. They were all true believers." [111] One counsel on the Senate committee described the House committee as "irresponsible." [112] Another described it as "a walking disaster from the beginning." [113] In some cases these views were reinforced by information obtained from the intelligence community. As a political scientist on the Church committee recalled:

> Intelligence-community people expressed relief that they were dealing with us and not the Pike committee. One story that was told us by some of the intelligence poeple: There was a young female staffer on the Pike committee who would question intelligence-community people in her bare feet. They sought to have sexy hearings. Chairman Pike in an open hearing disclosed sources and methods in the Middle East. They were sloppy and loose with security. We conducted our investigation in a "more responsible" way.[114]

Such views had a distinct impact on Senate behavior. This same staffer noted: "There were a number of us who were careful to disassociate ourselves from the Pike committee."[115] In addition Senate staffers sometimes took advantage of this situation. A senior staffer recounted: "When we were at NSA, we realized that the House committee was onto what we were. We told NSA: 'If you don't cooperate with us, you will have to deal with the House committee.' They cooperated."[116] In short, the Senate select committee tended to look down on its House counterpart.

At the same time, the House committee looked down on its Senate counterpart. Chairman Otis Pike had strong thoughts about the Senate committee and its chairman:

> The Church committee focused on aberrations and blowguns. We went after standard operating procedures. The Church committee did a fine job. They protected Henry Kissinger. You don't find Kissinger in the Chile report. My suspicion is that they cut a deal. One thing I really disagreed with Church on was his characterization of the CIA as a "rogue elephant." CIA never did anything the White House didn't want. Sometimes they didn't want to do what they did.[117]

Another House committee member agreed with Pike's assessment: "Frank Church, he leaves me unmoved. An artful dodge. They were removed generationally from the same constraints but they didn't take the issues on."[118] Moreover, House committee staffers also had very negative views of the Senate's work in general. One House committee investigator commented: "We were not Ivy Leaguers. The Church committee had a lot of nice fancy people. But we beat their pants off on getting information."[119] Finally, the House staffer who directed the Pike committee's investigation of the CIA and NSA compared the two committees: "The Church committee had more glamour and better members. But the Church committee focused more on abuses. The Pike committee focused more on problem solving, improving American intelligence, and intelligence failures."[120]

For the Senate select committee the importance of its relationship with the House committee was very low. About the only major area of mutual interest between the two was avoiding needless duplication. Once that issue was resolved there was no real need for extensive contact between them. The committees differed greatly in terms of chairmen, quality of members and staff, relations with their parent chambers, and relations with the executive branch. Some of the mutually hostile feelings can be attributed to traditional Senate-House jealousy, some to the personalities involved, some to the differing oversight strategies. During the investigative period such questions are not of great importance. However, these issues assume much greater importance when proposals such as a joint committee are considered and when both chambers move beyond the investigations toward permanent oversight.

The Committee and the Executive Branch

Crucial to the work of the Senate select committee was the committee's relationship with the executive branch. The executive branch controlled the committee's access both to evidence and to witnesses. S. Res. 21 had given the Church committee the power to subpoena evidence and witnesses, but it did not make use of this weapon. Chairman Church feared that use of the subpoena power would needlessly tie up the committee in court. At the same time the executive branch frequently rumbled about making claims of executive privilege with respect to information and testimony sought by the committee. Yet neither side was willing to push its claims to the limit. In this gray area of shared legislative-executive interests a series of accommodations was reached that permitted the committee's work to proceed.[121] Still, the executive branch retained control over access to evidence and witnesses. This control was vital because, as Counsel Joseph Di Genova noted, "there was very little independent work done by the committees. The committees don't have it in their power to generate their own product."[122]

Throughout the committee's fifteen-month history, the relationship between the committee and the executive branch was adversarial. Each side tried to protect its own legitimate interests. Counsel Joseph Dennin described the process:

It was what I would expect. As a lawyer in litigation, you have an obligation to comply with discovery requests. You also have a duty to represent the interests of your client. This is the heart of the adversarial system. You operate within the bounds of ethics but defend your client's interests to the utmost.[123]

Counsel Eric Richard also commented: "On the surface they were very cooperative. They did what any lawyer in court or an adversary proceeding would do: minimize the damage. If you used the wrong word or didn't know what to ask for, they were of no help." [124]

During the public hearings of the select committee, Senator Schweicker described the difficulties in obtaining information from the executive branch:

> The usual scenario that this committee follows is, first, we have to fight tooth and nail to get any document we can place our hands on. Second, we are told we do not have a right to see the documents anyway. Third, [we are told that] we have a bottleneck, that the [executive] staff is not available to provide us with that information, and we have to wait a couple more weeks [for them] to bring some staffers in. Next, they argue that under the Constitution, the Bill of Rights really does not cover the points that we are trying to raise in their testimony. After that they insist that no abuses existed; but whatever occurred, they stopped doing several years ago. [125]

Thus a key task confronting the select committee was obtaining from the executive branch the information necessary to conduct its investigation.

Initially the Ford administration had been caught by surprise when on December 22, 1974, Seymour Hersh's article appeared charging the intelligence community with engaging in illegal and improper activities. According to Philip Buchen, counsel to President Ford: "I don't recall ever any reference before the Hersh article that there were problems out there. Nixon had departed on August 7 and 8. There was so much else to be concerned about. We were not going out of our way to track down hints of trouble." [126] To understand the significance of the Hersh charges, the president sought information from the Director of Central Intelligence William Colby. As Buchen recalled:

> It was quite obvious that the president would have to call in Colby and make him disclose whatever he knew so that there wasn't a chance that we'd get blindsided. None of us knew Colby particularly well. Colby was kind of an obscure person. We were not sure what we were dealing with. He was very forthcoming. The trouble was he did know it all. He gave us [enough] information to know that we had a real problem. This was not something Hersh made up. [127]

In response to the information provided by Colby, President Ford created the Rockefeller commission to investigate domestic intelligence abuses. However, as Buchen sadly noted, when the Senate created the Select Intelligence Committee, it "disregarded the fact that there was a Rockefeller commission." [128]

The White House and the select committee conducted negotiations on: (1) ground rules, (2) access, and (3) secrecy. As Senator Church noted, the committee agreed to abide by two rules:

First, we would not ask for the names of agents, [thereby] protecting
sources. Second, we would not ask for the methods by which the CIA had
obtained its information. The basic need to protect sources and methods.
We agreed that we would abide by these rules. These were valid requests.
They didn't interfere with the investigation of illegal activities infringing
on the constitutional rights of Americans. We kept that agreement. In return we got a lot of information. Whether we got it all or not, I can't say.[129]

Within the White House, Phil Buchen was initially placed in charge
of coordinating executive-branch efforts regarding the congressional
investigations. As Buchen recalled:

There was disarray in the intelligence community. There was so much
beyond their control. We needed a central place to enforce coordination.
This was the role the White House played in this situation. We could get
the agencies talking to one another. The Congress might feel that this view
was taken to throttle the intelligence community or shape the flow of
information. We embarked upon low-key efforts. We concentrated the coordination effort in my office. We arranged to meet regularly with representatives of each agency at the CIA. Information was centralized. My
purpose was to get them [the intelligence agencies] talking to each other
for the first time in history. All requests for information were to be centralized so that the other agencies knew what was being asked. We insisted
that, if there would be damage done by the release of information, that
should be brought to the presidential level.[130]

Although Buchen was officially in charge of White House efforts,
there were significant areas beyond his control. As Buchen noted:

When Colby went up to the Hill, he was not under any injunction to clear
what he said with us. We couldn't clear witnesses. We'd need a whole huge
staff. If we'd asked to be present always, we'd have been accused of a
coverup. People criticized all the witnesses for being forthcoming. It was
awfully hard not to be forthcoming in that atmosphere.[131]

In the aftermath of Watergate and the resignation of President Nixon
the staff of an unelected president found itself in an extremely difficult
situation.

Because of problems Buchen and his attorneys encountered with
the House Select Intelligence Committee, John Marsh was placed in
charge of White House coordination. As James Wilderotter, associate
counsel to President Ford, observed:

The point of contact was moved from Phil Buchen's office to Jack Marsh's.
It became a congressional relations exercise rather than a legal situation.
Legal considerations are irrelevant in the context of a congressional investigation. Frank Church doesn't want a legal decision about why he can't
have documents.[132]

Within the White House, Marsh headed up the Intelligence Coordinating Group (ICG), which included Marsh as chairman, the director of

central intelligence, the director of the National Security Council, the attorney general, as well as representatives from the State and Defense departments and the Office of Management and Budget. The ICG met almost daily during the congressional investigations. Within the ICG there were often sharp disagreements over just what should be given to the Congress. For example, William Colby favored maximum disclosure while Henry Kissinger vehemently opposed such a policy.[133] There was no unified executive-branch position. On the Ford administration's dealings with the select committee Michael Madigan, a key aide to Senator Baker, observed that "there seemed to be considerable disagreement and disorganization within the administration." [134]

Despite the weaknesses within the Ford administration, the executive branch was still able to exercise considerable influence over the course of the select committee's investigation. In February 1975, less than a month after the select committee's creation, Vice-President Rockefeller met with Senators Church and Tower and turned over to them a copy of the "Family Jewels." As already noted, the Family Jewels contained items that raised questions of illegality and impropriety about actions undertaken within the intelligence community. With very few exceptions the committee's investigation centered on the items contained in the Family Jewels. So the committee's time was occupied to a large extent by a focus on past abuses. For example, among the Family Jewels were reports of assassination attempts. Additional information on this subject collected by the Rockefeller commission was also turned over to the select committee. In the end, the committee spent six months of intensive study on assassinations. The committee's agenda, then, was determined to a large extent by executive-branch decisions on providing information.

At times the executive branch refused to make available all the information the committee sought. In its final report, the committee observed:

> Despite its legal Senate mandate, and the issuance of subpoenas, in no instance has the committee been able to examine the agencies' files on its own. In all the agencies, whether CIA, FBI, NSA, INR, DIA, or the NSC, documents and evidence have been presented through the filter of the agency itself.[135]

Frederick Baron, a counsel on the committee, described the cooperation the committee received from the executive branch and the struggle to obtain documents:

> Cooperation was only given grudgingly. We were breaking new ground. The executive agencies strongly resisted the notion of congressional oversight. The assassination case studies were critical. At a certain point, Republicans like Baker and Tower realized that this was an issue in which the

entire Senate had an institutional interest. I remember a meeting with Vice-President Rockefeller that included Bill Miller, Fritz Schwarz, Senator Church, and some other senators. We wanted the original documents and not summaries. The White House gave in on this when they saw that the senators were determined to have the documents and would subpoena them if necessary. It was only the willingness of the Senate committee to provoke a Watergate-like confrontation with the executive branch that enabled this to be done. We got these documents because of: (1) the bipartisan consensus, (2) the determination of Church and Mondale, and (3) the threat to use subpoenas and litigation.[136]

Even then access was severely restricted. Baron himself did the committee's key work on the Lumumba assassination case study. As he commented:

I had a strong hunch that if I could see the cable traffic [between CIA headquarters and CIA stations in the Congo], I could get to the bottom of this. The CIA mightily resisted the notion that anyone outside the agency should have access to the CIA's cable traffic. Ultimately, the senators gave us strong support and we won on this. The key senators were Church, Mondale, and Baker.[137]

Thus, even with the strongest backing of the committee, there was still difficulty in obtaining unhindered access to information.

In its quest for information the select committee found different problems from agency to agency. The committee's relationships with the CIA and FBI illustrate the differences and difficulties encountered. Although William Colby was both head of the CIA and director of central intelligence, the intelligence community itself was more a system of independent baronies than a truly united entity. As a result Colby's influence was concentrated mainly within the CIA. In the congressional investigations Colby adopted a policy of cooperation and disclosure for the CIA. As Colby himself commented:

I made an early decision that it was in the interests of the agency that the true story get out about what the misdeeds were—which were few and far between. And the only way to get some credibility on that was to be forthcoming on the programs and activities [and] at the same time convincing the Congress to respect the necessity not to tell them the names of agents and things like that. I mean it was obviously a frustrating period because I think my own feeling is that we had in that whole process . . . brought [the] CIA within our constitutional system. Up to that time, we hadn't.[138]

Moreover, Colby believed there was no alternative: "It was a very clear feeling on my part that if I had stonewalled that they would have trampled me right down into the ground."[139] Colby also realized that even President Ford's ability to offer support was severely limited:

Nobody could be strong in the politics of the time. That was the problem. Also, it wasn't President Ford's problem. I think the whole White House was, their initial feeling was: "My God! What has this thing turned up?" It really was not their watch. Most of this stuff went back fifteen or twenty years so there's no reason for them to jump into the breach. They are not totally responsible for that. And I understand that and I said I'll be responsible for that and I'll take it.[140]

At the same time, Colby was very much aware that his actions were strongly opposed by some in the White House, especially Henry Kissinger: "Kissinger had his views and we were quite frank about it. He had views as to how things should be done and I had my views as to how they should be done, and they weren't entirely in accord. We were very open on these differences of opinion."[141] In short, Colby attempted to adopt a policy that disclosed past CIA abuses in order to move onward.

Colby's actions were viewed in varying ways by select committee staffers. According to a senior aide to Senator Tower: "Colby certainly had a conversion on the way to Damascus that was alarming. He was much more open in giving information to the committee than I would have wanted."[142] Howard Liebengood, a key aide to Senator Baker, expressed a similar view: "Colby was a chameleon. I didn't feel during Watergate that he was all that forthcoming or helpful. By contrast, during the Church committee, Colby began providing information to the committee in a manner that seemed out of character for him."[143] According to Michael Madigan, counsel to Senator Baker: "There were several congressional demands on Colby for information. In responding to the Church committee, Colby provided a considerable amount of information—more information than many people thought he had to give to the committee."[144] But not everyone agreed with this assessment. Chief Counsel Frederick A. O. Schwarz, Jr., observed:

> I wasn't totally certain that Colby came totally clear with us. It was difficult to figure him out. It appeared he wanted to make a clean breast of the situation. Yet, it sticks in my craw that on the assassinations investigation, we only got things after they thought we had them.[145]

So the question still persists whether Colby followed in practice what he was publicly proclaiming.

Despite the mixed reviews Colby's actions received from the committee, the record indicates that Colby was sincerely working to build a new oversight relationship between the Congress and the intelligence community. For those who had been supporters of the institutional oversight conducted by Senator Russell, Colby's approach did resemble a "conversion on the way to Damascus." For those who sought total access to all sensitive information, Colby's attempts to limit access to what he considered legitimate secrets provoked doubts that he was really forthcoming. Although Colby's goal was to build a new type of oversight relationship, he himself was subject to tremendous pressures from the committee, the CIA along with the rest of the intelligence community, and the White House.

In particular, support from the White House was slow in coming and almost nonexistent. As Seymour Bolten, then chief of the CIA's review staff for the House and Senate, recalled:

> The Ford administration was on the defensive. This was immediately after Watergate. There was a lot of suspicion. Ford was in a weak position vis-à-vis the Congress. The White House was very critical of Colby whenever something came up when Colby decided to compromise. But whenever the ball was tossed to the White House, they would cave in sooner. They were terrified of subpoenas. They did not want to force a resolution of constitutional questions that had remained in the twilight zone since the beginnings of the Republic. Whenever a subpoena or the threat of a subpoena occurred, the White House caved in. They wanted to distance themselves from Colby and the CIA. They would criticize Colby when he gave in to the committees. But they didn't give him the support necessary to stand up to the committees. The CIA was pretty much on its own.[146]

Despite the pressures, Colby conducted himself well. Although unnoticed and unrecognized, Colby's actions helped to lay the foundation for a new relationship between the Congress and the intelligence community. Moreover, Colby shared with Staff Director Miller a desire to focus on institutions, processes, and procedures. The permanent post-investigative oversight owes much to the unheralded and highly criticized labors of William Colby.

With the FBI the select committee also had to struggle for information. In fact the committee's experience with the FBI provides a case study in how a congressional committee obtains information from the executive branch. According to John Elliff, leader of the FBI Task Force, a long time was taken deciding on staff. Although the committee was created in January 1975, Elliff himself was not hired until April, and only in May were the first comprehensive requests for information submitted to the FBI. Throughout May and June, Elliff and his two key assistants—Michael Epstein and Mark Gitenstein—were at loggerheads with the FBI. According to Elliff the task force members carefully compiled a complete record:

> We worked in a painstaking, meticulous way. We were showing we were conducting no witch hunt. We framed the issues very carefully. We wanted to find out what happened. We had to see the internal reports. They wouldn't show us their internal reports. They were concerned about the impact this would have on their sources and methods. We tried to be as careful and as clear as we could. We had to make a record that there was no cooperation.[147]

In July, Elliff brought in Chief Counsel Schwarz and told him of the resistance the task force was encountering from the FBI and the Justice Department. Thus from April until July the FBI Task Force had been unable to obtain the information it sought.

In July, Attorney General Levi and FBI Director Kelley met with the select committee. Ironically, on the very morning of the meeting, several members received their own FBI files, which they had asked to see. John Elliff related what happened:

> The morning of the hearing Senator Morgan got his FBI file. They had sanitized them. Morgan had been the attorney general in North Carolina before coming to the Senate. He had attended a meeting of the Association of State Attorney Generals. In his file was a report the FBI representative to the meeting had written. The FBI had struck out the names of the people but not their offices. For example, "————, the attorney general of North Dakota." Morgan came to the hearing outraged about the stupidity of that. Attorney General Levi and Director Kelley were totally embarrassed. That, with all the work we had done, cleared the way for access to the FBI material. It was clear we had the backing of the committee. The next day Attorney General Levi said give them what they need. They did.[148]

As a result, it was not until August that the FBI Task Force started getting the information it had requested. The committee held seven days of hearings on the FBI, beginning on November 18. As Elliff observed, by the time of the hearings the task force had been able to fill in the gaps in its inquiries. In its hearings on the FBI, the Church committee presented dramatic evidence of the dangers an intelligence agency can present to those very freedoms it was originally created to protect. The success of these hearings was due largely to the hard work and persistence of the committee to obtain the necessary evidence.

Besides access to information, the select committee also negotiated with the executive branch over what information it could disclose publicly in its hearings and reports. According to Staff Director William Miller:

> What is made public is what we all agree upon: the committee, the White House, and the agencies. Enough came out from the committee to understand the principle and by example what we thought we were doing and did. There was enough to make a judgment about legislation.[149]

For example, in the committee's final report, the three chapters dealing with "Cover," "Espionage," and "Budgetary Oversight" were deleted. Sections of two other chapters were deleted along with the names of individuals whose lives might have been endangered or whose privacy might have been violated. The committee was sensitive to the need to preserve legitimate secrets.

At times, however, the committee was unable to resolve differences with the executive branch on whether information should be disclosed. As a senior Ford administration official commented: "We worked frantically to hold down disclosures." [150] On two occasions the administration refused to permit executive-branch personnel to testify before the select committee. The first occasion was the committee's disclosure of illegal activities conducted at NSA, and the second involved hearings on covert action by the United States in Chile. The decision to disclose NSA's "Operation Shamrock" was made very carefully in a process that amply illustrates the committee's difficulties in this entire area.

Initially the Select Intelligence Committee was steered towards the NSA by allegations contained in the Family Jewels and by a person who came in on a confidential basis "over the transom." [151] As a result, select committee staff uncovered Operation Shamrock, in which three American companies had provided the NSA with copies of international cables. Although Operation Shamrock had been terminated by Secretary of Defense James Schlesinger in 1974, both the NSA and the White House strongly opposed any public disclosure. In fact President Ford claimed executive privilege in keeping it secret.

To decide whether Operation Shamrock should be publicly disclosed, the select committee set up a special subcommittee of Senators Huddleston, Mathias, and Morgan. In the chain of command, the NSA is under the secretary of defense. However, Secretary of Defense Schlesinger refused to argue to keep Shamrock secret. As a result, John Marsh had Attorney General Levi meet with the special subcommittee on very short notice. A select committee counsel recounted:

> All of the subcommittee members—Huddleston, Mathias, and Morgan— were middle-of-the-roaders. This was an ad hoc subcommittee to decide if there should be public hearings. Levi was unprepared. Levi started to describe why the law didn't apply. Huddleston passed me a note: "We understand this stuff better than he does." The attorney general was caught knowing less than the senators. As a result, there was no doubt in the senators minds that: (1) something was wrong, (2) it could be investigated safely, and (3) they would do it. [152]

In addition, as Counsel Eric Richard noted, "[Director of Central Intelligence] Colby had a lot of integrity. On Shamrock we asked him if he agreed that disclosure of it would do grave harm to the national security. He said no, it was not a devastating thing." [153] Senators Baker, Tower, and Goldwater had all voted against public hearings on NSA. However, the refusal of either Schlesinger or Colby to argue against public hearings and Levi's bungling of the testimony made public hearings inevitable. The outcome was a carefully controlled one-day hearing in which the NSA told what happened. This testimony was carefully reviewed in advance. Thus the select committee used to its advantage disagreement and disarray within the executive branch.

Besides its control of access to evidence and witnesses and its critical role in deciding what was disclosed publicly, the executive branch also had the power to shape the political environment in which the select committee operated. On December 23, 1975, Richard Welch, the CIA station chief in Athens, was assassinated there. The executive branch exploited Welch's death to undermine the congressional investigations. As Senator Church recalled:

> The Welch murder was *the* event. It was stage-managed. There was a big public funeral which the president attended. An attempt was made to lay the responsibility on the congressional investigations. There is no substance to that charge. There is not one scintilla to that charge. We didn't have names. We didn't have the information to leak. I sensed the political interests of the administration to close down the investigation as soon as possible and to try to keep control of whatever remedies were sought.[154]

Chief Counsel Schwarz agreed: "They danced on the grave of Welch. They egregiously and unfairly took advantage of the situation. In a short-term, tactical way, they rejoiced in his death." [155] A special counsel for intelligence to President Ford acknowledged: "The Welch killing was exploited by the White House. A lot of people believed that the publication of a list of names by [former CIA agent Phil] Agee of station chiefs was encouraged and aided by the committees." [156] Welch's death, in the words of Chief Counsel Schwarz, "inhibited the committee, but only on the foreign side. On the domestic side, we were not inhibited." [157] But the Welch incident does show the ability of the executive branch to alter the political environment.

In its relations with the executive branch the select committee was establishing the principle that the Senate had a right to exercise intelligence oversight. Not only did the committee have to muster the political will to do this, it had to overcome the opposition and prejudice one executive-branch official described:

> The executive branch views itself as the locus of responsibility and restraint. It views Congress as having too many prima donnnas who every two or six years sells their souls for votes. Congressmen are seen as irresponsible in areas of national security. On their side, Congress views the executive branch with feelings of inferiority. There is a machismo factor driving Congress to try to assert their superiority over the executive branch in these matters.[158]

The select committee was bringing about a fundamental change in the way the executive branch perceived and dealt with the Senate regarding intelligence. In the past the Senate had preferred either not to be told intelligence secrets or to restrict the information to a select few individuals. Now many more members and, for the first time, significant numbers of staffers were being told the nation's most sensitive information. Along with this access came increased responsibility. The Senate now would have to protect the information given it and might have to accept a share of the responsibility for failed operations. No longer would a plea of ignorance be credible.

The Committee and the Press

Throughout the history of the select committee the press helped frame the issues the committee addressed and reported to the American people and the Senate on the committee's work. Two reporters were especially important in framing issues: Seymour Hersh and William Safire. Hersh's 1974 article in the *New York Times* first raised the questions about illegal and improper activities of the intelligence community that sparked the creation of the select committee. All of the abuses alleged by Hersh in his article were examined by the committee. In addition, William Safire influenced the committee with a series of columns he wrote for the *New York Times* accusing the committee of having a pro-Democratic bias and of covering up the abuses of the Kennedy adminstration. A task force leader described Safire's impact: "He wrote columns regularly predicting that we would not be hard on the Democrats. As a result, we felt that it was particularly necessary to get out what was done under the Democrats." [159] Both Hersh and Safire had a significant impact on shaping the committee's agenda and behavior.

For those on the committee, press coverage was both intense and extensive. As Church recalled:

> The press gave pretty steadfast coverage to the committee. In the first year that was all the more remarkable because, until we began public hearings, the press couldn't report much. That forced the press to speculate. Great pressure was brought to bear on the members to make disclosures. Tower and I became the spokesmen. He appeared with me at every press conference following executive sessions. We often took up in the executive branch sessions themselves what could be disclosed. [160]

At times Church's public comments caused controversy among the members. A committee counsel recalled that "Mondale read the riot act to Church in a private meeting of the senators after Church had made a public disclosure." [161]

Moreover, those on the select committee found the press attention a mixed blessing. Chief Counsel Schwarz noted that "they tended to go for the headline." [162] Counsel Joseph Di Genova was even more critical: "The coverage was sensational. They didn't attempt to find out anything more. They are faced with a limited number of sources and people who won't talk to them." [163] Similar sentiments were expressed by Michael Madigan, counsel to Senator Baker: "Press people are not any worse in the intelligence area than they are in any other area; in fact, some are quite good. A few press people, however, seem to want to make a scandal out of whatever they are covering—trying to become a new Woodward and Bernstein." [164] Finally, Counsel Eric Richard thought the press simply "liked the abuse stuff. The press didn't focus on the systematic stuff. The press focused on the covert actions and the darts and not on how it relates to foreign policy and under what circumstances it is appropriate to use covert action." [165] Thus, although the select committee received extensive press, the coverage tended toward the sensational.

In some instances the committee itself was responsible for sensationalizing the press coverage. On the very first day of public hearings the committee examined the unauthorized storage of toxic agents. Among the materials provided by Mitchell Rogovin, special counsel to DCI Colby, was a dart gun. As Rogovin recalled: "I myself brought the gun up and carried it like it was a dead fish. I wouldn't let Colby touch it. The press would have just loved to have gotten a picture of Colby carrying that gun." [166] Yet the senators themselves took the gun and pointed it at each other. On the evening newscasts and in the next day's papers, Senators Church and Goldwater appeared holding an "electric poison dart gun with a telescopic sight." Church reflected:

> By holding our first public hearing on this, we blew it out of all importance. The dart gun appeared at the committee table. It is pointed to as an act of exhibitionism. Every member wanted to pick up the gun. It was not planned. I'm sorry now it happened. It was a pitfall. Suddenly something occurs which you haven't expected. Then it's the focal point. [167]

A second example occurred during the hearings on the FBI. Gary Francis Rowe, an FBI informer, testified in a hood. Ironically, Church was out of town, and Tower was chairing. A committee counsel recounted what happened:

> Rowe didn't want to testify under the glare of TV. He had been given a new identity. Fritz [Schwarz] came up with the idea of having him testify in a hood. It was beyond the ridiculous. Schwarz told me that it was his idea. Kirbow was furious when he found out about the hood and went to Fritz. Fritz said the hood was my idea. Kirbow stormed in to see me. I took him to Fritz. Fritz said it wasn't me but that it was a Republican staffer.

> Kirbow stormed away trying to find out which one. I had almost been fired over this.[168]

Rowe still testified wearing the hood, receiving extensive coverage. The hood was the gimmick the media focused their attention on, thereby sensationalizing the testimony.

At times the committee's own conduct hindered effective press coverage. The committee's strict standards on secrecy restricted contact with the press. George Lardner, who covered both the Senate and House investigations for the *Washington Post*, commented: "Pike was easier to deal with than Church. The Senate committee has always been much more elaborate. They have always had much more of a fetish about unnecessary secrecy. The Senate committee still doesn't list itself as an occupant of the Hart Building." [169]

In attempting to educate the public, the committee sometimes neglected to educate the press first. For example, a major focus was on assassinations. Members and staff expected the press to devote considerable attention to the assassinations report. Yet, despite an initial burst of interest, the report quickly disappeared from the press. Why this happened was described by a senior staff member:

> I think we didn't let the press cover us. We didn't let them get sources inside and get leaks. They could cover what we wanted in public. For example, the assassinations report was a 280-page report with a million footnotes. If we'd had public hearings with leaks, we could have had it going for years. You could leak two thousand facts and it could have dragged on two thousand days. We failed to put the assassinations report in its full context. The fact is that this report is too much to eat up in one day. The press was just frozen. There was an editorial on this in the *Washington Post* on the day after the report was released: "This is a theme we'll return to in the days ahead." They never did. We made the subject of assassinations boring by telling everything we knew in one report.[170]

George Lardner addressed the same theme shortly after the committee finished its work: "What the Church committee ignored was the importance of the educational function—the need for lights, camera, action, day after day until the lessons are driven home." [171] To some extent, then, the committee was itself responsible for inadequate press coverage.

Despite Lardner's criticisms those associated with the committee were very much aware of the educational function that even sensationalized reporting could provide. As Counsel Burton V. Wides noted: "Dart guns and exploding clam shells were sexy and good television. The idea of them coming in with guns and vials could turn it into a circus. PR was for political reasons. It was also for getting the public interested and aroused and building support." [172] Chief Counsel Schwarz agreed, adding: "The key here is the importance of establishing the facts and drawing general lessons from them. The function of the press is to take the dramatic and bring the issues home to the public." [173] Finally, Counsel Frederick Baron felt the long-term impact of the coverage was extremely helpful in forwarding the committee's educational goals:

> In the end, the press was helpful. The press would dramatize certain aspects of intelligence. The power of the press disseminated information about intelligence issues more broadly than ever before. It influenced Jimmy Carter's eventual reforms of the guidelines for intelligence activities. You can always find fault with the press. There are inevitable inaccuracies and misquotations and overdramatizations. The press did a good job on the need for reform. The press was quite important in playing up the need for charter legislation and wiretapping controls. [174]

In balance, then, the committee was able to use the press as an instrument of education, but not to the fullest possible extent.

Within the fraternity of journalists, the Select Intelligence Committee was sharply criticized. Nicholas Horrock of the *New York Times* described it as "never good box office" and as at best only "a partial success." [175] Seymour Hersh saw the committee as having had the opportunity "to do something" but as "falling short" due to Church's run for the presidency and internal staff bickering. [176] George Lardner of the *Washington Post* characterized both the Senate and House investigations as "failures yet to be appreciated." [177] Despite it all, the Church committee had conducted an unprecedented and significant investigation. All too often the press focused only on the sensational aspects of the work. However, the major responsibility for the failure to use the press more effectively must be given to the committee itself. Members were not appointed nor were staffers hired because of their understanding of the media. In failing to secure better media coverage, the committee lost a unique opportunity to educate more fully the other members of the Senate and the country at large.

The Committee at Work

The Senate had authorized the Church committee in S. Res. 19 to investigate past activities in the intelligence area and to make recommendations for the future. In carrying out this assignment, the committee's work was divided into three stages. First, after the committee was created, the Rockefeller commission found itself unable to complete the examination of data on assassination attempts unearthed during the course of its own investigation. On May 9, 1975, the Church committee decided to conduct an investigation of possible United States involvement in assassination attempts. President Ford directed that the committee receive all of the information collected by the Rockefeller commission in this area. In this first phase the Church committee conducted an extensive closed-door examination of assassinations, issuing an interim report on November 20, 1975.

The second stage of the committee's work involved public hearings. Altogether, twenty-one days of public hearings were conducted, on the following subjects: the unauthorized storage of toxic agents (three days), the Huston plan (three days), the Internal Revenue Service (one day), mail openings by the intelligence community (three days), the National Security Agency and Fourth Amendment rights (two days), the Federal Bureau of Investigation (seven days), and covert action (two days).

In its third and final stage the committee prepared and released six final reports that included 183 recommendations to the Senate. The reports focused on: (1) foreign and military intelligence, (2) intelligence activities and the rights of Americans, and (3) the performance of the intelligence agencies in the investigation of the assassination of President Kennedy.

Study of Alleged Assassination Plots
The Church committee's study of alleged assassination plots was one of the most significant and extensive investigations it conducted. Altogether the committee took over eight thousand pages of sworn testimony behind closed doors from more than seventy-five witnesses during sixty days of hearings. The report, issued on November 20, 1975, as *Alleged Assassination Plots Involving Foreign Leaders*, stated that American officials had been involved in plots to assassinate five foreign leaders: Fidel Castro of Cuba, Patrice Lumumba of the Congo, Rafael Trujillo of the Dominican Republic, General Rene Schneider of Chile, and Ngo Dinh Diem of South Vietnam. The committee also reported that it had found no evidence that American actions had resulted in the deaths of any leader although, as DCI William Colby observed, "in Castro's case it was not for any lack of trying." [178] The same comment could be applied to American attempts against the other foreign leaders.

Within the entire government there was no other entity besides the Church committee that could have studied the assassinations issue. The Rockefeller commission, or any other presidential commission, would have been subject to the criticism that it was merely a case of the executive branch investigating itself. As Church commented: "The

Rockefeller commission punted this into our laps. This was something we had to get to the bottom of." [179] In conducting this investigation the committee performed a vital service to the whole country.

Although the committee did not link the United States directly to any successful assassination, what it did discover was equally disturbing. Church noted:

> The CIA operated as an arm of the presidency. This led presidents to conclude that they were "super-godfathers" with enforcers. It made them feel above the law and unaccountable. For years we tried unsuccessfully to assassinate Castro, Lumumba, and Trujillo. These men were no menace to the United States. The only time Castro was a menace in any physical sense was when he let Russian missiles in. Ironically, that was the only period when clandestine operations against his life were halted. [180]

Church and the other committee members had great difficulty finding a paper trail linking presidents directly to the assassination attempts. During open hearings on September 17, 1975, Senator Tower asked former DCI Helms directly:

Tower: Was it usual practice for you to give oral orders or instructions to your subordinates?

Helms: Constantly.

Tower: On extremely important matters or perhaps especially on very sensitive matters, is it policy not to transmit these things in writing?

Helms: Sir, when the day comes that in an intelligence organization, particularly a secret organization, everything has to be put in writing, it is going to come to a resounding halt, I am afraid. [181]

The lack of a paper trail enabled presidents to deny any involvement in activities such as assassinations. This doctrine was called "plausible deniability."

In its study of assassinations the Church committee did much to shatter forever the doctrine of "plausible deniability." On the committee, Frederick Baron was a special assistant to Chief Counsel Schwarz. During the assassinations study, Baron prepared the Lumumba report and was the only staffer to have free access to the files. He recalled:

> I was sent to the White House to look at the documents. I was brought to the Situation Room. I was the only person allowed to look at the documents. I had uncensored access to all the cable traffic. I was able to pick what I wanted. That was the rawest data provided to the committee. This was the case study where we produced the clearest evidence that a president had ordered an assassination attempt. This refuted the notion of the CIA as a rogue elephant. Eisenhower didn't say "Assassinate Lumumba." But the language was so strong and pointed that the CIA understood itself to be on sound ground in proceeding with the assassination attempt. [182]

The assassinations study also illustrated deeper institutional problems. As Baron noted:

We needed to find a way to underline the point that things had gone wrong and then to show the set of institutional relationships that are at play in the intelligence community in making significant policy decisions or in launching operations. The intelligence agencies were sometimes too responsive to executive-branch suggestions and pressures.[183]

That United States government officials had plotted to kill foreign leaders was not pleasant news to report. In addition, the committee established links—though sometimes tenuous ones—between presidents and other senior officials to these attempts. In this study, the committee served as the representative of not just the Senate but the American people. The assassinations report is one of the most valuable and important pieces of work it produced.

Public Hearings

Nine months after the passage of S. Res. 19 the Church committee conducted its first hearings open to the public. From September 16 to 18, 1975, the committee examined the unauthorized storage of toxic agents. President Nixon had announced in the fall of 1969 that the United States was renouncing biological warfare. On February 14, 1970, he ordered all existing stocks of toxins destroyed. However, a CIA scientist, Nathan Gordon, had decided by himself not to destroy eleven grams of shellfish toxin at the CIA.[184] The toxin that was not destroyed was extremely lethal. Only two-tenths of a milligram could kill a person. One gram could kill five thousand people. The CIA's supply of eleven grams represented one-third of the world's supply. In refusing to destroy the CIA's supply Nathan had disobeyed both a presidential order and an internal CIA memorandum on February 16, 1970, ordering the destruction of these toxins.[185] As Senator Church observed: "In this particular case, yes, there was a rogue elephant at the CIA." [186] This hearing demonstrated how elusive the chain of command could be in an intelligence community that was carefully compartmentalized to protect secrets.

Unfortunately, much of the impact of this particular hearing was lost due to an incident at the first session. At the direction of the committee Mitchell Rogovin had brought up some of the CIA's more exotic weapons, such as dart guns. As noted earlier, Rogovin placed a dart gun near the senators, who proceeded to play with it in public. The next day the *Washington Post* ran a page-one story focusing not on problems of command and control but on the CIA's "exotic weapons" [187] along with a picture captioned: "Senator Goldwater sights an electric dart gun at hearing as Senator Mathias looks on." [188] Thus the real point of the hearing was lost because of the way the story was reported.

From September 23 to 25 the Church committee examined what was known as the "Huston plan." In 1970 Tom Charles Huston had worked in the Nixon White House as an associate counsel and staff assistant to the president. At that time Huston had been assigned the task of developing a plan to improve intelligence collection within the United States, particularly concerning antiwar dissidents. Militant "New Left" groups and black extremist groups were singled out for special attention. Among the actions the Huston plan called for were electronic surveillance, mail openings, the recruitment of informers, and surreptitious entries (or "black-bag jobs"). Huston himself testified before the Church committee.[189] The Huston plan was terminated shortly after it was begun because of the opposition of FBI Director J. Edgar Hoover. However, in its hearings, the Church committee showed that the Nixon administration had applied heavy pressure on the FBI, the CIA, the DIA, and the NSA to become involved in improper and illegal activities within the United States. The hearings demonstrated the dangers these entities could pose to freedom and democracy within the country when an unscrupulous and outraged administration sought to use them against its political opponents.[190]

On October 2, 1975, the committee examined actions of the Internal Revenue Service. Commissioner Donald Alexander, the head of the IRS, testified that the IRS had maintained special lists of individuals and organizations that were to be subjected to tax audits. Altogether more than three thousand organizations and eight thousand individuals were on these special watch lists. More than half of all these had been suggested by the FBI. Among the names were: the American Jewish Committee; Associated Catholic Charities; the Legal Aid Society; Common Cause; Americans for Democratic Action; the National Education Association; Mayor John Lindsey; Senators Charles Goodell, Ernest Gruening, and Joseph Montoya; Linus Pauling; Jimmy Breslin; Shirley MacLaine; Jesse Jackson; and Coretta King.[191] The CIA also suggested names for the list. For example in 1967, when the CIA's relationship with the National Students Association was disclosed by *Ramparts*, the CIA requested a corporate audit of the magazine. In addition, the CIA supplied the IRS with a list of those Americans who visited North Vietnam so that their tax returns could be audited as well.[192]

The intelligence agencies, it turned out, were not the only entities that had sought to use the IRS to punish organizations and groups. During this hearing, committee member and Democrat Robert Morgan observed that a Democratic president, John Kennedy, had used the IRS against the steel manufacturers.[193] Senator Mathias noted that the Senate, through its Permanent Subcommittee on Investigations, had put pressure on the IRS to pursue extremist organizations. Mathias observed: "Congress itself was contributing pressure in the wrong direction in 1968 and 1969." [194] When asked for his advice on how to prevent similar abuses in the future, Commissioner Alexander recommended "continual, constructive oversight over the IRS and over other agencies having broad powers like ours. Tax enforcement is too important to leave to the enforcers." [195] In its one-day hearing on the IRS, the Church committee did a solid job of outlining the abuses that had occurred at that agency and developing the evidence to justify close and continuing oversight of the IRS in the future.

In late October the committee conducted three days of hearings into mail openings, finding that, from 1953 until the program was ended in 1973, 28,322,796 letters were subjected to a CIA mail-watch program run out of the New York Post Office. Of these letters, 2,705,726 envelopes were photographed, 389,324 envelopes were copied, and 215,820 letters were illegally opened and the contents photographed. The photographed letters were distributed to the FBI (57,846), the CIA's Soviet division (31,436), and counterintelligence units at the CIA (57,894). [196] Senator Church described the meaning of this program in well-chosen words: "I cannot think of a clearer case that illustrates the attitude that the CIA lives outside the law, beyond the law, and that, although others must adhere to it, the CIA sits above it, and you cannot run a free society that way." [197]

During these hearings, witnesses from the intelligence community attempted to justify the program. For example, former DCI Richard Helms testified that the program had provided valuable information about Algerians training guerillas who were United States citizens and about Mexican terrorists being trained in North Korea. [198] John Glennon, who had been a member of the CIA inspector general's staff, noted that the program had provided intelligence about the Soviet Union. And Glennon could not understand why the committee was so upset:

> I think this mail that we are talking about has already been intercepted by the Soviet Union and the Russian intelligence service. . . . Personally, if I had a letter opened from the Soviet Union, I would not object because I would not mind the FBI knowing what the Russian intelligence service knows. [199]

According to Glennon, since the Russians did this, the CIA was perfectly justified in doing it too.

When former Postmasters General Day and Blount defended the mail-opening program in a similar fashion, Mondale exploded:

> Well, I must say that the testimony I have just heard from you, Mr. Day, and from Mr. Blount, scares me more than I expected. Not only have we found gross and unconscionable interference with the mail which threatens

the civil liberties of every American, but we have the testimony from two former postmasters general that they do not think it is wrong, even today.[200]

Blount responded to Mondale in language equally as harsh:

> Everybody can sit up here and make a speech if they want to. But if you are trying to get at the facts, I would suggest you try to construct an atmosphere where you can deal with these sensitive questions of citizens' rights versus national security. I happen to believe that national security is very important in this country. I also believe that citizens' rights are very important, and I think those two can be and have been over the years, reconciled.[201]

Although the mail-opening program had ended in 1973, the hearings captured the tension between national security and the rights of American citizens. The Church committee came down hard on the side of citizens' rights, and the tension continued throughout the hearings.

Only after long and hard deliberation did the Church committee decide to hold public hearings on the National Security Agency. The NSA hearings, which lasted two days, examined two programs that agency had conducted. Although the NSA had been established in 1952, the Church committee hearing on October 29, 1975, was the first time the director of the NSA had ever testified in a public Senate forum. The committee exercised extreme caution. Committee Counsel and Task Force Leader Barry Carter reviewed Director Allen's testimony with him line by line prior to the hearing, which was carefully scripted.[202] As General Allen noted: "I appreciate the care which this committee and staff have exercised to protect the sensitive data we have provided."[203] At the October 29 hearing Allen reviewed "Project Minaret." From 1967 to 1973 the NSA monitored the foreign cables and telephone calls of more than sixteen hundred Americans. The operation began in 1967 to counter domestic unrest and antiwar protests. Eventually secret "watch lists" were submitted to NSA by the CIA, the DIA, the FBI, and the Bureau of Narcotics and Dangerous Drugs.[204] At the November 6, 1975, hearing, the committee disclosed "Operation Shamrock" over the opposition of the Ford administration and three committee members (Tower, Goldwater, and Baker). From 1947 until May 1975 the NSA had obtained copies of cables transmitted by ITT, RCA, and Western Union. Although the companies were assured by the secretary of defense in 1947 and again in 1949 that this cooperation would never be disclosed,[205] the Church committee did just this in November 1975. The U.S. government had conducted Project Minaret and Operation Shamrock without ever seeking a judicial warrant for these intrusions into the privacy of American citizens.

The disclosure of these two NSA operations was denounced in the strongest language by Vice-Chairman Tower: "The question here is whether or not this information should be made public. Yes, there is a right of the people to know, but that must be balanced against the fact that when these matters are made public record, they are available also to our enemies." [206] Chairman Church disagreed with Tower, stating that disclosure of the operations was required because "legislation is necessary to prevent their repetition." [207] Senator Huddleston agreed: "I do not see how you can pass legislation in a vacuum. I believe that there has to be a certain amount of knowledge made available to the public and made available to the Congress before reasonable and meaningful legislation can be processed." [208] The decision to disclose these two NSA operations in public session divided the committee. However, this was the first step in a process that led to the passage of the Foreign Intelligence Surveillance Act of 1978, which required warrants for such activities. In conducting these two hearings, the Church committee exercised great care not to harm the national security; at the same time, it established the foundation for legislation that safeguarded the Fourth Amendment rights of American citizens.

The most significant of the committee's public hearings were those on the FBI, conducted on seven days in November and December 1975. The picture that emerged was not pleasant. Senator Philip Hart, weak from his struggle with cancer, attended his first public sessions of the committee and put what was presented in context:

> As I'm sure others have, I have been told for years, by among others, some of my own family, that this [the FBI actions being examined by the committee] is exactly what the bureau was doing all of the time, and in my great wisdom and high office, I assured them that they were wrong—it just wasn't true, it couldn't happen. They wouldn't do it. What you have described is a series of illegal actions intended squarely to deny First Amendment rights to some Americans. That is what my children have told me was going on. I did not believe it.
>
> The trick now, as I see it, Mr. Chairman, is for this committee to be able to figure out how to persuade the people of this country that indeed it did go on. [209]

Led by Chief Counsel Frederick A. O. Schwarz, Jr., the committee carefully laid out for the American people how the FBI had harassed and tried to intimidate both the powerful and the weak. For example, they documented how the FBI had harassed civil rights leader Dr. Martin Luther King, Jr. Commenting on this case, Mondale observed: "I must conclude that apart from direct physical violence and apart from illegal incarceration, there is nothing in this case that distinguishes that particular action much from what the KGB does with dissenters in that country." [210] But the committee did not stop with the FBI's actions against Dr. King. It showed how the FBI in its COINTEL program had conducted 2,370 actions between 1956 and 1971 that had harassed and tried to destroy dissidents within the United States. For example, the FBI tried to foment violence between black militant groups. Furthermore, case after case showed where the FBI had tried to harass dissidents both at home and work. In seeking to protect American freedoms, the FBI had adopted the tactics and techniques of the KGB. [211]

The factual record compiled in Volume 6 of the Church committee hearings is a testimony of not only how an intelligence agency can run amok but of how a free and democratic people can unearth abuses and take concrete measures to correct them. As Senator Philip Hart noted during these hearings:

> It is right that the committee and the press be worried about the treatment of a Nobel Prize winner, Dr. King; but there are an awful lot of people who never got close to a Nobel Prize whose names are Jones and Smith, that my review of the files show had violence done to their first amendment rights. Nobel Prize winners will always get protection, but Joe Potatoes doesn't, and the committee should focus on him, too. [212]

In its hearings on the FBI the committee had developed the factual record demonstrating how the freedom of all Americans is denigrated when the rights of even one person are violated. Here the committee's actions paved the way for reforms implemented within the FBI that remain strong protections in insuring that such abuses do not reoccur.

The final set of hearings was on covert action abroad. Two days of hearings were held. Because the Ford administration refused to permit any administration or CIA officials to testify, four Church committee staffers described in detail U.S. covert actions in Chile from 1967 to 1973. They reported that the United States used the following techniques in Chile: propaganda for elections and other support of political parties ($8 million), producing and disseminating propaganda and supporting mass media ($4.3 million), influencing Chilean institutions ($900,000), and promoting a coup against President Allende ($200,000). [213] Altogether the committee studied six covert actions in detail, but Chile was the only case study revealed to the public. Church explained that Chile was chosen specifically to educate Americans:

> It was the interest of the committee to determine the character and scope of covert actions. We heard six covert operations in executive session. The Chilean operation had to a great extent already been exposed in such things as the Jack Anderson columns. The world had already come to know that we were engaged in a covert action in Chile. So we were not exposing any great secret in using Chile as a case study. [214]

Again the Church committee was presenting facts to establish a clear record of past abuses and improprieties. Although the public hearings received mixed reviews in the press, they built the foundation upon which reform proposals and legislative initiatives could be launched. The success of this part of the committee's work was due largely to the efforts of Chief Counsel Schwarz.

Final Reports
Following the conclusion of its public hearings, in December 1975, the Church committee's principal task became the writing of its final reports and recommendations. At this time investigative oversight was superceded by institutional oversight. The tone and emphasis of the committee's work shifted. Instead of an almost single-minded pursuit of abuses (the mindset that had characterized its public hearings), the committee now sought to understand functions, processes, and procedures of the institutions. The final reports included considerable material supplementing the testimony and information released during the public hearings. In addition, a final report critical of the intelligence community's performance in the investigation of the assassination of President Kennedy was issued. However, the most significant action was the issuance of two reports examining foreign and domestic intelligence. In these two reports the committee's work culminated in 183 recommendations to the Senate.

In the final report entitled *Foreign and Military Intelligence* the Church committee made eighty-seven recommendations related to foreign intelligence activities. At the core of these recommendations was the proposal that the Senate create a permanent oversight committee. As the committee noted: "A major conclusion of this inquiry is that congressional oversight is necessary to assure that in the future our intelligence community functions effectively, within the framework of the Constitution." [215] Each year the new Senate intelligence committee would authorize funds for national intelligence. It would also be informed about funds authorized for tactical intelligence. To oversee intelligence budgets the new committee would use such tools as General Accounting Office audits. Besides budget oversight, the committee's prior consent would be required before any covert activity could be undertaken. With respect to the budget and covert action the Church committee proposed a highly informed and powerful entity.

The committee also proposed new legislation to replace the National Security Act of 1947 that would clearly delineate the responsibilities of the president, the National Security Council, and the director of central intelligence. New legislation also would be needed to enact charters setting forth the roles and responsibilities of the intelligence agencies: CIA, DIA, and NSA. The executive branch was encouraged to give more authority and power to the general counsels and inspector generals within the intelligence community so as to better police itself for any illegal or improper activities.

Finally, the committee recommended that some activities be prohibited entirely. First, all political assassinations were to be banned. Second, no efforts were to be undertaken to subvert democratic governments. Third, no support was to be given to the police or internal security forces of any country that violated human rights. Fourth, use of American clergy or journalists in intelligence activity was to be prohibited, and severe restrictions were to be placed on any links with academics. Fifth, no drug testing or other such activity was to be undertaken without the informed consent of the participants.[216] These were the major recommendations on foreign intelligence.

In the final report entitled *Intelligence and the Rights of Americans* the committee made ninety-six recommendations with respect to domestic intelligence activity. Again the committee called for "vigorous Senate oversight."[217] This report was dominated by prohibitions and safeguards to protect the rights of Americans; clear links to the hearings could be seen. For example, the intelligence agencies were reminded that they must obey the law. The committee recommended that the CIA, the NSA, and the military as well as the IRS and the Post Office be barred from all domestic security activities. As to safeguards, the committee proposed that the attorney general assume the responsibility to oversee domestic security. The committee specifically advocated that the FBI director's term be limited to eight years (Hoover had served for forty-eight), and that the attorney general closely supervise the FBI and its director. Once again the committee recommended that the general counsels and inspector generals throughout the intelligence community be given a key monitoring role. The committee additionally recommended new legislation to ensure that the rights of Americans were not violated by the new technologies being used. Finally, the committee recommended that the victims of such covert pro grams as COINTELPRO be notified of what had been done to them and, where appropriate, that compensation be paid.[218] Building upon the findings of its hearings, the committee recommended that actions be taken to correct past abuses and to prevent future abuses.

The Pike committee's final report was never officially printed by the House. As will be seen in Chapter 5, the Pike committee ended in disarray with its final report and recommendations totally ignored by the House. Still, there are important similarities and differences between the final reports of the Church and Pike committees.

Like the Church committee, the Pike committee recommended that its parent body, the House, create a permanent intelligence oversight committee. The proposed House committee would have budget authority for all intelligence activities; the Church committee had limited its proposal to foreign intelligence. The Pike committee proposed that the new House committee be informed of covert actions prior to their taking place; the Church committee had recommended veto power for the Senate committee. Like its Senate counterpart, the Pike committee proposed prohibitions on assassinations and on links with academics, journalists, and clergy. They also recommended that the DCI be separated from the CIA (the Church committee said only that this should be studied) and given the tools necessary to direct the entire intelligence community. Finally, the Pike committee called for the abolition of the Defense Intelligence Agency while the Church committee had proposed passing a legislative charter for the DIA.[219] The key point is that both committees recommended the continuation of vigilant intelligence oversight to be conducted by separate Senate and House committees.

On June 6, 1975, the Rockefeller commission submitted its report to President Ford. The commission had been directed by the president to focus on CIA activities within the United States such as those described in articles by Seymour Hersh. Altogether there were thirty recommendations made by the commission. Unlike either the Church or the Pike committees, the commission recommended the creation of a joint Senate-House intelligence committee. Like the two select committees, the commission proposed amending the National Security Act of 1947 and strengthening the general counsels and inspector generals within the intelligence community. In addition, it recommended that the president issue an executive order in this area and that the activities of the President's Foreign Intelligence Advisory Board (PFIAB) be expanded to include oversight of the CIA.[220]

Following the Rockefeller commission's report, the Ford administration worked behind the scenes to draft an executive order on intelligence. Finally, the seventeenth draft was brought up to the Congress not for consultation but merely to inform. This entire exercise was an attempt by the administration to prevent legislative action that would permanently inscribe congressional oversight into law.[221] On February 18, 1976, President Ford issued Executive order 11905 reconstructing the intelligence community, giving executive charters to the various intelligence entities, creating a three-member Intelligence Oversight Board within the White House to investigate questions of "illegality" and "impropriety," and taking steps to protect classified information.[222] Yet this executive order had nothing to say about congressional oversight. As John Oseth noted:

EO 11905 was as much—and perhaps more—an attempt to maintain executive control of the reform movement as it was an attempt to accommodate reform pressures. Indeed, the order had very little to say with respect to participation by Congress in intelligence controls. It made only one reference to Congress, in a provision designating the DCI as the primary spokesman for the executive on intelligence matters.[223]

The executive order failed to prevent the Church committee and its parent chamber from continuing to seek a greater role for the Senate in intelligence oversight.

Evaluation of the Church Committee

When the Church committee ended its work after fifteen months, it had successfully completed the two tasks the Senate had entrusted to it. First, it had investigated the charges of abuses. Second, it had proposed legislative and executive remedies to correct the abuses and deficiences it had found. In view of the enormity of the tasks entrusted to the committee and the short time within which it had to operate, these were considerable accomplishments. The success of the Senate Select Intelligence Committee was due in large measure to the determination, dedication, and hard work of the chairman, the members, and the staff. However, the key factor was the incorporation on the committee of both the investigative and institutional oversight models, which neatly complemented each other. Adherents to the first model enabled the committee to complete its investigative tasks while advocates of the second enabled it to propose remedies. Besides the success it had in carrying out its delegated responsibilities, the select committee had a significant impact on the press and the public, on the executive branch and the intelligence agencies, and on the Senate itself.

With respect to the press and the public, the committee vastly increased awareness of the intelligence agencies and their work. Just as important were the committee's reports on the alleged abuses. Unfortunately many of the charges investigated were proven true. The facts of senior officials in the U.S. government plotting to assassinate foreign leaders and trying to discredit individuals like Dr. Martin Luther King are unpleasant but very real parts of American history. In investigating and exposing abuses, the committee served as the representative of the American people as well as the Senate. Moreover, in its reform proposals, the committee started the process of restoring the credibility and legitimacy of the intelligence agencies in the eyes of the press and the public.

The select committee had an enormous impact on the executive branch and the intelligence agencies. A new political environment was created in which accountability was stressed and standards established for intelligence activities. The committee identified the issues and concerns the agencies should be thinking about. As for the executive branch the committee had a significant impact on President Ford's Executive Order 11905 and on the guidelines Attorney General Levi developed for the FBI. Within the agencies internal memos, guidelines, and policy statements reflected the influence of the select committee.

Regarding the Senate, the select committee demonstrated that a congressional committee could conduct intensive oversight of intelligence. In light of the House Select Intelligence Committee's dismal failure, the ability of the Senate select committee to successfully complete its investigation had significant implications for the House as well as the Senate. Moreover, the committee established principles and standards that were to guide future Senate oversight of intelligence. For example, a tradition of bipartisanship was established. The creation of permanent files and the development of knowledge and expertise among members and staff developed an institutional memory in the Senate that would greatly assist future oversight endeavors. Furthermore, professional relationships were developed with people in the intelligence community. Trust and regular procedures were established. Business was conducted on an ongoing basis, and the process was institutionalized. Finally, the recommendations of the select committee, especially those concerning permanent intelligence-agency charters and controls on potential intrusions on individual rights, provided an agenda for future overseers.

In 1983, Senator Church reflected on the work of the select committee:

> Permanent committees were established. Today, continuing congressional surveillance is built into the woodwork. We did the necessary job. Political will can't be guaranteed. The most we could do was to recommend that a permanent surveillance be established. We did that knowing that the Congress being a political animal will exercise its surveillance with whatever diligence the political climate of the time makes for.[224]

Committee Counsel James Dick agreed and added: "The select committee established the principle of congressional oversight. Even though that principle might be expanded or reduced in the years ahead, it won't be abolished or eradicated."[225] The creation of the select committee signified a revolution in the way the Senate conducted intelligence oversight. By successfully completing the tasks delegated to it by the Senate, the Select Intelligence Committee ensured that this revolution would continue.

3 Institutional Oversight Triumphant: The Inouye, Bayh, and Goldwater Senate Select Committees, 1976–84

In early 1976 the Senate began the legislative task of creating a permanent Senate intelligence oversight committee with the introduction of S. Res. 400. Three different standing committees—Government Operations, Judiciary, and Rules and Administration—considered the resolution, and each submitted its own recommendation to the Senate. There was considerable disagreement over what action to take. For example, the Rules and Administration Committee recommended merely creating another investigative committee to study abuses while the Government Operations Committee proposed a new committee to function as an intelligence oversight czar. All three versions of S. Res. 400 were unacceptable to the Senate, and the chamber was deadlocked. On May 10 to 11, 1976, Majority Leader Mansfield assumed a leadership role toward the resolution, and a compromise version was hammered out and introduced in the Senate by Rules and Administration Chairman Cannon on May 12, 1976. Four days of debate followed and the compromise version crafted by Senator Mansfield was approved on May 19 by a vote of seventy-two to twenty-two.

When the Church committee was created, Seymour Hersh's charges in the *New York Times* of illegal and improper actions by the intelligence agencies had shaped the country's mood. By the time the permanent Senate intelligence committee was created, other forces, along with the abuses uncovered and the rest of the work done by the Church committee, had come to shape Senate perceptions and behavior. First, on December 23, 1975, Richard S. Welch, the CIA's station chief in Greece, was shot to death outside his suburban Athens home shortly after he was identified in an English-language Greek newspaper as a CIA agent. Two weeks before his murder Welch had met in Athens with Republican Senator James McClure of Idaho. As a member of the McClure party recalled:

> We were coming back from the Middle East. We met with Welch at the American Embassy in Athens. I remember talking about the Church com-

mittee. I remember his words: "The publication of the names of agents is terrible. What I am afraid of, which concerns me even more than the names, is that this emboldens our enemies to take even more direct action." [1]

Senator McClure blamed Church and his committee for Welch's murder. McClure and his allies in the Senate opposed S. Res. 400. During the debate Senator Milton Young of North Dakota directly accused the Church committee of identifying Welch as a CIA agent and causing his death. Senators Mondale and Huddleston noted that the committee "did not seek and did not have the identity of Mr. Welch." [2] Despite these emphatic denials, conservatives like McClure and Young opposed S. Res. 400 because of the murder. The record does not support such a charge, but it persisted nonetheless and affected the political environment in which the resolution was considered.

Two other factors affected this environment. First, the Pike committee, the House counterpart of the Church committee, self-destructed. The investigators of the Pike committee became the investigated as the House conducted its own inquiry to see who had leaked the Pike committee's final report. The effect on the Senate was to increase pressure to make certain that any permanent Senate intelligence committee would be trustworthy. Finally, conservative members of the Senate Armed Services Committee, led by Senators Stennis and Tower, sought to protect their turf, especially the Department of Defense. A Stennis-Tower amendment to S. Res. 400 that would have retained special prerogatives for the Armed Services Committee was decisively rejected on May 19, 1976, by a vote of sixty-three to thirty-one. Despite the continuing opposition of Stennis and Tower, the Senate proceeded to pass the resolution seventy-two to twenty-two. Unnoticed at the time was a key concession to the Stennis-Tower supporters. During the floor consideration of S. Res. 400 on May 19, Senator Ribicoff noted:

The substitute [the version of S. Res. 400 passed by the Senate] does not give the new [intelligence] committee any legislative, authorization, or oversight responsibility for tactical intelligence. Responsibility for this type of intelligence will remain solely within the jurisdiction of the Armed Services Committee. [3]

The Armed Services Committee was later able to use this concession to severely restrict the budget oversight of the new intelligence committee.

With the passage of S. Res. 400 the Senate had created a permanent select intelligence oversight vehicle. For the first time in the Senate's history one committee had oversight responsibility for the entire intelligence community. From 1976 to 1984, the Senate Select Committee on Intelligence had two major initiatives. From its creation on May 19, 1976, until mid-1980 the committee worked to pass legislation that built upon the revelations and proposals of the Church committee. The new committee's centerpiece for this period was its attempt to bring about a comprehensive legislative charter. For almost five years the committee's work was dominated by this effort, focusing its proposals to a large extent on prohibitions, identifying specific activities not to be undertaken by U.S. intelligence entities. In the middle of 1980, in the aftermath of the rise of Islamic fundamentalists in Iran, the Russian invasion of Afghanistan, and the opposition of President Carter to any effort to restrict executive power, the committee abandoned the effort to enact a comprehensive intelligence charter. From mid-1980 through 1984 the committee assumed a new posture. Instead of seeking to proscribe certain intelligence activities, it worked to build up American intelligence capability. It abandoned the legacy of the Church committee, becoming an active proponent and ardent supporter of the intelligence community.

More than a year after the permanent Senate Intelligence Committee was created, the House created its own permanent intelligence committee. As will be seen in Chapter 5, the House committee from 1977 to 1984 had one chairman, one staff director, one chief counsel, and a fairly stable membership. The Senate committee had no such stability. From 1976 to 1984 the Senate Intelligence Committee had three chairmen, three staff directors, two general counsels, and, with the Republicans winning control of the Senate in 1980, its majority shifted from the Democrats to the Republicans in 1981. As one student of both committees observed, the Senate committee "more vividly mirrored the changing political environment"[4] from 1976 to 1984.

When the Senate passed S. Res. 400 on May 19, 1976, the new committee was the legitimate successor to the Church committee. It adopted as its legislative agenda the reform proposals made in the Church committee's final reports. Yet the new committee did more than just inherit the agenda; five of the eleven members of the Church committee were appointed to the new one. Fourteen of the Church committee staffers joined the new staff. William Miller, the staff director of the Church committee, retained this role with the permanent committee. Although the Church committee's Chief Counsel Frederick Schwarz returned to private practice, several of his key investigators remained on the staff of the new committee. As was noted in the last chapter, the Church committee adopted both the institutional and investigative oversight models. On the new committee the institutional model gradually came to prevail as those staff members most strongly supporting aggressive investigative oversight were slowly purged by Staff Director Miller, who favored institutional oversight. Some members, however, left on their own as the novelty of oversight simply wore off and as practices and procedures became routine.

Recruitment of Committee Members

The committee created by S. Res. 400 was a select committee, meaning that the choice of members was left in the hands of the respective party leaders. The Senate Select Intelligence Committee had a membership of fifteen. For all of the nine years examined here, the majority party had eight seats while the minority was allotted seven. This ratio was deliberately set to foster bipartisanship. In addition, S. Res. 400 called for the representation of the four standing committees dealing with intelligence: Appropriations, Armed Services, Foreign Relations, and Judiciary with one Democrat and one Republican to be appointed from each. From 1976 to 1984 this guideline was violated only once when, from 1981 to 1984, there was no Republican member from the Judiciary Committee. The other seven seats were reserved for members of the Senate at large. Also, no member could serve for longer than eight years. In setting up the permanent Select Intelligence Committee along these lines, the Senate leaders sought to reflect all points of view with a rotating membership that would lead to a good mix of committees and perspectives.[5]

From 1976 to 1984 Mike Mansfield and Robert Byrd officially chose the Democratic members while Hugh Scott and Howard Baker designated the Republicans. The usual path to becoming a member was to formally request appointment either through a formal letter or by a personal appeal to the party leader. For example, in 1976, Republican Leader Scott received formal letters requesting appointment from Senators Baker, Case, Garn, Hatfield, Hayakawa, Stafford, and Thurmond. All but Hayakawa, a first-year senator, were appointed.[6] Scott himself described how he and Mansfield determined who would serve: "Mike would say: 'Who do you want to put on?' I would say: 'Tell me yours.' We chose those with the best background and interest. We put people on who would do a good job. Because this is a select committee, this gave us great flexibility."[7]

Party leaders sometimes sought to recruit specific individuals. For example, Senator Daniel Inouye was recruited personally by Majority Leader Mansfield to serve as the first chairman. As Inouye recalled: "I myself had had no role in the debate and negotiations over the size of the committee and the tenure of the members. Mansfield worked on

Table 3.   Membership of Inouye Committee (1976)

Member	Age	Years in Senate	1974 ADA Rating	1974 NSI Rating
Inouye	52	13	63	43
Bayh	48	13	93	17
Stevenson	46	5	77	0
Hathaway	52	3	94	10
Huddleston	50	3	56	25
Biden	34	3	78	0
Morgan	51	1	19	89
Hart	39	1	94	0
Democratic average	46.5	5.3	71.8	23.0
Goldwater	67	19	6	100
Baker	51	9	13	100
Case	72	21	83	11
Garn	44	1	14	88
Thurmond	74	21	0	100
Hatfield	54	9	88	0
Stafford	63	5	72	80
Republican average	60.7	10.6	39.4	68.4
Committee average	53.1	7.9	56.7	44.2

Source: *Almanac of American Politics 1976.*

me for ten days before I accepted the chairmanship."[8] Because of the importance and sensitivity of the committee's work, the party leaders exercised great care in their appointments. Senator Inouye, a member of the committee from 1976 to 1984, observed:

> The process of selecting the members is not discussed openly. In the selection of members, the selecting committees and the leadership would set aside seniority for one factor and desire for another. Membership on the Intelligence Committee is very prestigious in the Senate. The fact that you apply for membership on this committee doesn't mean you'll get it.[9]

Similar care was exercised on the Republican side. A senior aide to Senator Baker who assisted him in the process noted: "Baker largely

Table 4.   Membership of Bayh Committee I (1977-78)

Member	Age	Years in Senate	1976 ADA Rating	1976 NSI Rating
Bayh	49	14	94	17
Stevenson	47	6	75	0
Hathaway	53	4	85	10
Huddleston	51	4	61	25
Biden	35	4	83	0
Morgan	52	2	31	89
Hart	40	2	94	0
Moynihan	50	0	—	—
Inouye	53	14	64	43
Democratic average	47.8	5.6	73.4	23.0
Goldwater	68	20	0	100
Case	73	22	95	11
Garn	45	2	0	88
Mathias	55	8	81	0
Pearson	57	15	50	78
Chafee	55	0	—	—
Lugar	45	0	—	—
Wallop	44	0	—	—
Republican average	55.3	8.4	45.2	55.4
Committee average	51.3	6.9	62.5	35.5

Source: *Almanac of American Politics 1978.*

selected the Republican members himself. Potential members must be smart enough to understand the issues and careful enough to give them careful consideration. You try to avoid members who shoot their mouths off and leak to the press." [10] The decision to appoint is critical because, as a senior Republican staffer on the Senate committee observed, "once they are on, there is little that can be done." [11] Both parties, then, have exercised great care in picking members.

On the permanent House Intelligence Committee seats were allotted to the parties on the basis of the Democratic-Republican ratio in the

Table 5.   Membership of Bayh Committee II (1979–80)

Member	Age	Years in Senate	1978 ADA Rating	1978 NSI Rating
Bayh	51	16	85	11
Stevenson	49	8	65	30
Huddleston	53	6	30	50
Biden	37	6	50	0
Moynihan	52	2	60	30
Inouye	55	16	60	25
Jackson	67	26	55	50
Leahy	39	4	65	22
Democratic average	50.4	10.5	58.8	27.2
Goldwater	70	22	10	90
Garn	47	4	5	100
Mathias	57	10	50	13
Chafee	57	2	55	11
Lugar	47	2	10	100
Wallop	46	2	10	100
Durenberger	45	0	—	—
Republican average	52.7	6.0	23.3	69.0
Committee average	51.5	8.4	43.6	45.1

Source: *Almanac of American Politics 1980.*

House. Therefore the Republicans deliberately appointed only very conservative members to the Boland committee (see Chapter 5). However, in the Senate, the party ratio was retained at eight to seven. (The result is seen in Tables 3 to 7.) While the ADA and NSI ratings show that the Democrats tend to be more liberal than the Republicans, there is not the wide chasm between members from the two parties that existed on the Boland committee. In addition, the membership of both parties on the Senate committee reflects the diversity of the Senate itself. For example, liberal Democrats such as Bayh, Biden, Gary Hart, and Leahy, were included along with conservative Democrats such as Bentsen, Jackson, and Nunn. Liberal Republicans such as

Table 6.   Membership of Goldwater Committee I (1981–82)

Member	Age	Years in Senate	1980 ADA Rating	1980 NSI Rating
Goldwater	72	24	0	86
Garn	49	6	17	100
Chafee	59	4	72	20
Lugar	49	4	17	80
Wallop	48	4	22	100
Durenberger	47	2	44	70
Roth	60	10	22	90
Schmitt	46	4	17	100
Republican average	53.8	7.3	26.4	81.0
Moynihan	54	4	72	10
Huddleston	55	8	44	44
Biden	39	8	67	33
Inouye	57	18	67	14
Jackson	69	28	72	30
Leahy	41	6	83	0
Bentsen	60	10	39	44
Democratic average	53.6	11.7	63.4	25.0
Committee average	53.7	9.3	43.7	55.0

Source: *Almanac of American Politics 1982.*

Case, Chafee, Hatfield, and Mathias were combined with conservative Republicans such as Garn, Goldwater, Lugar, and Wallop.

Membership on the permanent Senate Intelligence Committee had both advantages and disadvantages. The biggest benefit to members was the access to secret information and the public perception following that access. For example, a Republican member of the committee from 1976 to 1984 observed how he used this access in debates with opponents in his home state: "I go to debates with nuclear freeze types. I respond by saying that, as a member of the Intelligence Committee, I have access to information that you don't have or should not have. I can't discuss it here but it counteracts what you've said." [12]

Table 7.   Membership of Goldwater Committee II (1983-84)

Member	Age	Years in Senate	1982 ADA Rating	1982 NSI Rating
Goldwater	51	18	83	0
Garn	51	8	5	100
Chafee	61	6	80	11
Lugar	51	6	15	100
Wallop	50	6	10	100
Durenberger	49	4	70	63
Roth	62	12	50	56
Cohen	43	4	55	89
Republican average	55.1	9.0	36.9	75.9
Moynihan	56	6	95	30
Huddleston	57	10	50	56
Biden	41	10	80	22
Inouye	59	20	70	30
Leahy	43	8	90	10
Bentsen	62	12	40	80
Nunn	45	10	45	90
Democratic average	51.9	10.9	67.1	45.4
Committee average	53.6	9.9	51.0	61.7

Source: *Almanac of American Politics 1984.*

While he was a member of the committee, Senator Henry Jackson used similar tactics both with constituents and with members of the Senate. As a senior aide to Jackson recalled: "Jackson always liked to say that 'if you had the information I have from the CIA, you wouldn't disagree with me.'" [13] Another senior staffer noted how members were able to use this access to secrets to shape the way they and their work in the Senate were viewed: "By and large, the members of the committee don't have any information that is significantly better than anybody else who reads the newspapers. But the perception is the key. One's image is elevated by service on this committee." [14]

Besides enhancing one's image, access to information can assist a member's other committee work or provide entry into intelligence and national security. Because eight members of the committee are from the four principal standing committees that touch upon intelligence, these members can use their position to advance their standing committee work. For example, Gary Hart was a member of the Church committee who also served for four years on the permanent committee. He was also a member of the Armed Services Committee. Appointed to the Church committee as a first-year member of the Senate, Hart used both of his intelligence-committee assignments to develop defense expertise helpful in his work on the Armed Services Committee. Besides advancing standing committee work, membership also provided an entry into national security. Senators Bentsen, Durenberger, and Moynihan, for example, were all able to use their Intelligence Committee positions to gain access to national security even though their other committee assignments had no relationship to national security.

Another advantage to membership is that it allows the pursuit of important public policy goals. For example, Senator Huddleston, a former member of the Church committee, for more than four years led the Senate effort to pass a comprehensive intelligence charter. Similarly, Senator Chafee became the prime committee mover for passage of agent-identities legislation. Senator Stevenson looked into the intelligence product (i.e., the reports, personality profiles, and assessments produced by the various intelligence agencies) while Senator Jackson focused on the quality of analysis (i.e., just how good were the analytical skills used in compiling the intelligence product). Senators Hathaway and Wallop devoted their attention to intelligence budgets while Senator Schmitt, a former astronaut, studied the role of intelligence in the space program.[15]

A final advantage to service was that it demonstrated the party leadership's trust and confidence in the member. By definition, the leadership could and did control the members appointed to this select committee. As Senator Inouye observed, appointment carried a certain amount of prestige within the Senate.

But there were distinct disadvantages to being on this committee. There was very little electoral benefit since most constituents often were not even aware that their senator was a member. A Democratic member who devoted enormous blocks of time to closed-door budget oversight described this phenomenon:

> Not one in ten thousand, not one in a hundred thousand knew I was on the Intelligence Committee. Adlai Stevenson came up to speak on my behalf when I was running for reelection. He was on the Intelligence Committee,

and he mentioned I was on it too. Some friends of mine came up later and said they didn't realize I was on the committee. It had been in all the newspapers when I was appointed but that didn't sink in.[16]

Likewise a Republican who served on the committee from 1976 to 1984 noted, "Most of my constituents don't know I'm on it" despite his having served "six or seven years."[17] A senior intelligence-community official who worked with the committee somewhat wryly observed: "You don't make any brownie points with constituents by serving on this committee. You get nothing for your state. You won't make any mistakes because nobody knows what you're doing on the committee anyway."[18] There are no projects or funds that can be brought back to a member's home state. Clientele groups in intelligence oversight (see the section, "The Committee and Clientele Groups," below) are either nonexistent or irrelevant in comparison with the strength of such groups in other policy areas.

Another disadvantage to service on the committee is the time it consumes. Because so much of the activity occurs by necessity behind closed doors members frequently do not come to meetings at all. A Democrat who headed budget oversight early in the history of the committee observed: "I was disappointed in the attendance of the members. Of course, senators have too many responsibilities. I was chairman of four or five subcommittees. To attend the hearings of others besides your own is almost impossible."[19] A Republican who directed budget oversight later during the 1980s was "very disappointed in the committee. Its lack of involvement. We so rarely have full attendance at meetings."[20] Another member, disappointed in his own inability to take a more active role, expressed a common theme:

I have not lost my interest in the Intelligence Committee. Attendance is a poor indicator of interest in the committee. I am now the chairman of [my standing committee]. A lot of my time is taken up there. I constantly have bright staff members coming in to see me with a whole host of different issues. I have to switch constantly in my mind. The only way I get any time to think is to come in at 6:30 in the morning. That gives me two and a half hours before the phones start to ring. We go by the bells here. Schedules are crazy.[21]

Because it is a select committee its members do not have to give up their standing committee assignments. However, even when members would have liked to devote more time to the committee and its work, the schedules imposed by other duties often intervened.

A final disadvantage to membership is the constraint it placed upon members' public actions and statements. With respect to actions, members asserted a claim to be "fully and currently informed." Yet, in terms of covert actions, even when members were informed, they had no veto power. The executive branch was supposed to inform the committee, but it did not have to obtain prior committee approval. Moreover, because of the controversy over leaks from intelligence oversight committees, it was easier for nonmembers to speak out in public than it was for informed committee members. A senior staffer on the Senate committee summarized:

> The payoff is small for being a member of this committee. It is easier to talk publicly if you're not a committee member. There is not much legislation and the budget is secret. If things go well, nobody pays attention. If things go badly, people say what did you know, what did you do, when did you do it, why didn't you do better?[22]

In the 1980s, the committee became attractive to two types of senators. The first group was made up of relative newcomers (especially the class of 1980) who sought membership on a committee with jurisdiction over the nation's security. The second group comprised older senators who sought to enhance their standing committee work. Others sought access to national security and found the Intelligence Committee to be just as effective an entry as the Armed Services or Foreign Relations committee. However, as time passed, the committee became, on the whole, a less attractive assignment. Members received only a fraction of the publicity that the Church committee received, and morale suffered under the 1981–84 chairman, who repeatedly stated that the committee was unnecessary and should not exist.[23]

Leadership of the Chairmen

From 1976 to 1984 the Intelligence Committee had three different chairmen. Senator Inouye served in this capacity for the first two years. However, fearing that he would be co-opted if he remained in this position any longer, Inouye resigned as chairman but remained as a member through 1984. Senator Bayh succeeded Inouye, chairing through 1980 when he was defeated for reelection and the Republicans won control of the Senate. From 1981 to 1984, Senator Goldwater served as chairman.

Daniel Inouye

When the committee was created Majority Leader Mansfield personally recruited Senator Daniel Inouye to be the first chairman. Without question, from 1976 to 1984, Inouye was the most respected member of the committee. A Japanese-American, Inouye had been in Hawaii when the Japanese attacked Pearl Harbor on December 7, 1941. Like many of his Japanese-American peers Inouye joined the 442nd Regimental Combat Team, which fought in Europe. A decorated combat officer, Inouye was seriously wounded two days before hostilities ended in Europe. His right arm was amputated, and he had a total of eight operations and seventeen blood transfusions. But when Inouye returned to Hawaii, a barber refused to cut his "Jap hair." Incensed, Inouye became active in politics and, after receiving his law degree from George Washington University, he slowly worked his way up in Hawaiian politics. In 1959 he was elected to the U.S. House of Representatives, in 1962 to the Senate. He eventually became part of the old Senate Democratic establishment and was the ally and confidant of senior Democrats.[24] In 1973 Mansfield personally recruited Inouye to serve on the Senate Watergate Committee. Thus when Inouye assumed the chairmanship of the Intelligence Committee he had solid credentials.

When he became chairman, Inouye viewed institution building as his major task. He described his set of informal rules:

> (1) I set the precedent of holding the chairmanship for only two years. If it was longer than two years, you would have become not the chairman but one of the advocates of the intelligence community. There is too much danger of developing a buddy system.
> (2) I tried to keep the committee as nonpartisan as possible in an atmosphere of partisanship. During my tenure as chairman all decisions were unanimous.
> (3) This was not to be a patronage committee. I set the example. Instead of appointing a designee [staff person allotted to each member] to do my bidding, I let him work for the committee.[25]

Inouye set a more formal precedent in the close relationship he maintained with his vice-chairman, Senator Goldwater. On the Church committee, Senators Church and Tower had worked well together as chairman and vice-chairman. Inouye established the same type of relationship with Goldwater, and it was followed by his successors. For example, Inouye insisted on taking Goldwater with him to all meetings with the president. The Inouye-Goldwater relationship was so close that Goldwater even gave the chairman his proxy. As Inouye reflected, "Can you imagine that? I am supposed to be from the liberal wing and he's supposed to be from the conservative wing but I still had his proxy."[26] Inouye also took the lead in maintaining security. He observed:

> I developed a highly disciplined unit. Leaks were unknown. I went very far in disciplining people. That type of discipline had never existed in the Congress. For example, I recommended that we fire a staff member who took his notes out of the shop. The other members intervened. We suspended him without pay for three months. He did come back after the suspension but he finally left.[27]

Inouye was not reluctant to discipline members of the committee either. He and Goldwater would call in and speak to members who spoke too frequently in public about intelligence or who came close to disclosing sensitive information.[28] Chairman Inouye was adept at building the institutional supports necessary for effective oversight.

As an intelligence overseer Chairman Inouye adopted a "carrot and stick" approach. The stick he wielded was budget authorization. The carrot he offered was a secure committee with disciplined members and staff. Of the three chairmen during this period Inouye was the most respected and effective. As Admiral Inman, the deputy to the director of central intelligence, commented: "Chairman Inouye's major contribution was the gift of tough oversight combined with the best security for classified information in Congress and the executive branch."[29] Inouye himself summarized his chairmanship:

> The general public was confused after the Church committee finished its work as to whether or not the intelligence community was doing authorized activities. We [the committee] can't make the case for intelligence, but the committee performs a watchdog function. We are in a position to provide credibility. Once you begin to realize what these agencies do, you can't help but reach the conclusion that they comprise one of the most important and powerful arms of the executive branch.[30]

Chairman Bayh commented on his predecessor: "Senator Inouye was uniquely qualified to be the first chairman. He was sensitive to civil rights, and he also realized that one breach of security would destroy our credibility."[31] As chairman, Inouye devoted an enormous amount of time to the work of the committee. Unfortunately he stepped down after only two years. His legacy, however, was an effective oversight vehicle.

Birch Bayh

When Inouye stepped down, Senator Birch Bayh succeeded him as chairman since he was second in seniority among the Democrats. Bayh came with solid liberal credentials. Serving in his third Senate term, he had been the floor leader and was largely responsible for Senate passage of the constitutional amendments that strengthened the presidential succession, gave eighteen-year olds the right to vote, and approved the Equal Rights Amendment. In addition he had been the floor leader for the successful campaigns to defeat the Supreme Court nominations of Clement Haynsworth in 1969 and G. Harrold Carswell in 1970. On the Intelligence Committee, Bayh chaired the Subcommittee on Intelligence and the Rights of Americans and was a member of the Subcommittee on Charters and Guidelines.

As chairman of the Intelligence Committee, Bayh continued some of the precedents established by Inouye. For example, Bayh worked closely with his vice-chairman, Senator Goldwater. Unlike Inouye, Bayh met with the president on his own. Still, Bayh made a practice of keeping Goldwater fully informed of what he had been told. Then the two of them decided if and when other members of the committee would be informed.[32] Like Senator Inouye, Bayh sought to keep the committee together. For example, in October 1979 the committee released a brief five-page report entitled *Principal Findings on the Capabilities of the United States to Monitor the SALT II Treaty.* The report did not state definitively that the United States was capable of monitoring the treaty. Senator Bayh had made a deliberate choice not to divide the committee. As he noted:

> I opted in the end that it was better to get a unanimous report through there than to force through a report that would have divided the committee. It would have been strongly along party lines that we would have supported SALT II. I believe the benefit gained by doing that was not compensated for by the damage that would result to the committee's structure.[33]

Finally, Bayh attempted to maintain Inouye's strict standards of security by occasionally calling members in when their public comments endangered secrets entrusted to the committee.[34]

Yet Bayh did some things his own way. Inouye had chaired while the committee was being established and, not surprisingly, there was little legislative activity. Under Bayh the committee assumed intelligence leadership as the Senate passed into law the Foreign Intelligence Surveillance Act of 1978 and the Intelligence Oversight Act of 1980. Bayh's leadership was important in the passage of both. In addition Bayh brought a significant change in tone and emphasis. Senator Inouye had been concerned about becoming "co-opted" by the intelligence community and so stepped down as chairman after only two years. Bayh had no such concern. As he put it, "The concern I had was not being co-opted but rather how you have complete communication."[35] A turning point came when President Carter refused to tell the committee in advance about the Iran rescue mission in April 1980 because of security concerns. Under Bayh's leadership the committee fought for and won the provisions in the Intelligence Oversight Act of 1980 that gave it the right to be "fully and currently informed."[36]

In 1980 there were major changes in the U.S. political environment that had a significant impact on the committee and its chairman. The political changes were due largely to the revolution in Iran and the Soviet invasion of Afghanistan. The committee, sensing these changes, abandoned in mid-1980 the attempt to enact comprehensive legislation for an intelligence charter. Instead it adopted completely the institutional oversight model, and the attempt to enact the reforms proposed by the Church committee ended. Bayh's last year as chairman was a difficult one. The time he could devote to the committee was interrupted by a tough reelection campaign in Indiana, which he lost to Dan Quayle, and by his wife's slow and painful death as a result of cancer. Because he was preoccupied with these matters, the committee's discipline was loosened, especially among the staff. Staff became increasingly involved in other activities for their members, and some staffers even took an active part in the 1980 political campaigns. Inouye had attempted to establish a precedent by having his own personal designee be devoted totally to committee work. However, in the last year of the Bayh chairmanship, the members increasingly came to view the designees as patronage employees.[37] Under Chairman Bayh, the Intelligence Committee remained united and the committee itself became solidly established in intelligence policy. However, the tight discipline that had characterized the committee under Inouye had been loosened.

Barry Goldwater

After the Republicans won control of the Senate in 1980, Senator Barry Goldwater became the third chairman of the Senate Intelligence Committee. He served from 1981 to 1984. When Goldwater assumed the chairmanship he was seventy-two years old and had served in the Senate for twenty-four years. The *New York Times* described him as "the Senate's crusty curmudgeon, a man of blunt frankness and firm opinion who was never overly concerned with the diplomatic niceties that pervade Senate life."[38] In 1985 Goldwater himself acknowledged that he had been aptly called "the fastest lip in the West" but noted that he had become "more tolerant": "I even sit down and ask whether it just would be better to keep my mouth shut."[39] During his time as chairman, Goldwater had some serious health problems. He underwent triple-bypass heart surgery and had artificial joints implanted in both hips.[40]

Chairman Goldwater made no secret of the fact that he unabashedly supported the intelligence community. He had served on the Church committee and had been the vice-chairman of the permanent Select Intelligence Committee under both Inouye and Bayh. Goldwater also had some definite views about the type of oversight the committee should conduct. He sincerely believed and repeatedly stated while he was chairman that the committee was unnecessary and should be abolished. Former Staff Director John Blake, who was present twice while Goldwater publicly made such statements, noted that they damaged his ability to serve as chairman: "It hurts the senator to make such statements. It would be like the chief of staff of the air force saying: 'I don't believe in flying.' Senator Goldwater wants to go back to the 'whisper in your ear' days." [41] Although Goldwater never was able to abolish the Intelligence Committee, he had very firm views as to what type of oversight it should practice. He was a strong believer in institutional oversight and conceived of the intelligence community as a "family." At a committee hearing on July 21, 1981, he stated:

> Now, we have an oversight committee for the first time in the history of this country. It is not just for the purpose of our overseeing what the intelligence family does, but it is part of our duty to listen to the intelligence family as to what they think would be helpful. [42]

Throughout Goldwater's chairmanship the committee increased funding for the intelligence community and passed legislation such as the Agent Identities Bill and revisions of the Freedom of Information Act that advanced the interests of those it was charged with overseeing. The committee thus became an intelligence advocate.

Like his two predecessors Goldwater developed a close working relationship with his vice-chairman, Senator Moynihan. In his autobiography Goldwater discussed this relationship:

> Although he [Moynihan] was vice chairman of the committee, I considered him an equal. My secrets would be his secrets and vice versa. . . . CIA Director William Casey would at times give the committee highly sensitive information. That would be kept between the chairman and vice chairman alone. . . . In the four years we worked together, we never passed along the most sensitive information to the rest of the committee. The compartmentalization worked well. [43]

When Goldwater was forced by illness to miss Intelligence Committee sessions, Moynihan assumed leadership. At times Moynihan tried to protect the chairman from his own words. For example, at the July 21, 1981 hearing cited above, Goldwater had said he did not believe there should be an intelligence oversight committee. After Goldwater made this statement, Vice-Chairman Moynihan tried to soften its impact:

> Well, Mr. Chairman, sometimes you say things you do not really mean. (Laughter)
> And those of us who know you and love you sometimes have to extend your remarks. You believe there should be an Intelligence Committee. Down deep you know it's right. (Laughter)
> But you want to make our intelligence system work and our institutions work. [44]

The bipartisan spirit was similar to that of the Inouye-Goldwater and Bayh-Goldwater relationships that had preceded it.

Although Senator Goldwater was a strong supporter of the intel-

ligence community, throughout his chairmanship he maintained a
strained and at times testy relationship with the Director of Central
Intelligence William Casey. Sometimes the conflicts erupted in public.
For example Goldwater told Casey at his confirmation hearing to hire
Admiral Inman as his deputy director: "I don't think you need much
assistance, but I think Admiral Inman would be a great addition to your
staff if you could see a way to put him on it." [45] Later Goldwater criticized Casey severely for his appointment of Max Hugel as head of the
Operations Directorate. Additionally, when it turned out that Casey
had not revealed all the financial information the committee had originally sought for his confirmation, Goldwater directed a staff inquiry
into the matter.

On December 1, 1981, the committee declared with a distinct lack
of enthusiasm that "no basis has been found for concluding that Mr.
Casey is unfit to hold office as director of central intelligence.[46]
Throughout his time as chairman, Goldwater and the committee clashed
with the DCI over the CIA's actions in Nicaragua. The chairman spoke
out harshly in public when the committee learned in 1984 that it had
not been briefed adequately on the mining of Nicaraguan harbors.[47]
Goldwater, like Bayh before him, had difficulty at times in obtaining
information from the executive branch.

Of all the individuals who headed Senate and House intelligence
oversight committees, Chairman Goldwater was the only overseer who
believed his committee should not exist. The statements he made as
chairman calling for the abolition of the committee damaged his credibility. A further loosening of discipline on the committee ensued. Staff
members especially took advantage of this situation and engaged in
other types of work, occasionally even political activity. During the
Goldwater chairmanship, the committee continued to conduct institutional oversight.

Internal Relations

When the permanent Senate Intelligence Committee was created in
1976, the party leaders took two important actions to insure that the
committee would remain unified and bipartisan. First, the party ratios
were set at eight seats for the majority party and seven for the minority. Even when the Republicans won control of the Senate in 1980 they
did not alter this ratio. Second, the vice-chairman was made the second in command even though he was from the minority party. Section
2(c) of S. Res. 400 stated: "The vice chairman shall act in place and
stead of the chairman in the absence of the chairman." In practice,

when the chairman was absent, the vice-chairman ran the committee. These two actions sent a clear sign to the members appointed to the committee. From 1976 to 1984 each of the committee's three chairmen formed a close and solid relationship with each of the two vice-chairmen. This example of teamwork at the top helped the Committee stay together. As Chairman Inouye observed: "The Senate committee is as nonpartisan as any you'll find. The work is secret. A group of men—we haven't had any women members yet—get together under almost equal terms." [48]

Although the members did not take opposing positions in public, there were at times heated, closed-door disagreements. As a senior staff member observed: "Disputes are carried on behind closed doors. The result is that you get the lowest common denominator approach. The committee prides itself on its consensus approach." [49] The best example was the committee's report on U.S. capability to monitor SALT II. As noted in the previous section, instead of issuing a strong endorsement of SALT II, which would have divided the members, the committee issued a more tentative endorsement that was unanimous. For the most part the divisions that emerged were due more to ideology and issue orientation rather than party affiliations. As another senior staffer commented: "The cleavages have consistently cut across party lines. What happens on Senate Intelligence is that you have Republican moderates lining up with Democratic moderates and Democratic conservatives lining up with Republican conservatives." [50]

In the 1976–84 period, there was only one issue on which the members disagreed in public: aid to the Contras in Nicaragua. On June 18, 1984, committee members Inouye and Moynihan introduced an amendment to terminate all U.S. aid to paramilitary operations in Nicaragua. The amendment would also have provided $6 million for an orderly and humanitarian withdrawal and resettlement of the opponents of the Nicaraguan government. The amendment was defeated by a vote of fifty-eight to thirty-eight, and the committee divided eight to seven. Inouye and Moynihan were joined by Republican Cohen and fellow Democrats Bentsen, Biden, Huddleston, and Leahy. They were opposed by Democrat Nunn and Republicans Goldwater, Chafee, Durenberger, Garn, Lugar, Roth, and Wallop. Later Inouye introduced another amendment to terminate all aid to the opposition in Nicaragua, and that was defeated on October 3, 1984, by a margin of fifty-seven to forty-two. This time the committee divided nine to six with Bentsen joining Chairman Goldwater and his seven allies. These are the only two instances in which public divisions occurred in this nine-year period. Moreover, Nicaragua was more of a foreign policy issue than an intelligence issue. A guiding principle remained, then, for the committee to seek consensus.

The members were also united by their support of U.S. intelligence. A staff member who himself strongly supported U.S. intelligence described this phenomenon:

> The senators are all extremely conservative on intelligence. There are more apologists and defenders on Senate Intelligence than on any other committee. Are they co-opted or educated? The senators add money to the intelligence budgets and like to protect intelligence capabilities.[51]

Even Senator Inouye, who gave up his chairmanship for fear of being co-opted, described how his own attitudes had changed as a result of his service on the committee:

> Yes, my views changed. I had no idea of what I was getting into. I thought of Robert Ludlum and what you read in magazines and newspapers. In reality, it is such a complex, all-encompassing organization with fancy devices. After about a month I felt that this [Robert Ludlum, James Bond] was a grossly distorted view of reality.[52]

The evidence suggests that, once members came to know what the intelligence agencies really did, they became strong supporters. For members sharing this mindset the institutional oversight model was ideal.

As noted above, the 1976–80 period was dominated by attempts to enact reforms proposed by the Church committee while from 1980 to 1984 efforts to strengthen U.S. intelligence prevailed. Throughout this entire time, the members agreed on the general initiatives in each period and competed merely at the margins. For example, the Foreign Intelligence Surveillance Act of 1978 passed the Senate ninety-five to one. More conservative members of the Senate committee tried to weaken the bill. However, on the House side, the ranking minority member of the House Intelligence Committee led an ambush that caught Chairman Boland unprepared and briefly threatened the entire bill (see Chapter 5). Because of the close relationships between all three chairmen and their respective vice-chairmen such an action was unthinkable in the Senate. Ironically the permanent House committee appeared on the surface to be less partisan than the permanent Senate committee. There appeared to be no partisan distinctions on the House staff as there were on the Senate staff. Yet appearances were deceiving. The members and staff on the Senate committee were in reality more bipartisan than their House counterparts.

Another characteristic of Senate Intelligence Committee members was their lack of time for committee work. As Senator Hugh Scott observed: "Senators are frustrated people. There is never time to think. There is no opportunity for original concepts or thinking. They are constantly badgered by constituents. They are computerized. They are hounded by special interest groups."[53] In response to such pressures, members tended to defer to the chairman and vice-chairman and the heads of the various subcommittees. In the House, members of the Budget Subcommittee took pride in the amount of time they devoted to their work. On the Senate Intelligence Committee, comparable time was given but, for the most part, only the chairman and staffers of the Senate Budget Authorization Subcommittee attended. Lack of member attendance plagued all of the other subcommittees as well. Staff members, and especially the designees, therefore came to wield enormous power on the committee. As former Secretary of Defense Harold Brown observed: "There is a tradition on the Intelligence Committee of the Senate as there was on the Armed Services Committee in the Senate that the committee works together and that the chairman runs it."[54] Consensus politics and the attempt to keep the members united dominated the internal relations of the Senate Intelligence Committee.

Committee Staff

Staff members had a critical role on the Senate Intelligence Committee. Because members' time was often severely limited the staff had to assume an important supportive role, in some cases becoming almost surrogate senators. As the committee evolved, the chairman was responsible for selecting the staff director and the counsel. The vice-chairman designated the minority staff director and minority counsel. Two professionals were hired by the committee to do budget oversight. In addition each member of the committee was allotted one staff "designee" to track issues. All staff members had a background check conducted by the FBI, and the full committee voted on them before they were hired. Only once did the full committee reject a proposed staff member.[55] From 1976 to 1984 the committee had three different staff directors.

When the committee was established in 1976 William Miller became the first staff director, serving through 1980. He had been staff director of the Church committee, on which he had been the strongest advocate of institutional oversight. Miller brought to his new position not only experience but an institutional memory. He sought to build a staff that was "nonpartisan" and "professional."[56] He also sought to implement institutional oversight on the permanent committee even though some staffers were investigative overseers held over from the Church committee. However, as time went on, these staffers gradually left and were not replaced by other investigative staffers.

Besides implementing institutional oversight Miller worked diligently to enact the reform proposals of the Church committee. Although comprehensive charter legislation was not enacted, during Miller's tenure the Foreign Intelligence Surveillance Act of 1978 and the Intelligence Oversight Act of 1980 were passed into law. In addition the committee and Miller were key shapers of the Executive Order on Intelligence issued by President Carter in 1978. In his relations with the executive branch Miller was assisted by former Church committee staffers who had assumed key positions throughout the Carter administration.

During Miller's time as staff director a problem began to arise concerning the designees. For the members, designees had a vital function. As Chairman Bayh noted: "Congress people are so busy. The members just really need a good staff person to trust and rely upon. You need a designee who won't feather his nest and who won't bother you when it's unnecessary. You don't get that from a nonpartisan staff." [57] When Senator Inouye was chairman he had tried to set a precedent by having his own designee work for the committee. However, this precedent was not established; the members increasingly viewed designees as patronage appointments. The designee's salary was paid by the committee but set by the individual member, typically between $40,000 and $48,000 per year.[58] Although most of the members selected highly competent professionals for these posts, one member proposed and was granted an eighteen-year old constituent who had just graduated from high school. This individual became merely a messenger for the staff but a very well paid messenger at that.[59] Gradually designees became simply an extension of the individual member's personal staff, having loyalty only to their members and not the committee. A saying common to the designees was: "You live and die with your senator." [60] The principles that had initially led to the creation of designee positions were being eroded.

Also during Miller's directorship came the growth of what became known as the "Gang of Six," a group of conservative designees who sought to shift the focus of the committee's efforts. Led by Senator Wallop's designee, Angelo Codevilla, the Gang of Six wanted to divert attention from the Church committee proposals to such issues as: (1) competitive analysis, (2) fostering different points of view in the analytic process, and (3) counterintelligence. After the committee's 1980 abandonment of intelligence-charter legislation, this group's agenda became largely the agenda of the committee from 1981 to 1984. In zealously pursuing this agenda their actions at times stimulated considerable tension on the committee.[61] As staff director, Miller implemented institutional oversight while still attempting to enact the reforms proposed by the Church committee; only he had the prestige and skill to keep the members and staff working together.

When the Republicans won control of the Senate, Chairman Goldwater designated John Blake as the new staff director. Blake, who came from an intelligence background, was the president of the Association of Former Intelligence Officers (AFIO) at the time. Blake found the position of staff director very frustrating largely because of his inability to control the staff. He noted:

> I was deputy director of the CIA. I received a salary of $50,000 and, although the absolute numbers are classified, I had a big budget and numbers in the thousands under me. I retired in January 1979. As staff director of the Senate Intelligence Committee I received $52,600 a year, had about fifty on the staff, but had no authority. The designees told me as staff director to "go stuff eggs." [62]

After ten months Blake resigned and was succeeded by Robert Simmons, also from the intelligence community, who served through 1984.

During the Goldwater years the designees increasingly devoted their time to members' personal work unrelated to either the committee or intelligence. A new type of person started to fill the designee positions. Initially most of the designees had worked on the Church committee. However, in the Goldwater years, the designees tended to be young, bright, ambitious, and competitive with little background in intelligence. They usually viewed their positions as mere way stations on a career path. Typically they would serve for about two years in order to use the committee on their résumés. Because most of these designees were neophytes regarding intelligence, legislative liaison people from the various intelligence agencies cultivated relationships with them to win support for their agencies' budgets and programs. [63]

Additionally some staffers began to come from positions in the intelligence community, serve on the Senate Committee, and then returned to the intelligence community. Daniel Childs, for example, joined the CIA in 1957 as an accounting clerk. In 1966 he joined the Office of Planning, Programming, and Budgeting. From 1972 to 1976 he was assigned to the Intelligence Community Staff as chief of the Program and Budget Development Division. In October 1976 Childs resigned from the CIA and joined the Senate Intelligence Committee, where he served as the senior staff member for the Budget Authorization Subcommittee until June 1982. On July 5, 1982, Childs returned to the CIA as comptroller. [64] Childs was not the only staff member to have such a career path. Thus the committee became an opportunity for intelligence professionals to advance their own careers.

Under Goldwater's chairmanship the committee staff evolved in a way quite different from the original vision of Senator Inouye. The increasing use of the committee by intelligence novices and professionals alike as a tool for career advancement raises some serious questions. How effective was the oversight such individuals performed? Did they withhold criticism for fear of losing job opportunities? The answers are clouded in the secrecy surrounding the committee. William Miller had been effective as staff director because he knew the Congress, knew the issues, and had the complete confidence of the members. However, during the Goldwater years, the staff director became just another among several voices clamoring for staff assistance and support. The staff director became more of a ringmaster than a framer of the committee's agenda.

The Committee and the Senate

For any committee the relationship with its parent chamber is its most critical relationship. S. Res. 400, passed by the Senate on May 19, 1976, by a vote of seventy-two to twenty-two, had authorized the Intelligence Committee to act as the Senate's representative. From 1976 to 1984, at those points where the committee could be held accountable for its actions, it received the solid backing of its parent chamber. Legislation brought to the Senate floor by the committee was approved with substantial majorities, and additional sensitive tasks were delegated to the committee. The strong Senate support is not surprising since the committee reflected both the views of the political parties and the diversity to be found among the senators with respect to intelligence issues. Since the committee practiced consensus politics and tried to rally members' unanimous support for measures it considered, its own bargaining and compromising were merely ratified on the floor of the Senate whenever the entire body considered the legislation it proposed.

The backing the Intelligence Committee received is amply illustrated by the Senate's actions regarding its legislative proposals. For example, on April 20, 1978, the Senate approved the Foreign Intelligence Surveillance Act ninety-five to one. On June 3, 1980, the Senate passed the Intelligence Oversight Act of 1980 by eighty-nine to one. "Graymail" legislation, designed to protect classified information during criminal trials, passed the Senate by voice vote on June 25, 1980. The Agent Identities Act, designed to protect undercover U.S. operatives, was passed on June 10, 1982, by eighty-one to four. Finally, revisions to the Freedom of Information Act, designed to exempt CIA operational files from FOIA search requests, were approved by voice vote on September 28, 1984. Besides proposing legislation, the committee began in 1977 to bring an annual intelligence authorization bill to the Senate floor to provide funds for U.S. intelligence activities.

These measures were passed routinely by the Senate by voice vote; no floor changes were ever made. During the Senate's consideration of the 1978 Intelligence Authorization Act, Majority Leader Robert Byrd expressed how the rest of the leadership and senators viewed the committee:

> I take exceptional pride in the work that is being done by this committee and exceptional pride in the membership of the committee.
>
> I believe that the work of this committee, its supreme dedication to duty and to patriotism have entitled it to the esteem and high regard and respect not only of the Senate but of the country.
>
> I salute the committee and its chairman, and may I say in my judgment the Senate and the country are in the committee's debt.[65]

Besides legislative activity the committee was entrusted with additional intelligence assignments for the Senate and for other Senate committees. The committee examined intelligence issues related to the Panama Canal treaties and did an extensive study for the Senate on whether the SALT II treaty had adequately provided for verification.[66] Throughout this period the Senate leadership routinely assigned the committee sensitive intelligence issues. Such issues were also referred to the committee by other Senate committees. The Intelligence Committee did studies for the Foreign Relations Committee concerning the Shaba invasion of 1978[67] and the implementation of the Taiwan Relations Act.[68] When an auditor for the General Accounting Office brought charges of Soviet spying to the Government Operations Committee, that committee routinely referred the matter to the Intelligence Committee.[69] All these requests demonstrated that the committee was viewed as secure and competent by the leadership and other committees.

From 1976 to 1984 the only difficulty the Intelligence Committee encountered with other parts of the Senate concerned the Armed Services Committee. From 1977 to 1984 the two committees waged a long, at times testy, and unresolved struggle over who should authorize funds for the Defense Department and its intelligence activities. The debate was conducted primarily behind closed doors; however, it did surface once on the floor of the Senate. On July 20, 1978, Senator Hathaway of the Intelligence Committee asserted that S. Res. 400 gave the two committees "joint" responsibility over authorizing funds for "intelligence-related activities" in the Department of Defense while Senator Harry Byrd of the Armed Services Committee maintained that the resolution gave Armed Services "exclusive" jurisdiction over this area.[70] Despite the fact that members of the Armed Services Committee served on the Intelligence Committee, this struggle over authorization polarized relations between the two committees. In the House,

Speaker O'Neill personally resolved the differences on authorization between the House Intelligence and Armed Services committees. The Senate leadership was either unwilling or unable to exert similar influence.[71] Despite this one unresolved conflict, the Senate Intelligence Committee had solid relations with its parent chamber for the entire period.

The Committee and the House

In its relations with the House of Representatives the Senate Intelligence Committee dealt almost exclusively with the House Intelligence Committee. The House committee was established more than a year after the Senate committee, and for the first few years it simply reacted to Senate legislative initiatives. The permanent Senate committee inherited members, staff, an institutional memory, and a legislative agenda from the Church committee. The House committee started basically from scratch and responded to the Senate committee's attempts to enact Church committee proposals by holding its own hearings which were less detailed than the Senate committee's.

Nonetheless the House committee had a distinct advantage in one area: budget authorization. Learning from the problems the Senate Intelligence Committee had with Senate Armed Services, the House committee won authorization authority over all intelligence activities. The Senate committee had authorization authority only over "national foreign intelligence" while the Senate Armed Services committee retained control over intelligence related to the Department of Defense. As a result, in conference committees, the Senate committee was able to go only to conference on "national foreign intelligence" while Senate Armed Services went to conferences on Defense Department intelligence authorizations.

Although both Senate and House intelligence members and staff claimed they won in conference, there was a distinct difference between the two on budget authorization. Senators personally spent far less time than House members did on authorization. As one Senate Intelligence staffer observed, "A representative defending a cut has spent more time on this one issue than all the senators on the whole budget."[72] On budget issues House Intelligence had a tendency to reduce authorization requests while Senate Intelligence tended to increase them. Senator Bayh described relations with the House committee:

> It was a pretty good relationship. The only time we ever differed was on the level of appropriations for particular types of intelligence collection

systems. I got into a major difference of opinion with the House committee and the [Carter] administration. The Senate was facing the SALT treaty and the need for new systems in the down years. The House committee and the administration thought this was wasteful spending. We said you'd better go ahead and spend the extra money. We were successful in conference.[73]

For the most part, relations were harmonious between the two committees.

In S. Res. 400, the Senate Intelligence Committee had been directed to look into the feasibility of establishing a joint Senate-House intelligence committee. As the two intelligence committees evolved there was contact between members of the two when necessary. Staffers from both worked closely on budget authorizations and kept in touch on the interests, problems, work, and issues of their counterparts on the other committee.[74] Yet there were some clear-cut divisions between the two committees. As a senior staffer on the Senate committee observed:

> We are more nonpartisan than the House committee. We are more bipartisan here. And, instead of being impressed like the House members are by being invited and going out to breakfast with DCI Casey at Langley, Senate members would say why doesn't he come down and have breakfast with us here?[75]

In its first annual report to the Senate, the Intelligence Committee noted that it had looked into the question of establishing a joint intelligence committee and had found that "for the foreseeable future a joint committee does not seem desirable or possible."[76] The Senate committee never addressed the issue again. Because of structural, jurisdictional, and institutional differences between the two committees and between the two parent chambers, a joint committee truly was neither desirable nor possible.

The Committee and the Executive Branch

From 1976 to 1984 the Senate Intelligence Committee constantly struggled with the executive branch over access to the information it needed to perform oversight. Because of the inherent secrecy of intelligence and the limited impact of outside forces such as the press and clientele groups, the relationship between the committee and the executive branch was crucial.

The investigations of 1975 to 1976 had an impact on executive-legislative relations concerning intelligence that can best be described as "revolutionary." The closed-door, loose oversight that had characterized the period from 1947 to 1974 had come to an abrupt end when the Church committee looked into all aspects of intelligence activity in excruciating detail. Previously acceptable practices and procedures were no longer satisfactory. In response, mechanisms were created within the intelligence agencies and the executive branch to ferret out abuses. The executive orders issued by both Ford (1976) and Carter (1978) had strengthened the authority and power of the general counsels and inspector generals within the various agencies and created the Intelligence Oversight Board to investigate any illegal or improper actions. Regular reporting requirements were established so that both the permanent Senate and House committees were informed of what the executive branch learned.

The reporting requirements and the fear of being subjected to searching, public congressional oversight modified the behavior of the intelligence community. For example, at the CIA, a report was filed with the general counsel that a CIA employee had stolen a twenty-five cent candy bar from a blind man's stand at agency headquarters. Because of a fear of being accused of covering up an improper action, the candy-bar theft was reported to the Intelligence Oversight Board and both intelligence committees.[77] Sometimes it was difficult to get employees to act in this new climate. An undercover FBI agent, for example, infiltrated a Weatherman group, a radical leftist organization, in California. When the group asked the undercover agent for instruction in using weapons, a considerable debate ensued within the FBI and the Justice Department about the propriety of such an action and how the matter would "play" with Congress. The matter was eventually brought to Attorney General Griffin Bell, who suggested that the undercover agent "teach them to shoot so as to miss."[78] The suggestion was accepted and, as Judge Bell observed, "The people were taught to miss in such contorted positions that they said there must be some easier way to shoot."[79] The investigations, then, had a significant impact on behavior within the executive branch. In addition, key Church committee staffers were appointed to senior positions in the Carter White House and the various intelligence agencies, where they also pushed for proper behavior and procedures.

The executive branch also had to make structural changes to accommodate the drastically increased congressional workload. From 1947 to 1974 one CIA legislative counsel had handled the task of congressional liaison for the entire intelligence community. Now individual agencies had to develop their own congressional liaison offices. At the CIA alone, up to six individuals were assigned at any one time to congressional liaison.[80] At the FBI nine were assigned to congressional relations. The FBI viewed its relationship with the intelligence committee as a "partnership."[81] Finally, the NSA assigned professional intelligence officers to two-year duty tours working with the Congress.

Prior to the 1975–76 intelligence investigations few people in Congress had even heard of the NSA; now it ran a very effective legislative operation.[82] These structural changes made it more difficult for the White House and the DCI to control access to the Hill. Agencies were now able to establish independent relationships with the oversight committees to advance their own interests. The agencies tried to cultivate favor with the Senate Intelligence committee staff, especially with ambitious designees.[83] Senior Carter and Reagan administration officials alike were concerned about the implications as a senior Reagan policymaker observed in 1983: "Too cozy a relationship has developed between the agencies and the congressional committees. The agencies are supposed to be responsive to the president and not just to the committees."[84] Thus congressional oversight had resulted in some dramatic changes in structure and behavior within the executive branch.

While these changes were taking place, three different views of congressional oversight emerged within the executive branch. These views were to be found in both the Carter and Reagan administrations. The first, the Brzezinski-Casey view, saw congressional oversight as an unnecessary activity fraught with danger. This view, adopted by both Carter and Reagan, was best summarized by Brzezinski himself:

> There is a very debilitating tendency for Congress to inject itself into details for which it has neither the competence nor the mandate. The intrusion of Congress into these areas is like the liberum veto in the Polish Parliament. In the middle of the sixteenth century any single nobleman could veto the decision of the entire parliament. Today any single member of Congress can veto a covert action by going public.[85]

Adherents of the Brzezinski-Casey view saw congressional oversight as: (1) compromising sensitive information, (2) giving power to overseers who had no expertise to do oversight, and (3) revealing bits and pieces of a puzzle that might enable an enemy to complete a picture that would do great harm to U.S. national security interests (the mosaic theory).[86] Holders of the Brzezinski-Casey view had great contempt for the members of Congress as individuals and for the Congress itself as an institution. During the Carter administration this viewpoint led the president to fail to inform Congress in advance about the mission to rescue hostages in Iran. It led the Reagan administration not to be honest with the Congress about what it was doing in Nicaragua. Since this view of oversight was held by both Carter and Reagan, the Senate Intelligence committee had to contend with the president when it sought greater access to sensitive information.

A second view emerged which might best be termed the "Turner thesis" since it was developed by Admiral Stansfield Turner, DCI under President Carter. Here, oversight by the two intelligence committees is seen as a necessary evil with some distinct tactical advantages for the executive branch. As Turner observed: "Congressional oversight gives a lot of power to the DCI. With this oversight process, I have a way of getting off the hook. I'd like to do this, but I have these committees to report to." [87] Yet this view is not limited merely to the executive branch. As a close aide to Turner observed, this view can be elaborated to severely limit congressional options:

> Admiral Turner felt it was important to share information and responsibility with the Congress. Then when something was blown or a disaster occurred, this would shut them up entirely and immediately. They can't say anything. If other committees raise questions, you tell the intelligence committee to get the other guys in order. It's a very effective tactic. [88]

This view uses the oversight committees as a shield to fend off requests for information from other parts of Congress. Ironically it is a great device for co-opting the Congress and its overseers. Had President Carter or President Reagan adopted this approach, either one might have been able to minimize congressional criticism. But this view requires a modicum of trust in the Congress and a willingness to share power and responsibility with it, two prerequisites neither president was willing to concede.

The third viewpoint might be called the "Vance thesis." Here congressional oversight was a positive good in and of itself. As former Secretary of State Cyrus Vance observed:

> Congress should be informed of the whole range of intelligence matters. Congress should be able to express its views on the covert side to the president and the senior officials in the executive branch so that the common sense view of elected representatives can be brought to bear on such matters. [89]

Agreeing with this view David Newsom, a former ambassador who worked closely with both intelligence committees on covert action during the Carter administration, noted: "The committees performed a very useful role in looking at actions from a useful and different perspective and asking questions that the executive branch, under the pressures of time, did not ask. Congress represents the best repository of domestic attitudes." [90] All too often White House officials are not familiar with intelligence, and the intelligence agencies themselves tend to be insulated from political realities. In such a policy environment, congressional oversight offers the executive branch a perspective to identify what might be politically feasible. However, for this viewpoint to operate, the Congress and its intelligence oversight committees must be seen as coequal partners with the executive branch, a perspective neither Carter nor Reagan was willing to adopt.

From a historical perspective, the number of contacts between the executive branch and the intelligence committees and the amount of information given to the committees grew enormously. From 1947 to 1976 there was limited access. During the investigative period of 1975 to 1976, access to information and witnesses was only grudgingly given. However, the permanent committees had unprecedented access. Even with this tremendous change, though, there was some information that presidents and senior officials simply refused to share with the Congress. To further illustrate the problem, Presidents Carter and Reagan were unwilling to deal with the Congress as a full and coequal partner in intelligence policy.

The Committee and the Press

The relationship between the committee and the press also evolved during the 1976–84 period. The committee's varying degree of openness was largely determined by the successive chairmen. Under Inouye the committee presented a closed-door policy to the press. Inouye refused all requests for interviews about the work of the committee. Spencer Davis, a professional staff member on the committee, and formerly the press secretary for the Church committee, was in charge of all press contacts. Any other contact with the press was actively discouraged by Chairman Inouye.[91]

During the chairmanship of Senator Bayh the committee became more accessible to the press, conducting extensive public hearings on all aspects of the proposed charter legislation. The hearings were opened deliberately to gain press coverage so as to build public support for the proposed legislation. Yet, in many ways, Chairman Bayh adopted a posture similar to Inouye's. Unlike Inouye, Bayh did meet with reporters privately. But as Bayh noted:

> Some of those reporters were hot on a story. They were out there in Afghanistan and Pakistan. They're on top of what's happening. Sometimes it is not easy to discuss these problems with them. They and you know what is going on. They thought that we didn't know or were just plain idiots. You just have to accept that.[92]

Under Bayh the committee was more open with the press but restraints were still imposed.

During Senator Goldwater's chairmanship press contacts became much more extensive. Members and staff, especially the designees, were cultivated by the press, and they in turn used the press as a communications vehicle. As one senior committee staffer observed in 1983: "What do you do if you're a designee and the member who hired you and can fire you at any time directs you to talk to the *New York Times?* You talk to the *New York Times.*" [93] Yet, in being more open with the press, committee members and staff were merely following the example set by Chairman Goldwater. For example, in March 1982, the *Washington Post* ran a front-page story charging that President Reagan had approved a $19 million CIA plan to create a five-hundred member paramilitary force of Latin Americans to "disrupt" the Nicaraguan regime. The administration heatedly denied the story. However, in the March 22, 1982, issue of *Time,* Chairman Goldwater confirmed the *Washington Post* story: "Everything in the *Post* story was true. They didn't have everything, but everything they had was true." [94]

In an interview with Bob Woodward of the *Washington Post* on April 2, 1982, Goldwater stated why he had confirmed the story: "I thought the American people should know about that [the Nicaraguan operation]. In fact, I'm tickled to death it was made public. A lot of this stuff should be made public. 75 percent of what we hear in intelligence briefings should come out." [95] Goldwater went on to tell Woodward that Deputy Director of Central Intelligence Inman was re-signing and that the United States had limited sources within the Soviet Union: "We don't have many eyeballs in there now. I know about twelve years ago we had only five sets of eyeballs there working for us." [96] In comparison with both Inouye and Bayh, Goldwater was very candid with the press. This example was emulated by committee members and staff.

During the Goldwater years the press was used to inform the public of opinions held on the committee. Occasionally members used the press to communicate among themselves. For example, Philip Taubman, who covered the committee for the *New York Times,* could never get Senator Inouye to agree to an intelligence interview, but was increasingly able to penetrate the committee during the Goldwater years. On May 28, 1982, a Taubman article described the committee's failure to perform its assigned oversight task. Senators Biden, Durenberger, Huddleston, and Leahy sharply criticized the committee leadership on the record. Taubman reported that the chairman and vice-chairman had "failed to set a clear agenda for the panel or supervise its work closely and had conducted too much committee business without consulting the other senators." [97] In this instance members used the *New York Times* to communicate their dissatisfaction with the committee leadership.

Although the Intelligence Committee's accessibility to the press changed over the years, throughout the entire 1976–84 period the committee was stirred to act by stories reported in the press. Indeed, the press helped to frame the very issues the committee considered. A theme that dominated press coverage was the suspicion that the intelligence agencies might be trampling on the rights of American citizens. As Ben Bradlee, executive editor of the *Washington Post,* observed:

> When I hear the words "national security" I suspect I'm being conned. We [in the press] are hostile to intelligence people. This is because we've been lied to so much. We don't fall for their simplistic bull. We know them and how they operate. I believe that our society is better served if they do have to answer to the press for what they do.[98]

The committee was quick to follow up on the press's reports of improprieties. For example, in its first report to the Senate, the committee stated that it had "received close to one hundred allegations of improprieties by intelligence agencies."[99] The committee further noted that it had done its own investigations and had required the intelligence community to submit formal reports."[100]

Sometimes the committee launched successive probes on a single issue. For example, on October 1, 1978, the body of retired CIA official and Soviet expert John A. Paisley was found floating in the Chesapeake Bay with weighted diver's belts around the waist and a gunshot wound in the back of the head.[101] The case took some bizarre turns (such as whether it was murder or suicide) and appeared regularly in the press over the next two years. After each new story the Senate Intelligence Committee called the CIA for a response. Liaison people at the CIA developed a "Paisley response team," and each new allegation was carefully investigated.[102] In its third report the committee commented that it "found no information to support the allegations that Mr. Paisley's death was connected in some way to involvement in foreign intelligence or counterintelligence matters."[103] Thus the press became a powerful catalyst for the Senate Intelligence Committee, providing it with issues and questions to be addressed.

The Committee and Clientele Groups

There were only a few groups concerned with intelligence that had any influence on the Senate Intelligence Committee. While the committee was attempting to enact a legislative charter some pressure came from both the American Civil Liberties Union and Morton Halperin's Center for National Security Studies. The two groups were linked by Jerry Berman serving as legislative counsel for the ACLU and general counsel for the Center for National Security Studies. These two groups focused on the protection of civil liberties, especially free speech and the right to privacy. At the Center for National Security Studies a group of ten individuals, led by Morton Halperin, tried to educate both the committee and the public on safeguarding civil liberties. The center issued a monthly newsletter and offered witnesses to testify at hearings on legislation the committee was considering.[104] The influence of the ACLU and the Center for National Security Studies was greatest in the period prior to mid-1980 when the Senate committee abandoned the charter effort.

At the other end of the political spectrum were two groups that strongly supported the U.S. intelligence community. The Association of Former Intelligence Officers (AFIO), a group of CIA, FBI, and NSA alumni, provided witnesses to testify before the committee. Its influence was more substantial after 1980, when the committee itself more strongly supported the agencies.[105] The American Security Council, with a membership of 300,000, also embarked on educational efforts. Each year the council compiled the National Security Voting Index, which rated all members of Congress on how pro-defense their voting records were.[106] Of these two groups the AFIO was much more active.

Finally, one other group active in the intelligence area was the self-funded Committee on Law and National Security, associated with the American Bar Association. This group became the focal point within the legal community for issues relating to national security. Its monthly newsletter, *Intelligence Report,* had a circulation of five thousand. It has sponsored conferences on intelligence issues, developed a casebook on law and national security, and set up an advisory committee of lawyers on intelligence law.[107]

These were the principal groups that sought to exert leverage on the Senate Intelligence Committee. In intelligence the clientele groups were extremely limited in the pressure they could bring to bear.

The Committee at Work

From 1976 to 1984 the Senate Select Intelligence Committee publicly released sixty-four publications about its work. It produced five reports to the Senate giving an overview of its activities and issued five reports, required by law, about the implementation of the Foreign Intelligence Surveillance Act of 1978. It also issued reports on: (1) intelligence analysis and the oil issue 1973–74, (2) Soviet strategic capability and objectives, (3) the CIA's analysis of Soviet oil production, (4) the activities of "friendly" intelligence services in the United States, (5) United States capability to monitor the SALT II treaty, and (6) political violence in El Salvador. The first four reports were issued in the 1977–78 period while the last was the only such study released from 1981 to 1984. Besides reports the committee released transcripts of fifty-seven days of hearings. Ten of these days involved hearings on the seven individuals nominated to either the DCI or DDCI positions. An additional twenty-four days of public hearings concerned attempts in the 1976–80 period to enact legislation embodying the Church committee recommendations. During the years Goldwater was chairman, the committee released only eight days of hearings, four of which involved nominations. In legislative activity the committee's public workload was severely limited and "comparable to that of some so-called 'paragraph 3' Senate standing committees." [108]

In addition to this public activity a considerable amount of the committee's work was done behind closed doors, a significant problem to anyone attempting to compare the Senate committee to either the House committee or other Senate committees. One political scientist who has closely observed both the House and Senate intelligence committees sees any such attempt as not only "difficult" but

> methodologically hazardous, in that many congressional observers doubt the validity of available statistics on committee workload. In the case of the intelligence committees, because much of their work is confidential, their published activity reports are not always comprehensive in scope. Certain generalizations can safely be made however. Both committees are referred fewer measures than any standing committee in their respective chambers, and no clear-cut comparisons of relatively private committee work can be made easily. [109]

Despite these limitations and despite the inherent secrecy, enough information is available to discuss the work of the committee.

Budget Oversight
From 1976 to 1984 the Select Intelligence Committee devoted a significant amount of time to budget oversight. From its inception, the Subcommittee on Budget Authorization, with its consideration of the annual intelligence authorization bill, was the principal means for the committee to exercise such oversight. Three different members chaired this subcommittee. From 1976 to 1978 Senator Hathaway served as chairman, to be succeeded by Senator Inouye, who served from 1979 to 1980. Senator Wallop then chaired from 1981 to 1984. The committee viewed its budget authority not only as a means for oversight but as a way to support the intelligence community. As the committee noted in its September 23, 1981, report to the Senate:

> Annual budget authorization is an essential tool in conducting effective congressional oversight of the U.S. intelligence activities. It not only provides an effective means of ensuring accountability, but also enables the

Congress to exercise a positive influence by strengthening areas where it was needed.[110]

For a committee practicing institutional oversight, budget authorization was an ideal tool.

The Subcommittee on Budget Authorization held a series of annual hearings that began in late January and ended in early April. The subcommittee received an overview from the DCI and then heard testimony from the heads of the intelligence agencies. For the fiscal 1978 authorization bill the subcommittee conducted forty hours of hearings and took a thousand pages of testimony.[111] For the fiscal 1979 bill it conducted thirty hours of hearings, submitted questions for the record, and received eleven volumes of budget justification materials totalling over two thousand pages.[112] When the subcommittee came to consider the fiscal 1985 bill it received seventeen volumes of budget justification materials comprising over three thousand pages, prompting the subcommittee to submit several hundred questions for executive-branch officials to answer for the record.[113] Committee members and staff also visited intelligence facilities inside and outside the United States when not occupied by the January–April budget hearings.

Intelligence budget oversight is handled uniquely by the Congress. Because of the great sensitivity of the information all the hearings were conducted behind closed doors, and no budget figures were ever released to the public. Although the Senate committee had twice as many staffers as the House committee, the Senate committee had only two full-time staff members assigned to the budget while the House committee had four. On the Senate committee one staff member handled the CIA, the Intelligence Community Staff, and special Air Force programs while the other staffer was responsible for all Defense Department intelligence activities, including the "tactical intelligence" and "intelligence-related activities" accounts.[114]

Because of other demands on member time, the principal overseers on the Senate Budget Authorization Subcommittee were the subcommittee chairman and the staff members. The work was extremely time-consuming. As one subcommittee chairman noted:

I spent more time in my budget subcommittee work than all my other committees combined. It is important work. You can't take anything home to study, not even notes. I spent a lot of time at NSA preparing myself to get an overview. If you don't have any background in intelligence, it takes a long time.[115]

A staffer on the subcommittee described how the process evolved:

At first two to three of the senators would attend the budget subcommittee hearings. But it gradually fell off to one member, the chairman. Senators have busy schedules—they are too busy. As a result, the subcommittee had to rely on staff. In fact, staff were used as witnesses by the senators.[116]

Because the committee adopted the institutional oversight model its relationship to the people it was overseeing was both close and supportive. At times budget overseers went out of their way to assist those they were overseeing. As another staff budget overseer noted:

> We would receive three-thousand page budget books. There is an awful lot of complexity; it is a difficult area to understand. We would write up questions for the senators and the historical record. We gave the witnesses who were to testify the questions in advance. Everybody knew what the game was. In terms of increasing funds, we never lost. We consistently increased funds but we spent very little time on the financial implications of the programs.[117]

In conducting this type of budget oversight, the Senate committee came to function as a court of appeals for executive-branch officials upset with cuts or with limited increases approved by the House committee. As a result, in the intelligence budget area, the Senate-House relationship came to resemble the system Fenno described in *The Power of the Purse.*[118]

Another distinction between Senate and House budget oversight was in the focus of attention. The House Intelligence Committee favored a careful line-by-line scrutiny of all budget requests, largely as a result of its legacy from the House Appropriations Committee. While the House intelligence overseers adopted a micro approach, the Senate overseers adopted a more conceptual macro approach. As a senior budgeter on the intelligence community staff observed: "House budget overseers are less supportive, more critical, and do their homework to find flaws. Senate budget overseers are more supportive, more relaxed, and less critical."[119] This, too, closely resembled the Senate-House distinctions found by Fenno in *The Power of the Purse.*

During the 1976–80 period, the Senate Intelligence budget subcommittee sought to identify and to meet intelligence needs and to identify waste and duplication. The approach was described by a budget subcommittee chairman: "I tried to go across the board. Intelligence is an extensive field. I didn't want any gaps left uncovered. Also, our work meant that there was a better chance of eliminating unnecessary redundancy."[120] However, in 1981, Senator Wallop assumed the subcommittee chairmanship and implemented a different type of budget oversight. He described how he moved the subcommittee to a more functional approach:

> Before I got involved in budget oversight, we never did some very elementary things. We never did ask what we're buying for what we're spending.

I started asking these questions: (1) What is the quality of our intelligence? (2) Is the product that is produced of any use to intelligence consumers? (3) What do consumers think of the intelligence product they receive? and (4) How do the intelligence services and agencies relate to one another? We now have a ten-year look at the intelligence needs of the United States. We are now looking at the total picture.[121]

In conducting budget oversight the Intelligence Committee was a supporter of and an advocate for those it was charged with overseeing. As has already been noted, the budget oversight conducted by the committee was hindered by the refusal of the Senate Armed Services Committee to surrender its budget oversight duties toward the Defense Department. The Intelligence Committee was fully briefed by Defense, but its recommendations on "tactical intelligence" and "intelligence-related activities" were usually ignored by the Armed Services Committee. Moreover, it was Senate Armed Services, not Senate Intelligence, that went to conference committee meetings on defense.[122] As a result, although the Senate Intelligence Committee received information on all intelligence-community activities, its budget authorization oversight was impeded by its lack of authority, power, and influence over Defense Department intelligence.

Covert Action
With respect to covert action, the Senate Intelligence Committee exercised a crucial oversight role. In 1974 Congress had passed the Hughes-Ryan amendment which required that eight Senate and House committees be informed in advance about covert action proposals. Critics maintained that the act let 57 senators, 143 representatives, and untold numbers of staff know the most sensitive secrets the U.S. government possessed.[123] But in reality very few members or staff were informed. For example, from 1976 to 1980 the Senate Foreign Relations Committee had fifteen members and more than fifty staff members. When covert action briefings were given the information was severely restricted. One staff director of the Foreign Relations Committee described how they followed the process:

> The Foreign Relations Committee was one of the committees that had to be informed under the Hughes-Ryan act. Agency representatives would come and talk to me and my deputy. We write that all up. Me, my deputy, and the secretary who types it up know. [DDCI] Carlucci would come and brief [Chairman] Church and [Ranking Minority] Javits. I don't remember any instance where we went further. We were "established eunuchs."[124]

Such was typical of the procedures followed by other committees that had to be informed. Instead of vast hordes of members and staff having access to this information, access was severely restricted. The Intelligence Oversight Act of 1980 eviscerated the Hughes-Ryan amendment by restricting notification of covert actions to only the Senate and House intelligence committees.

The Senate Committee took its responsibilities toward covert action very seriously during the entire 1976–84 period. S. Res. 400 had required that the committee be kept "fully and currently informed" with respect to "intelligence activities" and "significant anticipated activities." However, the resolution also stated that the committee had no veto power over such activities.[125] The Intelligence Committee developed a procedure that it followed throughout the nine-year period. All the members and four staffers were cleared for covert action briefings.[126] First, the committee was notified after the president signed a presidential finding approving a specific covert action but before the action was implemented. Briefings were then provided to explain and justify the details of the operation. The committee then had five options: (1) comment to the executive branch, (2) refer information to other committees, (3) seek public disclosure, (4) restrict funds, or (5) do nothing. For covert actions that were implemented the committee received semi-annual status reports on ongoing operations, briefings at the annual authorization hearings, and termination reports when an operation ended.[127] As the committee noted in its 1976 report, covert actions undertaken after such a process "will reflect the national will as expressed by both the legislative and executive branches and not by just the executive branch alone." [128]

This process allowed the committee to consider each covert action individually. After being briefed each member would vote on the proposed covert action. From 1976 to 1984 the only one of these options the committee chose was to comment to the executive branch. In contrast the House Intelligence Committee led efforts in 1984 that resulted in the House's denial of funds for covert actions in Nicaragua. In response to the reactions it received from the Senate Intelligence Committee, the executive branch terminated one proposed operation and modified several others.[129] The key problem for the Senate committee with respect to covert action —encountered during both the Carter and Reagan administrations—was gaining access to difficult information.

On April 25, 1980, a rescue operation ordered by President Carter to free Americans held hostage in the American Embassy in Tehran, Iran, was aborted, and an accident that occurred while American forces were leaving Iran killed eight U.S. servicemen. Prior to the operation, President Carter had ordered information about it very closely held. No one in the Congress was told in advance. Even within the executive branch, Carter severely restricted information. As one senior advisor to the president noted: "Carter personally approved the list of people to whom the existence of the plan was disclosed in advance. Carter refused to allow the Attorney General to be informed. The president felt so secretive he didn't want even his own attorney general to be informed." [130]

Reaction to Carter's decision not to inform the Congress was very sympathetic, even in Congress. The reaction of a senior Democrat on the House Intelligence Committee was typical: "The Congress should not have been informed in advance. This was not an intelligence-gathering operation. It was kind of a special military mission." [131] Similar sentiments were to be found on the Senate side. Minority Leader Hugh Scott observed: "Congress can't be trusted. If Ford had waited on Congress in the Mayaquez case, the ship would have been elsewhere by the time he was able to act." [132] On the Senate Intelligence Committee one senior Republican supported Carter's action, noting: "The more people you tell, the more danger there is of losing life. I say: 'To hell with the Congress.'" [133] A Democrat on the committee observed: "The problem is telling too many people. My sympathies lie with the administration." [134] Thus President Carter had support in both houses of Congress for not informing the Congress in advance of the mission.

One Senate Democrat, however, was extremely upset about not being informed. Senator Birch Bayh, the chairman of the Senate Intelligence Committee, noted: "It would have been so easy to tell us. Any leaker of that information would be hung up by his thumbs. I expressed my anger to Carter about not informing us. Carter had a thing about not being able to trust the committee." [135] The Iran mission was not the first instance of the Carter administration failing to keep the committee properly informed. There were other, equally as sensitive operations about which the committee and its chairman had not been informed. [136] Bayh had previously cooperated with the president. As he commented: "There were a couple of other areas where the president wouldn't tell the entire committee. He let me know but not the entire committee. I suggested to Goldwater we keep it to ourselves. Barry concurred. There were a couple of others we decided to tell to the entire committee." [137] Chairman Bayh proposed that one remedy might be to formally limit the number of members to be informed. Bayh suggested the creation of a special subcommittee of five or seven "so you'd know somebody in the oversight mechanism knew" [138] because "If oversight is to function better, you first need it to function." [139]

Although not widely recognized at the time, the failure to inform Congress in advance about the Iran mission led the Congress later in 1980 to pass legislation that more clearly delineated executive responsibilities in this area. The Intelligence Oversight Act of 1980 eviscerated the Hughes-Ryan amendment of 1974 by reducing the number of committees to be notified of covert action from eight to two. The executive branch was directed to keep only the two intelligence committees "fully and currently informed" of all intelligence activities. In addition, information was to be provided "in a prompt and timely fashion." Moreover, the intelligence agencies were required to provide to the two oversight committees advance notice of "significant anticipated activities." Also, in those circumstances where the president did not want to inform the entire committee membership, special provisions were written in to provide that prior notification be given to eight leaders (known as the "Gang of Eight"): the majority and minority leaders of each chamber and the chairmen and ranking minority members of the two intelligence committees. In those cases where prior notification was not given, the president was required to inform the select committees fully in a "timely fashion" and provide a statement why prior notice was not given.[140] In passing the Intelligence Oversight Act of 1980, the executive and legislative branches had fashioned a compromise. The president was left with some flexibility in sensitive situations and emergencies while the Congress believed it had secured access to the information necessary to carry out its oversight function.

In 1984 the Senate Intelligence Committee again struggled with the executive branch over access to covert action informaton. Unlike the House committee, the Senate Intelligence Committee continuously supported the administration's covert actions in Nicaragua. From 1983 to 1984 "at least a quarter of the [Senate] committee's time"[141] was devoted to covert action affecting Nicaragua. On September 20, 1983, the DCI and the secretary of state had presented to the Senate committee, at the committee's direction, a new presidential finding that defined U.S. goals in Nicaragua. However, in April 1984, the Senate Intelligence Committee was stunned to learn that it had not been told about the mining of Nicaraguan harbors by the CIA. On April 10, 1984, the Senate passed eighty-four to twelve a resolution condemning the mining of the harbors.

On April 10, 1984, Chairman Goldwater also issued a statement denouncing DCI Casey for not keeping the committee "fully informed" about the operation in accord with the Intelligence Oversight Act of 1980. Two days later Casey stated that the CIA had "fully met" all statutory requirements. That same day National Security Advisor Robert McFarlane stated, "Every important detail [of the mining] was shared in full by the proper congressional oversight committees." Because Chairman Goldwater was outside the United States, Vice-Chairman Moynihan was in charge of the Senate committee. On April 15, 1984, Casey sent a letter of apology to Chairman Goldwater. The next day Casey apologized to the full committee, and both the administration and the committee agreed that the executive branch should become more specific in its oversight responsibilities.

Finally, on June 6, 1984, the "Casey accord" was signed by Casey, McFarlane, Goldwater, and Moynihan. Approved by the president, this agreement refined the definition of "significant anticipated activities" in the Intelligence Oversight Act of 1980 as any matter with respect to covert action that the president specifically approved in advance. Moreover, the DCI was directed to keep the committee "fully and currently" informed about such activities. Although this was the last major struggle over access to covert information between the executive and legislative branches in the 1976–84 period it was not to be the last time the Senate Intelligence Committee had problems with access to information. Although from 1976 to 1984 the committee did develop and follow procedures to conduct such oversight, access to information and the lack of veto power over covert action remained key problems.[142]

Legislation

The Select Intelligence Committee's legislative work can be divided into two distinct periods. From its creation until June 3, 1980, the committee attempted to enact the major recommendations of the Church committee. Following the passage of the Intelligence Oversight Act of 1980 on June 3 the committee focused its legislation for the rest of 1980 through 1984 on advocacy for the intelligence community.

Senator Huddleston, who had also served on the Church committee, became the "father" of the effort to pass charter legislation implementing the principal recommendations of the Church committee. In 1976 Chairman Inouye appointed Huddleston to chair the Subcommittee on Charters and Guidelines, which Huddleston used as the base from which to launch this effort. On June 3, 1980, Senator Inouye noted the amount of time Huddleston and the committee devoted to charter legislation:

> The Intelligence Committee has held twenty-four open hearings and heard from seventy-seven witnesses concerning the charters. In addition, this committee has held eight full committee hearings in executive session concerning the same subject. . . . In addition, he [Huddleston] has had twelve meetings with Admiral Turner, three meetings with the president's legal counsel Lloyd Cutler, eight meetings with the vice president, and five meetings with the president of the United States. He has presided over four major drafts of this bill, and God knows how many modifications.[143]

For both Huddleston and the committee, the effort to pass charter legislation involved an enormous investment of time, resources, and emotional commitment.

When the Church committee had issued its final reports in the spring of 1976 the centerpiece of its recommendations was a comprehensive legislative charter for the intelligence community. The charter proposal involved three elements. First, there was a plan for "organic" acts that would recognize the different agencies that had developed organically within the intelligence community. For example, there were no organic acts for recognized entities such as the NSA, the DIA, or the FBI. All three of these agencies strongly supported this part of the proposal. Second, the charter effort tried to sort out roles and missions for the various intelligence agencies. Here no agreement was reached since each agency sought to protect its turf. Third, the charter effort tried to write into law restrictions on the type of activities in which the intelligence agencies could engage. Here again consensus was never attained. For example, the Church committee, as noted earlier, had recommended that no effort should ever be undertaken to overthrow or subvert a democratic government. But just what was a "democratic" government? This was an enormously difficult area in which to write hard and fast regulations. And there were literally hundreds of such issues to be decided. For those involved in the effort in both the legislative and executive branches the charter came to resemble the tax code in its complexity.[144]

Although the Church committee had issued its final report in April 1976 the permanent committee did not have legislation ready to consider until February 9, 1978, when Senator Huddleston introduced S. 2525. The select committee did not begin public hearings until April 4, 1978. Valuable time was lost from April 1976 until early 1978 in drafting S. 2525, which turned out to be a legislative behemoth. The bill was 263 pages long and was treated by supporters and opponents as a working draft. Even the principal staff member who drafted this bill noted in retrospect that it was "too complex."[145] Within the Carter administration Vice-President Mondale was the strongest supporter of the charter. Yet there was also strong opposition within the administration led by National Security Advisor Zbigniew Brzezinski and Secretary of Defense Harold Brown. As Brzezinski noted: "A detailed charter would be a mistake. You would need almost full-time interpreters to make sense of it. This would be a prescription for internal paralysis."[146] The Senate did not act upon S. 2525 before the Ninety-fifth Congress ended.

In the Ninety-sixth Congress the select committee tried once again to enact charter legislation. On February 8, 1980, Senator Huddleston introduced S. 2284, a revision of the bill he had introduced in 1978 pared down to 172 pages. However, S. 2284 was never considered by the full Senate. The Carter administration and the Senate Intelligence Committee deadlocked over the committee's claim to an absolute right to obtain any document or information concerning intelligence in the possession of the executive branch.[147] This was the ground where the constitutional prerogatives of the executive and legislative branches met. Both branches struggled over the allocation of constitutional power and responsibility and, in the resulting deadlock, S. 2284 died. As noted in the previous section, the failure of the Carter administration to inform the Senate in advance of the Iran rescue mission provoked a strong and negative reaction from Chairman Bayh of the Intelligence Committee. The charter supporters on the committee hammered out a compromise on access to information that was embodied in the Intelligence Oversight Act of 1980. With the passage of the Intelligence Oversight Act of 1980 by the Senate on June 3 the committee's efforts to pass charter legislation ended.

How is the committee's work on charter legislation to be assessed? In a very real sense it was a major failure. Despite an enormous investment of time and energy, success had eluded the committee. Critics such as Anne Karalekas noted that "the brief window of opportunity for change had closed."[148] Moreover, the Congress had failed to pass legislation to correct the deficiencies uncovered by the Church committee. Unfortunately much of the blame must be given to the permanent committee itself. The delay in drafting such legislation until 1978, and then producing a draft that became merely a working paper, meant that precious time had been lost. The investigative oversight practiced by the Church committee had unearthed past abuses that charter legislation was designed to prevent. Yet the institutional oversight practiced by the permanent committee made it unlikely that additional abuses would be unearthed. Moreover, the lack of clientele groups in intelligence meant there would be little additional outside support for further reforms. As a result, the climate for reform created by the Church committee hearings gradually dissipated while new events such as the Iranian revolution and the Soviet invasion of Afghanistan created a very different climate.

However, the effort that went into charter legislation was not a total failure, and the success the committee attained as a byproduct has been both overlooked and ignored. Critics such as Karalekas have overlooked some key factors. Although the Church committee did create a climate for reform and a "brief window of opportunity for change," that climate and opportunity existed only in the Senate. On the House side, the Pike committee left no similar legacy. In fact, even after the House created a permanent intelligence oversight committee in 1977, that committee never held meetings or produced any drafts of charter legislation. Therefore, even if the Senate had passed charter legislation, the prospects were dim at best for such legislation in the House. There was perhaps a missed opportunity in the Senate, but in the

House no base at all had been built from which any reform efforts could be launched.

The Senate's charter effort resulted in three significant developments that have been overlooked but are in fact genuine successes. First, the entire effort provided a valuable educational experience for all involved. As Senator Inouye observed: "This was part of the evolutionary process involved in growing up. It was an important part in our education." [149] Committee members and staff significantly increased their expertise. By maintaining its records the committee developed an institutional memory that could be drawn upon in the future. As a result of their involvement in the charter effort, individuals within the executive branch were educated as to the concerns of committee members and staff.

Second, the actions taken by the executive branch to forestall permanent charter legislation took into account many of the most important changes sought by advocates of the legislation. For example, on January 26, 1978, President Carter issued Executive Order 12306 embodying the very checks, controls, and accountability the Intelligence Committee was seeking. Moreover, committee members and staff were consulted extensively by the executive branch in drafting this executive order. Later, the committee assumed a similar role with President Reagan on Executive Order 12333, issued on December 8, 1981. Although permanent legislation was not enacted, the committee was a major player in shaping the actual rules that governed intelligence operations in both the Carter and Reagan administrations.

Third, there were two significant pieces of legislation passed in the 1976–80 period that encompassed major components of the general oversight effort. The Foreign Intelligence Surveillance Act of 1978 (FISA) established procedures for electronic surveillance within the United States by the FBI and NSA. Before such activity could be undertaken a warrant had to be approved by a special FISA court composed of seven U.S. district judges and three appellate judges appointed by the chief justice.

Judicial review of intelligence operations was thus established for the first time. For the intelligence community FISA provided legal authorization for electronic surveillance. For the citizen it provided the assurance that legal processes were to be followed. Because the FISA legislation also mandated the submission of regular reports to both intelligence committees, calling for them to report on the actions taken, FISA encompassed both judicial and congressional oversight. Originally FISA had been a part of the failed S. 2525. Its enactment was a major accomplishment. In addition, the Intelligence Oversight Act of 1980, as has already been noted, delineated executive-legislative relationships regarding covert action. Thus, although the comprehensive legislative package envisioned by the Church committee was never passed, the Senate Intelligence committee's efforts toward such legislation were not an unmitigated failure. Significant actions were taken.[150]

Since the select committee did not implement the investigative oversight model, little additional momentum for reform legislation could be generated by the committee itself. As the committee became farther removed in time from the Church committee's recommendations, reform efforts became more difficult to enact. In addition, the very existence of two intelligence committees conducting oversight obviated the pressing need to pass comprehensive charter legislation. As a senior CIA official active in the executive branch's work on charter legislation observed in 1983:

> The greatest irony is that the existence of Senate and House intelligence committees were negative factors in connection with charter legislation. If you have consistent, permanent oversight and a relationship of trust between the agencies and the oversight entities, everybody becomes a little less jumpy about what is going on and the need for formal legislation is less pressing. That is what happened here.[151]

Staff Director Miller agreed:

> This was a very interesting exercise. I lived through hundreds of drafts, thousands of pages, and numerous meetings. Even though the various bills we contemplated were agreed to by the executive branch, there were arguments about the preambulary language, adjectives, and tone—not the jurisdictional areas or main outlines. NSA, DIA, and the FBI would have been delighted to have the charters that were discussed at the time. We lost an opportunity to lay out a clear structure. But the most important issue was the relationship between the executive and legislative branches, and here access to information was the key. The executive orders and the access-to-information provisions were enough of a framework at this point.[152]

From 1976 to 1980 charter legislation preoccupied the committee. Despite its failure to enact a comprehensive charter, the committee nonetheless brought about some of the most important intentions behind the movement for such legislation.

Following its decision to abandon comprehensive charter legislation, the committee's legislative activity focused on measures designed to strengthen and support the intelligence community. The intelligence partnership the committee sought to foster with the executive branch was reflected in this legislation, almost all of which could be described as "housekeeping."

During the 1981–82 period, intelligence-identities legislation was approved by the Congress, making it a crime to deliberately reveal the names of covert U.S. intelligence operatives. Such legislation had been on the wish list of the intelligence agencies since the mid-1970s and was strongly supported by the Senate Intelligence Committee. In its report to the Senate of February 28, 1983, the committee noted that such legislation was deliberately designed to curb the activities of Philip Agee, an ex-CIA agent, and Louis Wolf, the coeditor of *The Covert Action Information Bulletin*.[153] The Senate approved this legislation eighty-one to four on June 10, 1982.

Besides the Intelligence Identities Act, the committee supported the successful passage of the CIA Spouses' Retirement Equity Act of 1982, giving former spouses of CIA employees the same claims to retirement benefits as former spouses of foreign service officers. In addition, Senator Wallop sponsored an amendment to the Fiscal Year 1982 Intelligence Authorization Act that established the Senior Executive Service for the DIA and the Senior Cryptologic Executive Service for the NSA. Such systems were similar to personnel management systems established in the civil service agencies. Finally, during the Senate's consideration of S. 907, committee member Schmitt introduced an amendment to this legislation, which was adopted, that made it a federal crime to assassinate, kidnap, or assault either the DCI or the DDCI.[154] Such legislation was of an order different from charter legislation. In its first few years the committee had addressed the key questions of executive-legislative relations that went to the very fabric of the American governmental system. Now the committee's work had come to focus upon routine housekeeping legislation.

This trend continued in 1983 to 1984, during which time the Senate Intelligence Committee successfully led the effort to free the CIA from restrictions imposed on it by the Freedom of Information Act. Operational files on the CIA's Directorate of Operations, Directorate of Science and Technology, and Office of Security were exempted in legislation that passed the Senate by a unanimous voice vote on September 28, 1984. The committee also led the effort to establish a National Historical Intelligence Museum, holding hearings on the subject and sponsoring S. Res. 267 in support of the project. S. Res. 267 was unanimously approved by the Senate by voice vote on November 17, 1983. The committee also conducted studies of polygraphing policies at the Defense Department and studied legislation proposing that the DCI and DDCI be appointed from among career civilian and military intelligence officers.[155] During the Goldwater years the committee's legislative activity slowed considerably. The only legislation to be considered and approved was designed to strengthen the intelligence community. The legislative activity was, in other words, what might be expected of a committee seeking to practice institutional oversight.

Nominations and Reports

Unlike its House counterpart, the Senate Intelligence Committee was entrusted with additional oversight responsibilities. Because of the Senate's constitutional responsibility to confirm presidential nominations, the Senate Intelligence Committee had the task of screening nominees for the DCI and DDCI positions. In addition, unlike the House committee, the Senate committee was used more frequently by its parent body's leadership, committees, and members as an ombudsman in the intelligence area.

During the 1976–84 period, the Senate committee considered three nominations for DCI and four for DDCI. The four DDCI nominees (E. Henry Knoche, 1976; Frank Carlucci, 1978; B. R. Inman, 1981; and John McMahon, 1982) were confirmed almost routinely. The committee used the opportunity of holding public confirmation hearings to gain commitments from the nominees. For example, during the June 23, 1976, hearing for E. Henry Knoche, Chairman Inouye directed questions that covered (1) committee access to National Security Council intelligence directives, (2) the possibility of the GAO auditing CIA expenditures, (3) internal reporting requirements to uncover improper and illegal activities within the intelligence community, (4) committee access to CIA studies of internal components, and (5) steps taken by the CIA to prevent its employees from using positions of trust to gain personal profits.[156]

Besides gaining commitments, members used the public hearings as an opportunity to share their own views with the nominees. During the questioning of Admiral Inman on February 3, 1981, Senator Biden used the hearing as an opportunity to lecture the admiral. A day earlier, Biden had grilled Justice William Clark with a series of questions that showed Clark's ignorance on foreign affairs. While Biden was lecturing Inman, the next questioner, Senator Moynihan, passed a note to Inman. When Moynihan's turn came, the following exchange took place:

Moynihan: I'm going to put it to the nominee straight. Can you spell the name of the prime minister of Sri Lanka? (Laughter)
Inman: Courtesy of the great support I have always enjoyed from this committee, Mr. Premadasa is the prime minister and Mr. Jayawardene is the president. (Laughter)
Moynihan: Thank you, Admiral.
Biden: He's tough, Admiral.[157]

Despite the humor on this occasion, members frequently made use of the confirmation hearings as an opportunity to let executive-branch officials know their views.

The committee routinely approved the nomination of Stansfield Turner as director of central intelligence. However, before Turner's nomination was submitted, the committee's confirmation process had led President Carter's first choice to withdraw his name from consideration. Initially Carter had named Theodore Sorensen to be DCI. However, the committee members were very uneasy over Sorensen's lack of experience in intelligence and foreign affairs. Moreover, as DCI, Sorensen would have been responsible for protecting "sources and methods." At the Pentagon Papers trial of Daniel Ellsberg, Sorensen had testified that he had used classified White House material in writing his book about the Kennedy administration and then had enjoyed a tax deduction based on his donation of the documents to the National Archives.[158]

Sorensen had also assumed an air of superiority toward members of the Intelligence Committee. For example, when Chairman Inouye had invited Sorensen to meet with him about the upcoming confirmation hearings, Sorensen had tartly replied: "I'm pretty busy. I don't think I have the time." Furious, Inouye exploded at the nominee, and Sorensen managed to make time for the chairman.[159] Such an attitude meant that an ongoing relationship between Sorensen and the committee would be fraught with tension and danger for the Carter administration. Two minutes before his confirmation hearing began on January 17, 1977, Sorensen notified Carter of his intention to withdraw his name from consideration, and Carter "made no attempt to dissuade him."[160]

Additionally the committee experienced some difficulties with William Casey after the Senate had confirmed him as director of central intelligence. As it turned out, Casey had not provided the committee with all the background information it had sought. From July 29 through October 31, 1981, the committee conducted an extensive investigation into Casey and his finances. Thirteen staff members examined more than thirty-eight thousand pages of documents and interviewed more than 110 people.[161] Although the committee found nothing that required Casey to resign his position, it was concerned about the propriety of some of Casey's actions, and at the end of its inquiry, issued a very lukewarm statement of support: "No basis has been found for concluding that Mr. Casey is unfit to hold office as director of central intelligence."[162] Both the Sorensen and the Casey nominations demonstrated that the committee was no mere rubber stamp when it came to the consideration of presidential appointments to senior intelligence positions.

Much more than its House counterpart, the Senate Intelligence Committee became an intelligence ombudsman for its parent congressional body. As already noted, the Senate leaders gave the committee specific tasks such as its work with respect to the Panama Canal treaties and SALT II verification. The committee also conducted investigations at the specific request of other Senate committees. In early 1982, for example, a former GAO auditor by the name of Ralph Sharer charged that Soviet spies had penetrated the GAO. Sharer's charges, made to the Government Operations Committee, received widespread coverage, appearing in the columns of Jack Anderson and on the "CBS Evening News." Chairman Roth of Government Operations asked Chairman Goldwater to investigate. Goldwater reported to the Senate on September 24, 1982, that "staff investigated these charges and found no substantiation for them." [163] In this case the Senate Intelligence Committee had the resources and security necessary to conduct a sensitive investigation for a Senate committee that did not possess such tools.

The committee also did investigations at the request of individual senators. For example, on April 3, 1984, Senator Kennedy requested that the Senate investigate alleged CIA links to El Salvador right-wing "death squads." Chairman Goldwater accepted Kennedy's request on behalf of the committee and, after an investigation, the committee reported that it found no such links. Classified and unclassified reports were issued.[164] In the intelligence area, the Senate Intelligence Committee became an ombudsman entrusted with sensitive investigative assignments throughout the entire 1976–84 period.

Summary and Evaluation of the Senate Select Intelligence Committee

With the passage of S. Res. 400 in 1976 the Senate had pledged to continue the searching oversight of the U.S. intelligence community that it had begun when it formed the Church committee in 1975. The best word that can be used to describe the permanent Senate Intelligence Committee as it went about its duties from 1976 to 1984 is that it was a truly "representative" Senate committee. Under three different chairmen and despite a shift in party control of the Senate the committee, throughout the nine years examined here, reflected all the major Senate views, including those of the other committees dealing with intelligence. Moreover during this time the committee practiced consensus politics in a spirit of true bipartisanship.

Unlike its House counterpart, the Senate committee was able to build upon the work of the Church committee. It inherited members, staff, an institutional memory, and an agenda from the earlier committee. One of the most valuable and least noticed accomplishments of the permanent Senate committee was the institutional memory it developed and maintained. The committee now possessed the paper trail that would allow members as well as staff to function as equals of the executive branch on intelligence issues. An invaluable contribution here was made by political scientist John Elliff. On the Church committee Elliff had been the FBI Task Force leader. On the permanent Senate committee Elliff served in a senior staff position from 1976 to 1984 and proved to be a valuable resource. The Senate committee developed an institutional memory—composed of paper and people—of benefit not only to itself but to future Senate overseers.

In practicing oversight the committee reflected the Senate at its best and worst. The leaders of both parties carefully assembled a team of members who sought to make their committee work. Unfortunately, like all other senators, the members of the Intelligence Committee were extremely pressed for time. All too often, even when members wanted to devote more time to the committee's work, pressures from constituents and other committee assignments intervened. It is a reflection of the seriousness with which they took their intelligence work that every member voted on every covert action brought before the committee during these nine years. However, in matters of lesser importance, the work was left to the chairman and vice-chairman, the subcommittee chairman, and the staff. As elsewhere in the Senate, the severe time constraints often meant that staffers became senators in fact if not in name.

Unlike the Church committee, the permanent committee practiced only institutional oversight, seeking to become a partner of the executive branch. At times this partnership led the committee to become a mere advocate. In addition, there were some limits on just how effective a partner the committee could become. For example, the power of the purse is the most potent oversight weapon the Congress possesses. Yet, in its own oversight of intelligence budgets, the committee was hindered by the Senate Armed Services Committee's refusal to relinquish control over the Defense Department's intelligence budget. At the same time, the committee's attempt to become a partner on covert action suffered a similar fate. Although the committee did halt one covert action proposal and helped modify others, it never fully gained the trust of either President Carter or President Reagan. The failure of the executive branch to keep the committee fully informed of operations in Iran and Nicaragua was a symptom of this distrust. Throughout this entire period the committee had to contend for access to the information necessary for it to do its work and become a full and coequal partner of the executive branch. In important respects the committee was unable to fully attain this partnership.

Although it had inherited a legislative agenda from the Church committee, the permanent committee had never been able to fully implement that agenda. The failure to enact comprehensive charter legislation had been tempered somewhat by the passage of key charter components such as FISA, the Foreign Intelligence Surveillance Act of 1978. Moreover, the committee was an active participant in the development of both the Carter and Reagan executive orders on intelligence. But the failure to enact comprehensive charter legislation meant that, of necessity, the executive orders assumed great prominence and importance, and the president could change executive orders at any time. Would the committee be able to continue to muster the political will to remain an active and equal participant in intelligence oversight?

When the Select Intelligence Committee was created in 1976, Chairman Inouye successfully focused his and the committee's attention on institution building. By the end of 1984 the committee had become a firmly established institution. Moreover, like the White House, the committee was itself an intelligence consumer. Still, its oversight was increasingly becoming merely reactive to outside pressures. In an area where there were few clientele groups and where the press was hindered in its work due to the endemic secrecy, the committee faced major challenges in finding both the motivation and the political will to continue thorough and effective oversight. At the end of 1984 the committee continued to function, having survived a chairman who thought and said it should be abolished. The challenge to the successors of the Goldwater committee was to continue to improve upon the structures and oversight conducted from 1976 to 1984. By 1984 institutional oversight of the intelligence community was again an established reality in the United States Senate.

4 Investigative Oversight Triumphant:

The Nedzi and Pike House Committees,

1975–76

As in the Senate, serious questions were raised in the House of Representatives both about the propriety of activities of the U.S. intelligence community and about the adequacy of the legislative body's own oversight of intelligence. The issues that had set the context for Senate action—Vietnam, Watergate, and press charges of intelligence-agency improprieties—also shaped the context for House action. In addition, in the summer of 1974, Representative Michael Harrington (D., Massachusetts) had disclosed to the press secret testimony that had been given to the House Armed Services Committee about U.S. efforts to overthrow the government of Chilean President Salvador Allende. The staff director of the House Armed Services Committee recalled:

> Harrington was raising hell about Chile. He approached Lucien Nedzi, chairman of the Intelligence Subcommittee [of the Armed Services Committee], with some of the questions he had. Nedzi had a hearing with the hearing on the record. Harrington asked Nedzi to see the transcripts. Nedzi came to me and Chairman Hebert. I was afraid of what Harrington might do. I made Harrington sign a statement. The statement Harrington signed said: "I am aware of the House rule that prohibits the disclosure of executive testimony, this is classified, and I will not release it." Later Harrington admitted that he had released the information. He recognized the rules of the House, and he recognized he had signed the agreement. He felt he had a greater duty to release the information.[1]

House members were divided in their reaction to what Harrington had done. Some were concerned about the wisdom and propriety of the U.S. actions in Chile. At the same time, others questioned the propriety of Harrington's disclosure of classified material after he had signed a statement saying that he would not do so. On January 16, 1975, Harrington introduced a resolution in the House to create a select committee to investigate the intelligence community.

Within the House Democratic Caucus there was strong support for the creation of a select intelligence committee. A special ad hoc sub-committee was formed to study this matter further. Congressman Robert Giaimo (D., Connecticut) was appointed chairman; other members included Lucien Nedzi, Michael Harrington, John Moss, Jonathan Bingham, and Mendel J. Davis. On February 4, 1975, the subcommittee unanimously adopted a resolution calling for the establishment of a House select intelligence committee, and this decision was ratified on the same day by the Steering and Policy Committee. Commenting on the investigation to be undertaken by the proposed committee, Chairman Giaimo observed: "We do not know whether these allegations are true in fact or not but Congress has the absolute obligation and duty to the American people to exercise its oversight function to determine whether there is any merit to these allegations." [2]

On February 19, 1975, the House voted 286 to 120 to pass H. Res. 138, creating a House select committee to investigate allegations of improprieties and to make recommendations to the House about how it should exercise intelligence oversight. The House committee had ten members, seven Democrats and three Republicans, with Congressman Lucien Nedzi (D., Michigan) appointed as chairman. Nedzi was also the principal intelligence overseer for the House Armed Services Committee. At the same time, Congressman Michael Harrington was also appointed to the select committee. It was Harrington who had the year before disclosed to the press the secret testimony that had been taken by Nedzi about U.S. activities in Chile. To appoint both representatives to the same committee was to build in the potential for serious conflict. For more than three months the committee members were unable to agree on a staff director. Then shortly before the committee's first public hearing, in June, information was leaked to the press that in 1973 Nedzi had been briefed about improper CIA activities in his role as chairman of the Armed Services Intelligence Subcommittee and that he had done nothing about it. The other Democrats on the select committee caucused and voted to strip Nedzi of his powers as chairman. Throughout this time the House leadership tried to work out a compromise between Nedzi and his Democratic critics on the committee. Majority Leader Thomas P. O'Neill, Jr., went twice to see Nedzi and requested that he remain chairman. However, Nedzi realized his position had become untenable, and he resigned.[3] But on June 16, 1975, the House refused to accept his resignation by a vote of 64 to 290.

Despite his vindication by the House, Nedzi refused to continue as chairman. On July 16 and 17, 1975, the House debated whether to have a select intelligence committee. On July 16 the House defeated a motion to abolish the committee by a vote of 122 to 293. The next day the House passed by voice vote H. Res. 591 which created a new select intelligence committee. Representative Otis Pike (D., New York) was appointed to be chairman of the new committee, which had thirteen members, nine Democrats and four Republicans. Neither Nedzi nor Harrington was appointed to the new committee. Under the provisions of H. Res. 591 the committee was directed to submit its final report to the House by January 30, 1976, as well as a supplemental report with recommendations by February 1, 1976.

On July 31, 1975, the Select Intelligence Committee conducted its first public hearings. Altogether the committee conducted twenty-eight days of public hearings from the end of July until December 17, 1975, throughout which time it was divided by ideological and partisan differences. Meanwhile the committee struggled with the executive branch over access to information. In November 1975 the committee voted to approve three contempt citations against Secretary of State Henry Kissinger for failing to provide information it had subpoenaed. After the contempt citations were approved the administration grudgingly provided access to the information. Following this dispute, the committee became embroiled in another controversy with the executive branch over information in its final report. This dispute reached the House floor. On January 29, 1976, the House voted 246 to 124 not to release the committee's final report, thereby repudiating its own select committee and agreeing with the executive branch's argument against the report's release.

Before the House vote on January 29, 1976, not to release the committee's final report, major portions of the report had been leaked to and had appeared in the *New York Times*. In addition, Daniel Schorr, a reporter for CBS News, had obtained a copy of the entire report. On February 16 and 23 the *Village Voice* published the report,which it had obtained from Daniel Schorr. Outraged, the House voted on February 19 to pass H. Res. 1042 by a vote of 269 to 119, authorizing the House Committee on Standards of Official Conduct to conduct an investigation into who had leaked the report to Schorr. Between July 19 and September 15, 1976, the Committee on Standards of Official Conduct conducted eleven days of hearings into this matter, summoning all thirteen members and thirty-two staff members of the select committee. Under oath, each person was asked whether they had leaked the report to Daniel Schorr. As Congressman Ron Dellums commented when he testified before the committee: "The investigator has now become the investigatee."[4] Unable to find the leak, the committee compelled Daniel Schorr to testify, but he refused to disclose his source. The committee never found the leak. In the end the House decisively rejected its select committee. Unlike in the Senate, more than a year was to pass before the House established a permanent intelligence oversight committee. Thus the Nedzi and Pike committees deterred the House's ability and willingness to conduct intelligence oversight even though the House intelligence investigations of 1975 to 1976 represent the high point for the exercise of investigative oversight by the U.S. Congress.

Recruitment of Committee Members

In 1975 the House created two committees to investigate the intelligence community. The first was created on February 19 with the passage of H. Res. 138. Chaired by Representative Lucien Nedzi (D., Michigan), this committee had ten members, seven Democrats and three Republicans. On July 17 the House abolished the Nedzi commit-

Table 8.   **Membership of Nedzi Committee (1975)**

Member	Age	Years in House	1974 ADA Rating	1974 NSI Rating
Nedzi	50	14	79	22
Giaimo	56	16	68	50
Edwards	60	12	100	10
Stanton	43	4	90	8
Harrington	39	6	100	10
Dellums	40	4	96	10
Murphy	42	4	50	44
Democratic average	47.1	8.6	83.2	22.0
McClory	66	12	24	70
Treen	47	2	4 '	90
Kasten	33	0	—	—
Republican average	48.7	4.7	14	80
Committee average	47.6	7.4	68	35

Source: *Almanac of American Politics 1976.*

Table 9.   Membership of Pike Committee (1975-76)

Member	Age	Years in House	1974 ADA Rating	1974 NSI Rating
Pike	54	14	74	30
Giaimo	56	16	68	50
Stanton	43	4	90	8
Dellums	40	4	96	10
Murphy	42	4	50	44
Aspin	37	4	96	0
Milford	49	2	16	57
Hayes	35	0	—	—
Lehman	62	2	86	25
Democratic average	46.4	5.5	72	28
McClory	66	12	24	70
Treen	47	2	4	90
Johnson	45	2	29	44
Kasten	33	0	—	—
Republican average	47.8	4	19	68
Committee average	47	5.1	57.5	39

Source: *Almanac of American Politics 1976.*

tee and created a new committee when it passed H. Res 591 by voice vote. This new committee, chaired by Otis Pike (D., New York) had thirteen members, nine Democrats and four Republicans. Four of the Democrats on the Nedzi committee remained on the Pike committee, as did all of the Republican members. Because both were select committees, the members were picked by the party leaders. Because both were select committees, service on them did not affect the members' standing committee assignments. Speaker of the House Carl Albert officially appointed the members of both committees. Minority Leader John Rhodes designated the Republican members of both.

Majority Leader Thomas P. "Tip" O'Neill, Jr. (D., Massachusetts), was the key individual in selecting the Democratic members of both committees. A source close to Speaker Albert observed: "Tip was the one who really took charge of the appointments to the select intelligence committees."[5] In selecting members for the Nedzi and Pike committees, the Democratic leadership made two significant decisions. First, unlike in the Senate, the House Democrats gave themselves a supermajority on both committees. In the Ninety-fourth Congress the Democrats held 291 House seats to 144 seats held by Republicans. This was 66.9 percent of all House seats. However, on the Nedzi committee Democrats controlled 70 percent of the seats and, on the Pike committee, 69.2 percent. Meanwhile the Senate allowed only one more seat to the majority party on its select intelligence committee. Defending the actions of House Democrats in setting this party ratio, Representative Robert Giaimo (D., Connecticut), a member of both the Nedzi and Pike committees, noted:

> We in the majority in the Congress have a responsibility and an obligation to lead and to propose recommendations, legislation, all kinds of activities designed to remedy the ills which beset us. . . . The fact is that the majority does bear the responsibility to take positive action and make positive suggestions.[6]

Thus the Democrats had solid majorities on both the Nedzi and Pike committees.

The Democratic leadership also chose to appoint representatives who tended to be ideologically liberal (see Tables 8 and 9). The *New York Times* described the Nedzi committee as having "a liberal cast."[7] On the Nedzi committee, the seven Democratic members had a mean ADA rating of 83.2 percent with only one rated below 68 percent. Two of the Democrats on the Nedzi committee—Don Edwards (D., California) and Michael Harrington (D., Massachusetts)—had ADA ratings of 100 percent. At the same time the Democratic members had low NSI ratings. None had an NSI rating of more than 50 percent, and the mean average for the Democrats was 22 percent. A similar situation existed on the Pike committee. With the exception of Dale Milford (D., Texas), all of the Democratic members had high ADA ratings and low NSI ratings. The Pike Democrats had a mean ADA rating of 72 percent and a mean NSI rating of 28 percent. A close aide to both Speaker Albert and Majority Leader O'Neill observed:

> The key to understanding the members selected for the intelligence committees was the climate of the time. There was a very negative attitude towards intelligence. This was part of the aftermath of Watergate, Vietnam, the press charges, Angola, and the Pentagon Papers. The leadership

didn't want the committees loaded down with hard-nosed conservatives like Nedzi.[8]

Thus the Democratic leaders in the House chose to create select intelligence committees with Democratic majorities comprised primarily of liberal Democratic members of the House.

Although the party leaders were free to choose whoever they wished as members, in reality there was considerable pressure behind the scenes from representatives seeking to gain appointment. On the first committee Lucien Nedzi was appointed chairman. Yet, as Majority Leader O'Neill observed, "Nedzi asked for it, and the fellow that was going to be chairman was called in by the Speaker and he acquiesced to allow—to step aside and allow Nedzi to be chairman."[9] As both a member of the Armed Services Committee and chairman of its Special Subcommittee on Intelligence, Nedzi had become the principal intelligence overseer in the House. Thus the House leadership elected to appoint as chairman of its investigative committee the very person responsible for past intelligence oversight. This meant a conflict of interest since one of the tasks given to the select committee was to examine past oversight. Nedzi was in the awkward position of having to assess the quality of the oversight his own subcommittee had conducted. In the Senate, Majority Leader Mansfield had selected as chairman an outsider who had not been involved in intelligence oversight to head that body's committee. However, the House leadership chose to act in a different manner.

As has been noted, the Nedzi committee self-destructed. Following Nedzi's resignation the House leadership reconstituted the committee and appointed Representative Otis Pike (D., New York) as chairman. Pike himself didn't know why he was picked by the Speaker but accepted the position because he "liked the challenge."[10] Before transferring to the Ways and Means Committee, Pike had been a member of the Armed Services Committee. In 1969 Pike had been selected to conduct a House investigation into the North Koreans' capture of the intelligence ship Pueblo. In 1967 he had gained considerable attention by charging that the Defense Department was paying large sums of money for spare parts that could be bought for less through regular mail-order catalogues. With Pike's appointment to chair the new committee the leadership had selected an aggressive investigator. In addition Pike knew intelligence because of his past work on the Armed Services Committee. Unlike Nedzi, Pike was not burdened with a record of past oversight activity that he himself had to defend.

For the Nedzi committee the Democratic leaders selected six Democratic members besides the chairman. These were Robert Giaimo of

Connecticut, Don Edwards of California, James V. Stanton of Ohio, Michael Harrington of Massachusetts, Ronald Dellums of California, and Morgan Murphy of Illinois.

Giaimo, a member of the Appropriations Committee, had been one of the leaders in the Democratic Caucus in the effort to create a select intelligence committee. Edwards, a former FBI agent, was a member of the Judiciary Committee and chaired the Subcommittee on Civil and Constitutional Rights. Having been an early opponent of the Vietnam War, the floor manager for the Equal Rights Amendment, and a past chairman of Americans for Democratic Action, Edwards had strong liberal credentials. Stanton served on the Government Operations Committee and the Subcommittee on Legislation and National Security. Harrington was on the International Relations and Government Operations committees and had strongly supported the creation of a select investigative committee on intelligence. Dellums, a member of the Armed Services Committee, was the only black member of the select committee. Representing the Eighth District in California, which the *Almanac of American Politics* termed "the most self-consciously radical district in the country," [11] he was a self-described "progressive," the committee member most hostile to the intelligence community during the investigative period. A senior staffer on the Pike committee described Dellums as "a good demagogue who didn't lack anything." [12] A close aid to Majority Leader O'Neill added that "Dellums was viewed fondly by Tip as the supreme idealist." [13] Finally Murphy, a member of the Rules Committee, was part of the political machine of Chicago Mayor Richard Daley. During his first term in the House, Murphy had conducted an investigation of the wide extent of heroin addiction among U.S. servicemen. These were the Democrats on the Nedzi committee.

Representatives Giaimo, Stanton, Dellums, and Murphy continued as members of the Pike committee. Nedzi and Harrington were not appointed to the Pike committee, and Edwards resigned to concentrate on his Judiciary Committee work. Four additional Democrats were appointed to the Pike committee: Les Aspin of Wisconsin, Dale Milford of Texas, Phillip Hayes of Indiana, and William Lehman of Florida. Aspin, a member of both the Armed Services and Government Operations committees, had been a whiz kid at the Pentagon under Secretary of Defense Robert McNamara. The *New York Times* described Aspin as a "frequent critic of Defense Department spending and procurement policies." [14] Dale Milford, a television meteorologist before coming to the Congress, emerged as the most conservative Democrat on the committee. Philip Hayes, a first-year representative from Indiana, and William Lehman, a used-car dealer known as "Alabama Bill" before he came to the Congress, were also appointed. These last three—Milford, Hayes, and Lehman—had no committee assignments that touched upon intelligence. These were the Democrats appointed to the Pike committee.

The Nedzi committee had Democratic members from the principal standing committees that dealt with the intelligence community: Appropriations, Armed Services, International Relations, and Judiciary. Of the Nedzi committee members, Giaimo served on Appropriations; Nedzi, Harrington, and Dellums had all served on Armed Services; Harrington served on International Relations; Edwards served on Judiciary. Of the members on the Pike committee Giaimo was the only Democrat to serve on Appropriations. Pike, Dellums, and Aspin all served on Armed Services. At the same time, no Democrat on the Pike committee served on either the International Relations or Judiciary committees. As a result, the principal standing committees that conducted intelligence oversight were better represented on the Nedzi committee. In addition, with the exception of Nedzi, none of the Democratic members appointed to the Nedzi and Pike committees had been intelligence overseers themselves. Consequently, with the exception of Lucien Nedzi, the Democratic members of both committees represented a clean break from past House intelligence oversight efforts.

Minority Leader John Rhodes made the Republican appointments. He selected Robert McClory of Illinois to be the ranking minority member of the Nedzi committee. McClory, the second ranking Republican on the Judiciary Committee, had a key role in the Nixon impeachment hearings conducted by that committee in 1974. In fact McClory himself had voted to impeach President Nixon for abuse of power. Rhodes also appointed David Treen of Louisiana and Robert Kasten of Wisconsin. Treen was the fifth ranking Republican on the Armed Services Committee while Kasten, serving his first term in the House, was the thirteenth ranking Republican on the Government Operations Committee. When the Pike committee was established the Republicans were allotted one additional seat. All three Republicans from the Nedzi committee remained on the Pike committee. In addition Rhodes appointed James Johnson of Colorado. Described as a "party moderate" by the *Almanac of American Politics*,[15] Johnson served on no standing committees directly related to intelligence or national security. As the work of the Pike committee progressed, Johnson was the only Republican who consistently sided with the Democratic members.

The Republicans appointed to both the Nedzi and the Pike committees were ideologically very conservative. They tended to have high NSI ratings and low ADA ratings—just the opposite of their Democratic counterparts. Thus while the Democratic leadership tended to appoint liberals to both committees the Republican leadership tended to appoint more conservative members.

Unlike the Democrats, the Republicans did not have representatives from all of the key standing committees that conducted intelligence oversight. The Republican leaders were hampered by the limited number of appointments they could make. McClory served on the Judiciary Committee while Treen served on the Armed Services Committee. There were no Republican representatives from either the Appropriations or International Relations committees.

Even though members of both the Nedzi and Pike committees were appointed by the respective party leaders, only those who actively sought the position were appointed. Those who sought membership usually approached their party leaders directly. For example Dale Milford, a Texas Democrat appointed to the Pike committee, noted: "I put in a bid. This was to Carl Albert. I was not asked about my views."[16] The same was true for James Johnson of Colorado after he contacted Minority Leader Rhodes and "asked on."[17] Some who sought membership were rejected. For example Democrats Leo J. Ryan of California and Samuel Stratton of New York sought assignment to both committees but were not appointed.[18] While the Democratic members of both the Nedzi and Pike committees tended to be liberals extremely critical of the intelligence community, the Republican members tended to be conservative defenders of both the intelligence community and the Ford administration.

Both House intelligence committees were composed of members whose stature in their parent chamber and in national security was considerably less than that of their Senate counterparts. For example eight of the eleven Church committee members had served at least six years in the Senate, and five had served for at least eleven years. On the other hand only five on the Nedzi committee had served in the House for at least six years. In addition, on the Pike committee only three of the thirteen members had served in the House for more than two terms. Mitchell Rogovin, special counsel to the director of central intelligence, dealt with both the Senate and the House committees. He observed that the House intelligence committees

> had no idea of the importance of the work they were doing. Some members treated this like it was an FHA investigation into whether housing examiners were on the take. [Chairman] Pike understood what he was doing. The rest of them did posturing and didn't pay attention.[19]

On the members selected for both the Nedzi and Pike committees Representative Morgan Murphy, a member of both, noted:

> I think one of the problems with the Select Committee on Intelligence has to go back to the leadership of the House. When you appoint members to a sensitive committee like the Select Committee on Intelligence, I think it is incumbent on the leadership of the House to make sure they appoint a type of member that they have looked at over the years and can repose some faith in. . . . I think the responsibility [rests] with leadership as Speaker and majority leader, and on the minority side when you put members on a committee like this, it shouldn't be just because he is a member of a certain caucus or she is a female. This quota business just has to be put aside when you get into membership on such a sensitive committee.[20]

Unfortunately the inexperience of some of the members was to hinder the work of both committees.

Membership on the Nedzi and Pike committees had some definite costs. The most important cost for House members, just as for members of the Senate Intelligence Committee, was time. Besides the chairman and ranking minority member, some members of both House committees spent considerable time on their intelligence work. According to Representative Dale Milford: "There was no input from constituents. Very few people from my district knew about my work on the Pike committee. It actually hurt me to be on the committee. I had to spend a lot of time away from the district on the work of the committee."[21] Representative James Johnson remembered membership on the Pike committee as "a full-time job. . . . I didn't do any other work on any other committee I was on because I spent my full time on this."[22] Some members were unwilling to invest the time required. An investigator who was among the first staff members hired for the Nedzi committee and who had served on the staff of the Senate Watergate Committee as an aide to Senator Lowell Weicker noted:

> The quality of the Pike committee was not of the same quality as the Senate Watergate Committee. A good example is the time given by the members. If you needed Senator Weicker for his work on the Watergate Committee, he was there. He rearranged his whole life for the committee. On the other hand, the members of the Pike committee were not of good quality and did not give the committee enough time. I was unimpressed by them.[23]

Service on the Nedzi and Pike committees had other costs as well. Because both were select investigative committees there were no pork-barrel benefits for the members' districts. Nevertheless membership was extremely attractive, and competition was keen among House members for the limited number of available appointments.

Why were the Nedzi and Pike committees attractive?

There are several reasons. First, because members were picked by their party leaders, appointment was a sign that the member had influence with, if not the respect of, his party's leadership. As Lucien Nedzi noted, the primary reward was "respect in the House."[24]

A second attractive feature was the significance of the work. Representative Robert Giaimo saw the task of the House investigations as "to reestablish adequate and proper oversight over the intelligence community."[25] Representative Philip Hayes, a member of the Pike committee, discussed this significance:

> I felt there was a public interest being expressed through the Congress in investigating our various intelligence agencies, and in trying to get a grip on how and in what manner we could have some public control over the way they operated or were alleged to have operated in order to improve their effectiveness.[26]

Similar sentiments were expressed by Representative Robert McClory, the ranking minority member on both the Nedzi and Pike committees:

> I felt it was important to take part in this investigation of alleged intelligence abuses and improprieties in order to help assure that it would be carried out in responsible fashion. I have never had any quarrel with those who seek to look into individual instances of alleged wrongdoing. However, we must remember that while individuals may sometimes take it upon themselves to act in an unauthorized and improper fashion, the overall integrity of our intelligence agencies must be preserved. Without it, these agencies cannot perform the functions which are so vital to the continued existence of our nation.[27]

A third factor making the intelligence committees attractive was the information members could gain. As Chairman Nedzi observed: "There is a sense of personal satisfaction. You are knowing something that somebody else doesn't know. Sometimes it is something of a good feeling to know something isn't taking place."[28] Representative Lehman, a member of the Pike committee, expressed similar thoughts: "In the time I have been on this committee, I have learned to appreciate the integrity of the CIA and its capabilities."[29] Information gained from serving on the Nedzi and Pike committees could be used in intelligence-related standing committee assignments. But this use of information was much more prevalent among members of the Church committee in the Senate.

Members of the House intelligence committees were more likely to use their committee assignments to advance constituent interests. For example, during the Pike committee's public hearings Representative Lehman of Florida focused on the competition companies in his district received from CIA proprietary companies.[30] Lehman also asked questions about intelligence activity directed against the drug problem in southern Florida.[31] Murphy of Illinois raised questions about intelligence activities engaged in by Illinois Bell.[32] Finally, Dellums, the only black member on either of the House committees, directed attention to the FBI's hiring of women and minority group members.[33] Membership on the intelligence committees thus provided access to information that could be used in a member's committee or district work. In addition, membership provided an entry into national security for members who did not serve on the relevant standing committees. Finally, some members of the Pike committee used their position to advance district issues, the only examples of this particular activity among House or Senate intelligence overseers.

A fourth and final characteristic was the national attention, which as one committee staffer noted "members on the Pike committee saw . . . as a guarantee for headlines for six to nine months. This is a part of the nature of the members."[34] Representative Robert Kasten, a Republican member of both the Nedzi and Pike committees, was even more direct in his criticism. According to Kasten members of both committees went "headline hunting" and sought to use their work to "put their name in the headlines."[35] At times even Chairman Otis Pike got frustrated with the members' attention to press coverage. During a poorly attended public hearing on reform of the intelligence community Pike commented: "I want to apologize for the poor turnout of members. We do find that if we are not locked into an acute controversy the television cameras seem to disappear, and with the disappearance of the television cameras goes some of the momentum for attendance."[36] In 1976 three members of the Pike committee—Chairman Pike plus Hayes and Stanton—all launched serious bids for seats in the Senate.[37] Service on the intelligence investigating committees therefore carried with it the opportunity for advancing public policy and personal career goals extending beyond the House.

The quality of the members on the Nedzi and Pike committees was not as high as that of their Senate counterparts on the Church committee. Nevertheless the committees were still very attractive to House members. They provided the opportunity to conduct a historically significant investigation, thereby furthering members's public policy goals. The work also enabled members to gain respect within the House and to advance personal and career goals outside of the House.

Leadership of the Chairmen

During the House investigations Lucien Nedzi and Otis Pike had pivotal roles as the chairmen of the two successive House select intelligence committees. Both Nedzi and Pike had served in the House for

seven terms before the investigations began. They were close friends
and had served on the Armed Services Committee together as members of the "Gang of Five," a group of liberals consistently outvoted
by the more conservative members. Despite these similarities Nedzi
and Pike adopted radically different styles of leadership as chairmen
of the successive House select committees. Their styles of leadership
and the actions they took as a result steered the course of the House's
investigation of the intelligence community.

Lucien Nedzi
When he was appointed chairman of the House Select Intelligence
Committee in February 1975 Lucien Nedzi had just completed fourteen years of service as a member of the House. During his time in the
Congress, Nedzi had established solid liberal credentials as an early
opponent of the Vietnam War, the B-1 bomber, and the antiballistic
missile system. In addition he was the last of the white liberal Democrats in the Michigan delegation to succumb to constituent pressure to
publicly oppose busing as a device to integrate public schools. Nedzi
had established a reputation as the Armed Services Committee's "most
liberal member." In 1974 he received an ADA rating of 74 and an NSI
rating of 22.

In 1971 Armed Services Committee Chairman F. Edward Hebert
appointed Nedzi chairman of the Special Subcommittee on Intelligence. Despite their being philosophical opposites, Hebert appointed
Nedzi because of the close relationship they had developed on the
Armed Services Committee. As Nedzi recalled:

> Becoming chairman was not something I aspired to. It was just dumped on
> me. Within a month after Hebert became chairman of Armed Services,
> there was some grumbling about the CIA not having sufficient oversight.
> Hebert called me in and just asked if I was interested and willing to assume
> the chairmanship. It was very flattering. He had insulated me on the com-
> mittee so that I could not prevail politically. I decided then to be as objec-
> tive and fair as I could.[38]

Within the intelligence community there was some concern over the
appointment of "liberal" Lucien Nedzi as chief overseer. Yet Nedzi
came to impress intelligence officials with his fairness, diligence, and
dedication in a post that carried long hours of work and virtually no
political benefits. As former CIA Legislative Counsel George L. Cary
observed:

> Chairman Hebert was sensitive to charges being made by critics of the
> House Armed Services Committee that the committee was not doing as
> effective a job of intelligence oversight as it should; that oversight was
> being carried out almost exclusively by senior, conservative members of
> the committee. (The "old boy" network, if you will.) Hebert saw the hand-

writing on the wall. Not enough attention had been given to intelligence oversight. He also knew that Nedzi was as honest as the day is long, diligent, smart, and had a little bit of a liberal bent. Hebert named him chairman of the Intelligence Subcommittee and named other "solid citizens" as members of the subcommittee. Before there was any real heat to do it, Nedzi jumped in and carried out tight, close, responsible oversight. Nedzi was a responsible guy! He had a healthy respect for intelligence professionals, but he gave us a hard time when he felt we needed a hard time. On more than one occasion he held our feet to the fire and forced us to change our course. It gave some of our people fits at the time, but, in the long run it was to our advantage. He had a lot of hearings and compiled a good oversight record.[39]

The appointment of Nedzi as chairman of the Intelligence Subcommittee in 1971 enabled the Armed Services Committee to establish more substantive activity in this area. Nedzi felt honored by the appointment but realized that it carried few tangible benefits: "You can be introduced to banquets as 'a man privy to the country's most secret secrets.' However, you don't have the opportunity to speak before bankers, postal workers, or teachers like members of their committees do and receive nice honoraria."[40] Nedzi also realized that his freedom of action was sharply limited by the power of Chairman Hebert:

I was on a very short leash. Chairman Hebert could have ousted me at any time. Those were the days when chairmen had power. Today the position of chairman is much less powerful. There is chaos and an absence of discipline on the standing committees. The chairman today has no power. He's less powerful than subcommittee chairmen. When I first came to Congress and was put on the Armed Services Committee, the chairman was all-powerful.[41]

Despite these limitations, from 1971 to 1974 Nedzi made some real advances in intelligence oversight. As the Armed Services Committee's general counsel recalled: "Nedzi was the brightest member I've seen in the fifteen years I've been here. Nedzi worked night and day on the oversight hearings he conducted into Watergate and the Ellsberg matters. He had a tremendous memory and a brilliant mind."[42] In other words, Nedzi had begun to institutionalize intelligence oversight in the House of Representatives.

As chairman of the Intelligence Subcommittee, Nedzi was immediately informed of CIA involvement in the Watergate break-in in June 1972. Nedzi recalled:

The Watergate break-in occurred on a Friday night. I was called on Saturday and told there were individuals—former CIA types—involved. Later I was told a camera and a wig were furnished. I heard of these things right after the CIA learned of them. [Director of Central Intelligence] Schlesinger called me one time and apologized after they found the McCord memo.

The press would find out about all these things afterwards but I was the first to know.[43]

Under Nedzi's leadership the Intelligence Subcommittee conducted an intensive inquiry into the CIA's involvement in Watergate and the Ellsberg matters. Altogether twenty-eight days of hearings were held and thirty-eight witnesses were summoned. As Nedzi recounted:

I conducted closed-door hearings with McCord, Hunt, Ehrlichman, and Liddy. Liddy refused to even be sworn in. I got him for contempt on that. I heard from Walters, Colby, Helms, Schlesinger, Haldeman, Ehrlichman, and Colson in my office privately. All this occurred before the Senate Watergate hearings. I held closed hearings and would meet with the press afterwards.[44]

Nedzi's oversight in this instance had some tangible results. Because of his sharp questioning of Howard J. Osborn, the CIA's director of security, and Osborn's failure to answer several questions to Nedzi's satisfaction, CIA Director William Colby was extremely upset. The next day Osborn retired from the CIA.[45]

Nedzi also sharply questioned Lieutenant General Vernon Walters, the deputy director of the CIA. As one Armed Services staffer recalled:

Nedzi wouldn't open his hearings to the press and public. He wanted to really get to the bottom of things. There were misstatements of witnesses under oath. Nedzi almost had Walters indicted for his misstatements. This was the one and only time Walters was reduced to size.[46]

Nedzi himself remembered the Walters confrontation quite well:

I questioned Walters sharply about his trip to see [FBI Director] Gray after he and [DCI Richard] Helms had met with [White House Counsel John] Ehrlichman. Walters testified that when he was called in to do these things he really strongly protested. Walters was trying to make himself out to be a hero. Subsequently, a memorandum that he had prepared at the time was found in his safe and ran quite differently from his testimony. I was offended by that testimony and dressed him down. Later he got back at me in his book.[47]

In his autobiography Walters described Nedzi as "a troubled little man."[48] In sum, Nedzi's oversight had a definite impact on the intelligence community.

During Nedzi's tenure as Intelligence Subcommittee chairman the "Family Jewels" were developed at the CIA. "Family Jewels" was the name given a report prepared for the director of central intelligence, a list of possibly illegal or improper activities engaged in by the intelligence community. Nedzi was briefed by the CIA about what was being unearthed but took no action. As former CIA Legislative Counsel John Maury explained:

> I briefed Nedzi about what was being uncovered at the agency. Nedzi said: "I know it's part of my job to go over this issue so that any abuses won't be repeated. I'm satisfied these mistakes won't be repeated. There's nothing to be gained by passing this information around Congress and out for public consumption. I'm satisfied that the safeguards there now are adequate." [49]

Former CIA Legislative Counsel Walter Pforzheimer added: "Nedzi was not a great believer in screwing up the intelligence community when abuses were already corrected." [50] Nedzi chose not to pursue the investigation into the Family Jewels because, besides the reasons advanced by Maury and Pforzheimer, Nedzi was under severe time restrictions due to his Watergate investigation. In addition, while he was chairman of the Intelligence Subcommittee, Nedzi had only two staffers. Thus his ability to conduct oversight was severely limited by time and staff restraints. However, the fact that Nedzi had not pursued the Family Jewels further was to destroy him as chairman of the House Select Intelligence Committee in 1975.

In his time as an intelligence overseer, Chairman Nedzi developed a distinct style of leadership. His institutional oversight orientation led him to seek an understanding of institutions, processes, and procedures. Wanting to make intelligence oversight a reality in the House, Nedzi preferred closed-door hearings and a very low-key approach. Although he conducted a comprehensive inquiry into Watergate, time and staff limits hindered his ability to pursue additional oversight activity. In addition, Nedzi had a positive attitude towards the intelligence community. As he commented: "You have to start out with the premise that people in the intelligence community are trying to do what's best for the country. The CIA has always had a strong commitment to personal freedom and the democratic way of doing things." [51]

In reality Nedzi created intelligence oversight in the House Armed Services Committee. He established some important standards. Of his interest in the intelligence community Nedzi noted:

> We were just getting over a period when things in the intelligence area were very closely held in Congress. I had the CIA come in for rather extended briefings on their whole operations. We went out to the CIA and saw their operations. We visited the National Security Agency and the Defense Intelligence Agency. I took a field trip to the State Department to see their intelligence component. This was the first time this was even done. When James Schlesinger was director of central intelligence there was a major reorganization. I got to see his cuts in personnel and the savings impact. They didn't seek our advice but our advice was offered. [52]

Besides establishing an institutional link between the Congress and the intelligence community, Nedzi also served as an ombudsman for individual congressmen. As he recalled:

There were a number of instances where members would come to me with problems and questions about intelligence that either they or their constituents were concerned about. These were forwarded by me to the appropriate intelligence people. They were resolved on a one-to-one basis.[53]

Thus Nedzi was a pioneer in establishing intelligence oversight in the House.

When Nedzi became chairman of the Select Intelligence Committee in February 1975 the political environment in the House had been altered dramatically from the period in which Nedzi's legislative style was formed. Major institutional reforms had been adopted in the House that greatly reduced the power of standing committee chairmen. In the 1974 elections ninety-two first-year representatives were elected to the House. In this group were seventy-five new Democrats. Following the 1974 elections three standing committee chairmen were deposed in the House Democratic Caucus as the absolute seniority system for selecting chairmen was ended. Among the deposed chairmen was F. Edward Hebert of the Armed Services Committee.

Within the House Select Intelligence Committee, Lucien Nedzi was viewed with great suspicion by the other Democratic members. The general perception was that he was a "co-opted congressman." As Michael Harrington, a member of the Nedzi committee, observed: "Speaker Albert should never have appointed Nedzi as chairman of the select committee. The problem really rests there. It would have been the same problem if Mike Mansfield had appointed John Stennis to investigate himself in the Senate."[54] A liberal Democrat on the Nedzi committee commented: "Nedzi was dovish by Armed Services standards. He was well intentioned but a weak guy."[55] Nedzi himself was well aware of his credibility problem. After Seymour Hersh's articles on the CIA appeared in late 1974, Nedzi went before the House Democratic Caucus to defend himself against charges that he had not exercised responsible oversight. Nedzi laid out his record before the caucus including the number of hearings he had held and the number of hours he had spent doing oversight. As a result he was able to beat back the caucus challenge.[56]

To be effective as chairman of the Select Intelligence Committee, Nedzi attempted to foster consensus through the selection of the committee's staff director. As Nedzi noted:

To eliminate any taint that the committee might become partisan or affected by predilections on the subject, I was endeavoring to achieve some kind of consensus on the selection of the staff director. This consumed a great deal of time. In one form or another we considered two-score candidates. We finally hired Searle Field. He had been recommended by Giaimo.[57]

The committee's search for a staff director had indeed been a long one. The Nedzi committee had been formed on February 19, 1975. Searle Field was not hired as staff director until May 13, 1975. At the same committee meeting where Field was selected, Representative Harrington nominated former Attorney General Ramsey Clark as a "symbolic" candidate for the post and told Chairman Nedzi that his appointment as chairman was "a symbol of failed oversight." [58] Unfortunately the hiring of a staff director had preoccupied the committee's work for three months and had not healed the split between the chairman and his fellow Democrats.

Next came Nedzi's attempt to set an agenda for the committee. Nedzi recalled: "One of the first things after Field's selection was to sit down and try to set a program for the committee. We had scheduled a meeting for the commencement of hearings. Our intention was to fully disclose everything, including the Family Jewels." [59] However, before the hearings could begin, the *New York Times* revealed on June 5, 1975, that Nedzi had already been briefed secretly by the CIA about the Family Jewels and had done nothing about it. Nedzi acknowledged the damage caused by this revelation: "The *New York Times* article said that I was informed about the Family Jewels. How could I have done anything differently? I was confronted with a fire storm. At that point, I'm dead." [60] Representative James V. Stanton, a Nedzi committee member, commented on the *New York Times* disclosure:

> Any member who knows of illegal acts committed by the CIA and who has oversight responsibilities involving CIA and who fails to try to correct them by informing the members of the House of Representatives would appear to have impaired his ability to conduct an important investigation. [61]

Fellow committee member Harrington accused Nedzi of a "deliberate effort to mislead us"; Dellums said Nedzi had compromised himself beyond repair. [62]

On June 12, 1975, Nedzi announced his resignation as chairman after the other Democrats voted 6 to 1 to form a separate CIA subcommittee under Representative James V. Stanton. However, after Nedzi was visited by Majority Leader O'Neill, he agreed to delay his resignation at the request of both O'Neill and Speaker Albert. On June 13 Stanton attempted to hold his first CIA subcommittee meeting with DCI Colby testifying. However, at the urging of Nedzi, the committee's three Republicans boycotted this meeting. Under committee rules, which required the presence of at least one minority party member, the hearing could not proceed. A stalemate had been reached. On June 16 the House voted 64 to 290 to reject Nedzi's resignation. Five Nedzi committee members—Democrats Dellums, Edwards, Giaimo, Harrington, and Stanton—voted to accept Nedzi's resignation. Democrat Murphy and Republicans McClory and Treen voted to reject the resignation while Nedzi and Republican Kasten voted "present." After this vote of vindication Nedzi was allowed to step down as chairman. As he noted: "I fell into total apathy after this with respect to intelligence. It helped contribute to my decision to leave the Congress." [63] Thus the controversy over Nedzi's appointment as chairman of the select committee and his eventual resignation from that post set back the House's investigation more than six months.

Otis Pike
After Nedzi resigned as chairman and the House Select Intelligence Committee was reconstituted, Otis Pike was appointed as the new chairman. Like Nedzi, Pike had served in the House for fourteen years and had been a member of the Armed Services Committee. Pike also had solid liberal credentials. In 1974 he received a mean ADA rating of 74 percent and an NSI rating of 30 percent. Yet Pike had a legislative style quite unlike Nedzi's. In a real sense Nedzi was institutional, devoted to both the House and his work on the Armed Services Committee. Pike, on the other hand, was an outsider. Despite his fourteen years in the House, Pike was still very much a maverick. A political scientist who served on the staff of the Pike committee observed:

> Pike himself was never an institutional man. As a result, the Pike committee was looking more outward than inside the House. You wouldn't expect an institutional view from Pike. [Staff Director] Field and [Chief Counsel] Donner were also outsiders. They didn't see much beyond the Pike committee. This was to be a one-shot deal. [64]

Finally, Otis Pike was a hard-nosed investigator. In 1969 he had directed a House subcommittee investigation of the North Korean seizure of the American spy ship Pueblo. Pike's history in the House demonstrated that he could be an effective and aggressive investigator.

When Pike took over as chairman of the Select Committee on July 17, 1975, the internal struggles over the hiring of a staff director and the controversy over Nedzi's ability to be an impartial and effective chairman had already consumed six months. This legacy of dissonance and drift had hindered the work of the committee. In some ways Pike was limited in what he could do. For example, he had no input on the selection of members for his committee. As Pike himself noted: "I inherited the staff. I only brought in [General Counsel] Aaron Donner from Long Island." [65] Nevertheless, Pike's assumption of the chairmanship marked a dramatic change in the history of the House's investigation.

Pike was able to set the agenda for the select committee. Within two weeks of his assumption of the chairmanship, the Pike committee conducted its first public hearing. To a committee that had been bogged down in disputes and controversy Pike brought a new sense of direction. At the first public hearing, on July 31, 1975, Chairman Pike set out the plan for the committee's work:

> We are to investigate the intelligence gathering activities of the U.S. government. We are to complete our investigation by January 31 and by that date report to the House our conclusions and recommendations. . . . We start by looking at the cost. . . . As we learn what the costs are, we will look at the benefits achieved as well as the risks created by gaining this intelligence. What benefits have we the right to expect? . . . We must draw reasonable lines between security and freedom, between "need to know" and "right to know." . . . While the budget seemed a reasonable place to start, we will pursue our investigation where it seems most useful to go. . . . We will try not to travel well-traveled paths and we will pursue facts rather than headlines.[66]

According to General Counsel Aaron Donner:

> The House committee started out with the philosophy of Pike himself. Pike is very conscious of fiscal matters. The committee asked these questions as a result: (1) How good are they? (2) Are we getting our money's worth? and (3) Are they doing what an intelligence agency should do? This is what we tried to stick with. We asked, How much is the cost? We found that a large amount of the information obtained was useless. It couldn't be digested. Too much was being collected. We examined the question of the gathering of foreign intelligence and the operation of foreign policy. And we were led finally to the question of intelligence failures.[67]

Ironically, of the three major investigations of the intelligence community from 1975 to 1976—President Ford's Rockefeller commission, the Senate select committee, and the House select committee—only the Pike committee did not allow itself to have its agenda shaped by the intelligence community and the focus on the Family Jewels abuses. The fact that the Pike committee did not fall into this trap was due largely to Chairman Pike. As Mitchell Rogovin, special counsel to DCI Colby, remarked:

> The Pike committee had an immature and incompetent staff. The makeup of the committee was substantially less competent than the Church committee. However, the agenda of the Pike committee was much better than that of the Church committee. For all the talent and competence in the Senate, they floundered. They didn't run an effective investigation. But, ironically, Pike did. Pike had an incompetent staff and got precious little help from other members, but he got to the heart of the issues. Pike himself was the driving force on that committee. He knew what he wanted and had a much better agenda and understanding than the Church committee.[68]

In setting the agenda, Pike made his most significant contribution to the select committee.

Pike also made sure that the committee focused on the major issues. For example, at a public hearing on August 6, 1975, Representative Lehman asked Pike to instruct the committee staff to study the possible adverse effects of CIA proprietary companies on American business. DCI Colby, testifying at the time, directed his response to Lehman's query toward Pike, saying: "I would welcome such a study Mr. Chairman." Chairman Pike responded first to Colby and then to Lehman:

> I am sure you [Mr. Colby] would, and I don't think it would be terribly revealing, and I think it would spread our staff pretty thin, if we try to study what the CIA proprietaries are doing to the American business community as a whole.
>
> Mr. Lehman, I just don't think I want the staff to devote too much of its efforts and energies to that particular concern, although I assure you that I will discuss it with the staff director further and members of the staff to see what we can do.[69]

Pike also declined to look at some of the more outlandish contingency plans developed by the intelligence community. These included such proposals as trying to develop a powder to cause Fidel Castro's beard to fall out. Unlike the Church committee Pike was not interested in spending time on such issues. Pike noted: "There have been somewhat wild schemes proposed in the past, which we gather never got carried out, and I don't see much sense in whipping them."[70] By such actions Pike made the committee focus on the broader and more substantive aspects of its inquiry.

Two other actions taken by Pike helped define the committee's role. First, unlike Nedzi, Pike sought to keep all of the committee's sessions open to the press and the public. He defended this openness at a public hearing on November 6, 1975:

> One of the things which I have tried to do is to be as open as possible in these hearings. I don't like executive sessions. I believe that the American people are entitled to the truth, and I would rather not settle issues like this in secret caucuses. It is my view that it is much better to let the people know what our problems are, what the issues are, and the manner in which we are proceeding. I will take the responsibility for that.[71]

Second, again unlike Nedzi, Pike refused information that only he as chairman would see. As he explained at a public session on November 14, 1975:

> It has been indicated to me that I would be permitted to go down and look at these documents. That is not satisfactory to me. We subpoenaed these documents for the committee. One of the difficulties which my predecessor

had was that he was in possession of information which the rest of the committee did not have. This chairman has made it clear from the outset that when we subpoena documents for the committee, and when there is information which the committee feels it is essential that it have, I am not going to look at the documents and deprive the rest of the committee of seeing the material themselves.[72]

Pike's determination to keep the sessions open afforded members the opportunity to educate both the press and the public. At the same time, Pike's unwillingness to allow himself sole access to secret information was a rejection of past oversight methods. Both actions are a reflection of Otis Pike's legislative orientation.

Some other decisions—both by Pike and by party leaders—were much less positive. For example, unlike Senator Church, Pike was unable to keep his committee together. The Church committee constantly strove for consensus, for unanimous agreement among the members. On the Pike committee it was rare for all the members to agree on anything. Much of this was beyond Pike's control. The Democratic leadership had set the party ratios and had appointed primarily liberal Democrats to the committee. In retaliation the Republican leadership had appointed primarily conservative members. The political division hurt the committee's work and was a major factor in the House's decision to reject the committee's final report in January 1976. Unlike Church, Pike was not as concerned with building consensus. He was not interested in institutionalizing intelligence oversight in the House. Instead his primary focus was the investigative activity in which his committee was engaged.

Moreover, while Pike set an agenda that was much more substantive than that of the Church committee, Pike's determination to complete his investigation by January 31, 1976, meant that his committee had only about six months to do its work. As one Pike committee investigator noted: "Pike was into the right approach. But the committee needed not six months but two years to do its work."[73] A Pike committee staffer who worked for Congressman McClory also cited the limited time: "Otis had his priorities wrong. His priority was to finish on time. Pike's principles were to do it cheaply and finish on time. He was not all that interested in the quality of the product. Otis could have had an extension but he didn't want one."[74] Thus by insisting on completing the committee's work by January 31, 1976, Chairman Pike prevented the committee from completing the extensive inquiry it had undertaken.

Pike also tended to overlook procedural details. For example, the committee was sharply criticized for being unable to keep secrets entrusted to it. When the Committee on Standards of Official Conduct held hearings on who had leaked the Pike committee's final report, Chairman Pike was upset about the focus of that committee's inquiry. Pike testified angrily on July 19, 1976:

> I really think we have spent too much time with the procedures of our report and not enough with the substance of it. You refer to the obtaining, safeguarding, and distribution of classified information, and I would only say that as far as Congress is concerned, the biggest problem still remains getting it. [75]

Later in that same meeting, committee member Thad Cochran (R., Mississippi) summed up a major criticism:

> I think the difficulty was whether there was evidence of our being able to place trust and faith in a committee that was established and operating in such a way that raised some doubts about whether we could maintain secrecy of legitimately classified material that might be given to the committee. [76]

Cochran also criticized the committee's failure to adequately regulate staff access to seventy-five thousand classified documents in its possession together with staff access to photocopy machines. Pike responded: "You either trust your staff or you don't. You are talking about staff. You are not talking about outsiders." [77]

As chairman, Pike failed to demonstrate real concern with maintaining security, just the opposite of Senator Church's position with the Senate committee. Consequently, when information leaked, fairly or unfairly, the Pike committee was blamed. In the end much of the committee's substantive work was overlooked or ignored because of the concern over procedural matters, a problem due largely to a lack of leadership in this area by Chairman Pike.

Another difficulty Pike had as chairman was maintaining relations with the executive branch. These relations were hostile and testy since senior officials in the Ford White House viewed Pike as unpredictable, unscrupulous, and roguish. [78] Mitchell Rogovin, special counsel to the director of central intelligence, described Pike as "a very smart man. But Pike is his own worst enemy. He was too glib, too quick." [79] Some of the hostility between Pike and the executive branch resulted from Pike's personality. But the manner in which Pike handled secret documents and the information they contained came directly from Pike's stance as an aggressive investigator unwilling to be sidetracked. It is not surprising that there was tension in this relationship. The degree of tension, however, was exacerbated by the personality of Pike himself.

At times Pike demonstrated a legislative style that could be described as eccentric at best or unprofessional at worst. One McClory staffer who worked on the Pike committee described this style:

Otis Pike was a real character. He was a real unique member of Congress. He did a lot of his own work. He had a very limited staff. He fashioned himself as a sort of character. He liked that role. He was somewhat irreverent. Pike had a great sense of humor. He looked for the humorous side.[80]

At times this side of Pike had very negative effects. For example after the House voted on January 29, 1976, to suppress the committee's final report, Pike became very irritable. Instead of seeking to salvage what he could, he threatened not to even file "a report on the CIA in which the CIA would do the final rewrite."[81] Pike was willing to destroy everything in a moment of pique. As a senior committee staffer noted:

> The only thing that the Pike committee needed to do was that its primary goal was not to be the end of congressional oversight of intelligence. It needed to convince the House that there was a need for a permanent committee and that oversight could be done responsibly.[82]

Pike failed to see these broader goals. At the completion of the Pike committee's public hearings on February 10, 1976, it is not surprising that Pike ended with these words: "Let's adjourn to another room where we can perhaps celebrate in a more fitting manner."[83] Thus at times Pike's own comments and actions undermined the respect he needed as chairman.

Chairman Pike conducted a comprehensive investigation of the intelligence community that raised many substantive issues. However, because of the way the investigation was conducted the important questions were ignored, and the focus devolved upon procedural issues such as whether a House committee could be trusted with classified national security information. In the end the Pike committee's final report was rejected by the House, and a permanent intelligence oversight committee was not formed until more than a year after the death of the Pike committee. As chairman, Otis Pike deserves credit for conducting a thorough investigation that raised extremely important issues. However, Pike was a dismal failure at advancing the cause of institutionalized intelligence oversight in the House of Representatives.

Internal Relations

The Nedzi Committee

There was sharp division and conflict within the Nedzi committee from its creation until it was reconstituted following the resignation of Chairman Nedzi. When it was learned that Nedzi had been informed of the Family Jewels in 1973 but had not acted on what he was told the committee's Democrats revolted. A senior staff member with both the Nedzi and Pike committees remembered:

> I was at the closed-door hearing when it had just been disclosed that Nedzi had been given this information and had held it. He was lambasted by the other members. I never saw one man take so much shit. His biggest attackers were Giaimo and Harrington. Giaimo was the main assassin. Harrington was a villain. Don Edwards was an assassin to a lesser extent. His was the knee-jerk liberal response. Some sincerely believed that a holdover from the bad old days was not right. Some people were hungry themselves for the limelight.[84]

Ironically, although Nedzi was opposed by his fellow Democrats, he retained the support of the three Republican members. Robert McClory, the ranking minority member, explained the Republicans' support:

> A majority of the Democratic members of the committee had learned of Chairman Nedzi's prior knowledge of certain covert operations which they felt compromised his leadership of the investigation and required his resignation. Meeting in private and without minority members present, they attempted to "depose" Nedzi and name a new chairman from their midst. Although Nedzi announced his intention to resign, he did not approve of, or acquiesce in, this unusual action by his colleagues—and he so informed me in my role as the ranking minority member of the committee. There shortly followed a hearing scheduled by the new "chairman" named by the rump caucus of Democrats at which the director of central intelligence was to testify in the committee's opening session. Chairman Nedzi, having not yet tendered his resignation, informed me that he did not sanction the rump caucus's attempt to hold a hearing. It was further clear to me that the chaos and disruption caused by the internecine squabbling threatened to destroy the entire investigation. Therefore, since it was clear that the caucus of Democrats was attempting to act in violation of both regular parliamentary order and the committee's own rules, I invoked a committee rule which required the attendance of a member of the minority for a valid quorum at a hearing and, having organized my colleagues in my office, refused to attend the rump caucus's hearing, thereby cancelling what would have been a sorry spectacle. The House repudiated the unfair tactics of the Democratic caucus by refusing to accept the resignation by an overwhelming margin.[85]

After McClory's action the committee was hopelessly polarized and deadlocked. Chairman Nedzi and the three Republicans were on one side, and the remaining six Democrats were on the other. Earlier the committee had spent three months trying to agree on a staff director. With the Republican boycott of the rump caucus's hearing, the work of the Nedzi committee came grinding to a halt. Further progress was not possible until the committee itself could be revamped and reconstituted.

The Pike Committee

Like the Nedzi committee, the Pike committee was characterized by constant conflict and the inability to form a consensus. In its public hearings and meetings sixty-six committee votes were recorded. On only five of these was there unanimous agreement among those voting, and four of the five votes involved whether the committee should go into executive session.[86] Of the divisions within his committee, Chairman Pike observed: "The committee has the broadest possible philosophical range."[87] And again: "Given the philosophic spread on the committee—Ron Dellums to Bob McClory and Dave Treen—it is amazing we got along as well as we did."[88] While the Democratic and Republican members of the Church committee had striven to foster consensus, no such attempt was made on the Pike committee.

There were six Democrats and five Republicans on the Church committee, with the chairman and the ranking minority member working together to foster consensus. On the Pike committee there were nine Democrats and four Republicans, and no attempt was made by the chairman or the other Democratic members to keep the committee united. On the Church committee when the chairman was absent the vice-chairman (from the other party) presided. On December 10, 1975, the Pike committee conducted hearings into covert action. Chairman Pike noted that he had to leave:

> Pike: I have a longstanding commitment to be somewhere else at 10:30. It is not on Capitol Hill, and I am going to have to leave. I hope I can find some warm body on the Democratic side to preside in my absence. If I can't, everything will come to a screeching halt.
>
> McClory: Mr. Chairman, I am able to preside.
>
> Pike: Mr. McClory, you know I trust you implicitly, and I would be delighted to have you do so. But unfortunately that would violate our rules and you are such a purist in those matters, I don't think it would work.[89]

Eventually Mr. Aspin presided at this hearing. Thus even the rules on the Pike committee had a tendency to hinder cooperation.

The most significant internal development on the Pike Committee was a bipartisan nine-to-four ideological division among the members. The nine in the majority included Chairman Pike and seven other Democrats (Giaimo, Stanton, Dellums, Murphy, Aspin, Hayes, and Lehman) plus one Republican (Johnson). The four in the minority included the three remaining Republicans (McClory, Treen, and Kasten) and one Democrat (Milford). The nine in the majority tended to be hostile and critical toward both the intelligence community and the

Ford administration while the four in the minority tended to be staunch defenders of both.

Compared to the others on the committee, both Johnson and Milford were party mavericks. Johnson, a Republican, had kept his real views about intelligence hidden from his party's leaders when he sought committee membership. He noted: "I asked on [the Pike Committee]. The leadership didn't know I would take the positions I did or I would never have been appointed to the committee."[90] Johnson's views on the intelligence community summarized the feelings of the nine-member majority:

> They were lying sons of bitches. They lie every chance they get. They are no-good people. They are no goddamn good. [Former DCI Richard] Helms lies to Congress, gets convicted of perjury, and says he will wear his conviction like a "badge of honor." I went out with staff one day to CIA headquarters. I told [CIA official Seymour] Bolten: "You, the CIA, are the enemy." The military establishment dominates this country today.[91]

At the same time, Milford was the ideological opposite of Johnson. Like Johnson, Milford had not been asked about his views before being appointed to the committee.[92] Milford's outlook summarized the views of the four minority members:

> Intelligence oversight should be done in a responsible way. You never should announce the names of the members. It should be very responsible members who work in complete privacy. Lucien Nedzi's type of oversight is the way it has to be done. Congress is not equipped to handle or protect intelligence information. Of necessity, certain things within the intelligence community are nasty. They are not the type of things you talk about in Sunday school.[93]

With such ideologically opposed positions being held by the members it is understandable why the committee found it impossible to unite.

In testimony before the House Committee on Standards of Official Conduct, Staff Director Searle Field stated that the nine members in the ideological majority of the Pike committee were a "bipartisan" majority.[94] Yet bipartisanship here meant that one Republican had chosen to align with the Democrats and one Democrat with the Republicans. As Chairman Pike himself noted:

> I am perhaps being a little picky here, but any time somebody says to me, "have a bipartisanship membership" on any committee, I don't think it accomplishes an awful lot. It depends on who the members are, rather than what their political party is.
>
> I can look at this committee right here [the Pike committee] and think that a liberal Democrat choosing the committee members would have Mr. Jim Johnson of Colorado as his ranking Republican member, and a conser-

vative Republican choosing the committee members would have Mr. Dale Milford as his ranking Democratic member. I just don't think that gets you anywhere.[95]

Thus the majority and minority on the Pike committee were indeed bipartisan but only in a very limited sense. The Pike committee was composed of two groups of ideological pursuits holding diametrically opposed views of their work and the intelligence community.

During the Pike committee's public hearings these ideological differences frequently resulted in verbal skirmishes. For example, on February 3, 1976, Mr. Dellums stated what he would like to see the committee do: "I think this committee ought to come down hard and clear on the side of stopping any intelligence agency in this country from utilizing, corrupting, and prostituting the media, the church and our educational system."[96] The very next day, Mr. Milford responded to Dellums: "There has been talk about corruption of the press, the church, and so forth. Mr. Chairman, I submit that such remarks can be construed to be an insult and a slap in the face to thousands of loyal, dedicated Americans working in our intelligence community."[97] Such conflict discouraged members from attaining common ground.

The most significant consequence of the committee's ideological polarization was the House vote of 246 to 124 on January 29, 1976, to suppress the committee's final report. Mr. McClory summarized the issue:

> On October 1, 1975, the committee adopted a procedure for receipt of classified information by which it agreed with the president to guard the confidentiality of sensitive material and not release such material unless certain clearance procedures, involving consultations with the executive, were employed. Until the committee began to consider its final report, this agreement was respected. However, a majority of the committee [the 9 to 4 bipartisan split] took the position that the agreement with the president, which was responsible for the orderly flow of information to the investigation, was inapplicable with respect to the publication of the final report. It remains a mystery as to how the committee could argue logically that classified information received under a solemn agreement, which contained no exceptions for unilateral release, could be included in a document without following the terms of that agreement simply because it was designated a "final report."[98]

Chairman Pike's assessment was quite different: "They [the executive branch] wanted to pre-censor our final report. This was unacceptable."[99] Within the Pike committee the key vote on this issue was held on January 21, 1975. Milford moved to strike out all classified material from the final report. The motion was defeated 8 to 4. The majority consisted of Pike, Giaimo, Stanton, Dellums, Murphy, Aspin, Lehman, and Johnson; the minority of McClory, Treen, Kasten, and Milford. Hayes did not vote.

On January 26, 1975, McClory announced to the committee that he had taken a special order on the floor of the House to oppose the committee's decision on its final report. McClory told his colleagues on the committee:

> I think initially I had great faith that the House intelligence committee or oversight committee could participate rather actively with respect to the whole intelligence function, and that the oversight capability of the House could be such that we could review the nature of the intelligence activities, the budget and a great variety of things. I must confess, Mr. Chairman, that I am not confident at this moment that a House committee can be trusted with that kind of responsibility.[100]

McClory was bitterly attacked by Representative Johnson for his remarks. Besides McClory, Milford also lobbied hard against the committee's majority position. As Milford recalled:

> I led the fight against the release of the report on the floor of the House. I went to John Young who was on the Rules Committee from Texas for help there. The debate in the House on the release of the Pike committee's report was one of the two times in my congressional career where members came and listened to the debate in order to make up their minds on how to vote. The House did reject the committee. It voted down the recommendations of the chairman and a majority of the committee.[101]

According to a senior committee staffer, "Milford was critical in the debate on the floor. He said, 'You can take it from me, and I've been able to see this first hand, it would be damaging to make this report public.' "[102]

The House voted 246 to 124 to suppress the committee's report. In the House vote, members of the Pike committee voted 9 to 4 not to suppress the report. However, this time, the 4 minority members were joined by 242 other members on the floor of the House. On February 3, 1976, McClory made a motion in the Pike committee that the Speaker be asked to submit the final report to the president so that it might be sanitized and released. However, this attempt at compromise on the part of McClory was rejected 7 to 4. The majority of the Pike committee was unwilling to bend to the minority of the Pike committee and the majority in the House. Ideological divisions within the committee and the resulting failure to practice consensus politics were the key factors in the House's rejection and repudiation of the Pike committee.

The Pike Committee was plagued by partisan as well as ideological divisions. Mr. Johnson, the one Republican member of the bipartisan majority, noted that some of the work of the Pike committee "involved partisan politics. You had Democrats going after a Republican administration." [103] One partisan division flared up on September 29, 1975. McClory reacted sharply to charges by Mr. Giaimo that the Republicans were trying to delay the Committee's work: "The delays are not caused by this side of the aisle or by me. I have been pushing ahead here. We had some serious delays for a matter of months, while you reorganized your side of this committee. That is where the big hangup has been." [104] On February 5, 1976, Giaimo bitterly rebuked McClory's suggestion that House Republicans should be given a ratio of committee seats comparable to those received by the Republican minority in the Senate: "I say that as far as this member of Congress is concerned, the minority has been trying to hamper and block effective oversight over these agencies since day one." [105]

In addition, relations between the individual members of the committee were frequently characterized by mistrust and suspicion. For example, members frequently leaked and counterleaked secret information to advance their positions. A senior staffer with both the Nedzi and Pike committees observed: "The biggest offenders with respect to leaks were members of the committee: Aspin, Harrington, Stanton, Dellums, and McClory when it suited him. Those guys were absolutely shameless when it came to leaks, especially Aspin." [106]

Democrat Les Aspin had an agenda of his own. A Pike committee investigator commented: "Les Aspin was a manipulator. Nobody really trusted him on the committee." [107] Against the wishes of Chairman Pike, Aspin worked out a compromise with Henry Kissinger on committee access to State Department materials. As Chief Counsel Donner noted, "Aspin was too close to Kissinger. They met frequently." [108] When Aspin testified before the Committee on Standards of Official Conduct on July 20, 1976, he acknowledged that he had secretly given copies of the Pike committee's final report to Mitchell Rogovin, special counsel to the director of central intelligence, and the Reuters news agency. Later Mr. Kasten told the Committee on Standards of Official Conduct what he thought of Aspin's testimony: "I was just flabbergasted when I read in the newspaper an account of your hearing that he had provided the report to the CIA. I think that is a breach of security that is just as serious as any of the other ones." [109] Mr. Giaimo was also viewed with suspicion. As a senior Pike staffer noted: "There was a lack of trust in Giaimo by the other members. He was seen as Nedzi's assassin. Giaimo was viewed as always having some angle at stake. There was a sense that he was trying to use the Intelligence Committee to get something else." [110] Thus relations between the members were frequently characterized by intrigue, suspicion, and mistrust.

Unlike the Church committee, the Pike committee was deeply and bitterly divided, especially across ideological and partisan lines. When the committee went to defend itself before the House of Representatives at the end of January 1976 its internal divisions contributed to its defeat.

Committee Staff

For the select intelligence committees, staff played an especially important role. The principal tasks of the staff members included the investigative and background work needed for hearings and reports. In the Senate, Majority Leader Mike Mansfield took a key role in recruiting Staff Director Miller for the Church committee. In the House, however, no such interest was displayed by either Speaker Albert or Majority Leader O'Neill. The Nedzi committee's major accomplishment after a search of almost three months was hiring a staff director. And the Pike committee's work and reputation were definitely affected by the quality of its staff.

Nedzi Committee Staff

For almost three months the Nedzi committee was paralyzed by its inability to select a staff director. Chairman Nedzi tried to use the hiring of a staff director as a means of building consensus within the committee. But the committee members were unable to come to any agreement. Finally, after interviewing more than twenty candidates, the committee selected Searle Field, who had worked on the Senate Watergate Committee with Senator Lowell Weicker (R., Connecticut). Senator Weicker and Nedzi committee member Giaimo were Field's strongest supporters. One House staffer described how Field was selected: "What sold Searle was that Weicker was behind him. Weicker is the kind of guy who when he wants something will lobby hard. He lobbied hard for Searle." [111] According to another staffer:

> Giaimo was pushing hard [for Field]. Field was willing to do it. Nedzi made a mistake in hiring Field. In his defense, a number of people had turned down the post including Thornburgh, the governor of Pennsylvania now, and Alexander Greenfield, the assistant attorney general in New Jersey. Ben-Veniste turned it down too. A whole lot of people were approached and said no. The Republicans were making a big deal about it. They wanted a Republican staff director. The committee was worried about the danger of fragmentation. The staff director post was not widely sought after. The members themselves are to blame for the fact that no better staff director was chosen. [112]

Field was to serve as staff director for both the Nedzi and Pike committees. His appointment to this post was therefore a significant decision in the history of the House investigations.

Searle Field's directorship was undermined because of his age, background, and temperament. As a Pike committee staffer noted: "Our staff director was only thirty-one. It is hard to have perspective when you are that young." [113] A senior staffer described how Field failed to measure up to expectations:

> House staff directors are very low key, invisible, deferential, and are allergic themselves to publicity. They buck up the members. Senate staff directors spread out and are visible and flamboyant. Field didn't fit the House role. The fact that he was very young was a problem. Also, he was too slick for the members of the Nedzi and Pike committees. The members had the impression he was talking too much to the press on a background basis playing both ends against the middle. Field as staff director was out too far from the members. [114]

Another senior staffer raised similar concerns:

> I don't think he was sufficiently tempered by experience. Searle had no House experience. He didn't know the players, the lay of the land, the way the House works. There are two sides of this: (1) directing the investigation, and (2) directing the committee through the shoals of House politics. Searle was young, bright, and driven. But he was not tempered by House experience. [115]

The Church committee had selected a Senate insider as its staff director. In hiring Field, the House committees opted for a young staff director with little of the qualifications required for the post.

Commenting on Field's work as staff director a committee staffer who worked for Representative McClory noted: "He was just outclassed." [116] Another staffer discussed how Field was twice outmaneuvered:

> The first time was when the Pike committee cited Kissinger for contempt for withholding documents. President Ford called the majority down, did a stroke job on them, and the committee backed down. Searle couldn't stop the members from going down to the White House. He knew what would happen if they went down there. The second time was with the final report. Had it been issued, nothing in it would have been of interest to anybody. Instead it leaked. It ended in an FBI and House Ethics Committee probe to see who leaked it. [117]

Field was a poor choice for staff director. The responsibility for his appointment must be shared equally by the House Democratic leadership and the members of the Nedzi committee.

When the controversy erupted over Lucien Nedzi's ability to serve as chairman the staff was left without a mandate. One staffer who worked on both the Nedzi and Pike committees described what it was like during the Nedzi controversy:

> It was embarrassing. You're stuck in the position of not being able to do any work. There is no direction. There are no projects. As a staff member you receive authority from the members. How do you do anything? You can't go to the agencies and say the chairman wants this. We just sat there a lot.[118]

Yet the staff was not totally inactive. Staff Director Field worked behind the scenes, as one staffer recalled, "to get Nedzi out. This surprised me. Searle's motivations were pure. He was afraid that Nedzi would taint our effort. There was a lot of tenseness. There was a lot of disloyalty involved in getting Nedzi out."[119] Thus the most significant action taken by the Nedzi committee was the appointment of Staff Director Searle Field. Ironically, Field worked very hard to oust the chairman who had appointed him.

Pike Committee Staff
When the Pike committee was formed Searle Field was retained as staff director. Chairman Pike brought in Aaron Donner to serve as general counsel. A senior staffer described Donner's role as:

> to be the eyes and ears for Pike. Pike wanted somebody he could trust, not somebody who knew intelligence but somebody who could give him good judgment. Donner was not meant to be a great general counsel. He was Pike's confidante, Pike's eyes and ears. He had a low-key get-it-done attitude and did very well.[120]

Unlike the Church committee, the Pike committee started out with a unified nonpartisan staff, the result of an agreement between Chairman Pike and the ranking minority member, McClory. As a McClory staffer noted:

> McClory had just come from a major constitutional confrontation [the House Judiciary Committee's impeachment of President Nixon, thwarted by Nixon's resignation before the process was completed] and he felt that this would be another one. The best way to approach it was from a nonpartisan point of view. The impeachment inquiry staff had been a group of Republicans and Democrats who had worked together on the case. That had proved satisfactory and probably would be best. So the idea was that the chief counsel would be particularly responsible to the chairman. There would be people designated by the ranking minority member. Everybody would work together. All the members would be informed equally. As a result, McClory was able to hire three people.[121]

However, as time went on, partisan and ideological divisions split the committee. Consequently the staff remained nonpartisan in name but became very partisan in its actions. According to one Republican staff member: "As time went on, we Republicans viewed it [the Pike committee] as a 'damage-limiting' operation. We worked with the White House to coordinate strategy." [122]

The Committee and the House

In the history of intelligence oversight, the Nedzi and Pike committees are the only ones to have been decisively rejected and repudiated by their parent chamber. Despite the importance of maintaining the support of the House, neither committee chose to do so. In fact both became renegades. Such behavior by intelligence oversight committees has never occurred elsewhere.

During the 1975–76 period the House made five key decisions that showed its concern over the work of its select intelligence committees. First, the Nedzi committee was created on February 19, 1975, by a vote of only 286 to 120. During the House debate some members questioned whether, in light of the Church committee in the Senate, it was really necessary to create a similar committee in the House. In addition Republicans were upset over the party ratio to be allotted. Although Democrats supported the creation of the committee by a vote of 231 to 43, Republicans opposed it by 77 to 55. The Senate, on the other hand, had created the Church committee by a vote of 82 to 4. The Nedzi committee was thus created by the House with considerably less enthusiasm and support than its Senate counterpart.

The second major decision took place on June 16, 1975. After the Nedzi committee's Democrats had revolted against their chairman, Nedzi resigned and the House publicly debated whether it should accept the resignation. Nedzi himself rose on the floor of the House to defend his oversight record. He denounced his critics on the committee as seeking "national self-flagellation" and as having "no historical memory and no institutional memory." [123] House Rules Committee Chairman Richard Bolling (D., Missouri) rose in defense of Nedzi, accusing the dissident Democrats of resorting to "cannibalism" in attempting to drive Nedzi from the chairmanship. [124] Representative Samuel Stratton (D., New York) summed up the sentiments of those who opposed the resignation:

> A vote of rejection is the only way we can demonstrate our strong disapproval of the manner in which the committee has treated its chairman and to vindicate the gentleman from Michigan [Mr. Nedzi] and to indicate our support for the responsible kind of an investigation that he has all along wanted to conduct. [125]

Although he refused to vote on the resignation motion—considering it a matter for the Democratic Caucus to decide—Representative Bill Frenzel (R., Minnesota) denounced Nedzi's Democratic committee opponents in these terms: "I have full confidence in the gentleman from Michigan, and I believe he has received shabby treatment from his Democratic committee members." [126] During the debate on Nedzi's resignation, committee member Don Edwards defended the actions of the committee's dissident Democrats:

> To have the gentleman from Michigan in charge of the investigation of the CIA when he had been privy to this information [the Family Jewels] for more than two years and had not reported it to the House or to the attorney general, would be totally inappropriate. [127]

Following the debate, the House voted 290 to 64 to reject the Nedzi resignation. Democrats opposed the resignation 193 to 64 while Republicans opposed it 97 to 0. Forty-four members voted "present." Nedzi committee members Dellums, Edwards, Giaimo, Harrington, and Stanton all voted to accept the resignation, but their position was decisively rejected by the full House.

The third key decision took place a month later, on July 16 and 17, 1975, as the House debated whether it should even have a new select intelligence committee. Although the Nedzi committee was abolished and the Pike committee was established by a voice vote on July 17 there were several votes that indicated how divided the House was on whether to continue the investigation. On July 16 the House defeated by 293 to 122 a motion to simply abolish the Select Intelligence Committee. Later the same day the House rejected 230 to 178 a motion to set up a joint House-Senate intelligence committee in the near future. Finally on July 17 the House rejected by 274 to 119 an amendment specifically designed to permit Nedzi committee member Michael Harrington to remain on the new Pike committee. The first two recorded votes indicated the great division in the House over continuing the intelligence inquiry. The Harrington vote was a repudiation of Michael Harrington's conduct as a member of the Nedzi committee. As one political scientist who worked as a Pike committee staffer observed, the debate had grave implications for the new investigative committee: "The vote to create the committee a second time was close. There was no mandate for Pike." [128]

The fourth key decision came at the end of January 1976. On January 26 Mr. McClory, the ranking Republican on the Pike committee, took a special order on the House floor and expressed his belief that the committee's final report would deliberately reveal secret information that would endanger the national security of the United States. On that same day the *New York Times* published leaked portions of the final report. The next day Chairman Pike made a unanimous consent request on the House floor that would allow the committee extra time to submit its report until midnight January 30 since it was having trouble completing its work on time. Representative Robert Bauman (R., Maryland) objected, and the House debated the issue. On January 29 the House considered an amendment to the resolution offered by Pike that directed the committee not to release a final report containing classified information until it "has been certified by the president as not containing information which would adversely affect the intelligence activities of the CIA." This amendment was introduced by Rules Committee member John Young (D., Texas) who meanwhile was working behind the scenes with Pike committee member Dale Milford to suppress the report.

The central issue to emerge during the debate on Young's resolution was whether the House approved the work of its intelligence committee. In fact most House members had not had time to read the Pike committee's final report. House Administration Committee Chairman Wayne Hays (D., Ohio) summed up the sentiments of House members who were upset with the Pike committee but who had not actually read the report:

> I will probably vote not to release it, because I do not know what is in it. On the other hand, let me say it has been leaked page by page, sentence by sentence, paragraph by paragraph to the *New York Times,* but I suspect, and I do not know and this is what disturbs me, that when this report comes out it is going to be the biggest non-event since Brigitte Bardot, after 40 years and four husbands and numerous lovers, held a press conference to announce that she was no longer a virgin.[129]

The Young amendment, showing the House's displeasure with the Pike committee, was approved 246 to 124 with Democrats voting 127 to 122 and Republicans 119 to 2 in support of the proposal. Chairman Pike bitterly declared: "The House voted not to release a document it had not read. Our committee voted to release a document it had read."[130] When it conducted its investigation the Pike committee was an authorized representative of the House. In its vote of January 29, 1976, the House dramatically showed its disapproval of the Pike committee as its representative.

Finally, the fifth key decision occurred on February 19, 1976. On February 11 the *Village Voice* had published a leaked version of the Pike committee's final report. CBS reporter Daniel Schorr acknowledged two days later that he had given the report to the *Village Voice.* On February 19 the House voted 269 to 119 to pass H. Res. 1042 directing the Committee on Standards of Official Conduct to investigate the leaking of the report. An extensive investigation including eleven days of hearings was conducted. All 13 members of the Pike committee and 32 of its staff members were compelled to testify. On January 29 the House had rejected the work of the Pike committee; on February 19 it authorized the Committee on Standards of Official Conduct to thoroughly investigate its investigators. Such was the end of the House's investigation of the intelligence community.

Any committee of the House or Senate is an authorized representative of its parent chamber. In the Senate the Church committee sought to maintain the support and trust of its parent chamber during every step of its investigation. In the House the Pike committee and, to a certain extent, the Nedzi committee were renegades assuming the role of a free agent. In the end the House felt compelled to take drastic measures to rein in and discipline the Pike committee. The repudiation of the Pike committee held serious implications for the future of intelligence oversight in the House of Representatives.

The Committee and the Senate

As has already been noted, there was relatively little contact between the House and Senate intelligence committees during the investigations of 1975 to 1976. For the Nedzi committee internal problems resulted in a total lack of contact with the Senate. The Pike committee also had very limited contact with the Church committee. Because the Pike committee was not a legislative committee, there was no legislation requiring a conference committee. About the only real need for contact between the Pike and Church committees was the desire of both chairmen to avoid needless duplication of effort. As Otis Pike commented shortly after he assumed the chairmanship of the House Intelligence Committee:

> It would be perfectly possible for us to duplicate what the Church committee is doing over in the Senate except that Frank Church and I have gotten together and decided that we are not going to duplicate each other. We are going to work together. He will do certain things. We will do other things. And, there's plenty for both of us to do.[131]

The Church committee examined alleged assassination attempts by the CIA, the unauthorized storage of toxic wastes, the Huston plan, alleged abuses by the IRS, mail-openings by the CIA and FBI, electronic surveillance of Americans by the NSA, alleged abuses by the FBI during the directorship of J. Edgar Hoover, and covert CIA actions in Chile. The Pike committee examined intelligence costs and fiscal procedures, the performance of the intelligence community—including

some specific intelligence failures—and domestic intelligence programs not studied by the Church committee. Thus the House and Senate committees were able to avoid overlapping their inquiries.

Despite their limited contact, there was considerable ill feeling between the Pike and Church committees as a result of their tremendous
differences. The composition and quality of the members and staff
differed greatly, as did the committees' approaches to their investigations. The Pike committee assumed a much more hostile stance towards the executive branch; the Church committee was much more
responsible. A good example of the differences is found in the manner
in which each committee dealt with a memorandum unearthed at the
CIA during the investigations concerning Senator Henry Jackson (D.,
Washington). On February 23, 1973, Senator Jackson had met with
representatives of the CIA and suggested how the agency could contain
inquiries from Senator Church's Subcommittee on Multinational Corporations on CIA involvement with ITT in Chile in 1970. The Church
committee delicately avoided the entire issue. The Pike committee, on
the other hand, printed the entire memo revealing Jackson's acts in its
final report.[132]

Moreover on the Pike committee there was considerable resentment
at the attention the Church committee commanded from the press and
the public. Occasionally this resentment surfaced publicly, as at a
hearing on December 9, 1975. Chairman Pike addressed this remark
to Professor Norman Dorsen in testimony about legal issues in the
intelligence field: "It is rare that we get a witness before Senator
Church."[133] A senior Pike committee staffer summarized their frus-
trations:

> We in the Pike committee were competing with the Church committee.
> They had more glamour and better members. We received less attention
> from the media. We had a harder time getting on the evening news. We
> weren't getting a prominent play in the newspapers. The Senate is always
> better at PR than the House. The Pike committee was sort of a graveyard.
> Anybody on the House side has a lot of disdain for the Senate side. The
> Senate side tends to be plastic and not very deep.[134]

As a result of these differences it is not surprising that there was considerable ill feeling between the Church and Pike committees even
though contact between them was limited.

The Committee and the Executive Branch

For any committee of Congress attempting to conduct oversight, relations with the executive branch are crucial. In examining activities
conducted by the executive branch the committee is dependent upon

the executive branch itself for access to evidence and witnesses. This oversight relationship produces tension and friction by its very nature. During the House investigations of 1975 and 1976 the adversarial relationship between the two successive House select intelligence committees and the executive branch degenerated into open warfare. While the director of central intelligence attempted to control the focus of the House investigation the secretary of state worked strenuously behind the scenes to undermine the House investigation. In the end the weaknesses within the Nedzi and Pike committees combined with the vigorous activity of the executive branch to destroy the House intelligence investigation.

The Nedzi Committee
Throughout the almost six-month history of the Nedzi committee the executive branch was a quiet observer of the committee's self-destruction. Perhaps the best illustration was a hearing scheduled with DCI William Colby on June 12, 1975. As noted earlier, Colby showed up but the hearing did not materialize. The hearing had been called by Representative James Stanton, who had been elected chairman of the Nedzi committee's CIA investigation by maverick Democratic members in revolt against Chairman Nedzi. However, when the Republicans at Nedzi's urging boycotted the hearing, the committee was unable to proceed because, according to the rules, a minority party member had to be in attendance. The *Christian Science Monitor* reported that Colby "listened impassively" to the announcement that the hearing was cancelled and then chided the committee on its failure to take adequate security measures to safeguard the highly sensitive material it had requested from him.[135] Thus during this time the executive branch was more observer than participant.

Meanwhile, however, opinions were being formed within the executive branch about the nature of the inquiry the House was prepared to undertake. Looking at the Democratic membership the executive branch saw a committee of ultraliberals bent on destroying the U.S. intelligence community. As former Secretary of Defense Melvin R. Laird observed: "They did a lot to weaken intelligence operations. They felt that it [the details] was something to take to the press to feather their own nests."[136] Officials within the executive branch placed the blame for this situation squarely on Democratic Majority Leader Thomas P. O'Neill. As Bryce Harlow commented:

Tip is a ward-heel pol from Massachusetts. He is a Boston pol and no deep thinker. He never attempted to be anything else. Tip can't keep politics out of anything he does. He is a Democrat even when he goes to the john. It's in his pores. Everything is made for politics. The CIA as much as anything else.[137]

Critical in shaping this assessment by the executive branch was the appointment of Michael Harrington to the Nedzi committee.

When Michael Harrington was appointed he was viewed as an extremely liberal idealist even among his House colleagues. As Representative Morris Udall observed: "Harrington was very energetic. He was impatient with the process of change. He wanted to do everything tonight or at the very latest tomorrow morning. He didn't want to wait. For Harrington, it had to be done today, tonight, tomorrow morning." [138] House Rules Committee Chairman Richard Bolling had even stronger views: "Harrington was so fundamentally wrong about the world. He is misguided. Harrington believes Joe McCarthy invented the CPUSA [Communist Party of the United States]. He has a totally different perception of the world. He is a complete wild man." [139] To appoint Harrington and like-minded investigative liberal Democrats to a select intelligence committee chaired by the institutionally oriented Lucien Nedzi meant that the Democratic House leadership had created an investigative unit with the potential for self-destruction.

For the executive branch Harrington's appointment was a clear and present danger. Within the executive branch the House Democratic leadership was widely perceived as playing politics with its intelligence inquiries, an impression shared by many intelligence insiders, who felt that the appointment was the result of a political deal. As former CIA Legislative Counsel Walter Pforzheimer stated:

> Michael Harrington was a left-wing dog in the Massachusetts delegation. Harrington was a sneak who revealed Colby's testimony about the CIA in Chile to the *Washington Post*. What Harrington did was known to us [the CIA] and Nedzi. When Carl Albert was selecting the members of the select committee, Tip walked in and said Harrington wants to be a member. Albert said: "Are you mad?" Tip said: "I gave him my word. Harrington came to me before the November elections and said if there's an intelligence investigation, I want to be on the committee." Tip's son was running for lieutenant governor. Harrington told Tip: "If your son's running for lieutenant governor, I'll give him every backing and support." Harrington's appointment was an out-and-out political deal. [140]

Former CIA Legislative Counsel George Cary agreed: "Harrington had a bad track record. He was headline hungry and totally irresponsible. He violated every norm of the House." [141] When I asked Harrington about this he denied that his appointment to the Nedzi committee was the result of a political deal. [142] A close aide to then Majority Leader O'Neill who assisted in the Nedzi committee appointments denied the charges of a political deal but noted: "Harrington's father and Tip were very close. The relationship between Tip and Harrington was like the story of the prodigal son. Tip saw this assignment as an opportunity for Harrington to grow and mature." [143] A former staff director of the Armed Services Committee felt that "Harrington's appointment was due to politics and political pressures. Harrington was a noisy bastard. Tip was anxious to appease the liberal element of the party. Harrington's appointment was purely political." [144]

Within the executive branch there was a widespread belief among intelligence insiders that Harrington's appointment was the result of a political deal. Even if it wasn't, appointment to a committee as sensitive as Nedzi's is hardly an assignment to foster the "growth" and "maturity" of members. In Harrington and like-minded liberal Democrats on the Nedzi committee the executive branch perceived a serious threat to its own interests. Because the committee self-destructed no executive action was necessary to contain the threat. However, the Nedzi committee's legacy was mistrust and suspicion toward House oversight in the minds of executive-branch officials. When the Pike committee was created with a membership again dominated by very liberal Democrats, executive officials were prepared to contain or if necessary destroy the committee to preserve executive interests.

The Pike Committee
After the Pike committee was established the executive branch sought an agreement with Chairman Pike on procedural matters such as staff clearance and the protection of classified materials. As Mitchell Rogovin, special counsel to DCI Colby, observed:

> The first thing we did when the new committee was formed was to write a letter to the chairman outlining procedures that had been worked out with the Senate select committee and giving Chairman Pike the advantage of our experience and, indeed, Senator Church's experience as to how procedures could be worked out. The chairman would not accept any of the procedures and, indeed, every time we had a conference it turned into a head-on confrontation. There was an awful lot of disputation and confrontation in those early days. When we raised the question of what kind of a security check or clearance would be made of the staff, we were told it was none of our business. We understand the separation of powers and we understand what congressional committees believe they should legitimately do. We merely wanted to render some assistance because we knew they were short of time. We suggested that some of the people from the security staff of the CIA may be of some assistance in helping the committee staff determine whether their facilities were sufficiently secure, to sweep the hearing rooms in case of bugs or transmitters and similar problems familiar to the CIA.
>
> All of this was rejected. When it came to classified material that was compartmented, where you needed special clearances to enter into these compartments, the chairman refused to have any of the staff go through the briefing or the security features of compartmented clearance. These were all extensive and abrasive early relationships. I am afraid they continued through the hearings. This was not the case in our dealings with the

Senate select committee, in our dealings with the Rockefeller commission before that, or with the CIA's twenty-seven year history of dealings with other congressional committees. So, I do believe it was a very unusual, but a very abrasive relationship.[145]

Rogovin believed that there was a definite reason for Pike's hard line:

The chairman [Pike], I believe, felt that the largest problem he faced was that his committee would be viewed as having been co-opted by the CIA, a charge that had been made with respect to his predecessor [Nedzi] and he took an extremely hard line in his dealings at the very outset.[146]

Pike himself acknowledged that the committee had set its own standards in this area: "We [the committee] have established our own rules on security and on secrecy. We have established our own agreements on secrecy security." [147] However for Pike the key reason for doing this was not to defend himself against charges of co-option but to assert the constitutional prerogatives of the legislative branch. As Pike stated: "In the final analysis the issue is: shall Congress be a coequal branch of the government?" [148]

By elevating disputes on procedural issues to the level of serious constitutional clashes Pike was wasting his most precious resource, time, on issues peripheral to the investigation. And, as Rogovin commented: "Pike was being impossible about a situation involving gray areas between the executive and legislative branches." [149] Pike was thus poisoning his committee's relations with the executive branch. Moreover he was enabling the executive branch to cite his record of noncooperation and irresponsibility compared to the cooperation and responsibility of the Church committee.

When the White House and the intelligence community realized that the Pike committee was just as threatening to them as the Nedzi committee, if not worse, then specific actions were taken to sidetrack the investigation. For example, both the Rockefeller commission and the Church committee focused their attention on past abuses. Attempts were made to get the Pike committee to do the same. As one Pike staffer recalled:

Our focus was to look at the overall failure of the intelligence community to analyze data. Especially in the beginning there was no cooperation from the agency. It was like pulling teeth. Their [the CIA's legislative liaisons'] job was to get as little out as possible. They just dribbled it out. They also tried to get us to refocus on the Family Jewels.[150]

Because most of the members and staff of the Pike committee had little experience with intelligence or national security, there were also attempts to divert the committee with toys and gimmicks. As Mitchell Rogovin, special counsel to DCI Colby, recalled:

> One day we held an executive session for the House committee and brought in a whole bunch of toys. The phone-in-a-shoe type thing. Most of the members were interested in all that James Bond stuff. But Pike and Aspin were not into that. Aspin said: "You guys are just like the air force. They let us come out and kick their tires." Pike told me: "You've got the children all excited." [151]

And this was not the only time such diversions were offered. As Aaron Donner, general counsel of the Pike committee, commented:

> They wanted to put on shows for us. This was to sidetrack us. They wanted to fly us down to Camp Peary to see how CIA people are trained. They even teased us with stories of pornographic movies. They offered to let us see secret movies of foreign officials in compromising circumstances. We could have had that forever. [152]

Even staff members were given special treatment. One Pike committee investigator described how the CIA's scientists responded to her examination of their work:

> We had heard during an interview with either a spook or an ex-spook that the CIA had developed multiflavored edible paper. This was for spies in the field. It would dissolve in the stomach. There were three flavors: vanilla, lemon, and chocolate. They took me on a tour of their laboratories where they dream up these wild things. They were mad scientists. That's the best way to describe these people. I joked: "Are you going to give me some of your edible paper?" They brought me a package: . . . "Bon Appetite." I got ten sheets. [153]

Finally General Counsel Donner described how at times there were efforts to create an air of awe and mystery around the work of the intelligence community. For example, when the Pike committee was to be briefed on the CIA's attempt to raise a sunken Russian submarine with the Glomar Explorer,

> The CIA men came in and swept the room with electronic gear. The CIA men had their arms folded. The CIA people came in with black salesmen's valises. The committee would hear about the Glomar Explorer. At the great moment, they took out polyethylene bags. The bags contained rusted pieces of iron. They were treated like pieces of the True Cross. Actually they were alleged to be pieces of the Russian sub. They were handled gingerly and reverentially. The CIA people had a serious look on their faces. People were shaking their heads with absolute awe. They were trying to give us a certain aura of great import and secrecy. [154]

Ironically the Church committee let its agenda be determined and set by the executive branch; in fact, it even held a public hearing where some of the more exotic "toys" were shown. The Pike committee did not do this. Despite strenuous exertions on the part of executive branch officials to redirect the focus of its investigation, the Pike committee refused to be sidetracked.

When it became apparent that the Pike committee would not be diverted toward past abuses or peripheral issues, the executive branch took additional steps to frustrate the committee. The Pike committee complained repeatedly in its final report:

> When legal preceedings were not in the offing, the access experience was frequently one of foot-dragging, stonewalling, and careful deception.[155]
>
> In reviewing the oversight experience, access to information, even when it was backed up by a subpoena, was not statisfactory.[154]
>
> The committee . . . endured more than three months of uninterrupted delays, cut-offs, silenced witnesses, amalgams, attacks, deletions, and privileges.[157]

Chairman Pike commented on this lack of executive-branch cooperation at a public hearing on August 4, 1975: "What we have found thus far is a great deal of the language of cooperation and a great deal of the activity of noncooperation."[158] Later, on September 29, 1975, Mr. Giaimo offered a similar assessment: "They [the executive branch] publicly allege they are willing to cooperate, but when we get down to the nitty gritty of it, we find they use all kinds of efforts and subterfuge to keep this committee and the Congress from conducting a thorough and necessary investigation."[159] Because the Pike committee had to complete its investigation in a little less than six months, delays by the executive branch in providing information had a serious negative impact on its work.

Within the executive branch two different strategies were adopted to respond to the perceived threat of the Pike committee. The first was the "Colby approach," named after its principal practitioner, William Colby, the director of central intelligence. On the surface Colby appeared to be cooperating with the Pike committee. In reality he was carefully regulating the amount and type of information the intelligence agencies provided. Later, in the face of subpoenas issued by the committee, Colby attempted to flood the committee with far more paper than, given its time and staff restraints, it would be able to handle. At the same time Colby attempted to use the committee to further the interests of the intelligence community.

Besides the Colby approach there was a second strategy that can best be termed the "Kissinger approach" since Secretary of State Henry Kissinger was its principal adherent. On the surface Kissinger also attempted to create the impression of cooperating with the Pike committee. However, in reality, Kissinger stonewalled the committee. He provided subpoenaed information only after the committee approved three citations of contempt against him on November 14, 1975. In addition, Kissinger worked actively behind the scenes in the Ford

White House and with his contacts in the press to destroy the Pike committee.[160]

For William Colby both the Pike and Church committees provided the opportunity to bring the intelligence community clearly into the American constitutional system. Colby testified before the Pike committee on December 12, 1975:

> I think the whole thing [the congressional investigations], from our point of view, has been of major assistance in bringing intelligence into the American Constitution in a fashion that was never even worried about before. I think we have been able to do it and we have been able to protect the necessities of intelligence.[161]

No longer was the United States intelligence community a state secret. Oversight was being conducted in public by formal "intelligence" committees. The secret, closed-door oversight of the past—conducted by congressional committees who did not even acknowledge that they were intelligence overseers—had come to an end.

Besides bringing the intelligence community into the American system, Colby also sought to protect ongoing intelligence operations directed towards the Soviet Union and covert actions in Angola and Italy from being examined by the Pike and Church committees. With respect to the Soviet Union, Colby testified before the Pike committee on December 12, 1975 that "with respect to the only major country that could threaten us today, intelligence on that country has not been a matter of the investigation of this committee."[162] However, Chairman Pike responded at the same hearing:

> I am a little disturbed when your statement is based on the allegation that we have not looked into our intelligence capabilities about the Soviet Union—when one of the things we have been fighting hardest to get is intelligence about the Soviet Union, and one of the things which has been most consistently denied to us is that sort of intelligence.[163]

The Pike committee's general counsel, Aaron Donner, commented that it was only due to solid investigative work by Pike staffers that covert CIA operations then taking place in Angola and Italy were uncovered by the committee.[164] Thus Colby's goals were to help legitimize the intelligence community under the framework of the Constitution and to protect sensitive intelligence operations from the scrutiny and criticism of the committee and Congress.

In seeking to achieve his goals Colby gave the appearance of full cooperation with the committee. In fact some within the intelligence community even viewed him as a traitor to his profession. For example, John Maury, former CIA legislative counsel, sarcastically described Colby's approach as: "For God's sake, tell them everything.

We want to be pure and clean." [165] Yet Colby's approach was in reality much more restrained. As he put it: "I thought that if I could be responsive on things that were proper, that Congress had a proper interest in knowing, that I could convince the congressmen not to get into the more sensitive stuff. And I think that essentially worked." [166] Despite Colby's public professions of cooperation, members of the Pike committee found Colby's performance to be quite different. As Chairman Pike remarked: "I think we have gotten that [information] which keeps Mr. Colby from being in contempt and nothing else." [167]

After Colby was fired as DCI by President Ford, Chairman Pike welcomed him back to testify before the committee with these words:

> I have heard comment to the effect that you have been too forthcoming with Capitol Hill.
>   It has been my own experience and judgment that if you are asked precisely the right question, you will give an honest answer. You do not lead us into those areas which would help us know what the right question to ask is. You do not make it easy for us to ask the right question. . . . I welcome you back here, not as a friend but as a respected adversary, because I feel that is the relationship we have had. [168]

Representative Johnson, addressing Colby, noted the advantage the intelligence community has over would-be congressional overseers: "You have indicated that you make available what is asked for. If a man doesn't know what to ask, obviously he is at a great disadvantage in trying to find something out." [169] Colby was not as forthcoming with the intelligence committees as his critics have alleged.

Unfortunately for Colby the Ford administration was in a very weak political position. When the Pike committee subpoenaed information Colby was forced to respond. In doing so Colby adopted the tactic of flooding the Pike committee with paper. As General Counsel Donner observed: "The CIA gave us a room with thirty-two file cabinets. You could die there." [170] Congressman McClory noted that the CIA alone provided the Pike committee with ninety thousand pages of documents. [171] Moreover the entire intelligence community provided over seventy-seven thousand documents. Pike staffer Jacqueline Hess explained what this flood of documents meant to the committee: "We had a situation where there were five months and thirty people to do a job that could have taken over five years and three hundred people." [172] Commenting on the Pike committee, Colby noted: "I thought they got totally in a hostile position." [173] Within the environmental constraints under which he operated— a weak executive branch and a hostile congressional committee—Colby sought to defend and advance the interests of the intelligence community.

For Henry Kissinger the Pike committee represented a serious threat to his personal reputation, the foreign policies pursued under the Nixon and Ford administrations, and the foreign policy–making mechanism he had carefully constructed and ruled. During the Nixon and Ford administrations, Kissinger had served as: (1) assistant to the president for national security affairs, (2) secretary of state, (3) a member of the National Security Council, and (4) chairman of the "40 Committee" which approves CIA covert actions. Not surprisingly, when the Pike committee began its investigation, Kissinger's actions as a policy-maker touched upon all of the areas the committee wanted to examine more closely. As General Counsel Donner commented: "Everyplace we turned, it was Henry Kissinger." [174]

During the Pike committee's public hearings Kissinger was frequently attacked. For example former CIA Deputy Director Ray Cline stated at one hearing: "A single policy-maker [Kissinger] ended up controlling dissemination and analyzing of intelligence, and yet intelligence provides the only possible basis for judging the wisdom of policy." [175] Individual committee members also attacked Kissinger. For example Morgan Murphy denounced him in these terms: "I think the American people should realize that as far as I am concerned, we have a one-man show in the State Department with Dr. Kissinger, and whatever he wants, he gets, and the Congress can be damned." [176] Moreover among the case studies of intelligence problems the Pike committee had decided to investigate were: SALT I, the 1973 Mideast War, the 1974 Cyprus crisis, the 1974 coup in Portugal, and the way covert actions were approved by the executive branch. All of these involved Kissinger, who, as a result, viewed the committee as a substantial threat.

Like Colby, Kissinger adopted a public approach of full cooperation. However, unlike Colby, Kissinger worked strenuously behind the scenes to stonewall the committee; he even worked actively to destroy it. [177] Unlike Colby, Kissinger could see no good coming out of the work of this committee. A good example of Kissinger's approach was his response to the Pike committee's attempt to examine the performance of U.S. intelligence in the 1974 Cyprus crisis in which Kissinger himself was the key American policymaker. The Pike committee learned that the State Department desk officer for Cyprus in 1974, Thomas Boyatt, had strongly criticized the handling of intelligence during the crisis and had filed a memorandum of dissent within the department. When the committee sought to question Boyatt and examine his memorandum, Kissinger used the incident to launch a powerful counterattack.

On September 25, 1975, Deputy Under Secretary of State Lawrence Eagleburger testified publicly before the Pike Committee, accusing it of "McCarthyism." Eagleburger said that Kissinger as secretary of state had forbidden Boyatt to testify because Kissinger wanted "to protect junior and middle-level officers of the Department of State." [178] At the same time Kissinger briefed his allies in the press, including James Reston of the *New York Times*. Aaron Donner described a telephone call he received after Kissinger had briefed Reston:

> He said: "This is Scotty Reston. What the hell's going on down there? You guys are reviving the McCarthy era. You are investigating the philosophy of foreign service officers. This was the same thing done over China. You guys are a bunch of McCarthyites." It was obvious that he had been briefed in depth about this matter. We tried to reason with him. It was clear that he had a full head of steam. I suggested that Pike go up and talk with the *New York Times* editorial board about this. The editorial board turned Pike down. After this incident, the *New York Times* became quite hostile editorially towards us. [179]

On October 19, 1975, the *New York Times* published an editorial entitled "Neo-McCarthyism" saying the Pike committee's attempt to question Boyatt and examine his memorandum was "clearly contrary to the national interest." [180] A similar editorial had appeared in the *Washington Post* on October 6. [181] On October 31 Kissinger testified before a public session of the committee, stating: "With respect to the charge of McCarthyism, I want to make clear that I do not accuse this committee of engaging in McCarthyism." [182] Yet behind the scenes this was just what Kissinger was doing. As Aaron Donner noted: "Maybe it was naïveté on our part to think that you can tinker in such an area and not have people get back at you." [183]

When Kissinger testified publicly before the Pike committee on October 31, 1975, some of the members believed they had found the ideal forum in which to hold him accountable. One who thought so was Mr. Dellums, who began his questioning of Kissinger this way:

> You occupy practically every position of importance in the 40 Committee structure. You are special assistant to the president for national security affairs. You are also secretary of state. We have testimony that you have participated in directing operations which were not fully discussed, analyzed, or evaluated by those authorized to do so. In fact, sometimes they were purposefully hidden.
>
> You have been involved in wiretaps of employees. We have heard testimony that the essence of your conversations with international leaders are not shared with the intelligence community.
>
> You now refuse information to Congress on a rather specious basis.
>
> Frankly, Mr. Secretary, and I mean this sincerely, I am concerned with your power, and the method of your operation, and I am afraid of the result on American policy, and I believe the direction of operations outside the

National Security Council and the full 40 Committee may indeed be contrary to law.

Would you please comment, sir?[184]

Kissinger responded: "Except for that, there is nothing wrong with my operation?"[185] As a key aide to Dellums noted: "Kissinger, by his answer, just deflated the whole atmosphere."[186] A Republican staffer on the committee analyzed the Kissinger hearing:

Some of the members asked good questions. You also see why Kissinger was so good. It was a major event. This was a thrill for a lot of these members. These members had not participated in the most recent thrill: impeachment. There is a certain excitement about getting on camera in your district questioning the secretary of state. Kissinger handled the members beautifully. He looks them directly in the eye. He changes the subject and diffuses the thrust very skillfully, and he is always deferring to the member.[186]

Consequently at its public hearing the Pike committee never even came close to holding Kissinger accountable for his conduct.

Despite the Pike committee's failure to hold Kissinger accountable when he testified publicly, further attempts were made to do just this. What especially angered the majority on the Pike committee was Kissinger's stonewalling. For example, on November 6, 1975, Mr. Stanton denounced Kissinger's conduct:

I would oppose the idea and the concept that we are getting cooperation from the State Department because we are not.

As of now, no one on this committee can honestly say we are getting a free flow of information; and it is strictly because of the policies of the secretary of state who has sat in front of this committee and has stonewalled it real tough. I think anybody who takes any different viewpoint hasn't been listening to him.[188]

On November 14 the Pike committee voted three contempt citations of Secretary Kissinger for his "contumacious conduct" in failing to turn over subpoenaed materials. The contempt citations were introduced by Mr. Dellums and noted that Kissinger had failed to turn over material relating to: (1) State Department covert action recommendations, (2) documents of the 40 committee, and (3) SALT I verification documents. After the contempt citations were voted by the committee, the State Department provided the materials. Moreover, the material contained in these documents was used in the committee's final report to criticize Secretary Kissinger's actions and policies.

However, the Pike committee's victory over Secretary Kissinger was short-lived. After the House voted to suppress the committee's final report and the report was leaked to the *Village Voice,* the substance of the report was overshadowed by the investigation into who had leaked it. Kissinger's victory over the Pike committee was insured.

In the history of congressional oversight of intelligence the Pike committee was unique in the amount of tension, hostility, and downright hatred that characterized its relations with the executive branch. Good illustrations are the controversy that erupted over Rod Hills's briefcase and "four words" released by the Pike committee. When the committee began its public hearings it focused on intelligence costs and fiscal procedures. A senior White House official described what happened:

> Pike started out going after our gonads. He wanted all the budget stuff. Jim Lynn was then director of OMB. Lynn and his deputy refused to disclose the intelligence budget unless and until assurances were given that the information would be held in confidence. This was an executive- versus a legislative-branch prerogative. This will never be worked out. The executive will always fight against the right of the legislature to make public information classified as secret by the executive branch. Pike threatened to hold Lynn and his deputy in contempt. Phil Buchen and Rod Hills were sent to see Pike by the White House in an attempt to work this out. It was worked out.[189]

Philip Buchen, counsel to President Ford, related what happened next:

> Hills had in his briefcase a classified document. By mistake, he left the briefcase in Pike's office. We were driving back to the White House when Rod realized what had happened. We turned around and went back. Hills was told he couldn't have the briefcase. The chairman insisted that it be kept there.[190]

Then, according to another White House official:

> Eventually, there came, a couple of months later, a very serious leak from the Pike committee. This leak involved Kissinger documents. Kissinger was enraged personally and institutionally. He was in a high dither. There was an early morning breakfast with the president. This group included President Ford, Donald Rumsfeld, John Marsh, Phil Buchen, James Wilderotter, Rod Hills, Brent Scowcraft, and Henry Kissinger. The issue was what do we do about the Pike committee leak? Rumsfeld and Marsh were both ex-congressmen and said we ought to do nothing else until we work out adequate arrangements. Kissinger said: "I'm worried about what he already has. He could destroy the national security and the country. We should not only say we won't give him [Pike] anything else but we should demand the return of what we've already given." Rummy and Marsh went white. Marsh pointed out that possession is nine-tenths of the law. Unless you're willing to send the fucking Marines down Pennsylvania Avenue, you're not likely to get them [the documents] back. Kissinger went bananas. The upshot of all this was that a letter was sent to Pike from President Ford demanding the immediate return of everything. Pike's return letter to Ford was a masterful letter. Pike said: "You've asked for the return

of documents. It is a matter of institutional prerogative. I as the chairman am bound by my oath of office to defend the legitimate prerogatives of the Congress. I have received documents that as a committee chairman it would be improper for me to return to you. I also am in possession of documents I received as a congressman. These I will be happy to return to you. However, I must insist on proper safeguards with respect to these documents. I will turn them over to uniformed officers with guards. I will treat these documents with the seriousness they deserve, unlike the official who did not do this. I will not behave as irresponsibly as your man." This was a beautiful classic letter. Pike added a P.S.: "I have not told you the name of the executive branch official responsible for this breach of security. He is the husband of one of your cabinet officers."

At that time, Carla Hills was the only woman in the cabinet. This was a very cheap shot. I have never seen a guy as humiliated and shattered as Hills. He was especially embarrassed over the fact that he was the instrument by which Pike had been able to get back at Ford. The P.S. was below the belt. I was with Rod when he read the letter. I thought he'd cry. I'd have cried. Pike was a real snake. Two weeks later Rod left the White House.[191]

Commenting on Pike's role in this incident a senior Ford White House staffer observed: "We were dealing with a real nut here." [192] One Pike staffer summarized the feelings of the committee when, discussing Pike's letter to President Ford, she observed: "Nothing very important was in Hills's briefcase but it was good to be able to hit them back with something." [193]

Although Pike did not return any of the documents demanded by the president, Ford did cut the committee off from further access to sensitive material. Ironically the source of this entire dispute was the Pike committee's release of just four words. On September 11, 1975, the committee released part of an intelligence summary of the situation in the Middle East that had been prepared on October 6, 1973. The key paragraph said:

> Egypt—The (deleted) large-scale mobilization exercise may be an effort to soothe internal problems as much as to improve military capabilities. Mobilization of some personnel, increased readiness of isolated units, *and greater communication security* are all assessed as part of the exercise routine. . . . There are still no military or political indicators of Egyptian intentions or preparations to resume hostilities with Israel.[194]

The four words that so upset Secretary Kissinger were: "and greater communication security," which meant the United States had the capability to monitor Egyptian communications systems. A former general counsel at the CIA believed Kissinger's concern was justified, noting:

> Pike released the four words despite a formal request by both the CIA and NSA that these words must be deleted. The release of these four words

was a serious compromise of communications intelligence. While the words themselves may not be revealing, they reveal the source we got it from.[195]

Yet this was a phony issue. First, the words themselves are ambiguous. Second, CIA sources had to identify the words and their meaning so that members of the press could understand why the executive branch was so upset. Third, Secretary Kissinger himself had leaked the same information but in a much more significant and dangerous manner.[196] In 1974 Marvin and Bernard Kalb had written a flattering book about Kissinger entitled *Kissinger*. In the acknowledgments section of their book the Kalbs thanked Kissinger, who had "been generous with his time and knowledge." [197] Discussing in a very favorable way Kissinger's leadership in the 1973 Mideast War, the Kalbs included in their discussion this passage based on information Kissinger had given them:

> Finally, from a secret U.S. base in southern Iran, the National Security Agency, which specializes in electronic intelligence, picked up signals indicating that the Egyptians had set up a vastly more complicated field communications network than mere "maneuvers" warranted.[198]

The entire dispute between the Pike committee and the executive branch over the release of the four words in 1975 was thus a phony issue. Secretary Kissinger himself had already committed a far more serious compromise of the same material in 1974. It was not proper for the Pike committee to release ambiguous language in criticizing a U.S. intelligence failure. However, it was proper for Secretary Kissinger to compromise the same intelligence sources in a much more serious way to bolster a sycophantic biography of himself!

This entire incident would be humorous were it not for the serious consequences that resulted from it. On September 26, 1975, President Ford met at the White House with Chairman Otis Pike, Representative Robert McClory, Speaker Carl Albert, Minority Leader John Rhodes, Secretary of State Henry Kissinger, Director of Central Intelligence William Colby, and White House aides Philip Buchen and Donald Rumsfeld to resolve the controversy over the four words. The president agreed to lift his order prohibiting the further release of classified material to the Pike committee. In return the committee agreed to let the president be the ultimate judge in any future disputes over the public release of classified material. Later, however, Chairman Pike and his ideological allies on the committee maintained that the agreement with President Ford did not extend to the committee's final report. Although Pike's position was upheld within the committee, the House itself rejected it by voting 246 to 124 on January 29, 1976, to suppress the report. Consequently the executive branch's adroit use of the phony dispute over four words led ultimately to the suppression of the Pike committee's final report.

Finally, the murder of Richard Welch, the CIA station chief in Athens, in December 1975 demonstrates how the executive branch was able to use an event to shape the political environment within which the Pike committee operated. Chairman Pike claimed that Welch's dead body was part of a "PR campaign by the CIA"[199] to undermine and destroy the committee. One committee member even expressed the belief that the CIA itself killed Welch:

There was an attempt to blame the Welch killing on leaks from Congress. The CIA manual in Nicaragua discussed the creation of "martyrs." I wouldn't be surprised if Welch had a terminal disease. The CIA could have terminated him themselves to create a martyr. For twenty years the house of the station chief in Athens had been known. Why kill him then?[200]

Pike staffers also observed how the Welch killing was used by the executive branch. As one noted:

We all had the sense that we were doing something that had to be done. Collectively, we were on a fairly good course. Now [after Welch's murder] we face the situation where you have an agent who, for a variety of reasons, gets killed. And you have the agency literally blame you for the killing. This was an incredible thing. This was their way to make their case. This was part of a smear campaign to discredit the committee. It was a real cheap shot.[201]

The committee's general counsel, Aaron Donner, added:

The public relations surrounding Welch's killing had absolute Hollywood direction. It was tragic that he died. No one ever established any link between our committee and the death of this man. It was turned into a media event. Everyone attended this funeral. It was like the discoverer of the cure for cancer had died. It was played up very skillfully in the press. The nexus between this man's death and the committee was that it created a hostile environment.[202]

Thus the executive branch was able to use Welch's death to alter the political environment within which the committee operated. The Pike committee's relations with the executive branch were extremely important, but, in the end, these relations became so bad that the executive branch worked actively to destroy the committee and its investigation.

The Committee and the Press

Throughout 1975 and 1976 the press had an impact on the inquiries conducted by the Nedzi and Pike committees quite different from its impact on the Senate investigation conducted by Church. In both cases Seymour Hersh's *New York Times* articles charging the CIA with violating its own charter were crucial in causing investigative units to be formed. The press charges of abuses by the intelligence community helped shape the agenda of the Church committee. But the press had very little influence on shaping the agenda of the Pike committee. Instead Chairman Pike himself set his committee's agenda. Moreover, both the House and Senate investigating committees differed significantly in the access they afforded to the press. While the Church committee tended to keep the press at arm's length the members and staff of the Pike committee actively cultivated the press. Finally, press coverage of the two committees differed. The Church committee tended to receive favorable coverage throughout its existence. However, the Pike committee, after initially receiving favorable press coverage, found that its internecine conflicts with the executive branch—which escalated into attempts by the executive to undermine the committee— hurt the committee-press relationship. Press coverage became increasingly hostile as time went on.

In the case of the Nedzi committee, press coverage was limited to reporting the committee's self-destruction. For example when Republicans boycotted the June 12, 1975, meeting of Stanton's CIA subcommittee, thereby preventing the hearing from beginning, the *Christian Science Monitor* noted: "The committee had egg on its congressional face because of the nonhearing." [203] With respect to the Pike committee, press coverage focused on both the committee's substantive work and its struggles with the executive branch. To ensure favorable press coverage, not only members but staff of the Pike committee actively cultivated members of the press. The Church committee strictly regulated and limited access to its secure areas whereas the Pike Committee allowed press people free access to wherever they wanted to go. As one Pike staffer commented:

> There were incestuous relations with the press. The name of the game on the Hill is clearly press coverage. God forbid that you piss off the press. For example, [CBS reporter] Dan Schorr was back in the classified area all the time. Also, [Italian reporter] Oriani Fallaci was also back in that area too. Her visit was a "happening." [204]

Not surprisingly there was considerable leaking from the Pike committee by both the members and the staff. Moreover because it cultivated the press the committee initially had great success in getting its view of issues a favorable presentation.

However, as the work of the Pike committee progressed, the press coverage became less and less favorable. Another Pike staffer noted:

During the beginning, they [the press] were overly zealous and swayed in our favor. There was a tendency to sensationalize our committee's work. The intelligence community is right about a biased press at the beginning. After a while, the administration was getting to people. They were trying to destroy our credibility. The press at the beginning was very different from the press at the end.[205]

Behind the scenes Henry Kissinger and others from the executive branch were using their own media contacts to turn the press coverage around. The executive branch was also able to use President Ford very effectively. For example, on January 31, 1976, Ford attended the swearing-in ceremony for George Bush as the new director of central intelligence and said it was time to move beyond the investigations:

The abuses of the past have more than adequately been described. We cannot improve this agency [the CIA] by destroying it. Let me assure you that I have no intention of seeing this intelligence community dismantled and its operations paralyzed or effectively undermined.[206]

Besides working behind the scenes Kissinger also spoke out publicly as part of the executive branch's effort to shift the committee's direction. For example, in a speech in Detroit in November 1975 Kissinger called for an end to the "self-flagellation that has done so much harm to this nation's capacity to conduct foreign policy."[207] In its deft handling of such incidents as Boyatt, the "four word" disclosure, and the Welch murder, the executive branch was able to use the press not only to defend its own interests but to undermine the credibility of the Pike committee.

The Pike committee was also hurt by the inferior quality of its work. George Lardner, who covered the committee for the *Washington Post,* offered a journalist's perspective:

Pike moved promptly and shrewdly into public hearings, provoking confrontations with the intelligence agencies that showed, eloquently at first, how secretive and aloof they had become toward the Congress that fed them. But the confrontations kept recurring, turning into thinly disguised diversions from the committee investigators' slender output. The Pike committee produced plenty of appetizers, but little more.[208]

Ironically so much leaking occurred from the Pike committee that members of the press sometimes had difficulty finding unleaked material to provide the basis for new stories. The following excerpts from Daniel Schorr's personal diary illustrate the problem:

January 20, 1976—Behind closed doors, the Pike committee studies a draft of its final report. . . . Despite the fact that the CIA is still fighting to "sanitize" this report—or maybe because of that fact—it is amazingly easy to

> learn details of the draft, even small details. . . . At
> the rate the draft report is leaking, there won't be
> much news left when it is released.
>
> January 26, 1976—I now have a copy of the Pike report! So much of it
> has already been touched upon in news reports that the
> immediate problem is to find a fresh story for broad-
> cast tonight! [209]

Ironically Schorr himself became the story when he leaked the copy, which he had received from another leaker, to the *Village Voice*. Instead of focusing on the substance of the report the press's attention was directed upon who leaked the report to Schorr and Schorr's ethics in releasing the report.

Over the course of its history the Pike committee earned the enmity of the executive branch and the House. In the end the House felt constrained to rein in its renegade committee. Yet the Pike committee still had the opportunity to try to educate the American public about intelligence issues. In any such effort the assistance of the press would be invaluable. Testifying before the Pike committee on December 11, 1975, before the imbroglio over the leaking of the final report, former Nedzi committee member Michael Harrington strongly criticized his colleagues for the educational opportunity they had missed:

> I don't think any printed report will ever make up for the chance that has
> been missed by this committee, and by its Senate counterpart, to educate
> the American public much more forcefully than has been the case over the
> course of this period. I do appreciate the truncated nature of this commit-
> tee's existence and the inherent limitations of time that have been imposed;
> but I don't think hearings in executive session and a report, as fine as it
> may be, will suffice as a civics lesson in this area for the public. [210]

Ironically the press, which the Pike committee had cultivated so carefully, did not assist in this educational effort. Instead the executive branch used the press to drive the last nails into the committee's coffin. In the beginning the *New York Times* had been instrumental in forming the environment that led to the creation of the committee. In the end even the *New York Times* would have nothing to do with it. Thus the press was both a witness to and participant in the undoing of the Pike committee.

The Committee at Work

The House of Representatives had authorized the Pike committee to investigate allegations of improprieties and abuses within the intelligence community and to make recommendations for the House's consideration. To carry out these assignments the Pike committee's work was divided into two stages. First it conducted twenty-eight days of public hearings directed at four areas: (1) intelligence costs and fiscal procedures, (2) the performance of the intelligence community, (3) domestic intelligence programs, and (4) risks and control of foreign intelligence. Second the committee prepared its final report to the House. Actually the Pike committee prepared two "final" reports. The first was written by political scientist Stanley Bach, who spent three months on the assignment. However, after the Pike committee completed its public hearings, Bach's report was simply discarded and a completely new one was hurriedly put together by Staff Director Searle Field, General Counsel Aaron Donner, and investigator John Boos. The second and truly final report discussed the committee's oversight experience and investigative record, but the House voted to suppress it on January 29, 1976. This is the report the *Village Voice* printed after CBS reporter Daniel Schorr provided it with a leaked copy. In 1977 Spokesman Books printed what had appeared in the *Voice* and added the recommendations the committee had made to the House.

Public Hearings
The Pike committee began its public hearings with seven days examining the cost of intelligence. The committee learned that money appropriated for the intelligence community was hidden throughout the entire federal budget and that the total amount of funds expended on intelligence was a closely guarded secret. Furthermore the committee identified a serious definitional problem. How was "intelligence" to be defined? For example, if a naval ship collects some intelligence, how much of the cost of running the ship should be placed in the intelligence budget? The committee also identified the two major wielders of power within the intelligence community: the director of central intelligence and the secretary of defense. Although the DCI is nominally in charge of the entire community, in actuality the secretary of defense has much greater power and controls a greater portion of the intelligence budget. The DCI is also the director of the CIA and controls about 15 percent of the total intelligence budget. The secretary of defense controls the remaining 85 percent and therefore is a force to be reckoned with on intelligence. In its hearings on the intelligence budget the committee closely examined William Colby, the director of central intelligence, and Dr. Albert C. Hall, the assistant secretary of defense for intelligence.[211]

In its questioning of executive-branch officials the committee learned that intelligence budget oversight was done by a very few individuals in the executive and legislative branches. In the executive branch OMB

Director James Lynn acknowledged that his agency had only six staffers working on the entire intelligence budget. Normally OMB would have had at least three hundred to four hundred staffers working on a budget the size of the intelligence community's. In addition three of the six OMB intelligence-budget staffers had long careers in the intelligence community themselves,[212] raising the question whether they could be truly objective. Finally the committee looked at budget controls within the various intelligence agencies, finding these units understaffed and hampered in their work by secrecy and compartmentalization requirements.

With respect to the Congress the committee found that the activities of the intelligence community were monitored by the Appropriations and Armed Services committees in both the House and Senate. Commenting on the oversight exercised by these committees DCI Colby told the Pike committee that "there are no secrets from them, that I will answer any question, and further that I have a positive obligation to bring to their attention things they might not know about that they should know."[213] Colby also noted that for fiscal 1976 he had testified six times before the Defense Subcommittee of the House Appropriations Committee. Besides testifying Colby had responded to two hundred written questions the subcommittee had submitted to him. When Chairman Pike remarked to DCI Colby that this meant that only thirty-eight members or 7 percent of the House was apprised of intelligence activities Colby responded: "I have advised the appropriate committees of the Congress as designated by them. I think it is up to the Congress to decide what further—where further to go."[214] In addition the comptroller general of the United States, Elmer Staats, told the Pike committee that, although the General Accounting Office had one staffer assigned to the National Security Agency, GAO had done nothing at the CIA since 1962 because of special security clearances and restrictions.[215]

During this part of the investigation the committee also received testimony from officials of the Federal Bureau of Investigation, the Internal Revenue Service, and the National Security Agency. The public session with NSA officials lasted less than forty minutes because of concerns over classified material. A great amount of the committee's study of the intelligence budget therefore took place in executive session. Nevertheless some major issues were raised during the public sessions. The committee sought to determine the total cost of U.S. intelligence activity and to examine past and present executive and legislative oversight in this area. In addition the committee addressed the issues of duplication and overcollection. For example Representatives Milford and Murphy asked sharp questions as to the necessity of having both the CIA and the DIA doing the same intelligence analysis.[216] Also Staff Director Searle Field raised the question whether the intelligence community was collecting so much information that it couldn't digest what it had collected.[217] In its public hearings on intelligence costs and fiscal procedures the Pike committee was addressing the questions at the very heart of effective budget oversight.

In its public examination of the intelligence community's performance the Pike committee focused on four intelligence failures and considered how the president exercises control both over the intelligence community in general and over covert action specifically. The four intelligence failures were: (1) the 1973 Mideast War, (2) the 1974 Cyprus crisis, (3) the 1968 Tet offensive, and (4) the 1974 Portuguese coup. In addition the committee examined how the National Security Council and the "40 Committee" enabled the president to exercise control of intelligence. Finally Secretary of State Henry Kissinger also testified about presidential control. Unfortunately the committee's work in this area was overshadowed by its disputes with the executive branch over access to information and its release of sensitive information from the executive branch.

The first intelligence failure the committee looked at was the 1973 Mideast War. Both American and Israeli intelligence had failed to warn of the Arab attack on Israel on October 6, 1973. In public hearings the committee received testimony from Ray Cline, former deputy director for intelligence at the CIA, who was extremely critical of Henry Kissinger. He charged that Kissinger had withheld vital intelligence—gathered on his travels and in discussions with foreign leaders—from intelligence-community analysts. In addition Cline was especially critical of Kissinger having simultaneously been both secretary of state and assistant to the president for national security affairs. Cline noted how this combination of positions corrupted the foreign poicy decision-making process:

> The highest level of our national security and foreign policy decisions is the National Security Council, where in effect the secretary of state and the secretary of defense argue out with the assistant to the president for national security affairs positions which are designed to influence the president and let him make a final decision. If two of those three key jobs are held by the same person, I fail to understand how what I would consider an adequate dialogue can take place.[218]

Unfortunately the Pike committee's public hearings on the 1973 Mideast War ended in disarray when the committee released the "four words" the executive branch maintained had seriously compromised U.S. intelligence.[219] Instead of examining why U.S. intelligence failed to anticipate developments in the Mideast in 1973 the committee found itself in a struggle with President Ford over access to classified material now forbidden to it by the president due to the disclosure of the "four words."

The second intelligence failure examined by the Pike committee was the 1974 Cyprus crisis. Once again the committee wanted to know why the intelligence community had failed to anticipate developments. And once again the committee's public investigation was sidetracked. At the time of these hearings the committee was still battling the executive branch over its disclosures on the 1973 Mideast crisis. In addition, when the committee sought to obtain the testimony of a State Department foreign service officer who had manned the Cyprus desk and had been critical of intelligence on Cyprus, the committee found itself charged with "McCarthyism." When the committee sought to obtain the "Boyatt memorandum," the foreign service officer's critique of intelligence failures in Cyprus, the committee found the executive branch claiming executive privilege to withhold the document. Thus the Pike committee's public examination of the 1974 coup in Cyprus never got off the ground.

The third intelligence failure considered by the committee was the 1968 Tet offensive in Vietnam. The public hearings focused on the testimony of Sam Adams, a former CIA intelligence officer, who charged that the "Tet surprise stemmed in large measure from corruption in the intelligence process." [220] Adams charged that senior officials in the executive branch—General William Westmoreland, DCI Richard Helms, and Walt Rostow (national security advisor to President Johnson)—had been part of a "conspiracy" in which Vietcong strength had been "deliberately downgraded" from 600,000 to 300,000. [221] Adams also asserted that U.S. intelligence in Vietnam suffered from too much collection and too little analysis. While testifying Adams noted that he was considered to be "something of a maverick." The Pike committee allowed those Adams had attacked to rebut his testimony. DCI Colby attacked Adams's credibility, charging that Adams's "conspiracy" charges were part of "his well-known tendency to make sweeping and unqualified generalizations." [222] Colby also attacked the substance of Adams's charges, stating that intelligence analysts in Vietnam often suffered from incomplete and conflicting data. [223] Moreover Lieutenant General Daniel O. Graham challenged Adams's claim that there were 600,000 enemy troops in South Vietnam. If there were so many, why had the enemy sent only 67,000 to 85,000 men into battle at Tet? [224] After the committee completed its hearings on the Tet offensive it was still unclear whether this incident really constituted an intelligence failure.

The fourth intelligence failure to be examined was the coup in Portugal on April 25, 1974, which American intelligence had failed to predict. The committee identified key incidents and developments that the intelligence community had failed to notice, reserving special criticism for the reporting by the six military attachés stationed in Portugal. Ironically the executive branch freely acknowledged that Portugal was an intelligence "failure." [225] However, Portugal was not at the top of anybody's list of key intelligence targets. Executive-branch officials knew the problems that had caused the failure in Portugal, but Portugal was considered to be of such limited importance that the executive could not see why anybody, especially the Pike committee, should be terribly upset about what had happened. In its public hearings on intelligence failures the Pike committee failed to conduct well-documented, complete, and effective hearings. At fault were both executive-branch hostility and the Pike committee's own incompetence in conducting hearings.

However, during the latter stages of this particular set of hearings the Pike committee made its most significant contribution to oversight. On October 30, 1975, the committee examined the role of the National Security Council and the 40 Committee. The National Security Council was composed of the president, the vice-president, the secretary of state, and the secretary of defense. Its function was to screen and coordinate foreign policy views and to provide the president with independent analytical advice. The 40 Committee was an adjunct of the National Security Council charged with the consideration of covert actions. During the Nixon and Ford administrations Henry Kissinger was the chairman of the 40 Committee. In public hearings the Pike committee established that Kissinger himself was the key decision maker when it came to covert actions. Moreover the committee found that, in making decisions to approve covert actions, the 40 Committee frequently had telephonic votes with no debates or discussion of the actions to be undertaken. At times the 40 Committee did not even meet!

As Mr. Stanton observed: "Between April 1972 and December of 1974, nearly forty sensitive covert activities were approved by the Forty Committee without a single meeting." [226] Discussing Kissinger's role in covert action decisions James Gardner, who had served as liaison between the State Department and the 40 Committee, testified that Kissinger "was fully informed and I think in the overwhelming majority of cases was the man who made the decision." [227] A major issue for both the House and Senate intelligence investigations was whether the CIA was a "rogue elephant" or under strict control of the president and the executive branch. The Pike committee hearing on October 30,

1975, established, in the words of Chairman Pike, that "the CIA does not go galloping off conducting operations by itself. . . . The major things which are done are not done unilaterally by the CIA without approval from higher up the line.[228] Thus, the Pike committee was beginning the process of demolishing the argument that the CIA was a rogue elephant.

This process was finished the very next day when Secretary of State Henry Kissinger testified publicly before the Pike committee. He was questioned by both Chairman Pike and Mr. Stanton about covert actions. The key portion of the testimony was the following exchange.

> Kissinger: . . . As secretary of state, it is peculiarly difficult for me to discuss covert operation in an open session.
> Pike: Nobody asked you about any covert operations.
> Kissinger: To discuss even the organization of covert operations. I will say that the assistant to the president makes no decisions. Every operation is personally approved by the president.
> Stanton: In other words, during the period of 1972 to 1974, any covert decision that was made was approved by the president of the United States?
> Kissinger: At any time; not just in that period.[229]

In this brief exchange the Pike committee had taken the most significant testimony received by either the House or Senate investigating committees. Secretary Kissinger had publicly acknowledged that the president himself approved all covert action and that this was the practice in every administration. The Church committee spent considerable time during its assassinations inquiry trying to document presidential involvement but was never able to do so. Since its creation the CIA had operated under the doctrine of "plausible deniability," which meant that the intelligence community took deliberate actions to shield the president from the decisions he alone made regarding covert intelligence actions. For twenty-seven years plausible deniability had been a viable policy. Now, in one brief exchange, Secretary Kissinger had irretrievably destroyed the doctrine for the Ford Administration and all of its predecessors.

Ironically the significance of the Pike committee's destruction of plausible deniability went virtually unnoticed. On the committee Mr. Johnson noted that they had solid documentation to support what Kissinger had said:

> We [the Pike Committee] went to investigate the reports of the 303 Committee [predecessor to the 40 Committee] and the 40 Committee. I saw these in the White House. We were referred to documents that involved McGeorge Bundy and his successor as assistant to the president for national security affairs. The documents referred to "Higher Authority" at

the LBJ ranch. "Higher Authority" was the president. These were the types of matters that were brought to the president's attention: (1) seeking approval for procuring girls for the King of Jordan, and (2) seeking approval for the transfer of five thousand rifles. If running girls and five thousand weapons were brought to the president's attention, assassination attempts were too. This all involved an abuse of presidential power. "Plausible deniability" was developed to protect the president.[230]

Testimony such as Kissinger's strongly affected the members. Chairman Pike observed how his own views changed:

I wound up the hearings with a higher regard for the CIA than when I started. We did find evidence, upon evidence, upon evidence where the CIA said: "No, don't do it." The State Department or the White House said: "We're going to do it." The CIA was much more professional and intelligent and had a far deeper reading on the down-the-road implications of some immediately popular act than the executive branch or administration officials. One thing I really disagreed with [Senator Frank] Church on was his characterization of the CIA as a "rogue elephant." The CIA never did anything the White House didn't want. Sometimes they didn't want to do what they did.[231]

What the Pike committee had accomplished was extremely significant. The CIA was not a rogue elephant; the president was firmly in command and control. In its final report the committee stated: "All evidence in hand suggests that the CIA, far from being out of control, has been utterly responsive to the instructions of the president and the assistant to the president for national security affairs."[232] For those exercising congressional oversight of intelligence, the Pike Committee had established that agencies like the CIA were merely the agents of the president and senior administration officials.

The Pike committee conducted four days of hearings on domestic intelligence programs. First it considered the general topic of illegal electronic surveillance, then the performance of the Drug Enforcement Administration and the FBI. Finally the committee concluded this series with three experts from the academic and legal community discussing recent court decisions and necessary legislation.

On October 9, 1975, the committee conducted public hearings on illegal electronic surveillance, learning that a lot of illegal bugging was done privately. In addition the committee took testimony about illegal bugging by members of the Houston Police Department from a former U.S. attorney in Houston and a former policeman sentenced to jail for his part in the bugging. However, by far the most entertaining testimony of the day came from Martin Kaiser who had his own electronics firm that sold more than three hundred types of electronic listening devices. Some of these devices were put into mattresses, golf clubs, and electric toothbrushes. Kaiser even put on a show-and-tell demonstration of some of his more exotic merchandise. Kaiser testified that he sold bugs to the FBI and that moreover he had been directed to sell his merchandise through the U.S. Recording Company which marked up the items 30 percent before passing them along to the FBI.[233] Pike committee investigators discovered links between senior FBI officials and senior officials in the U.S. Recording Company.

This hearing had two major functions. First, it was an educational experience. As Mr. Dellums remarked: "The hearing today is extraordinarily important because it raises one of the most dangerous risks of uncontrolled intelligence-gathering capability."[234] Second, the committee exercised real oversight. For example, Staff Director Searle Field sharply questioned James Kraus, head of the FBI's Antitrust and Bankruptcy Unit, why the FBI gave so little attention to prosecuting illegal advertising for electronic surveillance equipment.[235]

The committee also exercised oversight when it conducted hearings into the programs of the Drug Enforcement Administration. Chairman Pike was upset that only 10 percent of heroin coming into the United States was interdicted.[236] Mr. Giaimo criticized the antidrug efforts of the intelligence community.[237] Lehman sought to learn more about the effectiveness of antidrug programs in his home state of Florida.[238] Dellums was concerned that the DEA was going after just low-level sellers and not the "biggies" while Murphy, who had studied the drug problem extensively, identified the key problem for such efforts when he told those testifying: "Your agencies, both Customs and DEA, are ignored by the agencies and embassies around the world."[239] In its hearing on DEA programs the committee was making the executive branch aware of its displeasure with the low priority given to antidrug programs by the intelligence community.

The Pike committee also conducted hearings into the domestic intelligence programs of the FBI. The Church committee had conducted similar public hearings using as a case study the FBI's attempts to harass and destroy Dr. Martin Luther King. The Pike committee chose to do its work somewhat differently. First the FBI was allowed the opportunity to describe what it had done and to put its domestic intelligence work in perspective. Then the committee heard from a series of witnesses critical of FBI activities in this area.

For example the FBI had conducted surveillance of the Socialist Workers Party for thirty years and the Institute for Policy Studies for five and a half years. Witnesses from both groups testified about FBI attempts to undermine their activities. In addition the FBI was sharply criticized by a former FBI agent and a former FBI informer. The committee also heard testimony from Lori Patton, a high-school student who, as part of a high-school project, had written to the Socialist Workers Party for information. Her name was obtained by the FBI and she was investigated by the FBI for six months.[240] After the critical witnesses had testified, the FBI was allowed the opportunity to respond to their testimony and offer rebuttal evidence. Senior FBI officials viewed the Pike committee with great antipathy. As one senior FBI agent who worked closely with the committee noted:

> There was no real purpose for the Pike committee. The Pike committee was an effort by the House not to feel left out of the best game in town. There was the "exposure per week" syndrome. You got the feeling after a while that issues would remain viable so long as they were newsworthy. There was very little effort to understand what had occurred or to put it into perspective.[241]

However, the Pike committee was not unfair to the FBI. The witnesses critical of the FBI raised serious issues. Was it proper for the FBI to harass groups like the Socialist Workers Party and the Institute for Policy Studies? Were FBI informants misused? Were FBI domestic intelligence activities effective from both cost and intelligence perspectives? These questions were instances of the committee exercising real oversight.

Finally the Pike committee conducted a brief hearing on the legal issues in domestic intelligence. Three academic and legal experts talked about the effect of recent court decisions in this area along with possible legislative remedies. In contrast to other public hearings of the committee, this one was poorly attended by members and lasted for just a little over two hours.[242] Because the committee had adopted the investigative oversight model the members and the staff were interested primarily in unearthing abuses and scandal. This particular hearing dealt with practical legislative remedies to prevent the recurrence of improper activities that had been uncovered. Unfortunately the Pike committee had no practitioners of the institutional oversight model. As a result it is not surprising that the members had little interest in this hearing.

The hearings on domestic intelligence demonstrate both the strengths and weaknesses of this committee. The committee was able to use public hearings to point out areas where intelligence activity was deficient (drug policy) and where abuses had occurred (the FBI's relationship with the U.S. Recording Company). And the committee made effective use of witnesses like Lori Patton who themselves had suffered as a result of domestic intelligence activity. However, the committee, because of its mindset and oversight model, was unable to go beyond the mere accumulation of facts to develop a concrete program to insure that the abuses and deficiencies it had uncovered would not occur again.

The Pike committee concluded its public hearings by examining issues related to foreign intelligence. It began by looking at CIA procurement policies and went on to study CIA detail and media practices. Following this, the committee explored some of the intelligence aspects of the SALT I agreement with the Soviet Union. The committee ended by considering some of the major issues in foreign intelligence: legal issues, covert action, congressional oversight, reform of the intelligence community, and the future of intelligence. Despite the importance of these last five topics, the committee had neither the time nor the inclination to go into any of them in depth.

In this part of the public hearings the CIA was initially the focus of attention. The committee first examined CIA procurement practices. The members were extremely upset that secret CIA channels had been used to procure such "sensitive" items as limousines, golf hats, stroke counters, and putters. Unfortunately the committee's CIA procurement investigation was seriously handicapped by two factors. First, executive-branch witnesses refused to testify in open session about these matters. Second, divisions within the committee surfaced to shift the focus of attention from CIA procurement to the committee itself. For example Mr. Treen questioned William Nelson, the CIA's deputy director for operations, not about procurement but about how the investigations of CIA operations had damaged the intelligence community. Nelson responded by claiming that it was more difficult to recruit agents, that foreign intelligence services had difficulty trusting the CIA, and that Americans were no longer willing to assist U.S. intelligence.[243] Thus the committee's hearings on procurement were hindered by the decision to do much of this work in executive session and by some members' unwillingness to focus on the issue.

The Pike committee also looked at CIA detail and media practices. DCI Colby revealed that the CIA had detailed 104 of its employees to other agencies while 179 were detailed to the CIA.[244] The committee was concerned that CIA detailees were spies throughout the government and constituted a serious problem needing correction. Colby adroitly rebutted such assertions. In public session he refused to discuss the CIA's use of journalists. Moreover ranking minority member Robert McClory attacked the committee's Democrats, changing the focus of this particular hearing with the charge that during the 1964 presidential election a CIA detailee in the White House, Chester Cooper, had done political work for President Lyndon Johnson. Cooper had obtained advance copies of Barry Goldwater's speeches from intelligence sources and had written speeches for President Johnson designed to counter any attacks Goldwater made.[245] Thus once again the committee's attempt to conduct public hearings was sidetracked by the executive-branch witnesses' refusal to discuss certain material in public and by the minority's skill in shifting the focus of what was being examined.

The Pike committee held two days of hearings to examine intelligence issues related to the SALT I agreement with the Soviet Union. On December 2, 1975, the committee received the testimony of Admiral Elmo R. Zumwalt, former chief of naval operations. Administration witnesses were not allowed to testify at this hearing because the executive branch had refused to turn over to the committee materials relating to this subject that had been subpoenaed. Admiral Zumwalt strongly criticized Henry Kissinger. Zumwalt pointed out that Kissinger had negotiated the SALT I agreement with the Russians and that Kissinger was also the chairman of the verification panel that studied whether the Russians were adhering to the treaty. Zumwalt charged that the Russians had violated the treaty and that Kissinger had covered up these violations. Zumwalt considered Kissinger "a man who is extremely skillful at making strategic defeat look like tactical victory."[246] Chairman Pike raised the debate to a higher level by questioning to what extent political judgments affected intelligence reporting. At the same time Republican committee members defended Kissinger. Mr. McClory noted:

> I think there is real danger to our entire international relations structure through testimony or statements which indicate some kind of conspiracy or collusion in which the secretary of state is involved and in which it is alleged that he has deliberately ignored intelligence—which I deny.[247]

McClory also attacked Zumwalt's credibility by noting that Zumwalt was preparing to run for political office. McClory sarcastically suggested that Zumwalt become secretary of state instead of running for the Senate so that he could correct the misdeeds of Secretary Kissinger.[248] This hearing did manage to raise serious questions about how politics shapes intelligence. However, it degenerated into a bitter personal attack on Kissinger, and the Republican members of the committee responded in kind by defending a Republican secretary of state.

On December 17, 1975, the committee held a second hearing on SALT I. Chairman Pike set strict limits on what was to be considered:

> I am going to be rather tough on our jurisdictional limits today. It is not the jurisdiction of this committee to determine whether or not violations of the SALT I agreement have in fact occurred. That is not within our jurisdiction. What is within our jurisdiction is how intelligence is handled.[249]

Because the administration had declassified the documents the committee had been seeking, executive-branch witnesses were permitted to testify at this hearing. The committee established that Secretary Kissinger had taken complete control of monitoring Soviet adherence to the SALT I agreement. In addition Kissinger had withheld information about possible Soviet violations from the intelligence community as well as from then Secretary of State William Rogers. Pike noted in his questioning that Kissinger had publicly stated that no material was held for longer than two months, but Pike established that some items had been withheld for up to six months.[250]

In its hearings on SALT I the committee was raising significant questions about the impact of political concerns on the manner in which intelligence information was handled. However, the importance of this issue was overshadowed by the very personal attacks on Secretary of State Henry Kissinger. The committee was perceived as making ad hominem attacks on Kissinger rather than dealing with substantive intelligence questions. As a senior advisor to President Ford commented: "Otis [Pike] became obsessed in his efforts to get Henry Kissinger. He felt that Henry was the focal point of the problems. Once he got into the thing of getting Kissinger, it began to dilute his efforts. This divided the committee and even his own party."[251] The SALT I hearings thus became a source of division and partisan infighting for the Pike committee.

The committee's public hearings concluded with separate sessions on five major issues in foreign intelligence. In the first session the committee examined the legality of covert actions. Three witnesses testified. Mitchell Rogovin, special counsel to DCI Colby, defended the legality of covert actions, citing the inherent constitutional power of the president, the National Security Act of 1947, and congressional ratification of the CIA's authority to plan and conduct covert action. The other two witnesss, Norman Dorsen from the *ACLU* and Gerhard Casper, a professor at the University of Chicago's law school, challenged Rogovin's arguments.[252] After Dorsen vehemently attacked Rogovin, committee member James Johnson applauded. Chairman Pike observed: "Some of us are trying not to appear to prejudge."[253] But the committee had prejudged. Its selection of witnesses for these final hearings was dominated by those who agreed with the ideological majority on the committee.

The next hearing was devoted to covert action itself. Roger Fisher, a professor of law at Harvard, said that all covert actions were wrong and should be banned. McGeorge Bundy, former assistant to the president for national security affairs, opposed covert action in peacetime but stated that covert action was more permissible during wartime or when there was a serious threat to the national security, citing the U-2 overflights for intelligence gathering authorized during the Cuban Missile Crisis. Finally, former Attorney General Nicholas deB.

Katzenbach endorsed covert actions to collect intelligence but had reservations about covert actions designed to influence political actions.[254] Both Bundy and Katzenbach believed the executive branch itself would have to closely oversee the intelligence community and that the Congress would be a supplement to those efforts. Bundy commented: "I would put much heavier weight [for oversight] on the process of control inside the executive branch and monitoring by the Congress."[255] And again: "Congressional oversight committees on operational matters are not, based on the historical record, uniformly effective or vigilant."[256] Katzenbach also saw the Congress in a supporting role:

> Within the CIA, you ought to have an inspector general. Outside the CIA, you ought to have a Justice Department office charged with enforcement. Outside the executive branch, you ought to have a regular committee asking for regular reports with oversight. . . . You have to structure in the checks and balances.[257]

The Pike committee looked specifically at congressional oversight of intelligence in its next hearing. Two members of Congress, Michael Harrington (D., Massachusetts) and John Anderson (R., Illinois), testified in person, and Albert Quie (R., Minnesota) submitted written testimony. Harrington attacked the Congress for allowing the executive branch to dominate foreign policy. He stated: "For thirty years presidents have told the American people that only the executive branch has the information, competence, and discipline to conduct foreign policy, and by and large, Congress has acquiesced in that judgement."[258] Harrington criticized the way the committee had carried out its House mandate: "I think you have made your own problems by the reaffirmation of ending the existence of this committee at a fixed point in time."[259] He felt that he "would almost like nothing done, rather than to have the impression created and broadly held across the country that there has been success in this effort."[260] Harrington called for the outlawing of all covert action and the appointment of legal counsels to investigate improper activities in each intelligence agency. In addition he wanted an inspector general for the entire intelligence community along with a special prosecutor to ferret out intelligence abuses. Moreover Harrington wanted the Congress to have just as much access to products of the CIA as the president and sought to have the Congress radically revise secrecy restrictions.

Representative John Anderson, who also testified at this hearing, sought the creation of a joint congressional committee to oversee the intelligence community. Anderson warned against overreacting to past abuses and sought to leave some flexibility in the law. In addition he observed that "reforms are meaningless if we don't have the will and persistence to make them work." [261] Tragically Harrington and Anderson were the only two witnesses to appear before the committee on the subject. Harrington was a very liberal Democrat, Anderson a moderate Republican. The committee did not receive any testimony from more conservative members of the House or from members of the Appropriations or Armed Services committees. Thus the committee missed an opportunity to reach out to those in the House with key roles in intelligence oversight and to others in less than total agreement with the committee's ideological majority.

The Pike committee's work in this area was concluded by two hearings concerned with what would happen after its investigation was completed. The first hearing dealt with reform of the intelligence community. Historian Arthur Schlesinger, Jr., and Ambassador Robert Murphy testified. Schlesinger claimed the CIA was a "rogue elephant" and suggested that the only remedy was to drastically cut the intelligence budget and impose strict executive and legislative oversight. [262] Schlesinger was bitterly attacked by ranking member McClory who accused him of focusing "on the sins of Republican administrations" while overlooking or condoning similar offenses in Democratic administrations. [263] When Ambassador Murphy testified he was poorly prepared due to sloppy staff work on the part of the committee in telling him what was expected. He suggested that a joint committee was the best way for the Congress to conduct intelligence oversight and noted that the president must still be the maker of foreign policy in the American system of government. [264] This hearing was poorly attended by committee members, a symbol of their lack of interest in the institutional aspects of oversight.

The final hearing was concerned with the future of intelligence. Once again the committee members displayed a keen lack of interest. William Colby used this occasion to attack the Pike committee for having used the intelligence community's own postmortems as the basis for its hearings on intelligence failures. He remarked: "I hope that the CIA can stop being a scapegoat for sensation, created by its own critiques which were done so that it can improve its procedures." [265] The other three witnesses concentrated on the future. Leo Cherne noted that a new IBM computer system was able to print fifteen thousand lines per minute. Such technological developments would revolutionize future intelligence. Cherne suggested that the intelligence community would be critical in identifying and responding to political, economic, social, and military trends. [266] Admiral Earl Rectanus testified that the intelligence community must seek to attract qualified people. In addition he stated that there was a need to achieve better coordination in intelligence collection to avoid costly and needless duplication of effort.[267] Finally Arthur Cox advocated the separating of intelligence estimating from intelligence operations. Attention should be given to improving the quality of estimates themselves and using estimates to provide an early warning of critical developments.[268] Despite this significant testimony on the future role of intelligence the members once again had little interest in the more institutional aspects of their work.

The Pike committee's public hearings in many ways constituted a remarkable achievement. In choosing where to focus attention the committee wisely selected some of the most important intelligence issues, in sharp contrast to the public hearings of the Church committee. In light of the self-destruction of the Nedzi committee and the limited time in which it had to operate, the breadth and scope of the Pike hearings represent a tremendous accomplishment. However, in many other ways, the hearings were a dismal failure. A major function of such hearings is to educate the public, press, and Congress. Yet the Pike committee was frequently diverted from this key task by its bitter struggle with the executive branch over access to information, including executive-branch charges that the committee could not be trusted with sensitive information. The committee was also damaged by incessant internal partisan and ideological conflicts which severely constrained its ability to educate people on intelligence issues. Moreover the committee was severely handicapped by its adoption of the investigative oversight model. While this model greatly aided the committee in conducting the investigative aspects of its inquiry, it proved deficient in going beyond the investigation to devise institutional reforms based on what had been learned. It is not surprising that hearings devoted to such topics as the future of intelligence had little appeal for committee members. On balance the public hearings of the Pike committee were a costly and tragic failure.

Final Report
The Pike committee produced a final report. In reality two "final" reports were prepared, the first written by political scientist Stanley Bach. Searle Field had hired Bach on August 13, 1975, because of his experience on Capitol Hill. Bach was instructed to study the rules of the House and the relevant law and to begin working on the recommendations to be made by the committee. Later he was told to draft a final report. Bach used transcripts of the committee's hearings as the basis for his work. A Pike staffer described the report Bach prepared:

He was writing a congressional committee report. He was guided by the natural caution and moderation that guides such reports. He based the report he drafted on the transcripts. His draft was based on the record. There was a section on recommendations and the status of oversight. He thought that his stuff would be circulated among the staff people for comment.[269]

Despite Bach's work on a draft of the final report, his efforts were totally disregarded by the committee. A Pike staffer related:

What happened in reality was that, at some point, the draft was started from scratch all over again. The report that was finally published was something with which Bach had nothing to do. It was done in a couple of weeks by Searle Field and Jack Boos with help from Aaron Donner. Field and Boos closeted themselves in one of the interview rooms. There was a lot of typing, writing, cutting, and pasting.

What had happened was that Bach was a friend of Paul Ahearn [a top aide to Mr. McClory]. Paul knew that Bach was looking for a job and recommended him to Searle Field. They were looking for a couple of people on the staff to serve the needs of the minority. Bach was viewed as someone put on to placate the needs of the minority. As a result, they tried to keep Bach as harmless as possible. They were content to have Bach sitting with one or two others, spending three or four months, developing a briefing book. Bach and his cohorts were getting into the issues and the law and using CRS [the Congressional Research Service] to the hilt. They were content to have Bach play a game. This was a waste of time and money.[270]

Thus despite having had a Washington insider and political scientist prepare an institutionally oriented final report, the committee simply discarded this report.

When the House Committee on Standards of Official Conduct investigated the leaking of the Pike committee's final report, Stanley Bach testified. Asked how his draft had differed from the final report, Bach fudged his answer:

I didn't write every word myself. I worked with several other people on the staff in doing it. I think it covered essentially the same subjects that appeared in the report which the committee ultimately adopted. The difference was primarily one of organization, structure, and, in some respects, content, but the basic coverage of the two documents I think was essentially similar.[271]

In reality Bach's report differed significantly from the report ultimately produced by the Pike committee. A Pike staffer discussed the differences:

Bach had more sensitivity. Bach had a greater sense of emulating a committee report. The final report of a committee like this should be "responsible." Bach's draft was.

Bach's briefing book is still part of the committee papers. His working assumption was that there would be a joint intelligence oversight committee. That was to be the major recommendation. Bach devoted a good deal of time and attention to that. The Joint Atomic Energy Committee was to be the model. Ironically, Bach's final report was never utilized by the commitee but the report helped him get a job with CRS.[272]

Because the Pike committee had adopted the investigative oversight model, it is not surprising that an institutionally oriented report like Bach's would differ significantly from the final report produced by Field, Donner, and Boos.

This second draft was what ultimately became the Pike committee's final report. Originally it contained two major sections, the first dealing with the committee's oversight experiences, the second with its investigative record. Although the House voted to suppress this report, the leaked version given to CBS reporter Daniel Schorr was published in 1977 by Spokesman Books with a third major section consisting of the recommendations the committee made to the House. These three sections, then, constitute the actual final report of the Pike committee.

In its discussion of the committee's oversight experience the report captures the sense of frustration on an investigative committee encountering executive-branch opposition to providing easy access to information. Even though the committee contended that the Congress "has a right to all information short of direct communications with the president,"[273] in securing this right the committee found it necessary to issue subpoenas. However, as the final report noted, "Much of the time subpoenas were not enough, and only a determined threat of contempt proceedings brought grudging results."[274] In addition the final report describes some of the tactics the executive branch used to hinder access to information, including: (1) delays in responding to committee requests and subpoenas, (2) cutting off access to information after the committee's disclosure of the "four words" on September 21, 1975, (3) silencing witnesses such as State Department officer Thomas Boyatt who the committee wanted to testify about the Cyprus crisis, (4) flank attacks such as charging the committee with McCarthyism, (5) deleting information from materials turned over to the committee, (6) making claims of privilege, and (7) routine problems such as "footdragging, stonewalling, and careful deception."[275]

Moreover the committee encountered a serious problem in not knowing the right questions to ask. Witnesses for the executive branch were responsive to questions but did not volunteer additional information that would further the committee's work. A type of semantic warfare ensued. The final report summed up the atmosphere by quoting one executive-branch official: "After all, we're not a Coke machine; you don't just put in a quarter and expect something to come out." [276] As a result the Pike committee strongly recommended that effective oversight required "ready access to documentary evidence and primary source material." [277]

The Pike committee also found that the issue of secrecy posed a special dilemma for the Congress itself. Unlike previous congressional intelligence overseers the Pike committee refused to allow the executive branch to stipulate the terms under which the committee might receive—or committee staffers might be permitted—access to sensitive information. For example the executive branch wanted all Pike committee staff members to sign CIA secrecy agreements. But the committee believed this would violate the concept of Congress as an independent and coequal branch of the government. Another problem the final report described was the attempt by the executive branch to selectively brief certain members because of the sensitivity of the information involved. For example the report notes that on several occasions the executive branch sought to limit the dissemination of material to Chairman Pike and the ranking minority member, Mr. McClory, but Chairman Pike's opposition prevented this from occurring. [278]

In addition the final report disapprovingly printed the CIA memorandum of February 23, 1973, revealing how Senator Henry Jackson (D., Washington) had advised the CIA how to prevent Senator Frank Church's Subcommittee on Multinational Corporations from looking into CIA involvement with ITT in Chile in 1970. The CIA memorandum noted: "Senator Jackson is convinced that it is essential that the procedure not be established whereby CIA can be called upon to testify before a wide range of Congressional committees." [279] Pike committee investigator Sandra Zeune Harris had discovered the Jackson CIA memo, and a Pike committee staffer commented that not only was Jackson a "good soldier" for the CIA but he "carried its water and knew how to keep his mouth shut." [280] By printing such a memo in its final report the committee was directly attacking those members of the Congress who had failed to exercise vigorous intelligence oversight.

Finally, the report discusses the difficulty the Congress has in releasing intelligence information. The executive branch has 15,466 people who can classify information, and it claims exclusive jurisdiction over when this information can be declassified. The Pike committee found:

> This gives an administration the power to use the classification system in a manner that can result in manipulation of news by declassifying informa-

tion that can be used to justify policy, while maintaining classification of information that may lead to contrary conclusions.[281]

The committee went on to describe how the administration refused it permission to disclose a CIA covert project in Angola despite Secretary Kissinger having already discussed the operation quite freely with the press.[282] The Pike committee's oversight experience was not pleasant. In its final report the committee described not only the hostility of the executive branch but some of the difficulties the Congress has as an institution in conducting intelligence oversight.

The second section of the final report contained the Pike committee's investigative record, first the costs associated with intelligence activity and second an examination of the intelligence community's performance. This section concludes by examining the risks associated with intelligence. During the committee's public hearings these same issues had been addressed but at that time were frequently overshadowed by disputes both with the executive branch and within the committee itself. As a result this part of the report is the most important because it permits the committee's investigative work to be studied without distraction.

The Pike committee had begun its work by trying to determine the cost of intelligence. The final report stated why: "By following the dollars, the committee would locate activities and priorities of our intelligence services."[283] The committee had been disturbed by what it found. First it noted that intelligence budgets were deceptive. For example the Congress was not told of the CIA's reprogramming of funds. Also the military intelligence budget figures given to Congress did not include expenditures for tactical military intelligence, which would have doubled the intelligence budgets for the three armed services. Second the committee frequently found an absence of accountability, a "close, almost inbred relationship between OMB officials and intelligence budget-makers." Congress was hindered from exercising stringent budget control because the General Accounting Office was prevented by security constraints from looking carefully into intelligence budgets. The final report asserted that the end result was insufficient executive and legislative oversight. Consequently the committee found many examples of spending abuses. For example secret procurement channels had been used to purchase refrigerators, televisions, cameras, and watches. One medium-sized CIA station had spent over $86,000 on liquor and cigarettes over a five-year period. Another CIA station had spent $41,000 on liquor in 1971. Moreover the committee was especially concerned about purchases made by the intelligence community. It learned that 84 percent of all contracts entered into by the community were "sole source" contracts that frequently took advantage of the United States government.[284] Thus the committee found major deficiencies in the budget oversight conducted by both the executive and legislative branches.

The final report was also very critical of the performance of the intelligence community. The committee discussed six intelligence failures: (1) the 1968 Tet attacks in Vietnam, (2) the 1968 Soviet invasion of Czechoslovakia, (3) the 1973 Mideast War, (4) the 1974 coup in Portugal, (5) the 1974 testing of a nuclear device by India, and (6) the 1974 coup in Cyprus. For example the committee found that U.S. intelligence "lost" the Russian army for two weeks prior to the invasion of Czechoslovakia. In its examination of these failures the committee found that at times so much information was collected that analysts were not able to digest it all. On the other hand, sometimes intelligence collectors were not properly apprised of what information to collect.[285] The committee also examined domestic intelligence activity, criticizing FBI activities in internal security and counterintelligence. For example the committee saw little of value in the FBI's five-year investigation of the Socialist Workers Party. According to the committee a major cause of the poor performance of the intelligence community was inadequate oversight by the executive branch. The National Security Council's Intelligence Committee, for example, had met only twice in four years.[286]

The second section of the final report concluded by examining some of the risks associated with intelligence activity. The committee first examined ten years of covert action. This study led the committee to assert that covert actions are "irregularly approved, sloppily implemented, and at times have been forced on a reluctant CIA by the president and his national security advisor."[287] The committee was critical of three covert actions it had uncovered: (1) election support in Italy, (2) arms support to the Kurds, and (3) assistance to rebels in Angola.[288] The committee also found that sometimes the risks of intelligence collection were not worth what was obtained and that policy-level mechanisms for reviewing risk assessment were inadequate. In addition the committee discussed the risks in domestic intelligence operations. It was especially disturbed by the FBI's COINTEL program and the use of informants by law enforcement agencies. The committee concluded this section by criticizing Secretary of State Henry Kissinger for political control of intelligence regarding SALT. The committee was concerned that information about Soviet compliance with SALT had been withheld from intelligence analysts, decision makers, and members of Congress.[289] This second section of the final report consisted of a review of the committee's investigative record.

The third and final section of the final report consisted of recommendations to the House of Representatives discussed and approved by the committee during ten days of public sessions between January 20 and February 10, 1976. The committee recommended that a standing intelligence committee be created by the House to have exclusive jurisdiction over budget authorization for the intelligence community and covert action. In addition the standing committee would have the power to release information or documents in its possession by majority vote. Ironically the Pike committee approved this recommendation after the House had voted to suppress the first two sections of its own final report despite the committee's approval of both by majority vote.

The Pike committee also made several recommendations with respect to the organization of the intelligence community. The committee advised that the director of central intelligence be given central power over the intelligence community and that the DCI should no longer be the head of the CIA. The committee proposed that the director of the FBI have a limited term of office. Also an inspector general for intelligence with a ten-year term of office was to be created to seek out abuses. In addition the committee recommended that the Defense Intelligence Agency be abolished and that the General Accounting Office be given audit authority over intelligence. Finally, the committee recommended that intelligence agencies be prohibited from using journalists or individuals associated with religious or educational institutions.[290] These were the major recommendations proposed by the Pike committee to the House. Besides its public hearings the final report was the major work produced by the Pike committee.

Evaluation of the Nedzi and Pike Committees

The two select committees created by the House of Representatives to investigate the intelligence community in 1975 and 1976 were failures whose significance has still not been fully appreciated. The Nedzi committee self-destructed before its investigation ever really got started. Furthermore, although the Pike committee was able to conduct an intensive investigation and produce a final report, its inglorious ending overshadowed all of its positive accomplishments. The Pike committee held its last public session on February 10, 1976. It was not until July 1977, almost a year and a half later, that the House would vote to create the Permanent House Intelligence Committee. In the Senate, the permanent Senate Intelligence Committee was a natural outgrowth of the Church committee. In the House, however, the permanent committee established in 1977 would have few, if any, links to the Nedzi and Pike committees.

Why did the House fail in its 1975 and 1976 intelligence investigations? There were four major reasons. First, the leadership of the House of Representatives failed to exercise wise or proper supervision over either committee. The decision to appoint Lucien Nedzi as chairman of the first committee along with extremely liberal Democratic members resulted in the rebellion that destroyed the Nedzi committee. With respect to the Pike committee, the leadership failed to assemble a committee representative of the House itself. The vote on the House floor to reject and suppress the final report of the Pike committee was a judgment on the leadership of the House as well as on the work of the committee. The Pike committee had, like the Nedzi committee before it, become a runaway. And in both cases the House repudiated its committees. The Nedzi committee was repudiated when the House refused to accept the resignation of Chairman Nedzi, the Pike committee when its final report was suppressed. Because select committees are controlled by the leadership, a major portion of the blame for the failure of both committees must be attributed to the House leaders.

Besides the leadership of the House, the chairmen of the two select committees also contributed to the failures. Lucien Nedzi, by accepting the chairmanship of the first committee, put himself in the unenviable position of having to critique the oversight he himself had conducted as head of the Armed Services Committee's Intelligence Subcommittee. Otis Pike bears responsibility for the failure of the second committee since he was unable to keep the committee together. The inability of the Pike committee to form a consensus was in stark contrast to the consensus building of the Senate's Church committee. Although Pike was a good investigator he had little sense, feel, or concern for the need to build upon the investigative work of his committee by promoting institutional reforms.

The House select committees were also handicapped by the behavior of members and staff. The investigative assignment given to both committees constituted the first significant House examination of the intelligence community since the creation of the CIA in 1947. Yet the actions of members and staff frequently showed that they were not cognizant of this fact, as witness their inability to keep secrets. Intelligence was an area in which most of the staff had little or no expertise. The failure of both select committees—especially the Pike committee—to conduct an investigation in a professional manner seriously hindered their work. Having intelligence outsiders as staffers enabled the Pike committee to approach intelligence from a new and different perspective. However, the failure to include on the staff some experienced older Washington hands seriously handicapped the Pike committee in the long run.

Finally, the executive branch contributed to the failure of the House intelligence investigations. The Pike committee represented a new and dramatic break with the past. Instead of adjusting to this new situation, the executive branch went out of its way to hinder, frustrate, and ultimately destroy the House investigation. Ironically, by raising such issues as intelligence failures, the Pike committee was uncovering serious gaps and weaknesses within the U.S. intelligence community that needed to be addressed. But the hostility of the executive branch was so intense that the committee's potentially positive and important contributions were never realized. Consequently the failure of the House intelligence investigations reflected weaknesses within the House itself as a political institution and signified a rupture in legislative-executive comity.

Unfortunately the failure of the Nedzi and Pike committees has overshadowed the positive actions they undertook. The Pike committee was asking questions that needed to be asked. Was money being spent wisely by the intelligence community? How effective was the performance of the community? Many of the Pike committee's findings are deeply disturbing because of the weaknesses and deficiencies they reveal. But this solid and substantive work was lost in the conflicts within the committee, with the executive branch, and with its parent chamber. The final irony came in 1977 when the House created a permanent intelligence committee which went out of its way to distance itself from the Pike committee. But in doing so the new committee completely ignored the Pike committee's substantive accomplishments. As Pike committee member Robert Kasten commented: "It is tragic that it was necessary to establish this committee to inquire into the activities of agencies on which we depend so heavily for our security. But it would be even more tragic if the results of our investigation were now to be ignored." [291] Sadly, those words of Kasten, written in 1976, were prophetic. The legacy of the Pike committee has been ignored and forgotten.

5 The Reemergence of Insitutional Oversight in the House: The Boland Committee, 1977–84

Unlike the Senate, the House did not create a permanent intelligence committee to build upon the work undertaken by its predecessor. The House had no desire to eastablish a successor to the Pike committee. While the Senate established a permanent intelligence committee that inherited members, staff, an institutional memory, and an intelligence agenda from the Church committee, the Pike committee merely left a very bad taste in the mouths of most House members. A common view emerged that the Pike committee had demonstrated that the House could not be trusted to keep classified information secret and that the committee had somehow created the climate in which CIA Station Chief Richard Welch was murdered. Loch Johnson observed, there was no desire in the House to create a "son of Pike."[1]

In 1977, however, several forces converged that led the House to create a permanent intelligence committee. First, because there was no counterpart to the newly established Senate committee, every Wednesday morning the CIA gave an intelligence briefing to newly elected House Speaker Thomas P. O'Neill. As the Speaker recalled: "It was so confidential, I couldn't tell my wife. So after about three months I said to myself that this is crazy. There ought to be an intelligence committee."[2] Second, the House needed a committee to handle legislation being sent to it by the Senate and its intelligence committee. For example, on June 22, 1977, the Senate passed S. 1539 which for the first time in the history of Congress authorized funds for the operations and programs of the federal intelligence agencies. Although sent to the House, S. 1539 was never considered by it. In addition, there was no counterpart on the House side to consider such legislation as the intelligence charters the Senate Intelligence Committee was developing.

Third, the Carter administration desired a House intelligence committee. President Carter, Vice-President Mondale, and DCI Stansfield Turner all lobbied Speaker O'Neill to establish a House committee.[3] As Majority Leader James Wright noted, this committee "was requested by the president of the United States. He wants to have one place to which intelligence and intelligence-related spokesmen can come to give accurate information to the Congress secure in the knowledge that the confidentiality can be protected."[4] All these forces led the House to begin the process of creating a new intelligence committee.

Beginning in March 1977 the House leadership began work on creating a permanent House intelligence committee by forming a small working group that met in the Speaker's office. Members of this group included Rules Committee Chairman Richard Bolling, Minority Leader John Rhodes, and Representative Edward Boland. Charlie Ferris, a close aide to the Speaker and Boland aide Michael O'Neil were also present at these sessions. By this point the Speaker had already determined that his close friend Boland would chair the new committee.[5] Unlike in 1975, the House Democratic leadership maintained firm control over the entire process. The measure that finally emerged from the working group, H. Res. 658, was brought to the floor of the House on July 17, 1977, as a "privileged resolution," meaning that no amendments could be offered. In 1975 the resolution to create the Pike committee was considered under an "open rule," and amendments were offered and adopted. As Chairman Richard Bolling of the House Rules Committee observed during House consideration of H. Res. 658: "This is a select committee, a permanent select committee. It is basically a committee of the leadership."[6]

House Resolution 658 created a committee different in two significant ways from the permanent Senate Intelligence Committee. First, while the Senate committee had eight Democrats and seven Republicans, the new House committee gave the Democrats nine seats and the Republicans only four. Second, the Senate Intelligence Committee had authorization authority only for national foreign intelligence while the Senate Armed Services Committee retained control of tactical intelligence and intelligence-related activities. The House committee to be created under H. Res. 658, on the other hand, was given authorization authority over all three areas. These were the two principal structural differences between the permanent House and Senate intelligence committees.

During the floor debate on H. Res. 658 on July 17, 1977, Republicans attacked the resolution because of the party ratio and because of concerns for protecting classified information. Minority Leader John Rhodes suggested that the nine-to-four ratio would "blatantly politicize" the committee and expressed grave concern about the committee's ability to protect secrets.[7] Representative Robert McClory, the ranking Republican on the Nedzi and Pike committees, proposed that since in 1976 the Republicans had lost the popular vote for the House by only 55 to 42 percent, the party ratio on the new committee should be five to four instead of nine to four.[8]

In response to these attacks Speaker O'Neill went to the well of the House to strongly defend H. Res. 658. By going to the podium in front of the Speaker's chair to address the House, an unusual gesture, O'Neill showed the strength of his concern for the resolution. The Speaker dismissed Republican claims to a greater number of seats: "In the last election the constituencies in America sent 289 Democrats and 145 Republicans to the Congress. . . . Members of the minority party should not have a better chance of serving on this committee than members of the majority party."[9] As to claims that the new committee would be both partisan and a security risk, the Speaker clearly stated: "I expect this committee to deliberate and act in a nonpartisan manner."[10] More specifically, "this is a nonpartisan committee; there will be nothing partisan about its deliberations; and the members can be assured of it by the members that I appoint."[11] Following the Speaker, Representative Edward P. Boland, already known to be the Speaker's choice to chair the new committee, also argued for passage of the resolution: "This is important because the House ought to make itself a full partner in the congressional review and control of intelligence activities."[12] In sharp contrast to its attitude in 1975 toward the resolution that created the Pike committee, the House Democratic leadership strongly supported H. Res. 658.

Oddly enough, besides the Republicans, a number of liberal Democrats in the House also attacked H. Res. 658. Representatives Michael Harrington and Robert Giaimo, who had participated in the 1975 intelligence investigations, both spoke out sharply against the resolution. Harrington suggested that what was being offered to the House was "sham" oversight.[13] Giaimo charged that the new committee would easily be "co-opted" by the intelligence community.[14]

Despite the opposition of the Republicans and the liberal Democrats, H. Res. 658 was approved by the House by a vote of 227 to 171. All of the 9 House Democrats later appointed to the new committee voted for the resolution while all 4 Republican appointees voted against it. Although the Pike committee had recommended that an intelligence oversight committee be created, Representatives Pike, Dellums, Giaimo, Harrington, Kasten, McClory, and Treen all voted against H. Res. 658, as did Representative Nedzi. In fact, of those members who served on the Nedzi and Pike committees, only Edwards and Milford voted for the resolution. Although those members who had investigated the intelligence community for the House opposed the

resolution, it passed because of strong backing from the House Democratic leadership. During the House intelligence investigations of 1975
to 1976, liberal Democrats hostile to intelligence had dominated the
Democratic Caucus in the House and therefore controlled the agenda
of the Nedzi and Pike committees. Now, however, they were reduced
to being mere sideline critics and, during the 1977–84 period, had
little influence on the Permanent House Intelligence Committee.

In passing H. Res. 658 the House of Representatives created the
Permanent Select Committee on Intelligence, a unique legislative creation. It is similar to a standing committee in that it continues from
Congress to Congress, and it is the only House select committee to
have legislative authority and a standing committee staff. On the other
hand, because it is a select committee, the members are picked by the
Democratic and Republican party leaders, irrespective of the party
caucuses and the norm of seniority.

Even before the House passed H. Res. 658 it was common knowledge that Representative Edward Boland would be the first chairman
of the House Permanent Select Committee on Intelligence. Chairman
Boland dominated this committee from its creation in 1977 until the
end of the Ninety-eighth Congress in 1984. He had the full backing
and support of his long-time friend Speaker O'Neill. Ironically, after
the reforms of the 1970s, committees in the House became decentral-
ized with power resting in the hands of subcommittees and their chairmen. The Boland committee, however, represented a return to an
earlier era in which power was retained by the full committee chairman
and the Speaker. During Boland's chairmanship the House relied upon
and trusted the competency of the committee. The Boland committee
followed the institutional oversight model.

Recruitment of Committee Members

Following the passage of H. Res. 658, the Speaker officially named
Representative Boland to chair the new intelligence committee. Because the Boland committee was a select committee, appointments
were controlled by the Speaker and the minority leader. During the
eight years Boland chaired the committee Speaker O'Neill appointed
the Democratic members in close consultation with him. As a senior
aide to the Speaker observed, O'Neill deferred to Boland in this area.[15]
Speaker O'Neill commented on his appointments to the committee:
"Everyone I put on that committee I trusted. I knew of nobody more
trustworthy than Eddie [Boland]—of the greatest sincerity, dedicated

Table 10.   Membership of Boland Committee I (1977-78)

Member	Age	Years in House	1976 ADA Rating	1976 NSI Rating
Boland	66	24	79	44
Zablocki	65	28	50	90
Burlison	44	8	50	70
Murphy	44	6	55	50
Aspin	39	6	79	30
Rose	38	4	39	100
Mazzoli	45	6	65	40
Mineta	46	2	95	10
Fowler	37	0	—	—
Democratic average	47.1	9.3	64.0	54.2
Wilson	61	24	0	100
Ashbrook	49	16	6	90
McClory	68	14	20	70
Robinson	61	6	0	100
Republican average	59.8	15.0	6.5	87.5
Committee average	51.0	11.0	44.8	66.1

Source: *Almanac of American Politics 1978.*

to the country and dedicated to keeping his mouth shut." [16] At the same time Minority Leader John Rhodes and his successor Robert Michel designated the Republicans for the committee.

For Democrats there were two ways to gain appointment. First, members lobbied for appointment. For example in 1983 there were three Democratic openings on the committee. Nearly thirty members sought appointment and twelve were "serious candidates" who mounted extensive campaigns for appointment. [17] One Democratic member appointed in this manner described how he lobbied:

John Murtha was involved. I went in and had a long talk with Tip. This was the first time I had ever been in with Tip. We spent about thirty min-

Table 11.   Membership of Boland Committee II (1979-80)

Member	Age	Years in House	1978 ADA Rating	1978 NSI Rating
Boland	68	26	50	56
Zablocki	67	30	40	60
Burlison	46	10	45	50
Murphy	46	8	55	56
Aspin	41	8	60	33
Rose	40	6	50	43
Mazzoli	47	8	40	30
Mineta	48	4	80	20
Fowler	39	2	45	86
Democratic average	49.1	11.3	51.7	48.2
Robinson	63	8	10	100
Ashbrook	51	18	5	100
McClory	70	16	45	89
Whitehurst	54	10	15	100
Young	49	8	10	100
Republican average	57.4	12.0	17.0	98.0
Committee average	52.1	11.6	39.3	66.0

Source: *Almanac of American Politics 1980.*

utes together. I was one of the leaders of the Boll Weevils [conservative southern Democrats]. I asked for better representation for the Boll Weevils on the Appropriations and Armed Services committees. I asked directly for a spot for myself on the Intelligence Committee. I made the point that I had never lambasted the leadership on the floor.[18]

The other route to appointment for Democrats was to be recruited directly by either the Speaker, Chairman Boland, or the majority leader. One member who turned down appointment described how the leadership attempted to recruit him:

Originally Tip called me. Then Eddie [Boland] called me and we talked a couple of days on this. I did not want to give up my position on the Select

Table 12.　　Membership of Boland Committee III (1981-82)

Member	Age	Years in House	1980 ADA Rating	1980 NSI Rating
Boland	70	28	78	20
Zablocki	69	32	61	22
Rose	42	8	44	43
Mazzoli	49	10	33	33
Mineta	50	6	83	10
Fowler	41	4	61	50
Hamilton	50	16	44	22
Gore	33	4	50	40
Stump	54	4	0	100
Democratic average	50.9	12.4	50.4	38.0
Robinson	65	10	6	100
Ashbrook	53	20	6	100
McClory	72	18	17	88
Whitehurst	56	12	0	89
Young	51	10	11	100
Republican average	59.4	14.0	8.0	95.4
Committee average	54.0	13.0	35.3	58.4

Source: *Almanac of American Politics 1982.*

Committee on Aging. We were in the crunch on Social Security. The decision as to whether to go with Select Intelligence or Select Aging was the most excruciating decision of my congressional career. After three days of solid pressure, I turned down the offer. I was disappointed but you can only serve on one select committee. I was asked to recommend somebody and the member I recommended was appointed.[19]

Minority Leader John Rhodes and his successor Robert Michel designated the Republican members. Once again members both sought appointment and were recruited. As one Republican noted: "I aggressively sought a spot. I lobbied Rhodes hard and won appointment to this committee."[20] Another Republican member described how he

Table 13.   Membership of Boland Committee IV (1983-84)

Member	Age	Years in House	1982 ADA Rating	1982 NSI Rating
Boland	72	30	80	38
Mazzoli	51	12	70	30
Mineta	52	8	80	40
Fowler	43	6	65	70
Hamilton	52	18	70	60
Gore	35	6	70	50
Stokes	58	14	85	0
McCurdy	33	2	25	100
Beilensen	49	6	95	0
Democratic average	49.4	11.3	71.1	43.1
Robinson	67	12	5	90
Whitehurst	58	14	5	90
Young	53	12	10	100
Stump	56	6	0	100
Goodling	55	8	25	78
Republican average	57.8	10.4	9.0	91.6
Committee average	52.6	11.0	48.9	60.4

Source: *Almanac of American Politics 1984.*

"was recruited in early 1979 by Bob Wilson. Wilson was ready to step down and told me I was the type of person he would like to see replace him. He brought John Rhodes in and Rhodes handled it the rest of the way."[21]

During the eight-year history of the Boland Committee the Democrats retained control of the House. In the Ninety-fifth Congress the Democrats controlled nine of the thirteen seats on the committee (see Tables 10 to 13). While the Democrats controlled 67.1 percent of all House seats they had 69.2 percent of the seats on the Boland committee. During the Ninety-sixth Congress the Republicans were given an additional seat so that the party ratio was now nine to five. In the

Ninety-sixth Congress the Democrats controlled 63.7 percent of all House seats and 64.3 percent of the seats on the committee. In the Ninety-eighth Congress the Democrats controlled 61.8 percent of House seats and 64.3 percent of the committee seats. Only in the Ninety-seventh Congress was there gross underrepresentation of the Republicans with the Democrats controlling 55.9 percent of all House seats but retaining 64.3 percent of the Boland committee seats. The Republicans, who comprised 44.1 percent of all House members, had only 35.7 percent of the committee seats. Thus in each of the four Congresses during which the Boland committee was in existence the Democrats had on a percentage basis more seats on the committee than in the House as a whole. However, in only one Congress was there serious underrepresentation of the Republicans.

Under the provisions of H. Res. 658 members appointed to the Boland committee after the Ninety-fifth Congress could serve only six years on the committee. The committee had a fairly stable membership. Democrats Boland, Fowler, Mazzoli, and Mineta and Republican Robinson served from 1977 to 1984. Republicans Whitehurst and Young served from 1979 to 1984, and Democrat Zablocki and Republican Ashbrook served from 1977 until their deaths during the Ninety-eighth Congress. H. Res. 658 also required that at least one member of the Boland committee be from each of the following committees: Appropriations, Armed Services, International Relations, and Judiciary. Chairman Boland and fellow Democrat Burlison were on the Appropriations Committee as were Republicans Robinson and Young. Democrats Aspin, Stump, and McCurdy all served on Armed Services. (During his service on the Boland committee Stump switched parties.) Meanwhile Republicans Wilson and Whitehurst were also on Armed Services. The International Relations/Foreign Affairs Committee was represented by Democrats Zablocki and Hamilton and Republican Goodling. Finally, the Judiciary Committee was represented by Democrat Mazzoli and Republicans McClory and Ashbrook. Thus all four standing House committees dealing with intelligence issues were represented on the Boland committee.

Unlike Democrats on the Nedzi and Pike committees, the Democrats chosen for the Boland committee were not extremely liberal. Only two of the thirty-six Democrats who were members during the committee's eight-year history had ADA ratings of 90 percent or above. Seven of the sixteen Democrats on the Nedzi and Pike committees had such ratings. At the same time, as might be expected, the Democratic members of the Boland committee had higher NSI ratings than their counterparts on the investigative committees. While the Democrats were more moderate than their predecessors, Republicans were more conservative than their counterparts on the earlier committees. Because the Republican seats on the Boland committee were deliberately set at four and, later, after considerable Republican complaints, at five, the Republican leadership retaliated by insuring that only extremely conservative Republicans gained appointment. The only exception was Representative William Goodling who was recruited by the leadership to serve in 1983 but who left the committee in frustration in 1984.[22] But even Goodling was not terribly liberal. On the Pike committee Republican Johnson had frequently voted with the Democrats. This time the Republican leadership was more careful in screening members so that only ideologically safe members were appointed. The Boland committee was, in sum, composed of moderate Democrats and extremely conservative Republicans.

For those on the Boland committee there were both costs and benefits associated with membership. The two biggest costs were the time required and the silencing of members as a result of being told sensitive information. With respect to time, members were extremely devoted to the committee's work. Because much of the work took place behind closed doors it is impossible to ascertain just how much time members devoted, but, as a key budget staffer on the committee noted:

> Other committees are the committees on which they are graded. But members can and do take time to devote themselves to our efforts. Boland and Robinson are here all the time. But take Mineta. There are so many other demands on his time. He gets low marks on a member attendance scale but he'll see me at 6:30 or 7:30 at night. Also, take Zablocki. He will get his secretary to work me into his schedule when I need to see him.[23]

A ranking Democrat on the committee expressed the frustration and pressure members felt:

> Time is a real problem. Look at the scheduling of meetings. We are trying to squeeze in an hour, two hours so there will be no conflict in our schedules. It is tough to conduct good oversight. Your mind is on: (1) worries about work that needs to be done in your office or your other committees, (2) constituents to meet, and (3) votes on the floor.[24]

Although time is precious on the Hill, members on the Boland committee were willing to devote the time necessary to do the work.

Besides the cost of time, membership also imposed limits on speaking in public on classified information. A conservative Democrat on the committee commented: "If anything, being on this committee hampers you from being able to speak out."[25] A ranking Democrat acknowledged the difficulties this imposed on his meetings with constituents: "You can't talk about what you hear and do. When I'm asked a question at a town meeting, I have to stop and think. Did I read this in the *New York Times*, get it in a classified briefing, or both?"[26] Another senior Democrat expressed frustration at the limits on his ability to discuss developments in Nicaragua:

> The covert actions being used in Nicaragua have major policy implications. How does a member like myself, who I might add recognized that from the first day, respond to this? I wrote to the president, talked with the DCI, Shultz, and Weinberger. The secrecy provisions of this committee foreclosed any further action.[27]

Despite these costs members found it desirable to have a seat on the Boland committee, and for several reasons. First, the committee was a prestigious assignment signifying the trust and confidence of party leadership. Because so much of the committee's work took place behind closed doors, assignment was extremely beneficial only for members seeking greater influence within the House. Second, this was an important policy area. What emerges in interviews with committee members is that they saw themselves as buffers between the intelligence community and the Congress and American people. Third, this was an exciting or "sexy" policy area. As one Republican committee member noted: "To learn this area, I went through the CIA training program. I learned about guns, how to build and identify bombs, how to run a roadblock, and how to set one up."[28] Fourth, although most members' constituents did not even know they were on the committee, membership conveyed an aura of being an insider. One staffer described members of the committee as "cleaned" and other House members as "uncleaned." For example when on April 3, 1983, Boland committee member Albert Gore appeared on "Meet the Press," those members of the press asking questions cited four times the fact that Gore was on the Intelligence Committee. Being a member thus conveyed a sense of being well informed, at least in the minds of the Washington press corps.[29]

Finally, members were able to use information gained on the Boland committee in their other committees and House work. For example, Representatives Burlison and Robinson served on the Appropriations Committee. By also working on the Boland committee they had the unique opportunity to both authorize and appropriate funds for intelligence. In short, the Boland committee was attractive to House members, and its membership was carefully chosen by the Democratic and Republican party leaders.

Leadership of the Chairman

Unlike the Senate Intelligence Committee, which had three different chairmen from 1976 to 1984, the House Permanent Select Committee on Intelligence had only one chairman from its creation in 1977 until 1984, Representative Edward P. Boland of Massachusetts. It is highly appropriate to call this the "Boland committee" because during this time the committee was dominated by the personality and legislative style of its chairman. Boland was first elected to the House in 1952. Long a bachelor, Boland roomed in Washington with his close friend Tip O'Neill, whose wife remained in Cambridge. In his memoirs Speaker O'Neill notes that he and Boland roomed together for twenty-five years and describes Boland as "my pal and roommate."[30] Speaker O'Neill's memoirs tell how Edward Boland's life revolved around his work in the House. When Boland married in 1973 at the age of sixty-two, he and O'Neill stopped being roommates. But their close relationship continued through the years. When Boland accepted the chairmanship of the House Intelligence Committee, he did so with the complete confidence and backing of the Speaker of the House.

During his congressional career Boland had worked quietly behind the scenes on the Appropriations Committee. The *Almanac of American Politics for 1984* describes his legislative style:

> Boland has a reputation for getting bills and resolutions he manages adopted without major change. They are reported on time, he is prepared to answer queries, and the bills are usually passed without much challenge: he is one of the strongest Appropriations Subcommittee chairmen.[31]

In a 1986 campaign brochure, Boland himself noted that his work on the Appropriations Committee

> has paved the way for millions of dollars of federal funding that have been channelled into the Second District, for public works and veterans benefits, housing for the elderly and those with low and moderate incomes, for urban redevelopment and public health, education and transportation.[32]

Such a record made Boland electorally safe in his home district. When it came to national security issues in the House, Chairman Boland served as a bridge between senior big-city politicians and the younger, more ideological liberals in the Democratic Caucus. Although Boland occasionally questioned executive budget requests and actions, the *Almanac of American Politics 1984* observed that he had neither "total faith" in the executive branch nor the "endemic" suspicion of the national security bureaucracy possessed by many Democrats who entered the House during the Vietnam War era.[33]

When Boland assumed the chairmanship of the Intelligence Committee he acknowledged to his colleagues: "I know little more about the particulars of the intelligence community than other members present. I know nothing about covert or clandestine activities except what I have read in the newspaper."[34] Yet despite his ignorance Boland asked his colleagues to trust him as one willing to take the time to educate himself and his committee. His proven record of accomplishment on the Appropriations Committee led them to do so. A critical test of Boland's leadership occurred on June 6, 1978, when for the first time in its history the House had a public debate on an intelligence authorization bill, H. R. 12240. During the debate Representative James Johnson, formerly a member of the Pike committee, challenged the efficacy of the Boland committee's budget oversight. Chairman Boland himself took the floor to defend his committee's work. Although Johnson was joined in opposing the bill by intelligence critics Giaimo and Harrington, H. R. 12240 passed the House by a vote of 323 to 43,[35] a solid indicator of the firm support of Boland's House colleagues. This support stands in marked contrast to the support given to Chairman Pike in the past.

As chairman of the Intelligence Committee, Boland maintained a very low profile. He has never given an interview about his role as the first chairman of the committee. Boland defended his reticence: "I don't like the limelight in this situation. I think you have the responsibility of staying out of it." [36] This is typical Boland. The *Congressional Directory* entry on Boland, inserted by Boland himself, amounts to three terse lines: name, party, district, and congresses to which he was elected. Not surprisingly it is the shortest entry in the book.[37] A key moment during Boland's chairmanship occurred on December 8, 1982, when Boland took to the floor of the House to offer an amendment to the Harkin amendment restricting CIA activities in Nicaragua. Boland's remarks were carefully written out in advance, and he stuck fastidiously to his text. It was a measure of the respect in which the House held him that the Boland amendment was adopted by 411 to 0 that day.[38]

Boland's dual goals as chairman of the Intelligence Committee were to conduct effective oversight and to demonstrate that the House could be trusted with secrets. To accomplish these at times conflicting goals Chairman Boland worked hard to keep the committee together. As a senior Democrat on the committee observed:

> Boland is an able chairman. But he can only be prodded with some doing. He prefers not to ruffle the waters. He is excellent in terms of fairness and seeking consensus. He likes to get unanimous consent. He doesn't want to needlessly cause ripples or stir up criticism.[39]

As Representative Joseph P. Addabo observed: "Eddie doesn't feel that intelligence should be a partisan issue." [40] A ranking Republican on the committee noted: "He is an extremely fair-minded man. He does not enjoy controversy. He attempts to work out things so that there is a minimum of friction so that we can proceed with a total effort." [41]

Another Republican on the committee agreed: "Boland is outstanding. I have nothing but respect for him." [42] Similarly Representative Richard Cheney, chairman of the House Republican Conference, commented: "He took the Intelligence Committee when it was brand new and made it into something significant. On our side of the aisle you won't find anyone to say anything bad about him." [43] The committee's unity was due in large measure to the leadership exercised by the chairman.

Chairman Boland devoted considerable time to budget oversight. As one intelligence official involved in budget presentations before the committee observed: "He is a strong chairman. He makes sure that questions on our behalf are put into the official record that is compiled in closed session. At the hearings, more than a thousand questions have been put into the record. This is establishing a clear record of oversight." [44] Moreover senior White House and intelligence officials believe that Boland established a committee that could be trusted. A senior NSA official commented: "I have total trust in his ability to maintain the protection of information given to him." [45] Former Secretary of Defense Harold Brown described Boland as "conscientious and knowledgeable" [46] while former Admiral B. R. Inman gave Chairman Boland "high marks in a difficult job. He is a very cautious man and his judgment is sound. He is a liberal but a cautious liberal." [47] Such assessments are a far cry from the conflict and controversy that surrounded the Nedzi and Pike committees.

In the eight years Edward Boland chaired the Intelligence Committee his leadership in the intelligence area was rejected just once by the House of Representatives. On September 23, 1981, the House approved the Agent Identities Bill (H. R. 4) to protect undercover intelligence operatives and to punish those who deliberately sought to publicly identify undercover agents. By a vote of 226 to 181 the House adopted an amendment offered by committee member John Ashbrook to stiffen the measure and rejected a direct plea by Chairman Boland not to do so. [48] Earlier, on September 6, 1978, Chairman Boland had lost 178 to 176 on an amendment to the Foreign Intelligence Surveillance Act offered by committee Republican Robert McClory. However, after diligent work by the leadership and the administration, the House reversed itself on September 7, 1978, and backed Chairman Boland's position 246 to 128. Thus in eight years as chairman, Boland's leadership was rejected only once on the House floor.

Chairman Boland was a strong practitioner of institutional oversight. Although no staff members who served on the Nedzi or Pike committees were hired by the Boland committee, two members from the earlier investigative committees served on the Boland committee. One of them, Les Aspin, attempted to implement investigative oversight on the Boland committee from his position as chairman of the Subcommittee on Oversight. Describing the relationship between Chairman Boland and Subcommittee Chairman Aspin, political scientist Loch Johnson commented: "The full committee chairman [Boland] alternated between sharply pulling in the reins and begrudgingly loosening them a little." [49] After four years Aspin left the committee. In December 1986 former Speaker O'Neill, according to the *Congressional Quarterly*, "removed Aspin from the Intelligence Committee a year before his six-year term expired at the request of former Chairman Edward P. Boland, D.-Mass., and 'the highest authorities.' " [50] A senior intelligence official at the highest levels described Aspin's conduct: "You never knew when he was going to pull out secret intelligence information and use it. There were some times that he was very responsible but you never knew when he was going to crank out the Saturday press release." [51]

Representative Aspin attempted to implement investigative oversight on the Boland committee. From his appointment in 1977 until he left the committee in 1980 Aspin's actions stimulated considerable tension within the committee. Some on the committee and in the executive branch viewed Aspin as a "rogue elephant" out of control. [52] But the real cause of this tension was the conflict between the institutional and investigative oversight models. Aspin personified investigative oversight; his ouster meant that investigative oversight would not be implemented by the Boland committee. [53] Just as significantly, this incident demonstrated the power of Chairman Boland over the membership of the Intelligence Committee.

When Speaker O'Neill appointed Representative Boland to chair the Intelligence Committee he appointed his closest friend, but this appointment was due to much more than just friendship. As was not the case with the Nedzi and Pike committees, Speaker O'Neill was determined to maintain leadership control over the new committee. There would be no more mavericks or renegade committees in House intelligence oversight. The appointment of Chairman Boland signified that the Speaker himself intended to exercise political control, and Boland was someone the Speaker could trust to carry out the assignment. Chairman Boland would avoid the excessively public oversight that marked the investigative committees of 1975 to 1976. The relatively quiet institutional oversight practiced by the new committee was due largely to the influence and legislative style of the chairman. In this role as chairman, Boland retained the confidence of Speaker O'Neill and exercised powers reminiscent of those that House chairmen of standing committees possessed prior to the House reforms of the 1970s.

Internal Relations

The Boland committee was characterized throughout its history by a constant search for unity and consensus. Although the chairman had a critical role in this effort all of the committee members shared the desire to make intelligence oversight a reality in the House of Representatives. All the members also believed in the necessity of a good and strong intelligence capability. As a senior staffer on the committee noted: "There were no skeptics along those lines." Despite being supporters of intelligence, the members were not reluctant to take a hard and searching look at executive funding requests,[54] a bipartisan skepticism reflecting those members from an Appropriations Committee background.

Nearly all the committee members accepted a set of common assumptions. First, all of them realized the importance of preventing security leaks. As one aide close to Boland noted: "Keeping secrets was the *sine qua non* for this committee."[55] Second, there was to be no partisanship. Committee members sought to convey an image of responsibility. Ironically, while Democratic members tended to be moderate team players, the Republicans tended to be conservative ideological watchdogs. Third, members were careful to protect the committee's turf and were careful not to usurp the decisions of other committees, a policy facilitated by having representatives of all the other House committees that dealt with intelligence on the committee. Fourth, most members agreed that the work of the committee required a very low profile. The principal dissenter here was Representative Les Aspin who sought to maintain a very high public profile for both himself and his subcommittee. Finally, all of the members took their work on the Boland committee very seriously.[56]

During the debate on H. Res. 658 Representative Theodore Weiss had expressed a concern that the House was creating a group of intelligence "insiders": "We will have created two different classes of members of the House of Representatives: one class composed of thirteen members of this permanent select committee, and the other class consisting of the rest of the members of the House."[57] That concern has largely been realized. As described by one Boland committee staffer, there was an "insider" mystique that predominated:

> Members of the committee see themselves as being inside the circle while all other members are outside the circle. Outsiders are dangerous, unwashed, and uncleaned while among members of the committee there is this mystique of "We are the washed." Moreover, add on to this the fact that everybody on the staff is cleared by the FBI and you get a sense of being apart, being unique.[58]

When the Boland committee was first established thirty-two hours of closed-door informational hearings were held to familiarize the members with the intelligence field. For members appointed after 1977 a similar process of socialization mandated that their first two years on the committee be spent learning the terrain and terminology. Older members watched with patience as this process unfolded.[59]

Throughout its eight-year history the Boland committee had only four instances of public division along party lines. First, as noted previously, when the committee was created all the Democratic members supported H. Res. 658 while all the Republican members opposed it. Second, on September 6 and 7, 1978, the committee split along party lines on the McClory amendment to weaken the Foreign Intelligence Surveillance Act. Third, on September 23, 1981, the committee divided largely on a partisan basis when Representative Ashbrook introduced an amendment to toughen the Agent Identities Bill. Ironically, Ashbrook triumphed over Chairman Boland that day but was joined only by Republican Young and Democrat Stump. The rest of the Democrats stayed with the chairman and were joined by Republicans Robinson, McClory, and Whitehurst. Finally, the committee split twice over Nicaragua. The first time was on September 22, 1982, when Chairman Rose's Subcommittee on Oversight and Evaluation issued a report criticizing U.S. intelligence efforts in Central America. The second time was on July 28, 1983, when the chairman introduced a second Boland amendment to cut off all funds to opposition forces in Nicaragua and won by a vote of 228 to 195.

Except for these four exceptions, the Boland committee remained united for eight years. Furthermore, with the exception of Nicaragua— which was more a foreign policy than an intelligence issue—the issues on which the committee split along party lines were more a matter of degree than of disagreement over a particular proposal. Much more significant is that on budget and other legislative issues the committee maintained a united front for eight years. This consensus was due to the deliberate steps of the chairman and all the other members on this committee.

Curiously, the two most divisive incidents both arose within Democratic ranks. First Representative Aspin's attempts to practice investigative oversight provoked opposition from those members who preferred that the committee maintain a very low profile. Second a group of critics developed among the Democrats who sometimes questioned the approval the committee was giving to executive proposals given to it in secret, especially proposals for covert action. This group of skeptics included Representatives Aspin, Fowler, Gore, Hamilton, Mazzoli, and Rose. As one member of this group indicated: "This is not a highly partisan committee. It is an extremely conservative committee. All the Republicans and two or three of the Democrats are all strongly supportive of the CIA. The membership is stacked." [60] Thus the committee at times divided privately along ideological lines. In public, however, the Boland committee maintained a unified position with few exceptions throughout its eight-year history.

Committee Staff

After the passage of H. Res. 658 the first major decision made by the committee concerned the hiring and the role of staff. A decision was reached to hire a nonpartisan professional staff like those on the Appropriations and Armed Services committees. In addition the committee decided to hire a combination of staffers, some with and some without intelligence experience. The three most critical staff positions were staff director, chief counsel, and the chief staffer on the Budget Authorization Subcommittee. [61] For staff director the committee hired Thomas Latimer, who had served in the intelligence community and had been a special assistant to Secretary of Defense James Schlesinger. They hired Michael O'Neil, who had been a legislative assistant to Chairman Boland for four years, as chief counsel. Although O'Neil had no previous background in intelligence, he had worked on H. Res. 658 and his close relationship with the chairman gave him a strong power base on the committee. Finally, for chief budget staffer the committee hired James Bush, who had handled the intelligence budget for the secretary of defense. All three remained in their posts from 1977 to 1984, in stark contrast to the changes in key staff positions on the Senate side.

Even though the committee's staff was officially listed as nonpartisan, in reality the staff was divided between Democratic and Republican staffers. As a former legislative counsel for the CIA observed: "There are majority and minority staffers. They are not listed as such but in effect that's the way it shakes out." [62] One Boland committee staffer noted: "We have a professional staff system. You will not find majority and minority staff listed in the book but this doesn't mean politics ceases to operate. The staff work is professional, but you still see partisanship at the margins." [63]

The Republicans controlled three staff positions. And, as Loch Johnson had observed, the Republican staffers reflected the extreme conservativism of the Republican members of the committee: "Partly by design and partly by natural evolution, several of the minority staff soon became overseers (not to say obstructors) of the majority staff,

rather than devoting their time toward the monitoring of agency programs." [64] The only area where partisan distinctions were kept out was
on the subcommittee that did budget oversight. As chief staffer in this
area James Bush was permitted to hire three intelligence professionals.
A senior staffer on the committee observed: "He [Jim Bush] couldn't
bring in someone and train them. You have to hit the ground running." [65] Thus, although the Boland committee staff was officially
listed as nonpartisan, in reality there were clear partisan distinctions
among most of the staff.

The Boland committee's staff was much smaller than the Senate
committee's. The Boland committee had a staff of about twenty while
the Senate staff exceeded fifty. While senators hired designees responsible to them there was no such system on the House side. The only
"designee" on the House side was Chief Counsel Michael O'Neil,
who was close to Chairman Boland. While many of the Senate staffers
had been staffers on the Church committee, no Nedzi or Pike committee staffers were hired by the Boland committee. The staff recruited by
the Boland committee tended to be people who had served in the intelligence community. As one Democratic member of the committee observed: "The staff is very closely tied to the intelligence community.
Sometimes they are unwilling to challenge them directly. I don't buy
the argument that you need experts in this area because you don't need
that to do a good job. You can learn." [66] The danger exists that staff
members might be "co-opted." In a few cases staffers came to the
Boland committee from the intelligence community, served on the
committee, and then returned to another intelligence position. Although the turnover in staff was not as great and the intelligence community ties not as blatant in the House as in the Senate, the danger of
a co-opted staff is real.

Two of the most aggressive staffers on the Boland committee were
Loch Johnson and Dianne La Voy, both veterans of the Church committee staff. La Voy was the author of a 1982 study critical of the
performance of the U.S. intelligence community in Central America.
Both staffers, backed by their respective subcommittee chairmen—Les
Aspin and Charles Rose—attempted to conduct aggressive investigative oversight on the committee. However, the Boland committee was
not prepared or willing to undertake investigative oversight, and both
staffers eventually left the committee. The anti-investigative attitude
that characterized the Boland committee shows up in comments by
Chairman Boland shortly after the committee was established. A
staffer on the new committee had proposed an ambitious investigative
agenda; Boland had strenuously objected: "This committee will not be
an inquisition like the Church and Pike committees." [67] Nor was there

any staff continuity or institutional memory from the Nedzi and Pike committees. The negative legacy of those investigative committees required that the Boland committee hire staffers who were "careful," and "responsible"[68] adherents of "institutional" oversight.

The Committee and the House

When they created the Boland committee, House members had no desire to repeat the unpleasant experience of having to rein in a renegade intelligence-oversight committee. As already noted, the House Democratic leadership and Chairman Boland worked diligently to insure that the new committee would be a representative, not a renegade, committee. In its eight-year history, the chairman and the committee lost only once on the floor of the House, when the Ashbrook amendment to the Agent Identities Bill was passed on September 23, 1981, by a vote of 226 to 181. Special circumstances contributed to this lone committee setback. Representative Ashbrook, a conservative Republican member of the committee, and his allies on the House floor transformed the vote into an emotional appeal to avenge the murder of CIA agent Richard Welch. The American Civil Liberties Union, Philip Agee, and the magazine *Covert Action* were all attacked by name as deliberately endangering the lives of U.S. intelligence operatives.[69] As Representative C. W. Young observed: "What we're after today are the Philip Agees of this world. What we're doing today is announcing for all the world to see that we are going to protect the security of our nation. . . . We intend to protect those who are protecting us."[70]

The emotional appeal on this vote was so strong that, for the only time in the history of the committee, Majority Leader Wright voted in opposition to Chairman Boland. Nevertheless, only three committee members voted for Ashbrook's amendment as Republicans McClory, Robinson, and Whitehurst all voted in support of Boland's position. As one Democrat not on the committee noted in explaining why he resisted significant pressure and voted with Boland: "I gave Boland my vote on Agent Identities to show people he had support for his work in the House."[71] Thus, the Agent Identities Bill was the only occasion in its eight-year history that the Boland committee had a recommendation rejected by the House.

Far more typical of the relationship between the Boland committee and the House was the rather routine manner in which members passed authorization bills the committee brought to the floor. Also, members had the opportunity to go examine the classified annex in the offices of the House Intelligence Committee, although few ever did. In fact, when the House considered the first intelligence authorization bill on June 6, 1978, only fifteen House members had gone to examine the classified annex.[72] The annual number of visits declined in succeeding years.[73]

Why did so few members examine the classified annex? First, members were too busy. As one leading House conservative Republican not on the Boland committee noted:

> Outside of a very small handful, the Congress itself gives no oversight in this area. There is nobody up here who has intelligence oversight as one of their top twenty-five priorities. I have never gone to examine the classified annex. We are so swamped, so deluged with material, votes and paper that we don't know much beyond our own realm.[74]

As a ranking Democrat on the Boland committee observed in 1983: "Members tend to go to issue flashpoints and highly publicized areas. You don't get a lot of press now on intelligence."[75] Second, members preferred not to learn secrets in this manner. A former chairman of the House Rules Committee explained: "I never went to see the classified annex. I never wanted to know secrets. They get in the way of your ability to speak out about issues in public."[76]

Finally, and most important, the House members trusted Chairman Boland and his committee. When intelligence authorization bills would come up on the floor, members would tell Chairman Boland: "I know you spend more hours looking at this budget than we've got in any one week."[77] As one ranking southern Democratic member not on the committee commented: "I have never examined the classified annex because I trust that committee. Boland is a very respectable leader. He is not flamboyant and he is not a headline seeker."[78] Such comments were reinforced by the views of Chairman Morris Udall of the House Interior and Insular Affairs Committee:

> You need somebody looking at intelligence on a long-term, consistent, regular basis. That's what the Boland committee is doing. I have never looked at the classified annex. I have great respect and admiration for Boland. I'd worry a hell of a lot more if Boland weren't there. I think Boland would come to the same conclusions I'd come to if I were seeing the information that he's seeing.[79]

Thus it is fair to say that members of the House trusted Chairman Boland and his committee. As a representative of the House, the Boland committee had been tested and found acceptable.

Legislative proposals brought to the House floor by the committee were routinely passed, frequently by voice vote. One measure that encountered difficulty, however, was the Foreign Intelligence Surveillance Act, the first piece of legislation to emerge from the work of the intelligence investigations of 1975 to 1976. The measure passed the Senate by a vote of 95 to 1 with the only negative vote cast by Senator William Scott of Virginia, who had been named the "dumbest" member of the Senate by *New Times* magazine. (To rebut this charge Scott had called a news conference, and, as one senator noted, "Scott's rebuttal did not meet wholly with success." [80]) When this legislation came to the floor of the House on September 6, 1978, the leadership and Chairman Boland expected it to pass easily. However, Boland committee Republican Robert McClory and the Association of Former Intelligence Officers worked quietly behind the scenes [81] to ambush Boland and his committee. A McClory amendment gutting the bill passed the House 178 to 176.

After this stunning defeat Chairman Boland and the House leadership went to work. As a participant observed:

> When it came time to reverse the vote on the McClory amendment, the turning point was [after]: (1) the lobbying of the Speaker, (2) phone calls by Attorney General Bell, and (3) the involvement of Vice-President Mondale. As a result of all this, Jim Wright took the floor and urged a vote against the McClory amendment. This was a dramatic turning point. The majority leader was very persuasive and the result was a dramatic shift of the vote. Previously, the leadership had taken no role on shepherding this bill. [82]

The McClory amendment was subsequently defeated by a vote of 227 to 171 on September 7, 1978, a reversal demonstrating the use of raw power by the leadership and administration to support Boland and his committee. For its entire eight years the Boland committee had the solid support of its parent chamber.

In its relations with the House the Boland committee encountered the most difficulty with the other House committees involved in intelligence oversight, especially the Appropriations and Armed Services committees. Members of the Appropriations Committee, especially Chairman Mahon, initially opposed the creation of a permanent intelligence committee because they feared that such a committee would become an advocate of the intelligence agencies. Vice-President Mondale was personally recruited by the Speaker to come up to the Hill to reassure Chairman Mahon, and Appropriations dropped its opposition. [83]

Similarly, when the Intelligence Oversight Act of 1980 was passed and the number of congressional committees to be given covert action briefings was reduced from eight to just the two select intelligence committees, the Appropriations Committee objected. Privately the administration told Chairman Whitten that nothing would change, at least not the role of the Appropriations Committee. An exchange of letters between Chairman Whitten and DCI Turner confirmed this arrangement.[84] Although there were some difficulties in the relationship between the Boland committee and Appropriations, matters were eased somewhat by Chairman Boland and Intelligence members Burlison, Robinson, Stokes, and Young all serving on the Appropriations Committee.

A second committee that presented problems was Armed Services. Unlike the Senate, which had preserved the authority of the Senate Armed Services Committee over military intelligence, H. Res. 658 had given House Intelligence shared authority with the House Armed Services Committee over this area. This produced enormous tension and friction in 1977. As Armed Services Chairman Melvin Price noted: "They were duplicating the work we were doing. The more outlets you have, the worse it is for maintaining secrecy. You can't have two hundred to three hundred people knowing about it."[85] A senior staffer related how this situation was resolved:

> There was a question over who had jurisidiction over tactical intelligence and intelligence-related activities. It was not worked out at the staff level nor at the member level. As a result of the bickering, the Speaker called a meeting with the chairmen, Boland and Price, some members, and some staff. The Speaker said: "Gentlemen, the House resolution which passed the House and created this committee gave it jurisdiction over tactical intelligence and intelligence-related activities. The Intelligence Committee is to share this jurisdiction with the Armed Services Committee. Unless the members want to take it to the floor and change the rules creating this committee, let's get on with it. I don't want to see you again." There have been super relations ever since. There is now a fully cleared liaison from the Armed Services Committee to the Intelligence Committee.[86]

Once again the Speaker had intervened to advance the interests of the Boland committee. Throughout its life the Boland committee retained the trust and confidence of the House leadership and the House itself.

The Committee and the Senate

In its relations with the Senate the Boland committee dealt primarily with the Senate Intelligence and Senate Armed Services committees. Unlike the Senate Intelligence Committee, the Boland committee inherited no legislative agenda from the 1975–76 investigative work. On issues like intelligence charters and the Foreign Intelligence Surveillance Act, the Boland committee was content to let the Senate take the lead both in hearings and in legislative development. Here the Boland committee reacted to what Senate Intelligence was doing. Yet in one area the Boland committee did profit from the experience of the Senate Intelligence Committee. S. Res. 400 had divided budget authorization authority between the Intelligence and Armed Services committees. H. Res. 658, written more than a year later, built upon this to give the Boland committee authorization over all intelligence measures. As a result, the Boland committee, unlike the Senate committee, was able to get an overview of all U.S. intelligence activities. Moreover the Boland committee had conference meetings with Senate Intelligence only on national foreign intelligence authorizations. A separate conference had to be held between the Boland committee and the Senate Armed Services Committee with respect to tactical intelligence and intelligence-related activities. The principal reasons for House-Senate contact were thus budget authorizations and legislation affecting the intelligence community.

Although H. Res. 658 had directed the Boland committee to study the feasibility of a joint House-Senate intelligence committee, little was done to further this effort. There were considerable institutional rivalries between the two committees. One senior Boland staff member noted that the Senate designees were "irresponsible" and that Senate Intelligence members had adopted an "open mouth" policy when it came to protecting sensitive information.[87] There was little contact between either members or staff on the two committees. The following remark of a senior Boland committee Republican is typical: "Senators are spread so thinly. They take on too many responsibilities and delegate too much authority to staff members."[88] Thus institutional rivalry insured that a joint intelligence committee was not likely anytime soon.

The Committee and the Executive Branch

As with the permanent Senate Intelligence Committee, officials in the White House and the intelligence agencies had three different views of the oversight conducted by the Boland committee. First, some held the view that intelligence oversight was a dangerous risk and should not be done at all. Members of Congress were viewed as leaky sieves who could not be trusted with sensitive information. Second, others viewed the Boland committee as a necessary evil. Finally, a third view held that oversight was a positive good that held enormous benefits for improving U.S. intelligence. These views, examined in Chapter 3 with respect to the permanent Senate committee, were also held toward the Boland committee.

In addition, the Boland committee inherited the legacy of the Pike committee: that House committees could not be trusted with classified information. Chairman Boland and his committee went out of their way to prove themselves "trustworthy" overseers. And they were largely successful at accomplishing this. As a former director of the Defense Intelligence Agency who worked closely with the committee observed: "The Boland committee learned to keep secrets well. It was definitely not like the Pike committee where anytime you told anybody anything, it all ended up in the papers the next day."[89] Again and again executive-branch officials described the Boland committee as "trust-worthy."[90] As one CIA legislative counsel stated: "The Boland committee is absolutely trustworthy. We don't hesitate in giving them the most sensitive stuff. They even put in microwave surveillance to make their facilities physically secure."[91]

In attaining this trust, however, the Boland committee paid a heavy price. The concern for security led to the creation of an airless environment in which the committee became almost totally dependent upon the executive branch for all its information. For example, the committee did not use basic tools available to all congressional oversight committees: the investigative capacity of the General Accounting Office and the expertise developed at the Congressional Research Service.[92] Representative Lee Hamilton, a member of the Boland committee and chairman of the committee after Boland, described this unique situation and its implications:

> Look, the intelligence committees operate in a way that no other committees of the Congress operate. By that, I mean that almost the sole source of their information is the intelligence community. Those committees have almost no way of counterbalancing that information. If we have somebody giving us testimony with regards to education or Medicare or foreign policy, we can always counterbalance that with additional information. But the intelligence committees are dependent upon what the intelligence community says to the committees. Now there's a great deal of skepticism and even cynicism sometimes by some members, and on the other hand there is a total acceptance of what the intelligence community says by other members. But you do not operate on the intelligence committees in the same kind of forum that you operate on in any other aspect of American policy making.[93]

Thus in a very real sense intelligence overseers on the Boland committee were the captives, even if willing, of those they were overseeing.

Nonetheless, for the first four years of the Boland committee, this model was broken repeatedly by Representative Les Aspin and his Subcommittee on Oversight, which as Loch Johnson observed Aspin used to conduct vigorous public oversight of the intelligence community. Aspin was very public in both his praise and criticism of U.S. intelligence. He sought to make his subcommittee "a conspicuous in-box for the whistleblower."[94] At times, as Johnson noted, "the agency [was] skillful at footdragging."[95] Aspin was willing to do battle with intelligence officials to get the information he desired. It is not surprising that such actions made executive-branch officials uneasy and that they breathed a sigh of relief when Aspin left the committee.

Thus from its creation the Boland committee sought to prove to the executive branch that, unlike the Pike committee, it could be trusted with classified information. But the committee became almost totally dependent upon the executive branch for all the information it received. Members and staff alike described their access to sensitive information as "incredibly extensive."[96] In such an atmosphere it is not surprising that the Boland committee increasingly adopted a supportive role toward the intelligence community.

What was surprising was that, despite the committee's demonstrations of trustworthiness, both the Carter and Reagan administrations refused to really trust the Boland committee. In the Carter administration National Security Advisor Zbigniew Brzezinski was the severest critic of congressional intelligence oversight, and President Carter shared this attitude. In the Reagan administration similar positions were taken by DCI William Casey and President Reagan. During the the 1981–84 period some members of the Boland committee were quite public in their criticism of DCI Casey (see "The Committee and the Press," below). However, this was due more to Casey being a much more convenient target than Brzezinski. In the Carter administration DCI Turner viewed intelligence oversight as a necessary evil that he could turn to his advantage. In the Reagan administration DCI Casey made no attempt to hide either his scorn for congressional intelligence oversight or his contempt for the overseers themselves. The overseers developed a similar lack of respect for Casey. Yet Casey's attitude was not his alone; it was the dominant attitude towards congressional oversight in both the Carter and Reagan administrations and was held personally by both presidents.

The Committee and the Press

The press not only stimulated action by the committee but served as a means of communication with the executive branch and the American people. Loch Johnson is highly critical of the House committee's press relations compared to its Senate counterpart's:

The Senate committee was invariably more aggressive in its response to press stories. . . . [The Senate Intelligence Committee] was prepared to probe thoroughly any serious allegations. . . . [The House committee]—while not ignoring press stories on intelligence was more inclined toward a jaded outlook on intelligence exposés. Typically, the House committee would ascertain (over a secure telephone) the agency's response to a news item; more often than not, this ended the matter. Across the Hill, the standard operating procedure of the Senate committee was to establish a task force of staff investigators, devote days or even weeks to an analysis of the allegation, and produce a formal report for the committee members.[97]

Yet Johnson's criticism may be unfair since the Boland committee was just being organized while he observed it and the Senate committee benefitted from its staff investigators who had served on the Church committee. By 1983 the two committees had reversed roles in responsiveness to the press. As Philip Taubman, who covered intelligence for the *New York Times,* commented: "The House committee is more aggressive. I find on the House side that they'll already be working on what I call about while on the Senate side they often don't know what I'm talking about."[98] For the Boland committee the press, and especially the reporting of Taubman in the *New York Times,* helped "frame the issues" to be addressed.[99]

But frequently, although the press stimulated the Boland committee to act, the committee provided little public followup. For example on June 28, 1979, the *Washington Post* reported that the Boland committee had started a formal investigation into charges that a CIA liaison officer had rifled the files of the House Assassinations Committee.[100] However, a careful examination of the public record shows that the committee never issued a final report or even commented further about these charges. Were they true? The committee never said a word. Taubman himself had a similar experience. Throughout the fall of 1981 and into 1982 his series of articles in the *New York Times* discussed how ex-CIA agent Edwin P. Wilson had used his intelligence ties to make significant profits on the illegal sale of weapons to Libya.[101] Once again the Boland committee launched a formal investigation complete with closed-door hearings. Although mention of this was made in the committee's 1983–84 annual report,[102] as Taubman noted: "I did the stories on Wilson-Terpil, and the House committee did a formal investigation. But there was never any report or recommendations from the committee. It was all very frustrating. Their attention span is short. They are spread too thin."[103] Moreover Taubman commented on the difficulty of covering the House Intelligence Committee: "The greatest irony is that the leakiest place in Washington is the Congress but not on the two intelligence committees."[104]

Despite these limitations, a symbiotic relationship developed at times, between the press and the Boland committee. For example in late September 1984 an Associated Press reporter brought the committee a manual entitled *Psychological Operations in Guerilla Warfare*. The committee found that this manual had been written by the CIA in 1983 for use in the "covert" war against Nicaragua. Words such as "neutralization" of opponents were scrattered throughout the manual. The reporter ended up with a significant story, and the committee launched a major inquiry into how this "assassinations" manual was produced.[105]

Finally, the committee sometimes made use of the press to communicate with the executive branch and the American people. For example on June 1, 1978, a Seymour Hersh article in the *New York Times* accused the two intelligence committees of being mere "rubber stamps" when it came to covert action oversight.[106] Chairman Boland replied in a letter to the editor in which he carefully delineated how the committee reviewed covert actions as well as the limits that had been placed on the committee.[107] Similarly, as tensions over Nicaragua developed between members of the Boland committee and DCI Casey, some members used the press to communicate how upset they were with the director. For example in a news article in the *New York Times* of May 14, 1984, Boland committee member Mineta severely criticized the DCI in this on-the-record quotation: "We've dug, probed, cajoled, kicked, and harassed to get facts from the CIA but Casey wouldn't tell you that your coat was on fire unless you asked him."[108] Such comments sent a very strong message to Casey, the executive branch, the American people, and even Mr. Mineta's colleagues in the House. Thus the press goaded the committee to act, served as a partner in carrying out oversight, and provided a vehicle through which members could communicate their views to the executive branch and the American people.

The Committee and Clientele Groups

The same clientele groups that sought to influence the Senate Intelligence Committee (see Chapter 3) also sought to exert influence on the House committee. The most important groups included the American Civil Liberties Union, Morton Halperin's Center for National Security Studies, the Association of Former Intelligence Officers, and the American Bar Association's Committee on National Security. The ACLU and the Center for National Security Studies exercised significant influence on the committee in the first four years of its existence. However, in the aftermath of the seizure of American hostages in Iran and the Russian invasion of Afghanistan, the AFIO and the Committee on National Security came to play increasingly important roles. It is important to keep in mind that, in comparison with other policy areas, clientele groups have an extremely limited role to play in the intelligence domain. The relationship of clientele groups to the Boland committee can be summed up in the words of a senior committee staffer: "Few people know or care." [109]

The Committee at Work

During the eight years of its existence the Boland committee released thirty-four items to the public about its work. The committee produced four biannual reports giving an overview of its oversight activities. The committee also held fifty-two days of public hearings. (The Pike committee had held twenty-eight.) Oddly, the Aspin subcommittee was responsible for twenty-two of the fifty-two days of public hearings. During its final four years the Boland committee held only eight days of public hearings. During its eight years the Boland committee issued seven public reports (four produced by the Aspin subcommittee in 1979–80). Among the reports issued by the full committee were: (1) an evaluation of U.S. intelligence performance in Iran prior to 1978, (2) a controversial report on intelligence performance in Central America whose release split the committee along party lines, and (3) an evaluation of U.S. intelligence regarding the September 20, 1984, Beirut bombing. In legislative activity the committee's public workload was "comparable to that of some so-called 'non-major' House committees." [110] Besides this public activity a considerable amount of the work was done behind closed doors.

Budget Oversight
The most effective tool Congress has for intelligence oversight is the power of the purse. When the Boland committee began its work in 1977 its power to authorize funds for the entire intelligence community was the most potent weapon it possessed. In this area the Boland committee built upon the detailed and searching budget oversight that had been conducted by the House Appropriations Committee. The budget work of the Boland committee cannot be understood without first examining the role of House Appropriations.

From 1947 to 1975 the oversight the House Appropriations Committee exercised over the intelligence community was rather skimpy. Money was appropriated in closed-door sessions with five senior members of the committee. No record of these proceedings was kept. It was rare for the annual hearings to go beyond one day. All of this was in marked contrast to the House Appropriations Committee examined in the *The Power of the Purse* by Richard Fenno. Yet intelligence was handled in a special way at the express wish of the various chairmen of the committee.[111]

In January 1975 the special treatment of intelligence appropriations ended when staffer Chuck Snodgrass was transferred from the Agriculture Subcommittee to the Defense Appropriations Subcommittee. Snodgrass was picked personally by Chairman Mahon to begin in the intelligence area the hard-nosed scrutiny of executive budget requests that the Appropriations Committee did in all other areas.[112] Snodgrass himself came from training as a budget examiner with the Bureau of the Budget. A senior intelligence overseer in the Reagan administrations's Office of Management and Budget described the philosophy Snodgrass brought:

> Chuck was sort of like OMB. OMB is the place where the rubber meets the road. Chuck did it very effectively. Chuck's approach reflects the old BOB mentality: (1) define goals, (2) define how specific programs contribute to those goals, and (3) define the alternatives that contribute to those goals. The key is cost-effectiveness and the cost-benefit ratio.[113]

When Snodgrass arrived at the Defense Subcommittee he found a lack of proper documentation. However, all that was to change quickly.

From January 1975 until January 1979 Chuck Snodgrass was "Mr. Appropriations" for the intelligence budget. Snodgrass described how he approached intelligence oversight:

> I never treated the CIA any differently from the Agriculture Department or the FDA. This gave me my moral compass. In a pure structural sense, the intelligence bureaucracy is similar to the bureaucracy found in the rest of the government. There are two major differences: (1) there is no third-party involvement, and (2) defense contractors were completely missing in terms of lobbying me.[114]

At the beginning of his tenure Snodgrass was tested by the intelligence community, as he relates:

> There was one program that broke the camel's back. There was extraordinary security. They wouldn't tell us about it. We said tell us or no money. They called our bluff. We didn't give them the money. 9:00 A.M. the next day I was briefed. This committee does not make idle threats. I was the beneficiary of fifty years of history on the Appropriations Committee.[115]

Snodgrass adopted four key procedures:

> (1) written justification books, (2) a court reporter at all hearings with written transcripts, (3) the use of Survey and Investigations staff for investigations, and (4) a written classified report given to the intelligence community at the direction of Congress.[116]

Snodgrass himself worked around the clock on oversight. He noted:

> I did massive reading. I made lots of on-site inspections. I visited major
> facilities here and abroad. Altogether I visited thirty-five countries. I fo-
> cused on big dollar action. I paid limited attention to covert action, al-
> though I did look at a few high-profile covert actions. Most covert actions
> are too ambiguous, too far away, and there's too little money involved.[117]

For both the Appropriations Committee and the intelligence community the changes inaugurated by Chuck Snodgrass were revolutionary.

When Snodgrass was fully established the Appropriations Committee carried out in the intelligence area the reduction of executive budget requests and the close scrutiny discussed by Fenno in *The Power
of the Purse*. The executive branch tried to go around Snodgrass. A
senior House Republican on the Defense Appropriations Subcommittee noted that often he himself became a court of appeals: "In fact,
it got to the point that George Bush when he was DCI was charging
over to see me once a week to complain about Chuck."[118] The executive branch also appealed to the Senate, a typical tactic described by
Fenno. Snodgrass himself observed: "The intelligence community lobbied through the Senate Intelligence Committee and staffer Danny
Childs."[119] Intelligence oversight had arrived at the Defense Appropriations Subcommittee.

Since Snodgrass left the subcommittee, the Appropriations Committee has continued to be a major, if unnoticed, player in this area.
As Defense Appropriations Subcommittee Chairman Joseph Addabo
observed in 1983: "We have pointed out to the executive branch that
we have to dole out the dollars to them and we expect to be privy
to the same information that the Intelligence Committee receives.
99.9 percent of your work in this area is never known. We have no
leaks."[120] Snodgrass's two biggest contributions were: (1) the establishment of a written record against which subsequent community performance could be assessed, and (2) the creation of budget categories
so that the Appropriations Committee could examine the entire intelligence budget. Snodgrass divided intelligence into "national foreign
intelligence," controlled by the DCI, and "intelligence related activities" (changed in 1980 to "tactical intelligence" and "intelligence-
related activities" controlled by the Secretary of Defense). Snodgrass
demanded and got written justification books and was not loath to play
one intelligence agency off another. As Admiral B. R. Inman, the former deputy director of central intelligence, observed:

> Chuck Snodgrass was good for the oversight process. He had enormous
> energy and he was a hard worker. He used the investigations teams to great
> effectiveness. Also, he loved to ambush you. He brought out reports at

hearings that neither the members nor the witnesses had seen. There were *no* checks and balances on Chuck Snodgrass.[121]

The Boland committee was able to build on the foundation established by Chuck Snodgrass. After Snodgrass, the executive branch took Congress very seriously when it came to the power of the purse.

For its entire history the Boland committee exercised budget oversight through the Subcommittee on Program and Budget Authorization. From 1977 to 1980 Representative Bill Burlison chaired this subcommittee. Following Burlison's defeat in 1980, Chairman Boland himself chaired it from 1981 to 1984. Burlison and Republican Kenneth Robinson—who served on the subcommittee from 1977 to 1984—were also members of the Defense Appropriations Subcommittee. They brought the same approach to budget authorization on the Boland committee that they had seen Chuck Snodgrass use on Appropriations. Boland and Young also served on the Appropriations Committee, so this committee was well-represented on the Boland committee. The Boland committee's budget oversight was so thorough that a senior member of the Defense Appropriations Subcommittee noticed in 1983 an increasing tendency of his subcommittee to defer to the Boland committee: "Our subcommittee has backed off and done less as the Boland committee has become more important. My own view is that if you've got a committee dealing day in and day out with intelligence, that's the way it should be." [122] Thus the Boland committee had become virtually an extension of House Appropriations.

In conducting budget oversight the Boland committee had responsibility over national foreign intelligence, tactical intelligence, and intelligence-related activities. Each year the committee conducted two full months of budget hearings, with two main thrusts: (1) national foreign intelligence, and (2) tactical intelligence and intelligence-related activities. The committee reviewed the budget line by line and had access to the justification books developed by Chuck Snodgrass. By 1983 the Congressional Justification Books exceeded six feet on the shelf. As an intelligence community budget staffer observed: "We have to justify every line in the budget, and we do." [123] To assist in this area the Boland committee hired four professional staffers with previous experience in the intelligence community. The intelligence agencies and programs were divided between the staffers. The four staff responsibilities were: (1) supervision of the subcommittee staff, the Intelligence Community Staff, the CIA, and covert actions; (2) technical programs; (3) the entire tactical program plus NSA; and (4) general Defense, State, DOE, Drug Enforcement, FBI counterintelligence, and foreign intelligence. Although staff had a critical role, neither the subcommittee nor the full committee merely rubber-stamped the work of the staff.[124] The budget oversight done by the Boland committee was in sharp contrast to the oversight from 1947 to 1974.

In the budget area the Boland committee and its Senate counterpart brought into play the model set forth by Richard Fenno in *The Power of the Purse*. The House committee went over the intelligence budget in great detail and tended to reduce budget requests while the Senate committee took a more general approach to serve as a court of appeals for executive-branch officials upset at cuts made by the Boland committee. House and Senate members and staff claimed they won in conference. Since all of the appropriate figures remain classified, it is impossible to say who really won.[125]

Views were mixed on the impact of all this budget oversight. A director of one of the nation's largest intelligence agencies saw some definite benefits: "It forces us to recognize that we have to have priorities and can't do everything we'd like to. Prioritization is something the House and Senate committees have forced us to do."[126] At the same time a senior budgeter on the Intelligence Community Staff saw negative implications: "The staffers have tremendous influence and power. They tell us where to put people and that sort of thing. They are intruding into the DCI's prerogatives. This is micromanaging at its worst."[127] Regardless of how its budget work is assessed the Boland committee made itself a player whose views and positions the intelligence community took quite seriously.

Covert Action Oversight

Also behind closed doors the Boland committee reviewed covert actions proposed by both the Carter and Reagan administrations. Regarding covert action the Boland committee had special responsibility but some very severe restrictions. Prior to 1980 eight congressional committees were briefed on covert action. However, the Intelligence Oversight Act of 1980 officially restricted covert action briefings to just the House and Senate intelligence committees. In addition, the executive branch did not have to gain approval from the congressional overseers, merely inform them.

In conducting covert action oversight the Boland committee employed all members of the committee plus six staffers cleared for covert action briefings. The process began when the president signed a "finding" in which he gave his approval to the proposed action. The finding was brought to the two intelligence committees the same day. Within one or two days those staff members who had been cleared were briefed. Within a week the members themselves were briefed. As a senior CIA official in the Reagan administration observed: "This is not after-the-fact oversight. It is current oversight. It is pre-action oversight." [128] But, once the Boland committee was "informed," members were seriously restricted in what they could do. Member approval was not needed for the covert operation to proceed. Member options toward covert operations they opposed included:

> (1) convincing the president not to go forward, (2) informing other parts of the Congress or the public in an effort to increase opposition to the operation, (3) restricting funding, or (4) limiting the president's authority to order covert action operations. [129]

In real life, however, the members could do very little except reveal the operation to the public and run the risk of sanctions or even expulsion from the House. A senior Democrat on the Boland committee expressed his frustration:

> Some covert actions are necessary in this kind of a world. The bureaucracy follows its leader. If you know which way the president is leaning, you will know which way the bureaucrats will lean. Congress has an extraordinarily important role to play in giving a fresh perspective. The most important change that could be made is to have the Congress advised when the action is considered and not limit its role to when the operation has been decided on. Some in the executive branch look upon the Congress as an obstacle to be overcome rather than as a partner to be engaged. [130]

For most of its history the Boland committee gave clear majorities approving proposed covert operations. This was partly due to the way the committee was stacked. The Republican members were staunch supporters of all covert actions, and they were able to carry those Democrats deferential to presidential leadership in this area. As a committee critic of covert action observed: "The objectors are outnumbered just about every time. When I object, when the others object, we don't expect to win. I just want to preserve my personal integrity." [131] In its oversight of covert action the committee tended to be a supporter and advocate rather than an objective evaluator.

Ironically, the committee publicly opposed only one covert operation: the U.S. involvement in Nicaragua. Even here the committee and its chairman acted only when events compelled them. On November 8, 1982, *Newsweek* magazine ran a cover story on "America's Secret War" against Nicaragua. The article provoked a response in the House led by Representative Tom Harkin who introduced an amendment calling for the prohibition of all further funds for covert actions in Nicaragua. On December 8, 1982, Chairman Boland addressed the House with respect to the Harkin amendment. Boland stated that he himself and the members of the Intelligence Committee were concerned about the news stories on Nicaragua appearing in *Newsweek, Time,* the *New York Times,* and the *Washington Post.* [132] Boland observed that the House had already passed in the classified intelligence authorization annex language that prohibited the executive branch from using funds "to overthrow the government of Nicaragua or to provoke a military exchange between Nicaragua and Honduras."[133] He asked the House to substitute this language for the Harkin amendment and to trust him and the Intelligence Committee to see that it was obeyed by the executive branch. Members of the House then did just this by publicly passing what they had already passed in secret. This first "Boland amendment" was approved by a vote of 411 to 0. The *New York Times* observed later that such a step was both "unusual" and unprecedented.[134]

In taking this action Boland was attempting to fashion a compromise in an area in which there were considerable and emotional differences of opinion. House liberals such as Harkin, fearing that Nicaragua could become another Vietnam, sought to terminate all U.S. aid to opponents of the Nicaraguan government. House conservatives and the Reagan administration, greatly concerned about the growth of Soviet influence in Nicaragua, saw a serious threat to all of Central America.[135] The House Democratic leadership sought to forge a compromise with the administration. Majority Leader Wright and Boland committee members Young, Robinson, and McCurdy—along with Chairman Boland himself—were all very active in this effort to work out an agreement between the branches.[136]

Unfortunately for the administration the opposition forces that the United States was supporting subsequently announced that their only goal was to "overthrow" the Nicaraguan government. In light of such statements, made repeatedly by Contra leaders to American newspaper and television reporters, Chairman Boland and the Democratic members of the Intelligence Committee believed that the executive branch had flouted the expressed will of the Congress. Boland introduced a new amendment, similar to the earlier Harkin amendment, proposing to prohibit all covert funds to the Nicaraguan opposition. This amendment was passed by the House on July 28, 1983, by a vote of 228 to 195, and the committee split along party lines. Chairman Boland proceeded judiciously, acting to terminate aid to Nicaragua only when it was obvious that the will of the House was being flouted.[137] This was the only occasion in its eight-year history when a majority of the commitee opposed a covert action.

Legislation

The Boland committee's legislative work was characterized by two trends: (1) reaction to initiatives first undertaken by either the Senate or the executive branch and (2) legislative advocacy for those the committee was charged with overseeing. It is not surprising that the Boland committee was reactive. Unlike the permanent Senate Intelligence Committee, the Boland committee had to begin from scratch on legislation. The Senate committee had inherited a legislative agenda based on the work of the Church committee; the Boland committee had no such inheritance. Nor is it surprising that the Boland committee became a legislative advocate for the intelligence community. Institutional overseers view the oversight relationship as a partnership and, with this kind of mindset, members and staff of the Boland committee saw legislative advocacy as a proper oversight function.

In its final biannual report the committee looked back with pride at what it considered its four major legislative achievements: (1) the Foreign Intelligence Surveillance Act of 1978, (2) the 1980 Classified Information Procedures Act ("Graymail"), (3) the Intelligence Identities Protection Act, and (4) the 1984 revisions to the Freedom of Information Act exempting CIA operational files.[138] With the exception of FISA, the product of a process begun with the Church committee, the proposals were part of an executive-branch wish list. But the committee's legislative advocacy did not stop here. In its last report the committee noted: "Since its inception, this committee has made every effort to provide legislative support to the intelligence community whenever such support seemed warranted." [139] To the Boland committee such support was often warranted, as the committee reported:

> Although the total budget for U.S. intelligence activities remains classified, the amount of money authorized and appropriated has risen appreciably over the past few years. That increase has been necessary to enable the intelligence community to adjust from a prolonged period of cuts and freezes in the wake of the Vietnam War and to meet expanding requirements.[140]

In addition, the committee claimed credit for passage of bills that obtained: (1) a new CIA building, (2) a new DIA analytic center, (3) the freeing of CIA security officers from internal U.S. prohibitions,[141] (4) the strengthening of the CIA's retirement and disability system, (5) the restriction of CIA "whistle-blowers," (6) the prohibition of the GAO from auditing sensitive CIA files,[142] (7) incentives for NSA linguists, and (8) pay benefits for intelligence agents abroad similar to those of the Foreign Service.[143]

Moreover the Boland committee was always ready to protect its agencies on the floor of the House. For example on December 1, 1980, the House considered H. R. 5935, the Federal Privacy of Medical Information Act. Led by a unified Boland committee, the House voted 259 to 97 to give the intelligence community freer access to medical records. On June 23, 1982, the House—again led by a unified Boland committee—voted 353 to 57 to exempt all intelligence research funds from H. R. 4326, the Small Business Research Funds Act. Thus the Boland committee compiled a record of unblemished legislative support for the agencies it oversaw.

Evaluation of the Boland Committee

In contrast to all the excitement and controversy that surrounded the Nedzi and Pike committees, the Boland committee was rather a bland affair. Yet it was successful in establishing an intelligence oversight vehicle for the House. The Boland committee had to start from scratch in 1977 and, due to the leadership of Chairman Boland and the cooperation of the committee members and staff, the House had an oversight entity comparable to the Senate's. Learning from the experience of the Senate, the House gave the Boland committee budget authorization authority over the entire intelligence community. The committee, then, was able to use the most important weapon the Constitution gives to Congress: the power of the purse. For eight years Boland led a committee that remained together and conducted oversight on a nonpartisan basis, retaining the confidence of the House leadership and the House itself.

As a congressional overseer the Boland committee employed the institutional oversight model. The committee therefore sought to become a partner of the executive branch and an advocate for the intelligence community. This evolution was due to both education and co-option. Interestingly this is an area in which very few outside parties are visible or have influence. It is in reality a closed shop or oversight conducted in a cul-de-sac. The consistent support the committee received on the House floor indicated that it retained the support of its parent chamber. The Boland committee was a duly authorized committee, and the type of oversight it conducted won the approval of its parent chamber. Unlike its two predecessors, the Boland committee did not become a renegade.

Still, in some significant areas, the Boland committee failed to protect the public interest as effectively as it might have. The committee failed to communicate much information to the public about this vital area. Although the committee was stimulated by news stories to investigate, often there was little public follow-up beyond the mere fact that the committee was conducting an investigation. Also, the committee's failure to use such tools as the General Accounting Office or to listen to critics of intelligence meant that of necessity it would provide supportive oversight. In addition the limitations imposed on the committee on what it could do with information about proposed covert actions meant that even when the committee was informed there was little it could do to stop an ambitious executive.

Perhaps the greatest accomplishment of the Boland committee was its ability to conduct intelligence oversight for eight years without self-destructing. The committee demonstrated that it could keep secrets and be responsible. In the end the Boland committee had established the kind of foundation for House intelligence oversight that the Church committee had established for the Senate Intelligence Committee. According to H. Res. 658 members on the Boland committee could serve for no more than six years. Because of the closed-door nature of intelligence oversight, this limitation on service was a useful check to try to avoid co-option. Altogether the fourteen members of the committee represented only 3.2 percent of the entire House membership. At the end of 1984 seven of the fourteen members of the Boland committee had to step down because of this limitation. The retiring members left for their successors a viable vehicle for conducting oversight in this area. Intelligence oversight was finally a reality in the House of Representatives.

6 Congress and Intelligence, 1985–89:

A Look Back and a Look Ahead

It is now June 1989. Almost five years have passed since the events described in Chapters 3 and 5. In this interim much has occurred in the intelligence area. The Senate Intelligence Committee has had two new chairmen and sixteen new members. Since 1987 Senator David Boren (D., Oklahoma) has served as chairman, and he can remain in this post through 1992. The committee has retained its eight-to-seven party ratio and has emerged as a force to be reckoned with in national security. The House Intelligence Committee has had three chairmen in the past five years and will have another in 1991. Twenty-three new members have been appointed to the committee since 1984. The membership has been expanded so that the Democrats now possess twelve seats and the Republicans seven. The staff director and chief counsel remain the same two who were appointed in 1977. With all of the changes at the top, the House Intelligence Committee has lacked the stability and clear sense of direction given by its first chairman, Representative Boland. Both committees have continued to give considerable attention to budget oversight and covert action, and both have continued to practice institutional oversight.

However, the most significant development in intelligence oversight since the end of the Church and Pike investigations began to unfold at the White House on November 12, 1986. For the first time congressional leaders were told that the United States had secretly shipped weapons to Iran. Emerging from the White House, House Intelligence Committee member Dave McCurdy stated: "It's one of the dumbest things I've ever heard of. If Jimmy Carter pulled that stunt, he would have been hung from the rafters."[1] On November 13, President Reagan gave a nationally televised address to reassure the American people that the United States had not tried to ransom hostages with arms shipments. On November 19, the president held a nationally televised news conference to make the same point. But these efforts at damage control entered a new dimension when the president and Attorney General Edwin Meese announced on November 25 that profits from the sales of arms to Iran had been diverted to U.S.-backed forces opposing the Sandinista government of Nicaragua.

A little more than a decade had passed since the intelligence investigations of 1975 to 1976. Again, the United States undertook a major examination of U.S. intelligence activity. On December 1, 1986, President Reagan signed Executive Order 12575 establishing a three-member special review board headed by former Senator John Tower to investigate activities of the National Security Council with respect to the sale of arms to Iran and the diversion of funds to the Nicaraguan opposition. The Senate and House also established select investigative committees to look into the situation. The Senate committee, chaired by Senator Daniel Inouye, and the House committee, chaired by Representative Lee Hamilton, conducted a joint investigation into what became known as "the Iran-Contra Affair."

Following the conclusion of their investigations, congressional intelligence overseers took steps to improve the mechanisms through which they exercise authority. Although the Congress failed to enact legislation that built upon the recommendations of the Iran-Contra investigating committees, on August 7, 1987, President Reagan made an agreement with the two intelligence committees in which he pledged to establish a new relationship with the Congress. As already noted, similar steps were taken in 1980 and 1984 when the executive had failed to inform congressional overseers of activities in Iran and Nicaragua. The invitation to struggle which the Constitution extends to both the executive and legislative branches was accepted by both in the investigations of the Iran-Contra Affair. The very nature of constitutional government in the United States is such that, if the past is any guide, this struggle will continue.

The Durenberger and Hamilton Committees: 1985–86

The Senate Intelligence Committee: 1985–86
As 1984 ended a major reshuffling occurred on the Senate Intelligence Committee. Nine new members joined the fifteen-member committee. Senator David Durenberger (R., Minnesota), who had been a committee member since 1979, became the new chairman while Senator Patrick Leahy (D., Vermont) became vice-chairman. Realizing that he had only two years to be chairman, Durenberger decided to redirect the committee, to shake things up. First he abolished all of the subcommittees; all committee business was to be conducted at the full

committee level, enabling all the new members to learn about intelligence. Durenberger also hoped this would restore member interest and participation. At the same time he wanted to prevent members from developing power bases at the subcommittee level as Senator Wallop had just done with the Budget Subcommittee in the preceding Congress. Second, Durenberger purged the most extremely conservative members of the staff. Most prominent among these was Angelo Codevilla. Durenberger hoped to restore the staff to what it had been in the days of the first chairman, Senator Inouye. He envisioned a staff that would work together on committee business, not engage in personal work for the members, one that would eschew partisan political activity.

Besides these organizational changes Durenberger also sought to establish a new and more cooperative relationship with the executive branch primarily by means of an annual strategy report to be prepared by the intelligence community. Patterned after the annual Defense Posture Statement, this report would annually set forth a coherent set of guidelines for the intelligence community. It would address the following questions: (1) What are the country's intelligence needs for the next five to ten years? (2) How are we going to achieve them? (3) What are our priorities? and (4) What are our shortfalls? Durenberger saw such a report as a vehicle to strengthen the hand of the director of central intelligence. It would give the DCI clearer power over the various entities that make up the intelligence community and would force the intelligence community to look at itself and its problems from a broader and longer-term perspective. During Durenberger's two years as chairman, one intelligence strategy report was produced.[2]

Besides its continuing review of the intelligence community's budget and covert actions, the Durenberger committee also issued three significant public reports. On November 1, 1985, it released a staff report entitled *The Philippines: A Situation Report* highly critical of President Marcos and his government. It helped contribute to growing congressional pressure on the Reagan administration to support a noncommunist democratic alternative to Marcos. In addition the committee issued two reports dealing with counterintelligence. In May 1985 it issued a report entitled *Soviet Presence in the U.N. Secretariat* detailing how the Soviet Union used its citizens who worked for the U.N. to advance Soviet foreign policy and intelligence objectives. On October 3, 1986, the committee issued *Meeting the Espionage Challenge: A Review of United States Counterintelligence and Security Programs*. Ironically, DCI Casey strenuously opposed the public release of this report. He believed it would provide the Soviets a roadmap to exploit U.S. vulnerabilities. Yet this report was crucial for building broad support for doing something about foreign spying directed against the United States. The report helped to challenge U.S. policymakers to respond to this threat. Instead of making a political issue out of the Reagan administration's failures in counterintelligence, the committee worked hard to build a bipartisan consensus so that firm action could be taken. This effort paid off when the United States was able to expel more than eighty senior KGB officials in the United States during the imbroglio that followed the arrest of journalist Nicholas Daniloff. This extraordinary decapitation of the Soviet intelligence apparatus in the United States and an overall reduction of Soviet presence was due, in large part, to the unrecognized work of the Durenberger committee.[3]

Despite these substantive accomplishments the Durenberger committee encountered serious problems in its relationship with the executive branch. There were three key reasons for this. First, within Washington, Senator David Durenberger had to contend with the widespread perception that he was a "flake." Dealing with serious personal and family problems, Durenberger shocked outside observers with the candor of his public statements. For example, the *Almanac of American Politics 1988* compared Durenberger's candor to "the argot of a situation comedy supporting actress being interviewed on 'Entertainment Tonight' " and telling all.[4] Philip Shenon noted in the *New York Times*: "While such candor has helped make Mr. Durenberger one of the most popular elected officials in Minnesota, it has also prompted talk about the lawmaker's discretion. Questions have been raised . . . about his ability to deal with sensitive government information and about his emotional health."[5] In 1986 the *Washington Times* ran two front-page articles charging that Durenberger's "chaotic personal life" had compromised his ability to serve as chairman of the Senate Intelligence Committee.[6]

After his term on the committee ended, Durenberger was severely criticized for statements he made before two Jewish groups in Florida in 1987 suggesting that Israeli spying against the United States was justified because the U.S. had recruited an Israeli military officer as a spy in the early 1980s. On April 29, 1988, the Senate Select Committee on Ethics sharply criticized Durenberger for those Florida statements, claiming that they "jeopardized the mutual confidence which must exist between the Congress and the intelligence community."[7] Unfortunately for Durenberger, his personal behavior and statements had undermined his effectiveness as chairman long before the Ethics Committee criticisms of 1988.

The second factor that adversely affected the Durenberger committee was the behavior of Vice-Chairman Leahy. When he became vice-chairman in 1985 Leahy faced a difficult 1986 reelection campaign in

Vermont. In fact Leahy was viewed as "the most vulnerable Democratic incumbent running in 1986."[8] Leahy used the Intelligence Committee as a reelection campaign prop. For example, the Congressional Quarterly's *Politics in America* commented: "Leahy made certain, with newsletters and press releases, that his constituents would know about his activities. As the ranking Democrat on Senate Intelligence, he was often visible in Vermont through his national TV appearances."[9] One senior committee staffer described the effect on the committee:

> Leahy used the statute of the Intelligence Committee to help his reelection efforts. He used the committee to get favorable media coverage for himself. He did it pretty damm well. Leahy was always in the public eye. He was always screaming on the tube. It hurt him here at the committee. Leahy violated the traditional cooperative relationship that had existed between the chairman and the vice-chairman. He enforced that on the minority staff director. He told him: "You will demand the prerogatives of the minority and you will *not* work hand-in-hand with the staff director."[10]

In 1986 Leahy won reelection with 63 percent of the votes cast. This was the first time that any member, especially any vice-chairman, had used the Senate Intelligence Committee as a reelection vehicle.

The committee's third problem was DCI Casey, who not only detested congressional oversight but worked actively to undermine the oversight process. The committee had little confidence in Casey and he had little use for either Durenberger or the committee. A good example of this state of relations is an exchange that occurred in the pages of the *Washington Post* in November 1985. On November 14, David Ottaway wrote in the *Post* that Durenberger had criticized Casey for lacking a "sense of direction" and for failing to understand the Soviet Union.[11] Although Ottaway also noted that Durenberger had defended Casey as a "professional" and "a darn good guy in that job," these compliments appeared in paragraph three of Ottaway's story.[12] Casey immediately responded with a stinging public letter to Durenberger in which he attacked Durenberger as conducting intelligence oversight in an "off the cuff" manner that had resulted in the "repeated compromise of sensitive intelligence sources and methods."[13] Then Vice-Chairman Leahy joined the debate by attacking Casey and the CIA for "yearning to go back to the good old days" when Congress had no oversight of CIA covert operations.[14] On November 20 the ombudsman for the *Washington Post* criticized Ottaway and the *Post* for publishing the initial story. The ombudsman noted that the balance of the comments Durenberger had made about Casey in front of assembled journalists "should have discouraged treating the story so one-sidedly."[15] Nevertheless the lack of trust and the animosity this incident reveals amply illustrate the hostile relationship between the Durenberger committee and DCI Casey. Throughout his chairmanship Durenberger called for a new relationship between the executive branch and Congress. This was a good suggestion, but it was an impossible time to realize it.

The House Intelligence Committee: 1985–86
As in the Senate, major changes occurred in the membership of the House Intelligence Committee at the end of 1984. Boland left the committee after nearly eight years as chairman and was replaced by Representative Lee Hamilton. The committee's size was increased to ten Democrats and six Republicans. Six new Democrats and five new Republicans joined the Hamilton committee in 1985. In keeping with what their party had done previously the five new Republican members were all staunch conservatives while the new Democratic members included a mix of both liberals and conservatives. Thus Chairman Hamilton had six extremely conservative Republicans plus three Democrats (McCurdy, Daniel, and Roe) whose defection could give the conservatives working control of the committee.

During the Hamilton years the committee continued its close and intense scrutiny of the intelligence budget. As Chairman Hamilton observed, budget "oversight was done unanimously."[16] Legislative amendments strengthening the committee's budget oversight powers were enacted into law. For example Section 502—requiring the committee to specifically authorize and appropriate all monies to be spent on intelligence or intelligence-related activities—was added to Title V of the National Security Act of 1947. In addition the DCI was now required to give prior notice to the committee before releases could be made from the CIA Reserve for Contingencies and before any reprogramming or other fund transfer could take place. In its final report to the Congress the committee noted that these changes "ensured full congressional participation in intelligence-funding decisions, enabling Congress to exercise its power of the purse effectively."[17] Moreover the new section of the National Security Act required the executive branch to give the committee prior notice whenever a covert arms transfer of a single article or service exceeded $1 million in value.[18] The committee also routinely and unanimously passed several pieces of housekeeping legislation designed to strengthen the intelligence community.[19]

But there was one, in the words of Chairman Hamilton, "problem area"[20] for the committee: covert action. As Hamilton observed:

> The Reagan administration had an inordinate amount of faith in covert actions. They loved them. [DCI] Casey loved them. The DCI does not

control the intelligence community. The DCI controls little of the budget. The DCI is second fiddle to the secretary of defense. But the DCI *does* control covert action and Casey loved covert action. The advantage of covert action is that the action can be done without the approval of Congress. A covert action "finding" doesn't need the approval of Congress. This is the big attraction of covert action to the executive branch.[21]

From 1985 to 1986 two particular covert action areas divided both the Hamilton committee and the House. What was unusual was the degree to which these disagreements were carried out in public. First, like the Boland committee before it, the Hamilton committee struggled with covert actions proposed by the Reagan administration directed against the Sandinista government of Nicaragua. Committee members divided both within the confines of the committee and on the House floor where three critical votes were taken. On April 23, 1985, by a vote of 180 to 248, and again on March 20, 1986, by a vote of 210 to 222, the House defeated Reagan administration proposals for aid to the Contras. Then, on June 25, 1986, the House reversed itself on a vote of 221 to 209, approving $70 million in non-humanitarian military assistance for the Contras.

Second, in 1986, Chairman Hamilton strongly supported legislation barring aid to Angolan guerillas led by Jonas Savimbi unless such aid was publicly debated and approved in advance by Congress. Ironically, Congress had barred all such aid to Savimbi in 1976 but had later modified the ban in 1980 and repealed it in 1985. On September 17, 1986, the House defeated the Hamilton proposal by 229 to 186. On each of these four votes the committee divided. The Republicans, joined by conservative Democrats, opposed Chairman Hamilton and the more liberal Democratic members of the committee. However, with the exception of covert action, the Hamilton committee was characterized by consensus and nearly unanimous agreement on intelligence issues.

The Iran-Contra Affair
With the November 1986 disclosures that the United States had sold arms to Iran and that some of the profits from these sales had been diverted to the Contras in Nicaragua began a period of intense investigation similar to that of 1975 to 1976. Again the president appointed an executive-branch commission; again the Senate and House appointed select investigative committees. On December 1, 1986, President Reagan issued an executive order creating the President's Special Review Board, the "Tower Commission." In an investigation lasting over ten weeks the Tower commission reexamined the National Security Council system, took testimony from fifty-six witnesses, prepared

a detailed chronology of the Iran-Contra Affair, and released a final report on February 26, 1987, with conclusions and recommendations for the president. Select committees were formed in the Senate and House on January 6 and 7, 1987. The two committees agreed to conduct a joint investigation. More than 300,000 documents were reviewed and over 500 witnesses were interviewed. The committees also conducted forty days of joint public hearings. On November 18, 1987, the congressional committees issued a joint report summarizing their findings and making recommendations.

Much of what emerged from the investigations can best be described as "bizarre." A popular conservative Republican president, who had taken a strong stance in opposition to terrorists and the Iran of Ayatollah Khomeini, had secretly sold arms to Iran, a country his own State Department had branded as "terrorist." In a speech to the nation on March 4, 1987, President Reagan acknowledged that "what began as a strategic opening to Iran deteriorated in its implementation into trading arms for hostages." [22] Speaker of the House O'Neill pointed out the stupidity of such a policy: "You let a half-dozen hostages out today because you send 5,000 tons of replacement arms to them, then the next time they need replacements all they have to do is swoop in and grab half a dozen more Americans." [23]

Besides trying to exchange arms for hostages, the president had sent a secret delegation to Tehran in May 1986 in an attempt to bring about a "new relationship" between the United States and the Ayatollah Khomeini's Iran. Led by former National Security Advisor Robert C. McFarlane, this delegation carried with it a chocolate cake in the shape of a key which had been prepared in a kosher bakery in Tel Aviv. The cake was supposed to symbolize the new relationship being established. In fact, the delegation even carried a Bible for Iranian leaders with a handwritten scripture verse by President Reagan. This mission, not surprisingly, was a dismal failure. As McFarlane commented in a cable to the White House from Tehran: "It may be best for us to try to picture what it would be like if after nuclear attack, a surviving Tatar became vice president; a recent grad student became secretary of state; and a bookie became the interlocutor for all discourse with foreign nations." [24] Later this same crew "lost" $10 million that had been solicited for the Contras from the Sultan of Brunei after an incorrect prefix was given and the money was put into the wrong Swiss bank account. [25] As Representative Thomas Foley observed: "I'm struck by the tragedy of a popular president being served or used by such an odd collection of patriotic, pompous misfits." [26]

The Iran-Contra investigations were dominated by two individuals: Ronald Reagan and Oliver North. With respect to President Reagan, the key question was the same one Howard Baker had repeatedly posed during the Senate Watergate hearings of 1973: "What did the president know and when did he know it?" In its final report the Tower commission portrayed President Reagan as "a confused and remote figure who failed to understand or control the secret arms deal with Iran, and who thus had to take responsibility for a policy that in the end caused 'chaos' at home and embarrassment abroad." [27] The Ronald Reagan described by the Tower commission could not recall what specific actions he had approved or when. He was "out of the loop," a leader in name only.

The major focus of the congressional investigation's public hearings also became "What did the president know and when did he know it?" However, unlike Watergate, the members of Congress unearthed no "smoking gun." Instead former National Security Advisor John Poindexter testified that he had not kept the president informed. The buck had stopped with Poindexter, not Reagan. As *New York Times* television critic John Corry observed, Poindexter's testimony was devastating for the congressional investigators: "He [Poindexter] looked like a high-school principal. . . . Something had happened at the hearing. The drama wasn't there. It was as if everyone was paying less attention to television." [28] By staking so much on President Reagan's conduct the congressional investigators suffered a serious loss of media and public interest after the Poindexter testimony.

Curiously, at the 1989 trial of Oliver North, new questions were raised about how detached Ronald Reagan had really been from what was going on around him. New evidence presented in North's defense seriously challenged the portrait of the president painted by the Tower commission and the Poindexter testimony. As the *New York Times* noted, "Documents and testimony at the trial contradict this picture in showing Mr. Reagan as fully engaged in the details and the strategy in the effort to help the Contras." [29] At this point it is not clear whether President Reagan's involvement will ever be totally clarified. Nonetheless, the congressional investigators had chosen to focus primarily on the question of the president's role, and the Poindexter testimony was a crippling blow.

Besides Ronald Reagan, Lieutenant Colonel Oliver North also dominated the Iran-Contra investigations. North came into this position largely as a result of his testimony before the congressional investigating committees. In July 1987 North testified for six days. A wounded and decorated Vietnam veteran, North was the only witness permitted to appear without having his testimony screened in advance. As former Congresswoman Elizabeth Holtzman noted: "Having abandoned the procedures used for all other witnesses, the committees were unprepared for his [North's testimony] and did not effectively question him or rebut his contentions." [30] And North was not a witness to take for granted. For his July congressional appearances North wore his winter Marine uniform so he could display his military decorations. In his testimony North attacked the Congress itself as being untrustworthy and defended his shredding of documents and his lying to Congress. He called for aid for the Contras and attacked the Congress for failing to support these "freedom fighters."

Wrapping himself in patriotism and the American flag, North evoked an incredible response from the American public. For example, picking up on North's "can-do" philosophy, a billboard was erected in El Centro, California, proclaiming: "Elect Lt. Col. Ollie North for President: He'll Get the Job Done." [31] In Kansas City, Kansas, a retired utility executive announced the formation of the "Oliver North for President Clubs of America." [32] And in Oklahoma City youths lined up to get "Ollie" haircuts while adults lined up to purchase red, white, and blue "Ollie By Golly" T-shirts. [33]

This tremendous public response in support of "Ollie" had its intended impact on Capitol Hill. As *Washington Post* television critic Tom Shales observed at the time:

> The committee couldn't wait to get him, and now it must have occurred to some members, it would be great to get rid of him. . . . Having read the public opinion polls and the handwriting on the TV screen and having perceived North to be a great big wow with the viewing public, the congressmen behaved as though they planned to hit him with nothing harder than a powder puff. . . . The deference was appalling. North appeared to revel in it, and cranked his righteous glow up a few notches until it looked as if he were posing for an inspirational wall hanging. . . . He invoked God a lot, eyes aglisten. The piety was sliced pretty thick. [34]

But members of Congress were not the only ones to pull their punches at North. The television networks were also very circumspect in their coverage, as Watergate sleuth Carl Bernstein scathingly observed:

> There has been very little attempt to draw the real issues of the Iran-Contra Affair in terms that might risk offending some viewers. . . . The decision by the networks not to offer gavel-to-gavel coverage of the hearings . . . said, in effect, that the issues weren't important or dramatic enough to justify keeping people away from the soaps. When the networks got back on the air, they sent us a pack of theater critics, not reporters, who assured us that Ollie was playing boffo. [35]

Ironically like the Pike committee in 1976 the congressional Iran-Contra investigators found themselves forced to justify their investigation. In their search for a "smoking gun" with respect to President Reagan and in their handling of the public testimony of Oliver North, the congressional investigators lost an opportunity to educate the American people about the real significance of the Iran-Contra Affair.

Despite these deficiencies the Iran-Contra investigators were able to compile a documentary record that not only raises serious questions about executive-legislative relations in the formulation of American foreign policy but poses a serious challenge for those who would conduct congressional intelligence oversight. Even before the congressional Iran-Contra hearings began in 1987, Senator Inouye was very much aware of the stakes involved. Comparing the Iran-Contra Affair with Watergate, Inouye observed:

> Watergate was about a botched burglary, a campaign of dirty tricks and an attempted cover-up of those miserable deeds. It was a political scandal of major proportions to be sure, but solely that: a domestic political scandal.
>
> In contrast, the Iran-Contra Affair is an international event that has consequences that go beyond our shores. It involves the constitutional relationship between the executive and legislative branches in the shaping of foreign policy, the credibility of that policy, our relations with other countries, the actions of our intelligence service and some of America's most closely held national security secrets.[36]

These issues go to the very core of the Iran-Contra Affair.

What did the Iran-Contra investigators unearth? Since the creation of the CIA in 1947, the executive and legislative branches have had a partnership on intelligence. In the beginning the Congress had been content to defer to executive leadership. However, the intelligence investigations of 1975 to 1976 were a sign that the Congress no longer was content to defer to the executive and that it wanted to be a more equal partner. Therefore Congress created such structures as the covert action "finding" to ensure clear lines of responsibility and accountability. In its inquiry into assassination attempts the Church committee had not been able to fix responsibility because there were no such standards. Since 1976 all of the congressional intelligence overseers had sought to make certain that this type of situation did not arise again.

However, in the Iran-Contra Affair, the Reagan administration ignored these structures. In fact the Reagan administration actively sought to both undermine and destroy the accountability standards built up so carefully and painstakingly by congressional intelligence overseers since 1976. For example in a nationally televised address responding to the Tower commission's report President Reagan stated:

> One thing still upsetting me, however, is that no one kept proper records of meetings or decisions. This led to my failure to recollect whether I approved an arms shipment before or after the fact. I did approve it; I can't say specifically when. Well, rest assured, there's plenty of record-keeping now going on at 1600 Pennsylvania Avenue.[37]

Despite President Reagan's soothing words, the failure to keep adequate records was not inadvertent.

The Reagan administration played fast and loose with the requirements for covert action findings. As already noted, covert action findings were to be carefully recorded, and the two intelligence committees were to be informed as soon as possible. In extraordinary circumstances the "Gang of Eight"—the majority and minority leaders of each chamber and the chairmen and ranking minority menbers of the two intelligence committees—could be notified in Congress. However, as the Tower commission reported, the Reagan administration introduced some novel dimensions to covert action findings. In Iran-Contra, President Reagan had approved one action after it occurred.[38] Findings were supposed to be approved before, not after, the fact. On another occasion, the president had made a "mental," not a written, finding.[39] Furthermore on January 17, 1986, the president signed a covert action finding which deliberately ordered the DCI not to inform the Congress about the finding.[40] Testifying before the Tower commission on February 20, 1987, President Reagan stated: "I cannot recall anything whatsoever about whether I approved replenishment of Israeli stocks around August of 1985. My answer therefore and the simple truth is, I don't remember—period."[41] Such a situation should not have occurred. President Reagan is the individual responsible for this failure. This was not merely a case of poor record keeping; the Reagan administration simply refused to follow the rule of law.

In their final report the Iran-Contra congressional committees commented on the misuse of findings:

> The findings process was circumvented. Covert actions were undertaken outside the specific authorizations of presidential findings. At other times, covert actions were undertaken without a presidential finding altogether. Actions were undertaken through entities other than the CIA, including foreign governments and private parties. There were claims that the findings could be used to override provisions of the law. The statutory option for prior notice to eight key congressional leaders was disregarded throughout, along with the legal requirement to notify the intelligence committees in a "timely fashion."[42]

The Iran-Contra congressional committees made nine recommendations for covert action findings.[43] These proposals were designed to codify, in legislation, agreements previously made with the executive branch but repeatedly and shamelessly violated by the Reagan administration. One proposal was that all future covert action findings were to be made in writing.[44] This had not been required before but no one in the Congress had ever expected an administration to undermine this principle with "mental" findings. The Reagan administration had wanted no partnership with the Congress in this area.

Ironically, as noted earlier, in its final report to the House the Hamilton committee had cited with pride the enactment of legislation to improve congressional intelligence oversight. For example, Section 503 of the National Security Act now required that covert arms transfers of over $1 million be reported to Congress. During Iran-Contra, two covert arms sales to the Iranians exceeded $10 million, but they were never reported to Congress. Why weren't they? The justification was that, since no one item was worth more than $1 million, Section 503 did not apply.[45] This interpretation, although technically correct, violated both the spirit and the intent of the law.

In that same report the Hamilton committee noted how it had strengthened the power of the purse for intelligence overseers. Yet even here the Reagan administration was not content to follow the rule of law. In their most chilling finding the congressional Iran-Contra investigators unearthed plans to use the profits from secret U.S. arms sales to Iran to perpetuate a self-sustaining, overseas organization that would run future covert operations by the United States and friendly countries.[46] This off-the-shelf, stand-alone entity would require no money from Congress. In fact the Congress would not even need to be told about its existence. Senator William S. Cohen (R., Maine) found this to be "perhaps the most serious revelation" to have emerged from the Iran-Contra hearings.[47] As Congressman Jack Brooks observed:

> For me the most memorable and most important moment [of the Iran-Contra hearings] came on the afternoon of Wednesday, July 8, when Colonel North revealed that he and C.I.A. Director Casey had planned to put into operation a covert "government within the government," free from the accountability that our system of government provides.[48]

A senior Senate Intelligence Committee staffer described the implications of such a mechanism:

> What we saw was evidence of a search for means to escape the Constitution, to escape the intelligence professionals, and to provide in the hands of policymakers a tool that they could use at their whim, rather than through a careful deliberative process.[49]

Such contempt for the American constitutional form of government was unprecedented.

But in the Iran-Contra Affair the most serious contempt displayed by the Reagan administration was for the truth. Representative Lee Hamilton chaired the House Intelligence Committee when allegations were made about improper activities in which Oliver North was engaged. Hamilton received assurances from two national security advisors (McFarlane and Poindexter) that North was not involved in giving military advice to the Contras.[50] In fact, at a meeting in the White

House Situation Room, North told Chairman Hamilton and the other members of the House Intelligence Committee: "I am not involved [in giving military advice to the Contras]. I am following the letter and spirit of the law." [51] As Chairman Hamilton recalled:

> This was a difficult period for me personally and for the committee. The press was writing stories about Ollie North giving military advice to and soliciting funds for the Contras. But these were unsubstantiated stories. You have unsubstantiated allegations versus direct flat denials from two national security advisors and North himself. We didn't put anybody under oath. You don't put national security advisors under oath. There is no way that oversight works unless you tell them [the overseers] the truth. I got along well with [DCI] Casey. Bill was smart, dedicated to the country, and had a sure grasp of the importance of intelligence to the national interest. He realized we needed more assets, we needed to be at the technological cutting edge, and he was genuinely upgrading intelligence capabilities. There was never a cross word between us. His great failing was the ideological passion which clouded his judgment. [At times] policy would drive Casey's intelligence. If North is correct, Bill Casey deceived me. [52]

Truth is the vital ingredient that enables oversight to work. The truth was the most serious casualty of the Iran-Contra Affair.

When the Iran-Contra committees issued their final report they did not recommend a substantial number of new laws. Legislative remedies were not what was needed. As the final report stated:

> It is the conclusion of these committees that the Iran-Contra Affair resulted from the failure of individuals to observe the law, not from deficiencies in existing law or in our system of governance. This is an important lesson to be learned from these investigations because it points to the fundamental soundness of our constitutional processes.
>
> Thus, the principal recommendations emerging from the investigation are not for new laws but for a renewal of the commitment to constitutional government and sound processes of decisionmaking.
>
> The president must "take care" that the laws be faithfully executed. This is both a moral and legal responsibility.
>
> Government officials must observe the law, even when they disagree with it. [53]

In making these suggestions the committees were calling for a genuine partnership between the executive and legislative branches, the goal of intelligence overseers since the 1975–76 investigations.

When the final Iran-Contra congressional report was released to the public, it included a minority report signed by two of the four Republican senators and all six Republican representatives on the select committees. Unlike the majority, the minority did not view the Iran-Contra Affair as involving major constitutional issues. The minority report stated:

> The bottom line . . . is that the mistakes of the Iran-Contra Affair were just that—mistakes in judgement and nothing more. There was no constitutional crisis, no systematic disrespect for "the rule of law," no grand conspiracy, and no administration-wide dishonesty or coverup. In fact, the evidence will not support any of the more hysterical conclusions the committees' report tries to reach.[54]

The minority report defended the president's primacy in the conduct of foreign affairs. Like Oliver North the minority attacked the Congress itself as untrustworthy. In fact the minority report even included an entire chapter attacking the Congress as a "leaky sieve."[55] The remedies the minority called for included the acknowledgment of presidential supremacy in foreign affairs and the requirement that the Congress, not the executive, put its house in order.[56] Although the members who signed the minority report had attended the public hearings and sifted through the evidence, their ideological blinders prevented them from fully understanding what the Iran-Contra Affair was all about.

After the Iran-Contra investigations were completed, Oliver North spoke out publicly for the first time when he delivered the commencement address at Liberty University on May 2, 1989. Liberty University's founder, the Reverend Jerry Falwell, introduced the already indicted North by comparing him to Jesus Christ: "We serve a savior who was indicted and convicted and crucified."[57] Picking up on this theme, North responded: "Those accusations [charges that he lied to Congress, etc.] are not a brand—they are an honor. God willing, with your prayers and support, we will prevail, even in Washington."[58] North also lashed out at the Congress, accusing it of betraying both U.S. servicemen in Vietnam and the Contras in Nicaragua. North stated: "We must not just choose the right president in 1988; we need a better Congress."[59] On July 20, 1988, in Oklahoma City, North went so far as to accuse the Congress of treasonous conduct: "Other people who struggle for freedom desperately want the beacon of hope from America, and yet they are being sold out by a Democratic-controlled Congress intent on ignoring the meaning of freedom."[60] Earlier, during his Iran-Contra testimony, North had been asked if there was an alternative available to the executive branch besides lying to Congress. North replied that indeed there was: "I have suggested one of those better ways. Divulge nothing."[61] North's attitude was the same one held by the key decision makers in the Reagan administration and the authors of the Iran-Contra congressional minority report. The Congress was not a partner; the Congress was the enemy.

When Ronald Reagan left the presidency in January 1989 public opinion surveys showed that his job performance rating of 68 percent was the highest given any U.S. president at the end of his term since

World War II.[62] Historian Arthur M. Schlesinger, Jr., commented on Reagan's popularity: "He's like a nice, old uncle, who comes in, and all the kids are glad to see him. He sits around telling stories, and they're all fond of him, but they don't take him seriously." [63] Yet with respect to the Iran-Contra Affair Mr. Reagan had failed miserably in fulfilling his oath of office. The sale of arms to Iran in an attempt to ransom hostages was ill-conceived and ludicrous. Also despite Reagan's reputation as the "Great Communicator" and despite his repeatedly calling the Contras "freedom fighters," the American people never saw the danger he perceived. In fact in July 1983 only 13 percent of Americans knew the U.S. government supported the Contras.[64] In April 1986 only 38 percent knew the U.S. was supporting the Contras, and only 25 percent supported giving them funds to overthrow the government of Nicaragua.[65]

In the Iran-Contra Affair, President Reagan and his administration tried to do in secret what in a democracy they could not do in public. In showing contempt for the democratic process President Reagan implemented policies that embarrassed the United States, damaged the national security, and undermined the American constitutional system. History must render a much harsher verdict on Mr. Reagan's job performance as president than the American people did in January 1989.

The Boren, Stokes, and Beilenson Committees: 1987–89

The Senate Intelligence Committee: 1987–89
In the November 1986 midterm elections the Democrats regained control of the Senate. This meant that Democrat David Boren of Oklahoma would be the new chairman of the Intelligence Committee. Boren had joined the committee only in 1985 and was its sixth ranking Democrat. The *Washington Post* described Boren as a "consensus-builder" and noted:

> Temperamentally, Boren is a cautious and conservative person anxious to strike a judicious balance between [in Boren's words] "what is appropriate legislative oversight and what is appropriate executive action. I was a governor, and I understand such things." His Senate record shows him frequently siding with Republican conservatives on fiscal and foreign policy issues. Indeed, he has been one of the most conservative Democrats on the Hill. "I expect lots of face-to-face conversations with Mr. Casey and Judge Webster," Boren said. "This is my style of operation. I tend to be a consensus-builder. And we have to rebuild a relationship of trust between the committee and the agencies." [66]

Even though it was known shortly after the November 1986 elections that Boren would be the new chairman, Senator Durenberger retained the chairmanship until January 6, 1987.

When Boren became chairman he confronted a difficult situation. The Durenberger years had been marked by constant public confrontations between the committee leaders and the executive branch. Since 1980 the committee had rapidly lost the respect and clout it had possessed under its first chairman, Senator Inouye. In addition two serious issues confronted Boren immediately after attaining the chair. First, after the Iran-Contra Affair broke publicly in late November, the committee had launched an investigation. Strongly pressed by the administration and Majority Leader Robert Dole, Senator Durenberger had pushed for the release of a report detailing what had been uncovered. On January 5, 1987, the committee voted seven to six not to release this report. What should the committee do about this?

Boren confronted a second and even more serious situation. Shortly after Boren became chairman, Senator Leahy acknowledged responsibility for leaking the suppressed Durenberger Iran-Contra report to NBC News.[67] Leahy had been vice-chairman of the Durenberger committee and was not scheduled to leave the committee until June 1987. What should the committee do about this as well? How Boren and the committee addressed these two issues would determine Boren's credibility as chairman and the committee's effectiveness as an oversight vehicle.

The committee took decisive action in response to these two problems. Chairman Boren and the committee decided to produce a new version of the Iran-Contra report. A massive effort was mounted under the direction of Sven Holmes, the new staff director and general counsel. As a senior staffer on this project observed:

> The production of the new version of the Iran-Contra report recharged the committee. It gave the committee a specifically defined task. There was a clear message to the members and all the staffers, including the designees: everybody participates, everybody has a role to play. This effort discharged properly the committee's obligation to the Senate. We needed to button up the loose ends. The revised report put us in the position of transferring the committee's work to the Iran-Contra committee.[68]

The new report was approved by a vote of fourteen to one and discharged the committee's responsibilities in this area. Chairman Boren also took decisive action with respect to Senator Leahy. Boren and Vice-Chairman William Cohen accepted Leahy's resignation on January 13, 1987. This disciplining of a member of the Senate Intelligence Committee was unprecedented.[69] Under Chairman Boren the committee was regaining the reputation and respect it had under Chairman Inouye.

Chairman Boren restored the Senate Intelligence Committee to the position it enjoyed when it came into existence in 1976. He did so by practicing consensus politics. Boren outlined the crucial actions he and the members took when he first became leader of the committee:

> At the beginning, we as a committee went on a retreat together at a CIA installation. Fourteen of us gathered for the weekend. Also, I made the budget sessions the real focal point for the committee. We use the budget process to keep the committee members both involved and informed. We regularly average thirteen to fifteen members for budget meetings.
>
> We now do quarterly covert action reviews. The regularity of the covert action reviews imposes discipline on the committee. It keeps the members up to date. It also makes the executive look at all of them. It makes the executive function better. Those covert actions that should be terminated can be identified. To be effective, covert action oversight must be systematic and regular. In 1987 we established an audit unit for the first time. This gives us an independent source of information. It has had a good deterrent effect. We regularly average twelve to fifteen members for covert action reviews.
>
> There are no leaks on this committee. We have a new discipline and rules. Senators and staff members are not allowed to take classified material or notes which they take on classified hearings outside the secure committee rooms. Our staff is compartmented. Most of the committee's votes are unanimous and the members strive for consensus.[70]

In addition Boren developed a close working relationship with Vice-Chairman Cohen.

The actions taken by Chairman Boren and his committee have made the Senate Intelligence Committee a potent overseer. One of the committee's most significant actions has been to eliminate leaks, a crucial task that the committee has done well. Also the Boren committee has used the twin vehicles of budget and covert action oversight to guide its work. The committee has five staffers on budget oversight. In the covert action area the committee has the new in-house audit unit comprising three staffers headed by a certified public accountant. During its first year the unit produced nine audits. Although most audits are focused on the CIA, the audit unit can examine any component of the intelligence community.[71]

From 1987 to 1989 the Boren committee has dealt with a wide array of intelligence issues. Like the Bayh committee, it has come to play an important part in arms control issues. One of its most significant roles was in the passage of the INF treaty. Because of concerns about the procedures in the treaty concerned with on-site inspection, the committee worked closely with the Reagan administration to eliminate potential verification problems. As a result of the committee's work the secretary of state had to return to Geneva to renegotiate portions of the treaty. However, this action ensured Senate ratification of the INF Treaty.[72]

Both Chairman Boren and Vice-Chairman Cohen served on the joint congressional Iran-Contra investigative panel. On August 7, 1987, President Reagan met with Boren and Cohen at the White House. In a formal letter presented to Chairman Boren, Reagan agreed to: (1) put future findings in writing, (?) issue no retroactive findings, (3) inform the intelligence committees of all U.S. covert actions, (4) regularly review covert actions, and (5) notify the intelligence committees within forty-eight hours of the initiation of a covert action in all "but the most exceptional circumstances."[73] Although the Congress has not yet enacted these changes in permanent legislation, the commitment of the president, supported by a vigorous and vigilant oversight committee, will go far to make sure that these promises become a reality.

Throughout his career Chairman Boren has strongly advocated a bipartisan foreign policy. In the categories used in this book, he would have to be classified as an "institutional" overseer. As chairman of the Senate Intelligence Committee, Boren has sought to make the processes of government work and supported measures to improve the performance of the intelligence community. But the addition of the audit unit to the Senate Intelligence Committee's resources gives the committee the capacity to also implement "investigative" oversight, a capacity lacking in the Senate since the days of Senator Frank Church. Under the leadership of David Boren the Senate Intelligence Committee has been restored to a position of prominence and power it has not had since the chairmanship of Senator Inouye.

The House Intelligence Committee: 1987–89
In 1987 Louis Stokes succeeded Lee Hamilton as chairman of the House Intelligence Committee. Stokes was only the second black member of Congress to serve on the Intelligence Committee (Ron Dellums had been a member of the Pike committee), and he was the first black to serve as chairman. One more Democratic seat was added to the committee. The Democrats now possessed eleven seats and the Republicans six. Five new Democrats joined the committee in 1987—with Representative Barbara Kennelly of Connecticut becoming the first woman to serve as an intelligence overseer in the House—along with two new Republicans. For the Republicans, Henry Hyde became the new ranking minority member. Hyde was vigorous in his defense of the Reagan administration both in public and behind closed doors.[74]

Stokes had a nonconfrontational leadership style. He sought consensus while Hyde relished conflict and confrontation.

Under the leadership of Chairman Stokes the committee continued to oversee the intelligence budget and review covert actions. As one member of the Stokes committee observed, "Lou focused on the budget. He was a steady chairman who worked closely with the staff to help stabilize the budget." [75] Both Stokes and Hyde served on the select committee the House appointed to investigate the Iran-Contra Affair, and both spent considerable time on this work. Still, the Stokes committee examined U.S. counterintelligence efforts, considered legislation to strengthen reporting requirements for covert actions, and conducted an examination of the FBI's investigation of dissent to the Reagan administration's policies on Central America. [76] In large part the two years Stokes served as chairman provided continuity with no dramatic changes in the committee's basic oversight approach.

In 1989 Stokes was succeeded as chairman by Anthony Beilenson of California. An additional seat was added for both parties, giving the Democrats twelve seats and the Republicans seven. In 1977 the first Boland committee had only thirteen members; in 1989 the Beilenson committee had nineteen. Two new Democrats and three new Republicans joined the committee. However, the most significant committee action in 1989 was the reappointment of Representative Dave McCurdy. In 1988 McCurdy had resigned his committee seat after almost six years of service to be more involved in Richard Gephardt's presidential campaign. In 1989 Speaker Jim Wright reappointed McCurdy to the committee as the second ranking Democrat. No member may serve on the committee for more than six continuous years, so McCurdy's reappointment means that he may serve an additional six years and that he is in line for the chair in 1991 after Beilenson's term expires.

Not surprisingly Chairman Beilenson has been placed in a rather difficult position. With only two years to serve as chairman he does not have much time to put his own imprint on the committee or to maintain credibility with the executive branch and the intelligence community. Ironically Boland served as the committee's leader for almost eight years; in the five years since he stepped down, three representatives have led the committee with another scheduled to assume leadership in 1991. The original restriction on tenure was designed to prevent chairmen and members from becoming co-opted; instead this restriction has weakened the committee by causing a lack of stability in the top position. Notwithstanding, in 1989 50 percent of the staff had been with the committee since it was created in 1977. This group included Staff Director Latimer and Chief Counsel O'Neil. As the

1980s ended the committee had a fairly stable staff but an extremely rapid turnover in its leadership.[77]

Congressional Intelligence Oversight: 1989 and Beyond

In February 1989 I returned to Washington, D.C., and met with members and staffers from both the Senate and House committees. I also spoke with officials from the intelligence community and the executive branch. What became obvious immediately was the difference in activity levels and morale between the Senate and House committees. The Senate's Boren committee is permeated by a feeling of excitement. The dominant attitude, quickly gleaned from conversations with the chairman, members, and staff is that this is a committee at the cutting edge of intelligence issues. A radically different mood imbues the Beilenson committee. The House committee is in a holding pattern. Staffers who have been with the committee since its creation in 1977 are trying to plot out what to do with their lives when a new leader assumes the chair in 1991. At the House committee there is no sense of freshness, excitement, or being at the cutting edge.[78] What does the future hold for these two committees?

When David Boren became chairman of the Senate Intelligence Committee in 1987 he still had six years of committee service left. At the end of the 100th Congress a brief challenge was made to Boren's continuing as chairman, but he easily turned it aside.[79] Boren will be up for reelection in 1990 but, since he has not forgotten his roots and his constituents in Oklahoma, he should face no serious opposition. Consequently Boren should be able to remain as chairman of the Senate committee through 1992.

Under Boren's leadership the Senate Intelligence Committee has become a major player in the national security field. Like Senator Inouye before him, Chairman Boren offers the executive branch the "carrot" of a secure committee with disciplined members and staff. At the same time his committee wields the "stick" of budget authorization enhanced by the creation of the internal audit unit.

Chairman Boren sought to advance a bipartisan foreign policy in his dealings with President Reagan and his administration. He has sought a similar relationship with President Bush and his administration. In fact by early February 1989 Chairman Boren had already had nine one-on-one conversations with President Bush.[80] Moreover, after the resignation of DCI Casey, the committee considered the nominations of both Robert Gates and Judge William Webster. Although Gates withdrew his nomination, both he and DCI Webster now occupy important intelligence positions in the Bush administration, and the Boren committee has solid relationships with each of them. Despite these close ties, Chairman Boren has shown that he is not reluctant to challenge the administration when necessary. For example on April 6, 1989, Boren publicly warned the Bush administration that a failure to keep President Reagan's promise to modernize the nation's surveillance satellites "would seriously jeopardize our own near-term national security interests and could slow down completion of a strategic arms reduction treaty."[81] Chairman Boren has shown that he can use both the carrot and the stick.

When I interviewed Boren in early February 1989 I could easily see that he thoroughly enjoys being chairman of the Senate Intelligence Committee. Although he acknowledged that he receives little political benefit from his committee work, Boren noted: "This work carries with it a lot of satisfaction although I find myself working twice as hard to serve my Oklahoma constituents."[82] Chairman Boren will continue to push for a new national system of technical means for verifying present and future arms control agreements. In addition the committee is creating a technical advisory committee, which will meet three to four times a year, to advise and update the committee on intelligence developments. The committee is also seeking to tap new academic research on issues of concern to the members and staff.[83] For the duration of the Boren chairmanship, the committee will likely remain a key player in the national security field.

For the House Intelligence Committee 1989 was the year of a major change. Congressman McCurdy became the first member who had left the committee to return. In March 1989 *The Washingtonian* magazine called McCurdy a "rising star."[84] Also former *New York Times* reporter Hedrick Smith paid McCurdy the ultimate compliment when he referred to him in *The Power Game* as "an Oklahoma Democrat who has become a respected spokesman on defense issues."[85] McCurdy, elected to the Congress in 1980, was first appointed to the House Intelligence Committee in 1983. After leaving the committee in 1988 McCurdy was tapped by then Speaker Jim Wright to return to the committee in 1989 as the first ranking Democrat behind the chairman. A source close to Wright noted why McCurdy was picked: "McCurdy knows the intelligence community. He is respected by the intelligence community. He is respected by his peers in the House. And he will be effective because he will be hitting the ground running."[86] Although Wright has been replaced as Speaker by Representative Thomas Foley,

McCurdy remains on the committee as first ranking Democrat. In a February 1989 interview McCurdy noted what he would bring to the chairmanship in 1991:

> I have served on the [House] Intelligence Committee for over five years. That and my work on Armed Services have prepared me for this position. I will give the committee a very aggressive program and a different look. I do my homework and I am willing to listen. Intelligence is a vital area. On the Intelligence Committee, I have found that no one in the executive branch has a strategic vision. There is a real correlation between intelligence, military strategy, and foreign policy. It is almost like a triangle. None of these works well without the others.
>
> Intelligence needs a global vision. Tell me about five or ten years from now. Why spend so much here? What are our priorities? What are our long-range goals? What are the targets of opportunity? What threats do we face? How will they evolve, how will they change, how should we respond? These are the questions that need to be addressed.
>
> In doing oversight we must have long-term priorities. Look at the organization. Oversight can be improved. Start with the inspector generals. Start swearing in witnesses. Start auditing things. I would like us to broaden our view. Look first at the general policy and then go from there.
>
> The budget and covert action are oversight motivators. Too often all we get are snapshots. We need to consider the long-term issues: (1) developing missions for the agencies and the intelligence community, (2) looking at how analysis is done, (3) looking at how analysis flows, (4) looking at to whom it flows, (5) looking at how it is used, and (6) looking at the relationship of analysis to priorities.[87]

Even though Representative McCurdy is still in his thirties he has an understanding of the intelligence area I rarely encountered during the course of my interviews. McCurdy could serve as chairman from 1991 to 1994. Under his leadership the House committee will be able to implement both institutional and investigative oversight. A House Intelligence Committee headed by McCurdy should neatly complement the work being done in the Senate by the Boren committee.

The Evolution of Intelligence Oversight

After a careful consideration of intelligence oversight by the Congress from 1947 to 1989 certain issues stand out not only because they are substantive but because they recur down through the years. Some are problems of governance at the very heart of what is meant by the terms "democracy," "representation," "separation of powers," and "checks and balances." Some are problems of operation in making congressional intelligence oversight a reality and not just an ideal to be attained at some later date.

The system of separation of powers and checks and balances works in intelligence as well as in more public areas. The president has enormous power over intelligence by means of the command and control inherent to the office. Still, throughout the entire 1947–89 period, congressional intelligence overseers tended frequently to defer to executive leadership even though the Congress has significant powers of its own in this area. Through its power of the purse the Congress authorizes and appropriates all funds expended on intelligence. The Congress can use this power to shape executive activity if it so chooses. Increasingly in the post–Church and Pike era the Congress has wielded the power of the purse very effectively. Meanwhile Congress has been less effective in finding a voice and influence on covert action even though, by its ability to pass legislation and the Senate's power to confirm presidential nominees, the Congress has the means necessary to check and balance executive actions.

As congressional intelligence oversight evolved from 1947 to 1989 both the executive and legislative branches were confronted with a basic question that touches on the very meaning of representative democracy. How is the Congress to conduct oversight in a policy area deemed of great importance by both branches but characterized by a legitimate need for secrecy found in no other policy area? On the one hand, if Congress conducts oversight that is too public, the oversight process itself could gravely damage vital public policy. On the other hand, if the inherent secrecy of the policy area, the lack of input from press and public, and excessive congressional concerns about maintaining security lead to truncated and ineffective oversight, then the system of separation of powers and checks and balances will not be brought into play. Consequently congressional intelligence overseers must walk a fine line to avoid either irreparably damaging a vital governmental function or becoming so weak as to be meaningless.

During the entire 1947–89 period the Congress groped to find a way to conduct just such oversight. Viewed in this way congressional oversight has evolved, especially after 1974, to a point where both chambers have permanent intelligence committees, complete with staff and files, that have developed and strengthened congressional power and authority in intelligence. But the evolution of the permanent intelligence committees and the related struggle between the two branches in this policy area brings up a problem of democratic theory with serious implications for representative democracy in the United States.

Throughout this period the executive branch, and especially the presidents, have been extremely suspicious of congressional intelligence oversight. To put it simply, the executive branch just does not trust the Congress to handle intelligence responsibly. This is true whether the president is a Democrat or a Republican or whether the president's party is in control of the Congress. Distrust and suspicion between the executive and legislative branches are inherent in all oversight relationships. However, in intelligence, the problems are much greater due to the inherent secrecy unique to this area. In other public policy areas congressional overseers can receive assistance and support from the press, the public, and clientele groups. However, intelligence oversight, as practiced by the Congress from 1947 to 1989, has been pretty much a closed shop. The overseers have worked behind closed doors—with limited input from press, public, and clientele groups— almost totally dependent on the executive branch for access to information and witnesses.

This executive distrust of the Congress has serious implications for governance. For example, a constantly repeated theme of executive-branch officials over the entire period was that the Congress was a "leaky sieve" not to be trusted with sensitive information. Members of Congress and even some congressional intelligence overseers agreed with this assessment. However, such an assertion, despite its widespread acceptance, is just not supported by the historical record. Congress is indeed a notoriously leaky institution when it comes to keeping secrets. But in the intelligence area Congress is anything but leaky. Nonetheless this negative perception has had serious effects. The executive branch has used this perception to justify severely restricting or even at times entirely withholding information from intelligence overseers. At the same time intelligence overseers are so sensitive to charges of leaking that they have insulated themselves from the personal and institutional supports that would let them become more than mere puppets of the executive branch. For "separation of powers" and "checks and balances" to work, for governance to be a reality, the Congress must be a full and equal partner of the president on intelligence. This was the system designed by the Founding Fathers. In the intelligence area from 1947 to 1989 true governance in the relationship between the branches was more ideal than reality.

Solutions

What, then, is to be done? Some have suggested that it is not appropriate for the Congress to have any role regarding intelligence. The Congress should defer totally to the leadership of the president; the national security combined with congressional ignorance of this area demand it. However, such an approach has some serious defects. First, for representative democracy to survive in the United States, the Congress must become a full partner in this area or the country runs the risk of becoming totally subservient to presidential dictatorship in these policies. Such deference to the president, characteristic of the institutional oversight the Congress practiced from 1947 to 1974, runs the risk of undermining the very pillars upon which representative democracy continues to stand in the United States. Second, the executive branch actually benefits from oversight by congressional intelligence neophytes. Intelligence is such a closed area that the national security benefits from close scrutiny by outsiders who can not only offer objectivity but suggest possible public reception to policy proposals. Sometimes such objectivity is not sought by policymakers who think they know what is best for the people. Consulting with congressional overseers is time-consuming and, at times, frustrating and messy. But democracy itself is a messy business. For representative democracy to survive, the Congress must be a coequal intelligence partner rather than a body to be avoided and denigrated.

Another popular proposal is to form a joint committee to oversee the intelligence community. Just such a proposal was advanced by the Rockefeller and Tower commissions and in the minority report of the Iran-Contra congressional committees. A joint committee, as envisioned by its proponents, would reduce the number of members and staff exposed to sensitive information. The executive branch would be more likely to trust a smaller and more secure committee. However, like the first alternative discussed above, a joint committee is not feasible. As already noted, the notion of the present committees as leaking sieves is just not true. A joint committee might indeed reduce the amount of time executive officials spend testifying before such committees, but at what cost? A small joint committee would risk becoming the closed circle of intelligence advocates that Senate and House overseers became in the committees led by Richard Russell and Carl Vinson. This is not real or meaningful oversight; it is cheerleading at best, sycophancy at worst. Moreover, the serious institutional differences between the Senate and the House demonstrated in this book would make such a committee unworkable. The American system of governmental checks and balances offered by having two committees is too precious to surrender to the executive convenience of a single joint committee.

The proposal supported most strongly by the evidence in this book is to maintain the separate Senate and House intelligence committees. Moreover these committees, to be truly effective, should incorporate both the investigative and institutional oversight models. Both models are essential to uncover abuses and deficiences and to undertake concrete and meaningful actions based on the investigative findings. The permanent intelligence committees that emerged from 1976 to 1989 implemented only the institutional oversight model. The challenge that remains is to institutionalize investigative oversight. Members of both the Senate and House must be motivated to undertake such an action. What is at stake is the survival of representative democracy in this critical policy field. The system of government devised by the Founders works, and this proposal is the only way in which separation of powers and checks and balances can be maintained and strengthened in the intelligence area.

If the institutionalization of investigative oversight is to be accomplished, several measures must be undertaken. Because the select committees are appointed by party leaders, the party leaders have the responsibility to recruit members who will take the job of intelligence oversight seriously and act responsibly. The party leaders have the key task of recruiting the right members and giving them the support they need. Moreover incentives must be given to intelligence overseers to devote the time and effort such oversight demands. There are specific ways to do this. For example, although much in the intelligence area must of necessity remain secret, party leaders can announce the appointment of members with more emphasis on the trust and responsibility that such positions carry. Party leaders could follow up by visiting overseers' home states and districts to emphasize this respect to the members' constituents. In addition, committee members might be freed from work that wastes their time and energy. For example, voting procedures in both the Senate and the House need reform. Presently, continuing and meaningless votes in both chambers show merely that members can get to and from the floor before the time for voting has expired. Time for reflection is lost as members adopt a Pavlovian mindset to merely respond to the bells. Also, both chambers need to reexamine their present committee systems. Reducing the number of committees would bring more order and efficiency to both chambers.

The chairman and committee members also have the responsibility to hire the best staff available. Staff members must be provided proper direction, and they must act responsibly. The chairman and committee members must seek out staffers with an investigative mindset. National security careerists will always be available to conduct institutional oversight, but specific actions must be taken by the chairman and other members to recruit and retain staffers with an investigative mindset. Rewards of salary and meaningful work must be built into the oversight process to attract investigative staff.

Meanwhile the press must learn to focus on more than sensationalism when it comes to intelligence reporting. Pulitzer prizes and other awards need to be given to those in the media who explain and educate and not just to those who uncover spectacular scandals. In addition, the oversight committees must be much more sensitive to their task of educating both the press and the public about intelligence issues.

As for oversight itself, the committees should demand a much more meaningful role in covert action. At present the committees are what one interviewee called "established eunuchs" in this area. An absolute veto to halt proposed covert actions should be available when a majority on either committee opposes an action. The committees should also use such basic oversight tools as GAO audits, outside experts, and critics. These are some of the measures that should be adopted to improve the intelligence oversight conducted by the Congress.

A Look Back and a Look Ahead

When the Founders wrote the U.S. Constitution at Philadelphia in 1787 they created a governmental system characterized by separation of powers and checks and balances. They deliberately incorporated a dynamic tension so that each branch might have the means and the motives to prevent any other part of the government from becoming so powerful that it might threaten the existence of American representative democracy. Following the end of World War II the national security area for the first time saw permanent nonmilitary intelligence agencies created within the executive branch. What had once been a function used only during war became in the nuclear age necessary on a daily basis to safeguard the national security interests of the United States. Moveover the rise of permanent intelligence agencies brought a whole new series of questions over competing rights and interests. How were the legitimate needs for secrecy of the intelligence agencies to be balanced against the rights of citizens to know what their government was doing in the conduct of public policy? How were the needs of national security to be balanced against the need to safeguard the rights of individual American citizens? How was the need of the president to control a vital executive function to be balanced against the need of Congress for access to the information necessary for it to not only appropriate funds but prevent the executive from misusing power?

In attempting to fashion answers to these questions, the president and Congress ran into a dispute over the control of American foreign policy, a conflict deliberately created by the Founding Fathers. As Clinton Rossiter noted in his classic study *The American Presidency*, among the roles the Constitution gives the president are chief executive, commander-in-chief of the armed forces, and chief diplomat. At the same time the Constitution gives the Congress "brakes" on presidential freedom such as the power of the purse and the ability to pass legislation.[88] The control the Congress can choose to exercise over money and legislation leads directly to conflict over primacy in foreign affairs. This conflict has characterized executive-legislative relations over intelligence policy since 1789.

Beginning in 1789 during the First Congress and continuing in succeeding Congresses, the president requested and Congress appropriated "unvouchered funds" to compensate U.S. intelligence operatives. However, in 1847, when a congressional committee sought to examine how Secretary of State Daniel Webster had made use of these funds, President Polk refused to provide the requested information and successfully asserted a claim of executive privilege. This type of conflict was deliberately created by the Founding Fathers to both separate and check power. This contest is rooted in what Edwin S. Corwin describes as the Constitution's "invitation to struggle."

From 1947 to 1989 the relationship between the executive and legislative branches in this area evolved gradually. From 1947 until 1974 was a period of benign neglect in which the Congress was content to merely gloss over the budget and not look into intelligence in any great detail. Stimulated by allegations of improprieties and illegalities, the Church and Pike committees of 1975 to 1976 inaugurated a period in which the congressional investigators adopted an antagonistic and adversarial attitude. The creation of permanent intelligence oversight committees by both houses of Congress brought about an intense educational period in which the committees learned how the intelligence community was organized, how it performed its duties, and how intelligence people operated. The intelligence committees assembled their staffs primarily from former intelligence-community people and, for the first time, searchingly evaluated budgets and programs. As the committees grew older their attitudes evolved from adversarial to supportive.

The most striking development from 1947 to 1989 is how the Congress through its oversight committees emerged as a coequal partner of the executive branch. Congressional overseers became intelligence consumers just like the president and the president's foreign policy advisors. Moreover this new equality provided the committees with the opportunity to conduct real and legitimate oversight that no other part of the American governmental system could conduct. As Chairman Bayh noted:

> I don't believe that intelligence people can see the total implications of what they are doing. We in the Congress are political animals. We know how people will respond. We might see the possibility of something going

awry that the intelligence community can't. The president can't do this kind of oversight. He's got so many other things on his mind.[89]

Thus the committees serve as representatives for both the Congress and the American people. They not only provide a check on the executive but give an additional perspective. The positive role of intelligence oversight committees is to take another look. As a senior CIA official noted, congressional oversight provides the "greatest insurance policy" for the executive branch in a crucial policy area.[90]

On November 11, 1947, Sir Winston Churchill addressed the House of Commons on the Parliament Bill:

> Many forms of government have been tried, and will be tried in this world of sin and woe. . . . No one pretends that democracy is perfect or all-wise. Indeed, it has been said that democracy is the worst form of government except all those other forms that have been tried from time to time.[91]

This book has examined the way in which Congress has conducted intelligence oversight from 1947 to 1989. In this area the system of representative democracy devised by the Founders and characterized by separation of powers and checks and balances has creaked and groaned at times but, despite its imperfections, it still works. The dream of the Founders and of individuals like Churchill endures. To keep that dream alive in the years ahead is a challenge to intelligence overseers and citizens alike.

Notes

1. Congress and Intelligence

1. *The Federalist* (Indianapolis: Modern Library, 1937), 337.
2. Ibid., 419.
3. Ibid.
4. General George Washington to Colonel Elias Dayton, 26 July 1777, original in Walter Pforzheimer Collection on Intelligence Service, Washington, D.C.
5. Interview, Walter Pforzheimer, 18 January 1983.
6. Ibid. For a modern counterpart of these confidential funds, see Section 8(b) of the CIA Act of 1949.
7. *A Compilation of the Messages and Papers of the Presidents: 1789–1897* (Washington, D.C.: Government Printing Office, 1897), 430–36.
8. Roberta Wohlstetter, *Pearl Harbor: Warning and Decision* (Stanford: Stanford University Press, 1962); also Rear Admiral Edwin T. Layton, *"And I Was There"* (New York: Morrow, 1985).
9. Interview, Clark Clifford, 27 May 1983.
10. George F. Kennan, "The Sources of Soviet Conduct," *Foreign Affairs* 25 (July 1947): 566–82.
11. Interview, Lawrence R. Houston, 28 January 1983.
12. Interview, Jack Maury, 16 February 1983.
13. Interview, Walter Pforzheimer, 18 January 1983.
14. Interview, Clark Clifford, 27 May 1983.
15. Ibid.
16. Confidential interview.
17. Interview, Robert F. Ellsworth, 23 May 1983.
18. Confidential interview.
19. Confidential interview.
20. Richard Russell to Theodore Green, 16 January 1956, in Dr. Frank J. Smist, Jr., Collection, University of Oklahoma.
21. Interview, J. William Fulbright, 26 July 1983.
22. Confidential interview; also John Herbers, "Helms Says CIA Will Cancel Some Private Subsidies," *New York Times*, 22 February 1967.
23. Confidential interview.
24. Interview, Bryce Harlow, 1 June 1983.
25. Confidential interview.

26. Interview, George H. Mahon, 19 May 1983.
27. Confidential interview.
28. Confidential interview.
29. Confidential interview.
30. Confidential interview.
31. Confidential interview.
32. Interview, Walter Pforzheimer, 9 May 1989.
33. Interview, Lawrence R. Houston, 28 January 1983.
34. Seymour M. Hersh, "Huge CIA Operation Reported in U.S. against Anti-war Forces, Other Dissidents in Nixon Years," *New York Times*, 22 December 1974.
35. Loch Johnson, *A Season of Inquiry: The Senate Intelligence Investigation* (Lexington: University of Kentucky Press, 1985).
36. Bob Woodward, *Veil: The Secret Wars of the CIA* (New York: Simon and Schuster, 1987).
37. Richard J. Fenno, Jr., *The Power of the Purse* (Boston: Little, Brown, 1966).
38. David Easton, *A Systems Analysis of Political Life* (New York: Wiley, 1965).
39. Fenno, *The Power of the Purse*, xviii–xxiv.
40. Richard J. Fenno, Jr., *Congressmen in Committees* (Boston: Little, Brown, 1973), xiv–xv.
41. Ibid., 278–79.
42. Ibid., 280.
43. John F. Manley, *The Politics of Finance* (Boston: Little, Brown, 1970), 1.
44. William J. Keefe and Morris S. Ogul, *The American Legislative Process*, 5th ed. (Englewood Cliffs, N.J.: Prentice-Hall, 1981), 169–70.
45. William L. Morrow, *Congressional Committees* (New York: Charles Scribner's Sons, 1969), 35–37.
46. V. Stanley Vardys, "Select Committees of the House of Representatives," *Midwest Journal of Political Science* 6 (August 1962): 247–65.
47. See Scher, Sharkansky, and Bibby in Journals section of Bibliography; Kirst, Henderson, and Ogul in Books section.
48. Morris S. Ogul, *Congress Oversees the Bureaucracy*, (Pittsburgh: University of Pittsburgh Press, 1976), 21–22.
49. Interview, Frank Church, 25 April 1983.
50. Confidential interview.
51. Confidential interview.
52. Allen Dulles, *The Craft of Intelligence* (New York: Harper & Row, 1965), 50.

2. The Church Committee

1. Senate Committee on Government Operations, *Legislative Proposals to Strengthen Congressional Oversight of the Nation's Intelligence Agencies before the Subcommittee on Intergovernmental Relations*, 93d Congress, 2d sess., 9 and 10 December 1974, 20–21.
2. Ibid., 3.
3. Hersh, "Huge CIA Operation."
4. William E. Colby, *Honorable Men: My Life in the CIA* (New York: Simon and Schuster, 1979); 340, 348–49.

5. Interview, Philip Buchen, 6 June 1983; One of the members of the Rockefeller commission was Ronald Reagan. This was the only formal foreign policy–related position Reagan held prior to assuming the presidency six years later.
6. Colby, *Honorable Men*, 401–2.
7. Seymour Hersh, "Democrats Vote Wide CIA Study by Senate Panel," *New York Times*, 21 January 1975.
8. Ibid.
9. *Congressional Record*, 94th Cong., 1st sess., 21 January 1975, 1434.
10. Ibid.
11. Ibid.
12. Martin Tolchin, "Senators Assail Anarchy in New Chamber of Equals," *New York Times*, 25 November 1984.
13. Interview, William G. Miller, 3 December 1984.
14. Two interest group ratings are used in this book. The ADA rating is compiled yearly by the Americans for Democratic Action, founded in 1947 by a group of liberal Democrats including Senator Hubert Humphrey and Eleanor Roosevelt. The NSI (National Security Index) rating is also compiled yearly, by the American Security Council. Founded in 1965, this conservative organization is especially concerned with defense and foreign policy issues. The ratings given by these groups reflect the number of times a member of Congress has agreed with the group's position during key floor votes. Thus a rating of 100 percent means that the member voted the group's position all the time, while a rating of 0 percent means that the member never voted in support of that group's position.
15. Michael Barone, Grant Ujifusa, Douglas Mathews, *Almanac of American Politics 1976* (New York: Dutton, 1975); 396.
16. Confidential interview.
17. Interview, Frank Church, 25 April 1983.
18. Interview, William G. Miller, 7 December 1984.
19. Ibid.
20. Interview, Hugh Scott, 15 September 1983.
21. Ibid.
22. *Congressional Record*, 94th Cong., 1st sess., 27 January 1975, 1434.
23. Interview, Mitchell Rogovin, 28 January 1983.
24. Interview, Michael Madigan, 18 July 1983.
25. Confidential interview.
26. Confidential interview.
27. Confidential interview.
28. Hersh, "Democrats Vote Wide CIA Study."
29. Interview, Michael Madigan, 18 July 1983.
30. Confidential interview.
31. Interview, Frank Church, 25 April 1983.
32. Ibid.
33. Ibid.
34. Christopher Lydon, "Frank Church Is Moving Center Stage," *New York Times*, 15 June 1975, sec. 4.
35. Interview, Frederick A. O. Schwarz, Jr., 24 May 1983.
36. Ibid.
37. Interview, Frank Church, 25 April 1983.
38. Ibid.

39. Confidential interview.
40. Nicholas Horrock, "Senator Church's Committee: More Than One Voice," *New York Times*, 25 April 1976, sec. 4.
41. Confidential interview.
42. Confidential interview.
43. Lydon, "Frank Church Is Moving Center Stage."
44. Interview, Frank Church, 29 August 1983.
45. Ibid., 25 April 1983.
46. Ibid.
47. Ibid.
48. Ibid.
49. Confidential interview.
50. Interview, Frank Church, 25 April 1983.
51. Ibid.
52. Confidential interview.
53. Interview, Frank Church, 25 April 1983.
54. Interview, William G. Miller, 12 May 1983.
55. Interview, Frederick A. O. Schwarz, Jr., 24 May 1983.
56. Johnson, *A Season of Inquiry*, 86, 118, 150, 165.
57. Ibid., 165.
58. Confidential interview.
59. Confidential interview.
60. Confidential interview.
61. Interview, Joseph Di Genova, 15 June 1983.
62. Interview, David Aaron, 22 June 1983.
63. Confidential interview.
64. Johnson, *A Season of Inquiry*, 165.
65. Confidential interview.
66. Interview, Joseph Dennin, 8 September 1983.
67. Interview, Frederick A. O. Schwarz, Jr., 24 May 1983.
68. Interview, Howard Liebengood, 2 August 1983.
69. Confidential interview.
70. Senate Select Committee to Study Governmental Operations with Respect to Intelligence (hereafter "Senate Select Committee on Intelligence"),, *Alleged Assassination Plots Involving Foreign Leaders*, Interim Report, 94th Cong., 1st sess., 20 November 1975, 304.
71. Ibid.
72. David Rosenbaum, "Senate Panel Asserts U.S. Aides Were Involved in Plots to Kill Foreign Leaders," *New York Times*, 21 November 1975.
73. Interview, Frederick A. O. Schwarz, Jr., 24 May 1983.
74. Interview, William Colby, 14 July 1983.
75. Interview, Frank Church, 25 April 1983.
76. Interview, Frederick A. O. Schwarz, Jr., 24 May 1983.
77. Interview, William G. Miller, 12 May 1983.
78. Confidential interview.
79. Interview, William G. Miller, 12 May 1983.
80. Ibid.
81. Interview, Frederick A. O. Schwarz, Jr., 24 May 1983.
82. Interview, Joseph Dennin, 8 September 1983.

83. Interview, Frederick A. O. Schwarz, Jr., 24 May 1983.
84. Interview, Frederick Baron, 29 September 1983.
85. Interview, James Dick, 6 July 1983.
86. Interview, Joseph Dennin, 8 September 1983.
87. Confidential interview.
88. Interview, Joseph Di Genova, 15 June 1983.
89. Interview, Joseph Dennin, 8 September 1983.
90. Interview, James Dick, 6 July 1983.
91. Interview, David Bushong, 4 August 1983.
92. Confidential interview.
93. Interview, Joseph Di Genova, 15 June 1983.
94. Interview, Peter Fenn, 13 September 1983.
95. *CIA: The Pike Report* (Nottingham: Spokesman Books, 1977); 87.
96. Confidential interview. "Track I" was the Nixon administration's public accep-
    tance of Allende's election; "Track II" was Nixon's covert order to DCI Helms
    to do everything possible to overthrow Allende.
97. Confidential interview.
98. Interview, William G. Miller, 12 May 1983.
99. Edward Jay Epstein, *Inquest: The Warren Commission* (New York: Viking
    Press, 1970), 74.
100. Confidential interview.
101. Interview, John Elliff, 2 June 1983.
102. *Congressional Record*, 21 January 1975, 1432.
103. Ibid., 1434.
104. Interview, John Elliff, 2 June 1983.
105. George Lardner, Jr., "Lumumba, Castro Plots Told," *Washington Post*, 21
     November 1975, sec. A.
106. David Rosenbaum, "Senate Panel Asserts U.S. Aides Were Involved."
107. Ibid.
108. Interview, Frank Church, 25 April 1983.
109. Interview, Frederick A. O.Schwarz, Jr., 24 May 1983.
110. Johnson, *A Season of Inquiry*, 43.
111. Interview, Frederick A. O. Schwarz, Jr., 24 May 1983.
112. Confidential interview.
113. Confidential interview.
114. Confidential interview.
115. Ibid.
116. Confidential interview.
117. Interview, Otis Pike, 7 October 1983.
118. Confidential interview.
119. Confidential interview.
120. Confidential interview.
121. Johnson, *A Season of Inquiry*, 122–123.
122. Interview, Joseph Di Genova, 6 June 1983.
123. Interview, Joseph Dennin, 8 September 1983.
124. Interview, Eric Richard, 26 September 1983.
125. Senate Select Committee on Intelligence, *Internal Revenue Service*, Hearings,
     94th Cong., 1st sess., 2 October 1975, 22–23.
126. Interview, Philip Buchen, 6 June 1983.

127. Ibid.
128. Ibid.
129. Interview, Frank Church, 25 April 1983.
130. Interview, Philip Buchen, 6 June 1983.
131. Ibid.
132. Interview, James Wilderotter, 14 July 1983.
133. Interview, William Colby, 14 July 1983.
134. Interview, Michael Madigan, 18 July 1983.
135. Senate Select Committee on Intelligence, *Foreign and Military Intelligence*, Final Report, 94th Cong., 2d sess., 26 April 1976, 7.
136. Interview, Frederick Baron, 29 September 1983.
137. Ibid., 11 December 1983.
138. Interview, William Colby, 14 July 1983.
139. Ibid.
140. Ibid.
141. Ibid.
142. Confidential interview.
143. Interview, Howard Liebengood, 2 August 1983.
144. Interview, Michael Madigan, 18 July 1983.
145. Interview, Frederick A. O. Schwarz, Jr., 24 May 1983.
146. Interview, Seymour Bolton, 3 June 1983.
147. Interview, John Elliff, 12 May 1983.
148. Ibid.
149. Interview, William G. Miller, 12 May 1983.
150. Confidential interview.
151. Confidential interview.
152. Confidential interview.
153. Interview, Eric Richard, 26 September 1983.
154. Interview, Frank Church, 25 April 1983.
155. Interview, Frederick A. O. Schwarz, Jr., 24 May 1983.
156. Confidential interview.
157. Interview, Frederick A. 0. Schwarz, Jr., 24 May 1983.
158. Confidential interview.
159. Confidential interview.
160. Interview, Frank Church, 25 April 1983.
161. Confidential interview.
162. Interview, Frederick A. O. Schwarz, Jr., 24 May 1983.
163. Interview, Joseph Di Genova, 15 June 1983.
164. Interview, Michael Madigan, 18 July 1983.
165. Interview, Eric Richard, 26 September 1983.
166. Interview, Mitchell Rogovin, 28 January 1983.
167. Interview, Frank Church, 25 April 1983.
168. Confidential interview.
169. Interview, George Lardner, Jr., 14 December 1983.
170. Confidential interview.
171. George Lardner, Jr., "The Intelligence Investigations," *The Progressive*, July 1976, 16.
172. Interview, Burton Wides, 6 June 1983.
173. Interview, Frederick A. O. Schwarz, Jr., 24 May 1983.

174. Interview, Frederick Baron, 29 September 1983.
175. Nicholas Horrock, "The Meaning of Congressional Inquiries," *New York Times*, 30 April 1976, sec. A.
176. Interview, Seymour Hersh, 3 January 1983.
177. Interview, George Lardner, Jr., 14 December 1983.
178. Interview, William Colby, 30 December 1982.
179. Interview, Frank Church, 25 April 1983.
180. Ibid.
181. Senate Select Committee on Intelligence, *Unauthorized Storage of Toxic Wastes*, Hearings, 94th Cong., 2d sess., 26 April 1976, 101.
182. Interview, Frederick Baron, 11 December 1983.
183. Ibid., 29 September 1983.
184. *Unauthorized Storage of Toxic Wastes*, 51–89.
185. Ibid., 140–50.
186. Interview, Frank Church, 25 April 1983.
187. George Lardner, Jr., "CIA Tells of Exotic Weapons: Electric Gun, Untraceable Poison Pellets," *Washington Post*, 17 September 1975, sec. A.
188. Ibid.
189. Senate Select Committee on Intelligence, *Huston Plan*, Hearings, 94th Cong., 1st sess., 23, 24, 25 September 1975, 3–49.
190. Ibid., 141–88.
191. Senate Select Committee on Intelligence, *Internal Revenue Service*, Hearings, 94th Cong., 1st sess., 2 October 1975, 2, 9, 10, 29, 30.
192. Ibid., 23, 28.
193. Ibid., 26.
194. Ibid., 16.
195. Ibid., 24.
196. Senate Select Committee on Intelligence, *Mail Opening*, Hearings, 94th Cong., 1st sess., 21, 22, 24 October 1975, 31.
197. Ibid., 24.
198. Ibid., 109.
199. Ibid., 20.
200. Ibid., 53–54.
201. Ibid., 57.
202. Confidential interview.
203. Senate Select Committee on Intelligence, *The National Security Agency and Fourth Amendment Rights*, Hearings, 94th Cong., 1st sess., 29 October and 6 November 1975, 5.
204. Ibid., 10–13.
205. Ibid., 57–75.
206. Ibid., 52.
207. Ibid., 48.
208. Ibid., 62.
209. Senate Select Committee on Intelligence, *Federal Bureau of Investigation*, Hearings, 94th Cong., 1st sess., 18, 19 November and 2, 3, 9, 10, 11 December 1975, 41.
210. Ibid., 43.
211. Ibid., 4–255, 347–840.
212. Ibid., 73.

213. Senate Select Committee on Intelligence, *Covert Action*, Hearings, 94th Cong., 1st sess., 4, 5 December 1975, 95.
214. Interview, Frank Church, 25 April 1983.
215. Senate Select Committee on Intelligence, *Foreign and Military Intelligence*, 2.
216. Ibid., 423–74.
217. Senate Select Committee on Intelligence, *Intelligence and the Rights of Americans*, Final Report, 94th Cong., 2d sess., 26 April 1976, 339.
218. Ibid., 296–339.
219. *CIA: The Pike Report*, 257–63.
220. Commission on CIA Activities within the United States, *Report to the President*, 6 June 1975, 12–39.
221. Confidential interview.
222. Nicholas Horrock, "President Limits Surveillance of Lives of Citizens," *New York Times*, 19 February 1976.
223. John M. Oseth, *Regulating U.S. Intelligence Operations* (Lexington: University of Kentucky Press, 1985), 97.
224. Interview, Frank Church, 25 April 1983.
225. Interview, James Dick, 6 July 1983.

3. The Inouye, Bayh, and Goldwater Committees

1. Confidential interview.
2. *Congressional Record*, 95th Cong., 2d sess., 19 May 1976, 14645.
3. Ibid., 14648.
4. Anne Karalekas, "Intelligence Oversight: Has Anything Changed?," *Washington Quarterly* 6 (Summer 1983): 26.
5. Interview, William G. Miller, 12 May 1983.
6. Confidential interview.
7. Interview, Hugh Scott, 15 September 1983.
8. Interview, Daniel Inouye, 22 March 1983.
9. Ibid.
10. Confidential interview.
11. Confidential interview.
12. Confidential interview.
13. Confidential interview.
14. Confidential interview.
15. Confidential interviews.
16. Confidential interview.
17. Confidential interview.
18. Confidential interview.
19. Confidential interview.
20. Confidential interview.
21. Confidential interview.
22. Confidential interview.
23. Karalekas, "Intelligence Oversight," 26.
24. Daniel K. Inouye, *Journey to Washington* (Englewood Cliffs, N.J.: Prentice-Hall, 1967), 1–297.
25. Interview, Daniel Inouye, 22 March 1983.

26. Ibid.
27. Ibid.
28. Confidential interview.
29. Interview, B. R. Inman, 1 August 1983.
30. Interview, Daniel Inouye, 22 March 1983.
31. Interview, Birch Bayh, 26 April 1983.
32. Ibid.
33. Ibid.
34. Ibid.
35. Ibid.
36. Ibid.
37. Confidential interview.
38. Steven V. Roberts, "Some Kings of the Hill Bow to Time, Ambition," *New York Times*, 19 October 1986, sec. 4.
39. Pat Murphy, "Goldwater, Softer But Still Spicy, Reflects on a Fading Odyssey," *New York Times*, 22 September 1985.
40. Ibid.
41. Interview, John F. Blake, 23 February 1983.
42. Senate Select Committee on Intelligence, *Intelligence Reform Act of 1981*, Hearing, 97th Cong., 1st sess., 21 July 1981, 49.
43. Barry M. Goldwater, *Goldwater* (New York: Doubleday, 1988), 300–301.
44. Senate Select Committee on Intelligence, *Intelligence Reform Act of 1981*, Hearing, 97th Cong., 1st sess., 21 July 1981, 49.
45. Senate Select Committee on Intelligence, *Nomination of William J. Casey*, Hearing, 97th Cong., 1st sess., 18 January 1981, 38.
46. Senate Select Committee on Intelligence, *Report on the Casey Inquiry*, 97th Cong., 1st sess., 1 December 1981, 5.
47. David Rogers, "U.S. Role in Mining Nicaraguan Harbors Reportedly Is Larger Than First Thought," *Wall Street Journal*, 6 April 1984.
48. Interview, Daniel Inouye, 22 March 1983.
49. Confidential interview.
50. Confidential interview.
51. Confidential interview.
52. Interview, Daniel Inouye, 22 March 1983.
53. Interview, Hugh Scott, 15 September 1983.
54. Interview, Harold Brown, 16 August 1983.
55. Confidential interview.
56. Interview, William Miller, 12 May 1983.
57. Interview, Birch Bayh, 26 April 1983.
58. Confidential interview.
59. Confidential interview.
60. Confidential interview.
61. Confidential interview.
62. Interview, John F. Blake, 23 February 1983.
63. Confidential interviews.
64. Résumé, Daniel A. Childs, Jr., in Dr. Frank J. Smist, Jr., Collection, University of Oklahoma.
65. *Congressional Record*, 95th Cong., 1st sess., 22 June 1977, 20439.
66. Interview, Birch Bayh, 26 April 1983.

67. Senate Select Committee on Intelligence, *Report to the Senate*, 96th Cong., 1st sess., 14 May 1979, 6.
68. Senate Select Committee on Intelligence, *Report to the Senate*, 97th Cong., 1st sess., 23 September 1981, 10.
69. Senate Select Committee on Intelligence, *Report to the Senate*, 98th Cong., 1st sess., 28 February 1983, 34.
70. *Congressional Record*, 95th Cong., 2d sess., 20 July 1978, 22055–22058.
71. Confidential interview.
72. Confidential interview.
73. Interview, Birch Bayh, 26 April 1983.
74. Confidential interview.
75. Confidential interview.
76. Senate Select Committee on Intelligence, *Annual Report*, 95th Cong., 1st sess., 18 May 1977, 37.
77. Confidential interview.
78. Confidential interview.
79. Interview, Griffin Bell, 28 September 1983.
80. Confidential interview.
81. Confidential interview.
82. Confidential interview.
83. Confidential interview.
84. Confidential interview.
85. Interview, Zbigniew Brzezinski, 15 June 1983.
86. Confidential interview.
87. Interview, Stansfield Turner, 30 January 1983.
88. Confidential interview.
89. Interview, Cyrus Vance, 17 May 1983.
90. Interview, David Newsom, 30 September 1983.
91. Confidential interview.
92. Interview, Birch Bayh, 26 April 1983.
93. Confidential interview.
94. Walter Issacson, "A Lot of Show, But No Tell," *Time*, 22 March 1982, 20.
95. Woodward, *Veil*, 208–9.
96. Ibid., 209–10.
97. Philip Taubman, "Serious Problems Seen in Senate Intelligence Unit," *New York Times*, 28 May 1982, sec. A.
98. Interview, Benjamin Bradlee, 22 September 1983.
99. Senate Select Committee on Intelligence, *Annual Report*, 18 May 1977, 3.
100. Ibid.
101. Stephanie Mansfield, "No Blood Found on Paisley's Boat," *Washington Post*, 8 October 1978, sec. A.
102. Confidential interview.
103. Senate Select Committee on Intelligence, *Report to the Senate*, 23 September 1981, 24.
104. Confidential interview.
105. Interview, Walter Pforzheimer, 24 January 1983.
106. Confidential interview.
107. Confidential interview.
108. Confidential communication.

109. Confidential communication.

110. Senate Select Committee on Intelligence, *Report to the Senate*, 23 September 1981, 27.

111. Senate Select Committee on Intelligence, *Annual Report*, 18 May 1977, 24.

112. Senate Select Committee on Intelligence, *Report to the Senate*, 14 May 1979, 47.

113. Senate Select Committee on Intelligence, *Report*, 98th Cong., 2d sess., 10 October 1984, 45.

114. Confidential interview.

115. Confidential interview.

116. Confidential interview.

117. Confidential interview.

118. Fenno found that the House Appropriations Committee carefully examined and cut executive budget requests while the Senate Appropriations Committee heard appeals from officials distressed by House cuts and restored the funds. In conference, a compromise was hammered out between the House and Senate positions.

119. Confidential interview.

120. Confidential interview.

121. Interview, Malcolm Wallop, 28 June 1983.

122. Confidential interview.

123. Confidential interview.

124. Confidential interview.

125. Senate Select Committee on Intelligence, *Annual Report*, 18 May 1977, 17.

126. Confidential interview.

127. Senate Select Committee on Intelligence, *Annual Report*, 18 May 1977, 19–20.

128. Ibid., 19.

129. Confidential interview; Senate Select Committee on Intelligence, *Report to the Senate*, 14 May 1979, 48.

130. Confidential interview.

131. Confidential interview.

132. Interview, Hugh Scott, 15 September 1983.

133. Confidential interview.

134. Confidential interview.

135. Interview, Birch Bayh, 26 April 1983.

136. Confidential interview.

137. Interview, Birch Bayh, 26 April 1983.

138. Ibid.

139. Ibid.

140. Senate Select Committee on Intelligence, *Report to the Senate*, 23 September 1981, 3, 4, 31, 34.

141. Senate Select Committee on Intelligence, *Report*, 10 October 1984, 4.

142. Ibid., 4–10.

143. *Congressional Record*, 96th Cong., 2d sess., 3 June 1980, 13105.

144. Confidential interview.

145. Confidential interview.

146. Interview, Zbigniew Brzezinski, 15 June 1983.

147. Confidential interview.

148. Karalekas, "Intelligence Oversight," 23.
149. Interview, Daniel Inouye, 22 March 1983.
150. Confidential interviews.
151. Confidential interview.
152. Interview, William Miller, 12 May 1983.
153. Senate Select Committee on Intelligence, *Report to the Senate*, 28 February 1983, 2–3.
154. Ibid., 2–14.
155. Senate Select Committee on Intelligence, *Report*, 10 October 1984, 18–22.
156. Senate Select Committee on Intelligence, *Nomination of E. Henry Knoche*, Hearing, 94th Cong., 2d sess., 23 June 1976, 4–7.
157. Senate Select Committee on Intelligence, *Nomination of Admiral B.R. Inman*, Hearing, 97th Cong., 1st sess., 3 February 1981, 26.
158. James Wooten, "Carter Stands Firm, Supports Sorensen as Director of CIA," *New York Times*, 17 January 1977.
159. Confidential interview.
160. Wendell Rawls, "Sorensen Withdraws," *New York Times*, 18 January 1977.
161. Senate Select Committee on Intelligence, *Report on the Casey Inquiry*, 1 December 1981, 1–2.
162. Ibid., 5.
163. *Congressional Record*, 97th Cong., 2d sess., 24 September 1982, 512286.
164. Senate Select Committee on Intelligence, *Report*, 10 October 1984, 15–18.

4. The Nedzi and Pike Committees

1. Confidential interview.
2. "House Intelligence Panel," *Congressional Quarterly Weekly Report*, 22 February 1975, 367.
3. Confidential interview.
4. House Committee on Standards of Official Conduct, *Investigation of Publication of Select Committee on Intelligence Report*, Hearings, 94th Cong., 2nd sess., 1976, 330.
5. Confidential interview.
6. *Congressional Record*, 94th Cong., 1st sess., 19 February 1975, 3613–14.
7. "House Establishes Intelligence Inquiry," *New York Times*, 20 February 1975.
8. Confidential interview.
9. "Face the Nation," CBS News, 27 July 1975.
10. Interview, Otis Pike, 20 January 1983.
11. Barone, Ujifusa, and Mathews, *Almanac of American Politics 1976*, 66
12. Confidential interview.
13. Confidential interview.
14. John M. Crewdson, "A New Spy Panel Is Voted by House," *New York Times*, 18 July 1975.
15. Barone, Ujifusa, and Mathews, *Almanac of American Politics 1976*, 137.
16. Interview, Dale Milford, 8 February 1985.
17. Interview, James Johnson, 4 February 1985.
18. Confidential interview.
19. Interview, Mitchell Rogovin, 28 January 1983.

20. House Committee on Standards of Official Conduct, *Investigation of Publication*, 386.
21. Interview, Dale Milford, 8 February 1985.
22. Interview, James Johnson, 4 February 1985.
23. Confidential interview.
24. Interview, Lucien Nedzi, 9 February 1983.
25. House Committee on Standards of Official Conduct, *Investigation of Publication*, 226.
26. Ibid., 143.
27. Robert McClory to Frank Smist, 9 October 1981, in Dr. Frank J. Smist, Jr., Collection, University of Oklahoma.
28. Interview, Lucien Nedzi, 9 February 1983.
29. House Select Committee on Intelligence, *U.S. Intelligence Agencies and Activities: Risks and Control of Foreign Intelligence*, Hearings, 94th Cong., 1st sess., 4, 6 November, 2, 3, 9, 10, 11, 12, 17 December 1975, 1707.
30. House Select Committee on Intelligence, *U.S. Intelligence Agencies and Activities: Intelligence Costs and Fiscal Procedures*, Hearings, 94th Cong., 1st sess., 31 July, 1, 4, 5, 6, 7, 8 August 1975, 260.
31. House Select Committee on Intelligence, *U.S. Intelligence Agencies and Activities: Domestic Intelligence Programs*, Hearings, 94th Cong., 1st sess., 9 October, 13, 18, November, 10 December 1975, 1009.
32. Ibid., 1031.
33. Ibid., 1079.
34. Confidential interview.
35. House Committee on Standards of Official Conduct, *Investigation of Publication*, 402.
36. House Select Committee on Intelligence, *U.S. Intelligence Agencies and Activities: Risks and Control*, 1847.
37. Confidential interview.
38. Interview, Lucien Nedzi, 9 February 1983.
39. Interview, George L. Cary, 24 January 1983.
40. Interview, Lucien Nedzi, 9 February 1983.
41. Ibid., July 20, 1983.
42. Confidential interview.
43. Interview, Lucien Nedzi, 9 February 1983.
44. Ibid.
45. Confidential interview.
46. Confidential interview.
47. Interview, Lucien Nedzi, 9 February 1983.
48. Vernon A. Walters, *Silent Missions* (New York: Doubleday, 1978), 606–7.
49. Interview, John Maury, 16 February 1983.
50. Interview, Walter Pforzheimer, 24 January 1983.
51. Interview, Lucien Nedzi, 9 February 1983.
52. Ibid.
53. Ibid.
54. Michael Harrington, CBS News interview, 7 July 1975.
55. Confidential interview.
56. Interview, Lucien Nedzi, 9 February 1983.
57. Ibid.

58. George Lardner, Jr., "House Intelligence Unit Names Staff Director," *Washington Post*, 14 May 1975.
59. Interview, Lucien Nedzi, 9 February 1983.
60. Ibid.
61. Nicholas M. Horrock, "Nedzi Is Said to Have Kept House in Dark on CIA Violations," *New York Times*, 5 June 1975.
62. Ibid.
63. Interview, Lucien Nedzi, 9 February 1983.
64. Confidential interview.
65. Interview, Otis Pike, 20 January 1983.
66. House Select Committee on Intelligence, *U.S. Intelligence Agencies and Activities: Intelligence Costs*, 1, 2.
67. Interview, Aaron Donner, 3 June 1983.
68. Interview, Mitchell Rogovin, 28 January 1983.
69. House Select Committee on Intelligence, *U.S. Intelligence Agencies and Activities: Intelligence Costs*, 260.
70. House Select Committee on Intelligence, *U.S. Intelligence Agencies and Activities: Domestic Intelligence*, 1013.
71. House Select Committee on Intelligence, *Committee Proceedings*, 94th Cong., 1st sess., 10, 29 September, 1 October, 4, 6, 13, 14, 20 November 1975, 1342.
72. Ibid., 1401.
73. Confidential interview.
74. Confidential interview.
75. House Committee on Standards of Official Conduct, *Investigation of Publication*, 42–43.
76. Ibid., 57.
77. Ibid.
78. Confidential interviews.
79. Interview, Mitchell Rogovin, 5 October 1983.
80. Confidential interview.
81. David E. Rosenbaum, "House Prevents Releasing Report," *New York Times*, 30 January 1976.
82. Confidential interview.
83. House Select Committee on Intelligence, *Committee Proceedings II*, 94th Cong., 2d sess., 20, 21, 23, 26, 27, 28 January, 3, 4, 5, 10 February 1976, 2315.
84. Confidential interview.
85. Robert McClory to Frank Smist, 9 October 1981.
86. Summary based on recorded votes in Pike committee hearings.
87. House Select Committee on Intelligence, *The Performance of the Intelligence Community*, Hearings, 94th Cong., 1st sess., 11, 12, 18, 25, 30 September, 7, 30, 31 October 1975, 855.
88. Interview, Otis Pike, 20 January 1983.
89. House Select Committee on Intelligence, *U.S. Intelligence Agencies and Activities: Risks and Control*, 1771.
90. Interview, James Johnson, 4 February 1985.
91. Ibid.
92. Interview, Dale Milford, 8 February 1985.
93. Ibid.

94. House Committee on Standards of Official Conduct, *Investigation of Publication*, 207.
95. House Select Committee on Intelligence, *U.S. Intelligence Agencies and Activities: Risks and Control*, 1857.
96. House Select Committee on Intelligence, *U.S. Intelligence Agencies and Activities: Committee Proceedings II*, 2163.
97. Ibid., 2177.
98. McClory to Smist, 9 October 1981.
99. Interview, Otis Pike, 20 January 1983.
100. House Select Committee on Intelligence, *U.S. Intelligence Agencies and Activities: Committee Proceedings II*, 2063.
101. Interview, Dale Milford, 8 February 1985.
102. Confidential interview.
103. Interview, James Johnson, 4 February 1985.
104. House Select Committee on Intelligence, *U.S. Intelligence Agencies and Activities: Committee Proceedings*, 1258.
105. House Select Committee on Intelligence, *U.S. Intelligence Agencies and Activities: Committee Proceedings II*, 2228.
106. Confidential interview.
107. Confidential interview.
108. Interview, Aaron Donner, 3 June 1983.
109. House Committee on Standards of Official Conduct, *Investigation of Publication*, 398.
110. Confidential interview.
111. Confidential interview.
112. Confidential interview.
113. Confidential interview.
114. Confidential interview.
115. Confidential interview.
116. Confidential interview.
117. Confidential interview.
118. Confidential interview.
119. Confidential interview.
120. Confidential interview.
121. Confidential interview.
122. Confidential interview.
123. *Congressional Record*, 94th Cong., 1st sess., June 16, 1975, 19054.
124. Ibid., 19054.
125. Ibid., 19058.
126. Ibid., 19060.
127. Ibid., 19058.
128. Confidential interview.
129. *Congressional Record*, 94th Cong., 2d sess., 29 January 1976, 1639.
130. Ibid.
131. CBS News, Otis Pike interview with Bruce Morton and Morton Dean, 22 July 1975.
132. *CIA: The Pike Report*, 85–87.
133. House Select Committee on Intelligence, *U.S. Intelligence Agencies and Activities: Risks and Control*, 1744.

134. Confidential interview.
135. Louise Sweeney, "Republicans Boycott CIA Hearing," *Christian Science Monitor*, 13 June 1975.
136. Interview, Melvin Laird, 28 September 1983.
137. Interview, Bryce Harlow, 1 June 1983.
138. Interview, Morris Udall, 11 April 1983.
139. Interview, Richard Bolling, 11 April 1983.
140. Interview, Walter Pforzheimer, 24 January 1983.
141. Interview, George Cary, 25 July 1983.
142. Interview, Michael Harrington, 11 May 1983.
143. Confidential interview.
144. Confidential interview.
145. Interview, Mitchell Rogovin, 28 January 1983.
146. House Committee on Standards of Official Conduct, *Investigation of Publication*, 316.
147. House Select Committee on Intelligence, *U.S. Intelligence Agencies and Activities: Intelligence Costs*, 223.
148. House Select Committee on Intelligence, *U.S. Intelligence Agencies and Activities: The Performance of the Intelligence Community*, 681.
149. Interview, Michael Rogovin, 28 January 1983.
150. Confidential interview.
151. Interview, Michael Rogovin, 28 January 1983.
152. Interview, Aaron Donner, 3 June 1983.
153. Confidential interview.
154. Interview, Aaron Donner, 3 June 1983.
155. *CIA: The Pike Report*, 69.
156. Ibid., 66.
157. Ibid., 63.
158. House Select Committee on Intelligence, *U.S. Intelligence Agencies and Activities: Intelligence Costs*, 169.
159. House Select Committee on Intelligence, *U.S. Intelligence Agencies and Activities: Committee Proceedings*, 1244.
160. Confidential interviews.
161. House Select Committee on Intelligence, *U.S. Intelligence Agencies and Activities: Risks and Control*, 1925.
162. Ibid., 1877.
163. Ibid., 1900.
164. Interview, Aaron Donner, 3 June 1983.
165. Interview, John Maury, 16 February 1983.
166. Interview, William Colby, 14 July 1983.
167. House Select Committee on Intelligence, *U.S. Intelligence Agencies and Activities: Committee Proceedings*, 1277.
168. House Select Committee on Intelligence, *U.S. Intelligence Agencies and Activities: Risks and Control*, 1585.
169. House Select Committee on Intelligence, *U.S. Intelligence Agencies and Activities: Intelligence Costs*, 273.
170. Interview, Aaron Donner, 3 June 1983.
171. House Committee on Standards of Official Conduct, Investigation of Publication, 155.

172. Ibid., 436–37.
173. Interview, William Colby, 14 July 1983.
174. Interview, Aaron Donner, 3 June 1983.
175. House Select Committee on Intelligence, *U.S. Intelligence Agencies and Activities: Risks and Control*, 1932.
176. House Select Committee on Intelligence, *U.S. Intelligence Agencies and Activities: The Performance of the Intelligence Community*, 733.
177. Confidential interview.
178. House Select Committee on Intelligence, *U.S. Intelligence Agencies and Activities: The Performance of the Intelligence Community*, 729.
179. Interview, Aaron Donner, 3 June 1983.
180. "Neo-McCarthyism?" *New York Times*, 19 October 1975.
181. "Mr. Pike's Committee," *Washington Post*, 6 October 1975, sec. A.
182. House Select Committee on Intelligence, *U.S. Intelligence Agencies and Activities: The Performance of the Intelligence Community*, 862.
183. Interview, Aaron Donner, 3 June 1983.
184. House Select Committee on Intelligence, *U.S. Intelligence Agencies and Activities: The Performance of the Intelligence Community*, 852.
185. Ibid.
186. Confidential interview.
187. Confidential interview.
188. House Select Committee on Intelligence, *U.S. Intelligence Agencies and Activities: Committee Proceedings*, 1333.
189. Confidential interview.
190. Interview, Philip Buchen, 6 June 1983.
191. Confidential interview.
192. Confidential interview.
193. Confidential interview.
194. Daniel Schorr, *Clearing the Air* (Boston: Houghton Mifflin, 1977), 188. I have emphasized the four words with italics.
195. Confidential interview.
196. Schorr, *Clearing the Air*, 188.
197. Marvin and Bernard Kalb, *Kissinger* (Boston: Little, Brown, 1974), vii.
198. Ibid., 454.
199. Interview, Otis Pike, 20 January 1983.
200. Confidential interview.
201. Confidential interview.
202. Interview, Aaron Donner, June 3, 1983.
203. Sweeney, "Republicans Boycott CIA Hearing."
204. Confidential interview.
205. Confidential interview.
206. James M. Naughton, "Ford Promises Effort to Restore CIA," *New York Times*, 31 January 1976.
207. House Select Committee on Intelligence, *U.S. Intelligence Agencies and Activities: Risks and Control*, 1823.
208. Lardner, "The Intelligence Investigations," 17.
209. Schorr, *Clearing the Air*, 192–93.
210. House Select Committee on Intelligence, *U.S. Intelligence Agencies and Activities: Risks and Control*, 1827.

211. House Select Committee on Intelligence, *U.S. Intelligence Agencies and Activities: Intelligence Costs*, 109–224.

212. Ibid., 51–107.

213. Ibid., 139.

214. Ibid., 111.

215. Ibid., 3–50.

216. Ibid., 194, 207.

217. Ibid., 202.

218. House Select Committee on Intelligence, *U.S. Intelligence Agencies and Activities: The Performance of the Intelligence Community*, 648.

219. See "The Committee and the Executive Branch," above.

220. House Select Committee on Intelligence, *U.S. Intelligence Agencies and Activities: The Performance of the Intelligence Community*, 684.

221. Ibid., 700.

222. House Select Committee on Intelligence, *U.S. Intelligence Agencies and Activities: Risks and Control*, 1687.

223. Ibid., 1689.

224. Ibid., 1652. In January 1982 CBS broadcast a controversial documentary, "The Uncounted Enemy: A Vietnam Deception." Adams was allowed once again to make the charges he had made before the Pike committee. The committee was fairer to those Adams accused as it gave them the opportunity to rebut the charges. The CBS documentary failed to even mention this work of the committee.

225. House Select Committee on Intelligence, *U.S. Intelligence Agencies and Activities: The Performance of the Intelligence Community*, 777–78.

226. Ibid., 827.

227. Ibid., 828.

228. Ibid., 813.

229. Ibid., 849.

230. Interview, James Johnson, 4 February 1985.

231. Interview, Otis Pike, 20 January 1983.

232. *CIA: The Pike Report*, 189.

233. House Select Committee on Intelligence, *U.S. Intelligence Agencies and Activities: Domestic Intelligence*, 947–57.

234. Ibid., 959.

235. Ibid., 972.

236. Ibid., 996.

237. Ibid., 999–1000.

238. Ibid., 1008–10.

239. Ibid., 1005.

240. Ibid., 1019–86.

241. Interview, James Nolan, 1 November 1983.

242. House Select Committee on Intelligence, *U.S. Intelligence Agencies and Activities: Domestic Intelligence*, 1087–1117.

243. House Select Committee on Intelligence, *U.S. Intelligence Agencies and Activities: Risks and Control*, 1575–76.

244. Ibid., 1588–89.

245. Ibid., 1590.

246. Ibid., 1622.
247. Ibid., 1631.
248. Ibid., 1616.
249. Ibid., 1927.
250. Ibid., 1949–50.
251. Confidential interview.
252. House Select Committee on Intelligence, *U.S. Intelligence Agencies and Activities: Risks and Control*, 1729–70.
253. Ibid., 1743.
254. Ibid., 1772–1820.
255. Ibid., 1811.
256. Ibid., 1812.
257. Ibid., 1818.
258. Ibid., 1823.
259. Ibid., 1831.
260. Ibid., 1837.
261. Ibid., 1840.
262. Ibid., 1848–50, 1858.
263. Ibid., 1859.
264. Ibid., 1855–56.
265. Ibid., 1882.
266. Ibid., 1885–86.
267. Ibid., 1893–96.
268. Ibid., 1898–1900.
269. Confidential interview.
270. Confidential interview.
271. House Committee on Standards of Official Conduct, *Investigation of Publication*, 219.
272. Confidential interview.
273. *CIA: The Pike Report*, 27.
274. Ibid.
275. Ibid., 32–75.
276. Ibid., 72.
277. Ibid., 73.
278. Ibid., 76–94.
279. Ibid., 85–88.
280. Confidential interview.
281. *CIA: The Pike Report*, 90.
282. Ibid., 92, 94.
283. Ibid., 96.
284. Ibid., 96–128.
285. Ibid., 129–167.
286. Ibid., 168–178.
287. Ibid., 187–189.
288. Ibid., 192–218.
289. Ibid., 219–255.
290. Ibid., 257–263.
291. Ibid., 284.

5. The Boland Committee

1. Loch Johnson, "The U.S. Congress and the CIA," *Legislative Studies Quarterly* 4 (November 1980): 492.
2. Sidney Blumenthal, "The Boland Achievement," *Washington Post*, 15 June 1987, sec. C.
3. *Congressional Record*, 95th Cong., 1st sess., 17 July 1977, 22944.
4. Ibid., 22936.
5. Confidential interview.
6. *Congressional Record*, 95th Cong., 1st sess., 17 July 1977, 22935.
7. Ibid., 22937.
8. Ibid., 22943–44.
9. Ibid., 22943.
10. Ibid.
11. Ibid., 22944.
12. Ibid., 22947.
13. Ibid.
14. Ibid., 22945–46.
15. Confidential interview.
16. Blumenthal, "The Boland Achievement."
17. Confidential interview.
18. Confidential interview.
19. Confidential interview.
20. Confidential interview.
21. Confidential interview.
22. Confidential interview.
23. Confidential interview.
24. Confidential interview.
25. Confidential interview.
26. Confidential interview.
27. Confidential interview.
28. Confidential interview.
29. "Meet the Press," NBC, 2 April 1983.
30. Thomas P. "Tip" O'Neill, *Man of the House* (New York: Random House, 1987), 144–46.
31. Michael Barone and Grant Ujifusa, *Almanac of American Politics 1984* (Washington, D.C.: National Journal, 1983), 542.
32. Edward P. Boland, "It's Good to Have This Man around the House," campaign brochure, 1986.
33. Barone and Ujifusa, *Almanac of American Politics 1984*, 541–42.
34. *Congressional Record*, 95th Cong., 1st sess., 14 July 1977, 22948.
35. Ibid., 16374–96.
36. Blumenthal, "The Boland Achievement."
37. Ibid.
38. *Congressional Record*, 97th Cong., 2d sess., 8 December 1982, 9156–57.
39. Confidential interview.
40. Interview, Joseph P. Addabo, 6 June 1983.
41. Confidential interview.

42. Confidential interview.
43. Blumenthal, "The Boland Achievement."
44. Confidential interview.
45. Confidential interview.
46. Interview, Harold Brown, 16 August 1983.
47. Interview, B. R. Inman, 7 June 1983.
48. *Congressional Record*, 97th Cong., 1st sess., 23 September 1981, 21738.
49. Johnson, "The U.S. Congress and the CIA," 484.
50. "Four Battling for Armed Services Chairmanship," *Congressional Quarterly Weekly Report*, 17 January 1987, 104.
51. Confidential interview.
52. Confidential interview.
53. I have found that another member of the Boland committee was forced to leave. Intelligence officials claimed that both Aspin and this member were security risks. However, the evidence does not support these charges. Both Aspin and the other member were hard-charging but responsible investigative overseers. Their style was unacceptable to Chairman Boland, who had the power to force both members off the committee.
54. Confidential interview.
55. Confidential interview.
56. Confidential interview.
57. *Congressional Record*, 17 July 1977, 22942.
58. Confidential interview.
59. Confidential interview.
60. Confidential interview.
61. Staff members on the Subcommittee on Oversight and Evaluation assumed a prominent role whenever members attempted to implement investigative oversight.
62. Confidential interview.
63. Confidential interview.
64. Johnson, "The U.S. Congress and the CIA," 485.
65. Confidential interview.
66. Confidential interview.
67. Confidential interview.
68. Confidential interview.
69. *Congressional Record*, 22 September 1981, 21730, 21748–49.
70. George Lardner, Jr., "House Would Bar Naming of Agents," *Washington Post*, 24 September 1981, sec. A.
71. Confidential interview.
72. Confidential interview.
73. David Shribman, "Few Go to Study Intelligence Reports," *New York Times*, 19 October 1983.
74. Confidential interview.
75. Confidential interview.
76. Confidential interview.
77. Confidential interview.
78. Confidential interview.
79. Interview, Morris K. Udall, 11 April 1983.
80. Confidential interview.

81. Confidential interview.
82. Confidential interview.
83. Confidential interview.
84. Confidential interview.
85. Interview, Melvin Price, 5 May 1983.
86. Confidential interview.
87. Confidential interview.
88. Confidential interview.
89. Confidential interview.
90. Confidential interviews.
91. Confidential interview.
92. Confidential interview.
93. C-SPAN, 28 September 1987.
94. Johnson, "The U.S. Congress and the CIA," 487.
95. Ibid., 493.
96. Confidential interviews.
97. Johnson, "The U.S. Congress and the CIA," 489–90.
98. Interview, Philip Taubman, 18 March 1983.
99. Confidential interview.
100. George Lardner, Jr., "House Probing CIA 'Babysitter' Who Rifles Files on JFK," *Washington Post*, 28 June 1979, sec. A.
101. Philip Taubman, "Beyond the Wilson Case," *New York Times*, 14 September 1981, sec. A.
102. House Permanent Select Committee on Intelligence, *Report*, 99th Cong., 1st sess., 2 January 1985, 12–14.
103. Interview, Philip Taubman, 18 March 1983.
104. Ibid.
105. House Permanent Select Committee on Intelligence, *Report*, 2 January 1985, 15–16.
106. Seymour Hersh, "Congress Is Accused of Laxity on CIA's Covert Activity," *New York Times*, 1 June 1978.
107. Edward P. Boland, "Letter to the Editor," *New York Times*, 8 June 1978.
108. Martin Tolchin, "Of CIA Games and Disputed Rules," *New York Times*, 14 May 1987, sec. A.
109. Confidential interview.
110. Confidential communication.
111. Interview, George H. Mahon, 19 May 1983.
112. Confidential interview.
113. Confidential interview.
114. Interview, Chuck Snodgrass, 6 and 27 July 1983.
115. Ibid.
116. Ibid.
117. Ibid.
118. Confidential interview.
119. Interview, Chuck Snodgrass, 27 July 1983.
120. Interview, Joseph Addabo, 6 June 1983.
121. Interview, B. R. Inman, 1 August 1983.
122. Confidential interview.
123. Confidential interview.

124. Confidential interview.
125. Confidential interviews.
126. Confidential interview.
127. Confidential interview.
128. Confidential interview.
129. Memorandum for Mr. [Lee H.] Hamilton, [Jr.,] 23 March 1983, copy in Dr. Frank J. Smist, Jr., Collection, University of Oklahoma.
130. Confidential interview.
131. Confidential interview.
132. *Congressional Record*, 98th Cong., 1st sess., 8 December 1983, 9156.
133. Ibid.
134. Bernard Wienraub, "Congress Renews Curbs on Actions against Nicaragua," *New York Times*, 23 December 1982, sec. A.
135. Drew Middleston, "Nicaragua Buildup: Soviet Threat to Region Seen," *New York Times*, 9 March 1983, sec. A.
136. Hedrick Smith, "House Compromise Sought on Nicaragua," *New York Times*, 7 July 1983, sec. A.
137. Hedrick Smith, "Bobbing and Weaving on Nicaragua: Questions from an Anxious Congress," *New York Times*, 6 August 1983.
138. House Permanent Select Committee on Intelligence, *Report*, 2 January 1985, 10–11.
139. Ibid., 4.
140. Ibid., 2.
141. Ibid., 4.
142. House Permanent Select Committee on Intelligence, *Annual Report*, 95th Cong., 2d sess., 14 October 1978, 20–22.
143. House Permanent Select Committee on Intelligence, *Report*, 97th Cong., 2d sess., 17 December 1982, 6–8.

6. A Look Back and a Look Ahead

1. John Felton, "Reagan Tries to Put Out Fire on Iran Dealings," *Congressional Quarterly Weekly Report*, 15 November 1986, 2883.
2. Confidential interview.
3. Confidential interview.
4. Michael Barone and Grant Ujifusa, *Almanac of American Politics 1988* (Washington, D.C.: National Journal, 1987), 625.
5. Philip Shenon, "Senator Durenberger Stirs New Concern with Outspokenness," *New York Times*, 8 April 1987, sec. B.
6. Ibid.
7. Irvin Molotsky, "Senate Ethics Panel Criticizes Durenberger on Talk," *New York Times*, 30 April 1988.
8. Alan Ehrenhalt, ed., *Politics in America: The 100th Congress* (Washington, D.C.: Congressional Quarterly, 1987), 1540.
9. Ibid.
10. Confidential interview.
11. David B. Ottaway, "CIA, Casey Criticized by Hill Chairman," *Washington Post*, 14 November 1985, sec. A.
12. Ibid.

13. Patrick B. Tyler and David B. Ottaway, "Casey Accuses Durenberger of Compromising CIA," *Washington Post*, 15 November 1985, sec. A.

14. David B. Ottaway, "Leahy Joins Durenberger in Criticizing CIA," *Washington Post*, 16 November 1985, sec. A.

15. Sam Zagoria, "Durenberger, Casey and the Post," *Washington Post*, 20 November 1985, sec. A.

16. Interview, Lee H. Hamilton, 9 February 1989.

17. House Permanent Select Committee on Intelligence, *Report*, 99th Cong., 2d sess., 31 December 1986, 6–7.

18. Ibid., 7.

19. Ibid., 11–15.

20. Interview, Lee H. Hamilton, 9 February 1989.

21. Ibid.

22. "President Reagan Responds to Tower Board Investigation," *Congressional Quarterly Weekly Report*, 7 March 1987, 440.

23. Felton, "Reagan Tries to Put Out Fire," 2884.

24. *The Tower Commission Report* (New York: Random House, 1987), 296.

25. Fox Butterfield, "North's $10 Million Mistake," *New York Times*, 13 May 1987, sec. A.

26. "Panel Members Recount the Moments They Won't Forget," *New York Times*, 9 August 1987, sec. 4.

27. Steven V. Roberts, "Inquiry Finds Reagan and Chief Advisers Responsible for 'Chaos' in Iran Arms Deals," *New York Times*, 27 February 1987.

28. John Corry, "Poindexter Testimony: A Decrease in Drama," *New York Times*, 16 July 1987, sec. C.

29. Stephen Engelberg, "Bush Denies Role in Honduras Plan," *New York Times*, 5 May 1989, sec. A.

30. Elizabeth Holtzman, "Faulting the Iran-Contra Committees," *New York Times*, 7 August 1987, sec A.

31. "North For President Group Formed," *Shawnee, Oklahoma, News-Star*, 14 July 1987.

32. Ibid.

33. Kay Morgan, "North Fans Lining Up to Get 'Ollie' Haircuts," *Daily Oklahoman*, 17 July 1987.

34. Tom Shales, "What a Deference a Day Makes," *Washington Post*, 11 July 1987, sec. G.

35. Carl Bernstein, "TV Anchormen Are Missing the Big Story of the Hearings," *New York Times*, 14 July 1987, sec. A.

36. Daniel K. Inouye, "More Serious Than Watergate," *New York Times*, 3 May 1987, sec. 4.

37. "President Reagan Responds to Tower Board Investigation," 441.

38. *The Tower Commission Report*, 33.

39. Ibid., 172–77, 495.

40. Ibid., 78.

41. Ibid., 29.

42. Senate Select Committee on Secret Military Assistance to Iran and the Nicaraguan Opposition and House Select Committee to Investigate Covert Arms Transactions with Iran, *Report of the Congressional Committees Investigating the Iran-Contra Affair*, 100th Cong., 1st sess., 17 November 1987, 378–79.

43. Ibid., 423–24.

44. Ibid., 423.

45. Ibid., 425.

46. Dan Morgan and Walter Pincus, "Casey Sought Permanent Covert Set-Up, North Reveals," *Washington Post*, 11 July 1987, sec. A.

47. Fox Butterfield, "North Says Casey Proposed Using Arms Profit for Fund Kept Secret from President," *New York Times*, 11 July 1987.

48. "Panel Members Recount the Moments."

49. John T. Elliff, "Two Models of Congressional Oversight," *Houston Journal of International Law* 11 (Fall 1988): 150.

50. David Johnston, "Lawmaker Says Reagan Officials Mislead Panel on North and Rebels," *New York Times*, 23 February 1989, sec. A.

51. Interview, Lee H. Hamilton, 9 February 1989.

52. Ibid.

53. *Report of the Congressional Committees Investigating the Iran-Contra Affair*, 423.

54. Ibid., 437.

55. Ibid., 575–80.

56. Ibid., 583–586.

57. "North Says Criminal Charges against Him Are 'An Honor,' " *New York Times*, 3 May 1988, sec. B.

58. Ibid.

59. Ibid.

60. "Democrats Turn Backs on Liberty, North Says," *Daily Oklahoman*, 20 July 1988.

61. Butterfield, "North Says Casey Proposed Using Arms Profit for Fund."

62. Steven V. Roberts, "Reagan's Final Rating Is Best of Any President since '40s," *New York Times*, 18 January 1989, sec. A.

63. Ibid.

64. Adam Clymer, "Poll Finds Americans Don't Know U.S. Positions on Central America," *New York Times*, 1 July 1983, sec. A.

65. David K. Shipler, "Poll Shows Confusion on Aid to Contras," *New York Times*, 15 April 1986, sec. A.

66. Dusko Doder, "Hosting Favored Over Roasting," *Washington Post*, 21 November 1986, sec. A.

67. Stephen Engelberg, "Senator Leahy Admits He Leaked a Document," *New York Times*, 29 July 1987, sec. A.

68. Confidential interview.

69. Allan Cromley, "Leak Caused Senator's Ouster," *Daily Oklahoman*, 29 July 1987.

70. Interview, David L. Boren, 8 February 1989.

71. Confidential interviews.

72. Confidential interviews.

73. President Ronald Reagan to Chairman David Boren, 7 August 1987, copy in Dr. Frank J. Smist, Jr. Collection, University of Oklahoma.

74. Confidential interviews.

75. Confidential interview.

76. House Permanent Select Committee on Intelligence, *Report*, 100th Cong., 2d sess., 27 December 1988, 2–23.

77. Confidential interviews.
78. Confidential interviews.
79. Stephen Engelberg, "Bradley's Covert Effort to Become Panel Chief," *New York Times*, 28 February 1989.
80. Confidential interview.
81. Susan F. Rasky, "Bush Is Accused of Backing Away from Promise on 1988 Arms Pact," *New York Times*, 7 April 1989, sec. A.
82. Interview, David L. Boren, 8 February 1989.
83. Ibid.
84. "Bests, Mosts, Misfits, and Others," *The Washingtonian*, March 1989, 97.
85. Hedrick Smith, *The Power Game* (New York: Random House, 1988) 206–7.
86. Confidential interview.
87. Interview, Dave McCurdy, 24 February 1989.
88. Clinton Rossiter, *The American Presidency* (New York: Harcourt, Brace & World, 1956), 17–26.
89. Interview, Birch Bayh, April 26, 1983.
90. Confidential interview.
91. *Winston S. Churchhill: His Complete Speeches, 1897–1963* (New York: Chelsea House, 1974), 7:7566.

Bibliography

Books

Barone, Michael, Grant Ujifusa, and Douglas Mathews. *Almanac of American Politics 1976*. New York: E. P. Dutton, 1975.
———. *Almanac of American Politics 1978*. New York: E. P. Dutton, 1977.
———. *Almanac of American Politics 1980*. New York: E. P. Dutton, 1979.
Barone, Michael, and Grant Ujifusa. *Almanac of American Politics 1982*. Washington, D.C.: Barone & Co., 1981.
———. *Almanac of American Politics 1984*. Washington, D.C.: National Journal, 1983.
———. *Almanac of American Politics 1988*. Washington, D.C.: National Journal, 1988.
CIA: The Pike Report. Nottingham: Spokesman Books, 1977.
Cline, Ray S. *Secrets, Spies, and Scholars*. Washington, D.C.: Acropolis Books, 1976.
———. *The CIA: Reality vs. Myth*. Rev. ed., Washington, D.C.: Acropolis Books, 1982.
———. *The CIA under Reagan, Bush, and Casey*. Washington, D.C.: Acropolis Books, 1981.
Colby, William E. *Honorable Men: My Life in the CIA*. New York: Simon and Schuster, 1979.
Dulles, Allen. *The Craft of Intelligence*. New York: Harper and Row, 1965.
Easton, David. *A Systems Analysis of Political Life*. New York: Wiley, 1965.
Ehrenhalt, Alan, ed. *Politics in America: The 100th Congress*. Washington, D.C.: Congressional Quarterly, 1987.
Epstein, Edward Jay. *Inquest: The Warren Commission and the Establishment of Truth*. New York: Viking Press, 1970.
Fenno, Richard, Jr. *Congressmen in Committees*. Boston: Little, Brown, 1973.
———. *The Power of the Purse*. Boston: Little, Brown, 1986.
Froman, Lewis A. *The Congressional Process*. Boston: Little, Brown, 1967.
Goldwater, Barry M. *Goldwater*. New York: Doubleday, 1988.
Henderson, Thomas A. *Congressional Oversight of Executive Agencies*. Gainesville: University of Florida Press, 1970.
Inouye, Daniel K. *Journey to Washington*. Englewood Cliffs, N.J.: Prentice-Hall, 1967.

Johnson, Loch. *A Season of Inquiry: The Senate Intelligence Investigation*. Lexington: University of Kentucky Press, 1985.

Kalb, Marvin and Bernard. *Kissinger*. Boston: Little, Brown, 1974.

Keefe, William J., and Morris S. Ogul. *The American Legislative Process*. Englewood Cliffs, N.J.: Prentice-Hall, 1981.

Kent, Sherman. *Strategic Intelligence for American World Policy*. Hamden, Conn.: Archon Books, 1965.

Kirkpatrick, Lyman B., Jr. *The U.S. Intelligence Community and Domestic Activities*. New York: Hill and Wang, 1973.

Kirst, Michael W. *Government without Passing Laws*. Chapel Hill: University of North Carolina Press, 1969.

Kowet, Don. *A Matter of Honor: General William C. Westmoreland versus CBS*. New York: Macmillan, 1984.

Layton, Rear Admiral Edwin T. *"And I Was There."* New York: William Morrow, 1985.

Manley, John F. *The Politics of Finance*. Boston: Little, Brown, 1970.

Morrow, William L. *Congressional Committees*. New York: Charles Scribner's Sons, 1969.

Ogul, Morris S. *Congress Oversees Bureaucracy*. Pittsburgh: University of Pennsylvania Press, 1976.

O'Neill, Thomas P. "Tip." *Man of the House*. New York: Random House, 1987.

Oseth, John M. *Regulating U.S. Intelligence Operations*. Lexington: University of Kentucky Press, 1985.

Prange, Gordon W. *At Dawn We Slept*. Ontario: Penguin Books, 1981.

Rossiter, Clinton. *The American Presidency*. New York: Harcourt, Brace and World, 1956.

Schorr, Daniel. *Clearing the Air*. Boston: Houghton Mifflin, 1977.

The Tower Commission Report. New York: Random House, 1987.

Treverton, Gregory F. *Covert Action: The Limits of Intervention in the Postwar World*. New York: Basic Books, 1987.

Walters, Vernon A. *Silent Missions*. New York: Doubleday, 1978.

Wohlstetter, Roberta. *Pearl Harbor: Warning and Decision*. Stanford: Stanford University Press, 1962.

Woodward, Bob. *Veil: The Secret Wars of the CIA*. New York: Simon and Schuster, 1987.

Campaign Brochure

Boland, Edward P. "It's Good to Have This Man around the House." 1986.

Journals

Bibby, John F. "Committee Characteristics and Legislative Oversight of Administration." *Midwest Journal of Political Science* 10 (February 1966): 78–98.

Elliff, John T. "Two Models of Congressional Oversight." *Houston Journal of International Law* 11 (Fall 1988): 149–58.

Johnson, Loch. "The U.S. Congress and the CIA: Monitoring the Dark Side of the Government." *Legislative Studies Quarterly* 4 (November 1980): 492.

Karalekas, Anne. "Intelligence Oversight: Has Anything Changed?" *Washington Quarterly* 6 (Summer 1984): 26.

Scher, Seymour. "Conditions for Legislative Control." *Journal of Politics* 25 (August 1963): 526–51.

Sharkansky, Ira. "An Appropriations Subcommittee and Its Clients: A Comparative Study of Supervision and Control." *American Political Science Review* 59 (September 1965): 622–28.

Vardys, V. Stanley. "Select Committees of the House of Representatives." *Midwest Journal of Political Science* 6 (August 1962): 247–65.

Magazines

"Bests, Mosts, Misfits, and Others." *The Washingtonian*, March 1989, 97.

Felton, John. "Reagan Tries to Put Out Fire on Iran Dealings." *Congressional Quarterly Weekly Report*, 15 November 1986, 2883–84.

"Four Rattling for Armed Services Chairmanship." *Congressional Quarterly Weekly Report*, 17 January 1987, 103–4.

"House Intelligence Panel." *Congressional Quarterly Weekly Report*, 22 February 1975, 367.

Isaacson, Walter. "A Lot of Show, but No Tell." *Time*, 22 March 1982, 20.

Lardner, George, Jr. "The Intelligence Investigations: Congress Cops Out." *The Progressive*, July 1976, 16.

"President Reagan Responds to Tower Board Investigation." *Congressional Quarterly Weekly Report*, 7 March 1987, 440–41.

Newspapers

Christian Science Monitor, 1975–82.
New York Times, 1974–89.
Washington Post, 1975–87.
Wall Street Journal, 1984.

Correspondence

McClory, Robert. Letter to Frank Smist. 9 October 1981. Dr. Frank J. Smist, Jr., Collection. Carl Albert Congressional Research and Studies Center, University of Oklahoma, Norman.

Reagan, President Ronald. Letter to Chairman David Boren. 7 August 1987. Copy in Dr. Frank J. Smist, Jr., Collection. Carl Albert Congressional Research and Studies Center, University of Oklahoma, Norman.

Russell, Richard. Letter to Theodore Green. 11 January 1956. Copy in Dr. Frank J. Smist, Jr., Collection. Carl Albert Congressional Research Center, University of Oklahoma, Norman.

Washington, General George. Letter to Colonel Elias Dayton. 26 July 1777. Walter Pforzheimer Collection on Intelligence Service. Washington, D.C.

Television and Radio Interviews

C-SPAN. 28 September 1987.
"Face the Nation," CBS News. 27 July 1975.
Harrington, Michael. Interview with CBS News, CBS Radio Network. 7 July 1975.
Meet the Press, NBC News. 2 April 1983.
Pike, Otis. Interview with Bruce Morton and Morton Dean, CBS Radio Network, 22 July 1975.

Congressional Documents

Commission on CIA Activities within the United States. *Report to the President*. Washington, D.C.: GPO, 1975.
Congressional Record. 1975–83. Washington, D.C.
House Committee on Standards of Official Conduct. *Investigation of Publication of Select Committee on Intelligence Report*. 94th Cong., 2d sess., 1976.
House Permanent Select Committee on Intelligence. *Annual Report*. 95th Cong., 2d sess., 1978.
———. *Report*. 97th Cong., 2d sess., 17 December 1982.
———. *Report*. 99th Cong., 1st sess., 2 January 1985.
House Select Committee on Intelligence. *U.S. Intelligence Agencies and Activities Committee Proceedings*. 94th Cong., 1st sess., 1975.
———. *Committee Proceedings II*. 94th Cong., 2d sess., 1976.
———. *U.S. Intelligence Agencies and Activities: Domestic Intelligence Programs*. 94th Cong., 1st sess., 1975.
———. *U.S. Intelligence Agencies and Activities: Intelligence Costs and Fiscal Procedures*. 94th Cong., 1st sess., 1975.
———. *U.S. Intelligence Agencies and Activities: Risks and Control of Foreign Intelligence*. 94th Cong., 1st sess., 1975.
———. *U.S. Intelligence Agencies and Activities: The Performance of the Intelligence Community*. 94th Cong., 1st sess., 1975.
Senate Select Committee on Intelligence. *Annual Report*. 94th Cong., 1st sess., 1977.
———. *Foreign Intelligence Surveillance Act of 1978: The First Five Years*. Report, 98th Cong., 2d sess., 1984.
———. *Intelligence Reform Act of 1981*. 97th Cong., 1st sess., 1981.
———. *Nomination of Admiral B.R. Inman*. 97th Cong. 1st sess., 1981.
———. *Nomination of E. Henry Knoche*. 94th Cong., 2d sess., 1976.
———. *Nomination of William J. Casey*. 97th Cong., 1st sess., 1981.
———. *Report on the Casey Inquiry*. 97th Cong., 1st sess., 1981.
———. *Report to the Senate*. 96th Cong., 1st sess., 14 May 1979.
———. *Report to the Senate*. 97th Cong., 1st sess., 23 September 1981.
———. *Report to the Senate*. 98th Cong., 1st sess., 28 February 1983.
———. *Report to the Senate*. 98th Cong., 2d sess., 10 October 1984.

————. Senate Select Committee to Study Governmental Operations with Respect to Intelligence Activities. *Alleged Assassinations Plots Involving Foreign Leaders.* 94th Cong., 1st sess., 1975.

————. *Covert Action.* 94th Cong., 1st sess., 1975.

————. *Federal Bureau of Investigation.* 94th Cong., 1st sess., 1975.

————. *Foreign and Military Intelligence.* Final Report, 94th Cong., 2d sess., 1976.

————. *Huston Plan.* 94th Cong., 1st sess., 1975.

————. *Intelligence Activities and the Rights of Americans.* Final Report, 94th Cong., 2d sess., 1976.

————. *Internal Revenue Service.* 94th Cong., 1st sess., 1975.

————. *Legislative Proposals to Strengthen Congressional Oversight of the Nation's Intelligence Agencies before the Subcommittee on Intergovernmental Operations.* 93d Cong., 2nd sess., 1974.

————. *Mail Openings.* 94th Cong., 1st sess., 1975.

————. *The National Security Agency and Fourth Amendment Rights.* 94th Cong., 1st sess., 1975.

————. *Unauthorized Storage of Toxic Agents.* 94th Cong., 1st sess., 1975.

Interviews*

Senators

Birch Bayh (Democrat, Indiana): Chairman, Senate Select Committee on Intelligence.
Henry Bellmon (Republican, Oklahoma).
David Boren (Democrat, Oklahoma): Chairman, Senate Select Committee on Intelligence.
Frank Church (Democrat, Idaho): Chairman, Senate Select Committee to Study Governmental Operations with Respect to Intelligence Agencies; Chairman, Senate Foreign Relations Committee.
J. William Fulbright (Democrat, Arkansas): Chairman, Senate Committee on Foreign Relations.
Jake Garn (Republican, Utah): Member, Senate Select Committee on Intelligence; Chairman, Subcommittee on Budget, Senate Select Committee on Intelligence.
Daniel K. Inouye (Democrat, Hawaii): Chairman, Senate Select Committee on Intelligence.
James A. McClure (Republican, Idaho): Chairman, Senate Committee on Energy and Natural Resources.
Hugh Scott (Republican, Pennsylvania): Republican Minority Leader of the Senate, 1969–77.
John C. Stennis (Republican, Mississippi).
Malcolm Wallop (Democrat, Wyoming): Chairman, Subcommittee on Budget, Senate Select Committee on Intelligence.

Representatives.

Joseph P. Addabo (Democrat, New York): Chairman, Subcommittee on Defense, House Committee on Appropriations.
Carl Albert (Democrat, Oklahoma): Speaker, House of Representatives.
Richard Bolling (Democrat, Mississippi): Chairman, House Committee on Rules.
Jack Edwards (Republican, Alabama): Ranking Minority Member, Subcommittee on Defense, House Committee on Appropriations.

---

*A partial list of individuals interviewed by the author.

Mickey Edwards (Republican, Oklahoma).

Glenn English (Democrat, Oklahoma): Chairman, Subcommittee on Government Information and Individual Rights, House Committee on Government Operations.

Barney Frank (Democrat, Massachusetts).

William F. Goodling (Republican, Pennsylvania): Member, House Permanent Select Committee on Intelligence.

Lee H. Hamilton (Democrat, Indiana): Chairman, House Permanent Select Committee on Intelligence.

Michael J. Harrington (Democrat, Massachusetts): Member, House Select Committee on Intelligence.

James P. Johnson (Republican, Colorado): Member, House Select Committee on Intelligence.

James R. Jones (Democrat, Oklahoma): Chairman, House Committee on Budget.

George H. Mahon (Democrat, Texas): Chairman, House Committee on Appropriations.

Robert McClory (Republican, Illinois): Ranking Minority Member, House Select Committee on Intelligence; Ranking Minority Member, House Permanent Select Committee on Intelligence.

Dave McCurdy (Democrat, Oklahoma): Member, House Permanent Select Committee on Intelligence.

Dale Milford (Democrat, Texas): Member, House Select Committee on Intelligence.

Norman Y. Mineta (Democrat, California): Member, House Permanent Select Committee on Intelligence.

G. V. "Sonny" Montgomery (Democrat, Mississippi): Chairman, House Committee on Veterans' Affairs.

Lucien Nedzi (Democrat, Michigan): Chairman, House Select Committee on Intelligence.

Otis G. Pike (Democrat, New York): Chairman, House Select Committee on Intelligence.

Melvin Price (Democrat, Illinois): Chairman, House Committee on Armed Services.

J. Kenneth Robinson (Republican, Virginia): Member, House Permanent Select Committee on Intelligence.

Bob Stump (Democrat/, later Republican, Arizona): Member, House Permanent Select Committee on Intelligence.

Mike Synar (Democrat, Oklahoma).

Morris K. Udall (Democrat, Arizona): Chairman, House Committee on Interior and Insular Affairs.

G. William Whitehurst (Republican, Virginia): Member, House Permanent Select Committee on Intelligence.

C. W. Bill Young (Republican, Florida): Member, House Permanent Select Committee on Intelligence.

Congressional Staff.

David L. Aaron: Task Force Leader, Senate Select Committee to Study Governmental Operations with Respect to Intelligence Activities; National Security Advisor to Walter F. Mondale; Deputy Assistant to President Carter for National Security Affairs, 1977–81.

Peter A. Abbruzzese: Staff Consultant, House Committee on Foreign Affairs.

William B. Bader: Task Force Leader, Senate Select Committee to Study Governmental Operations with Respect to Intelligence Activities; Staff Director, Senate Foreign Relations Committee.

Frederick Baron: Counsel, Senate Select Committee to Study Governmental Operations with Respect to Intelligence Activities.

Michael F. Barrett, Jr.: Staff Director and Chief Counsel, Subcommittee on Oversight and Investigations, House Committee on Energy and Commerce.

Kenneth E. Belieu: Staff Member, Senate Armed Services Committee; Staff Director, Senate Committee on Aeronautics and Space Sciences; Staff Director, Preparedness Subcommittee, Senate Armed Services Committee.

Richard S. Betts: Political Scientist; Professional Staff Member, Senate Select Committee to Study Governmental Operations with Respect to Intelligence Activities; Senior Fellow, The Brookings Institute.

John Blake: Staff Director, Senate Select Committee on Intelligence; Deputy Director for Administration, CIA.

John Russell Blanford: Chief Counsel, House Committee on Armed Services, 1964–72.

John L. Boos: Staff Member, House Select Committee on Intelligence.

Steven H. Bourke: Staff Member, Democratic Steering Committee.

T. Edward Braswell, Jr.: Attorney, Department of Justice; Professional Staff Member, Senate Armed Services Committee, 1953–69; Chief Counsel and Staff Director, Senate Armed Services Committee, 1969–78.

Robert B. Brauer: Staff Member, House Select Committee on Intelligence.

William Holmes Brown: Parliamentarian, House of Representatives.

James O. Bush: Staff Member, House Permanent Select Committee on Intelligence.

David Bushong: Counsel, Senate Select Committee to Study Governmental Operations with Respect to Intelligence Activities; Staff Member, Senate Select Committee on Intelligence.

Barry E. Carter: Counsel, Senate Select Committee to Study Governmental Operations with Respect to Intelligence Activities.

Daniel A. Childs, Jr.: Comptroller, Central Intelligence Agency; Staff Member, Senate Select Committee on Intelligence.

Angelo Codevilla: Staff Member, Senate Select Committee on Intelligence.

William E. Cresswell: Administrative Assistant to Senator John C. Stennis.

William H. Darden: Vice President, Association of American Railroads; Professional Staff Member, Senate Committee on Armed Services.

Lynn F. Davis: Visiting Professor, National Security Affairs, National War College; Staff Member, Senate Select Committee to Study Governmental Operations with Respect to Intelligence Activities.

Spencer F. Davis: Press Secretary, Senate Select Committee to Study Governmental Operations with Respect to Intelligence Activities; Staff Member, Senate Select Committee on Intelligence.

Rhett B. Dawson: Counsel, Senate Select Committee to Study Governmental Operations with Respect to Intelligence Activities; Staff Director and Chief Counsel, Senate Committee on Armed Services.

Joseph F. Dennin: Counsel, Senate Select Committee to Study Governmental Operations with Respect to Intelligence Activities; Counsel, Intelligence Oversight Board.

James V. Dick: Counsel, Senate Select Committee to Study Governmental Operations with Respect to Intelligence Activities; Counsel, Intelligence Oversight Board.

Joseph F. Di Genova: Principal Assistant U.S. Attorney, District of Columbia; Counsel, Senate Select Committee to Study Governmental Operations with Respect to Intelligence Activities.

Aaron B. Donner: General Counsel, House Select Committee on Intelligence.

Earl Eisenhower: Minority Staff Director, Senate Select Committee on Intelligence.

John Elliff: Political Scientist; Task Force Leader, Senate Select Committee to Study Governmental Operations with Respect to Intelligence Activities; Staff Member, Senate Select Committee on Intelligence.

Peter Fenn: Professional Staff Member, Senate Select Committee to Study Governmental Operations with Respect to Intelligence Activities.

Stephen Flanagan: Staff Member, Senate Select Committee on Intelligence.

Thomas Fox: Barber, House of Representatives.

Sam Francis: Professional Staff Member, Subcommittee on Separation of Powers, Senate Committee on the Judiciary.

Leon S. Fuerth: Staff Member, House Permanent Select Committee on Intelligence.

John R. Galloway: Subcommittee Staff Director, House Committee on Government Operations.

Mark H. Gitenstein: Minority Chief Counsel, Senate Committee on the Judiciary; Counsel, Senate Select Committee to Study Governmental Operations with Respect to Intelligence Activities.

Ira H. Goldman: Staff Member, House Permanent Select Committee on Intelligence.

Sandra Zeune Harris: Staff Director, Subcommittee on Environment, Energy, and Natural Resources, House Committee on Government Operations; Staff Member, House Select Committee on Intelligence.

William F. Hildebrand: Secretary of the Senate.

William H. Hogan, Jr.: General Counsel, House Committee on Armed Services.

Sven Holmes: Staff Director, Senate Select Committee on Intelligence.

David Jameson: Staff Member, House Committee on Government Operations.

Loch Johnson: Political Scientist; Staff Member, Senate Select Committee to Study Governmental Operations with Respect to Intelligence Activities.

James H. Johnston: Counsel, Senate Select Committee to Study Governmental Operations with Respect to Intelligence Activities.

W. Procter Jones: Staff Member, Personal Staff of Senator Richard B. Russell, 1960–66, 1968–71; Professional Staff Member, Senate Committee on Appropriations.

Frederick Kaiser: Staff Member, Congressional Research Service.

Anne Karalekas: Staff Member, Senate Select Committee to Study Governmental Operations with Respect to Intelligence Activities.

John G. Keliher: Professional Staff Member, House Permanent Select Committee on Intelligence.

Robert K. Kelley: Counsel, Senate Select Committee to Study Governmental Operations with Respect to Intelligence Activities.

Clifford A. Kiracofe, Jr.: Legislative Assistant to Senator Jesse Helms.

Billie Gay Larson: Senior Legislative Assistant, Office of the Speaker.

Dianne E. La Voy: Research Assistant, Senate Select Committee to Study Governmental Operations with Respect to Intelligence Activities; Staff Member, House Permanent Select Committee on Intelligence.

Edward P. Levine: Staff Member, Senate Select Committee on Intelligence.

Jerome I. Levinson: Counsel, Subcommittee on Foreign Economics Policy, Senate Foreign Relations Committee; Counsel, Subcommittee on Multinational Corporations, Senate Foreign Relations Committee.

Howard S. Liebengood: Sergeant at Arms, Senate; Assistant Minority Counsel, Senate Watergate Committee; Consultant, Senate Select Committee to Study Governmental Operations with Respect to Intelligence Activities; Minority Staff Director, Senate Select Committee on Intelligence.

Mark M. Lowenthal: Staff Member, Congressional Research Service.

Michael J. Madigan: Assistant Minority Counsel, Senate Watergate Committee; Counsel to Senator Howard Baker; Counsel, Senate Select Committee to Study Governmental Operations with Respect to Intelligence Activities; Staff Member, Senate Select Committee on Intelligence.

David Martin: Staff Assistant to Senator Thomas J. Dodd for Internal Security, Foreign Policy, and National Defense, 1959–70; Senior Analyst, Subcommittee on Internal Security, Senate Committee on the Judiciary; Consultant, Standing Committee on Law and National Security, American Bar Association.

Elliot E. Maxwell: Counsel, Senate Select Committee to Study Governmental Operations with Respect to Intelligence Activities; Staff Member, Senate Select Committee on Intelligence.

Leslie L. Megyeri: Staff Member, House Committee on Government Operations.

Linda Melconian: Member, Massachusetts State Senate; Staff Member, Office of the Speaker of the House.

Paul R. Michel: Legislative Assistant to Senator Arlen Specter; Counsel, Senate Select Committee to Study Governmental Operations with Respect to Intelligence Activities; Associate Deputy Attorney General.

William G. Miller: Dean, Fletcher School of Law and Diplomacy; Staff Director, Senate Select Committee to Study Governmental Operations with Respect to Intelligence Activities; Staff Director, Senate Select Committee on Intelligence.

Thomas Moore: Staff Member, Senate Select Committee on Intelligence.

Robert Morgan: Staff Member, Senate Select Committee on Intelligence.

Peter J. Murphy, Jr.: Staff Director, Subcommittee on Defense, House Committee on Appropriations.

John Nelson: Staff Member, Senate Select Committee on Intelligence.

Tod Neuenschwander: Administrative Assistant to Senator James A. McClure.

Michael J. O'Neil: Chief Counsel, House Permanent Select Committee on Intelligence.

James G. Phillips: Professional Staff Member, Senate Committee on Labor and Human Resources.

George E. Pickett: Principal, Booz Allen & Hamilton, Inc.; Staff Member, Senate Select Committee on Intelligence.

John G. Plashal: Staff Assistant, Subcommittee on Defense, House Committee on Appropriations.

Andrew D. Postal: Counsel, Senate Select Committee to Study Governmental Operations with Respect to Intelligence Activities.

Ralph Preston: Staff Assistant, House Committee on Appropriations, 1954–82; Staff Director, Subcommittee on Defense, House Committee on Appropriations.

Eric Richard: Counsel, Senate Select Committee to Study Governmental Operations with Respect to Intelligence Activities.

Arch W. Roberts, Jr.: Staff Consultant, House Committee on Foreign Affairs.

Herbert Romerstein: Staff Member, House Permanent Select Committee on Intelligence.

Miles Q. Romney: Staff Member, House Committee on Government Operations.

Samuel J. Rouston: Legislative Assistant, Senator Steven D. Symms.

Paul Rundquist: Staff Member, Congressional Research Service.

Gregory Rushford: Journalist; Staff Member, House Select Committee on Intelligence.

Gary Schmitt: Minority Staff Director, Senate Select Committee on Intelligence.

Judith Schneider: Staff Member, Congressional Research Service.

Frederick A. O. Schwarz, Jr.: Corporation Counsel, City of New York; Chief Counsel, Senate Select Committee to Study Governmental Operations with Respect to Intelligence Activities.

Patrick Shea: Professional Staff Member, Senate Select Committee to Study Governmental Operations with Respect to Intelligence Activities.

Emily Sheketoff: Associate Producer, "The Journal," Canadian Broadcasting Company; Staff Member, House Select Committee on Intelligence.

William A. Shook: Minority Counsel, Subcommittee on Separation of Powers, Senate Committee on the Judiciary.

Abram N. Shulsky: Director, Strategic Arms Control Policy, Dep. of Defense; Staff Member, Senate Select Committee on Intelligence.

Frank Slatinshek: Staff Member, House Committee on Armed Services, 1957–77; Staff Director, House Committee on Armed Services, 1972–77.

L. Britt Snider: Principal Director for Counterintelligence and Security Policy, Office of the Deputy Under Secretary of Defense for Policy, Dep. of Defense; Counsel, Senate Judiciary Subcommittee on Constitutional Rights, 1972–75; Counsel, Senate Select Committee to Study Governmental Operations with Respect to Intelligence Activities; Chief Counsel, House Government Operations Subcommittee on Government Information, 1977; Chief Counsel, Senate Select Committee on Intelligence.

Chuck Snodgrass: Staff Assistant, House Committee on Appropriations; Assistant Secretary, Air Force.

Roscoe B. Starek III: Staff Member, House Select Committee on Intelligence.

Stan A. Taylor: Director, Center for International and Area Studies, Brigham Young University; Staff Member, Senate Select Committee on Intelligence.

George Tenet: Staff Director, Senate Select Committee on Intelligence.

Victoria Toensing: Chief Counsel, Senate Select Committee on Intelligence.

James S. Van Wagenen: Staff Assistant, Subcommittee on Defense, House Committee on Appropriations.

Ralph Vinovich: Administrative Assistant, Representative Robert H. Michel.

S. Ariel Weiss: Executive Director, Democratic Steering Committee, House of Representatives.

Stephen R. Weissman: Staff Member, House Foreign Affairs Committee.

Burton V. Wides: Minority Counsel, Subcommittee on Immigration and Refugee Policy, Senate Committee on Judiciary; Counsel, Senate Select Committee to Study Governmental Operations with Respect to Intelligence Activities; Counsel, Intelligence Oversight Board.

R. James Woolsey: Program Analyst, Office of the Secretary of Defense, 1968–70; National Security Council, 1970; General Counsel, Senate Committee on Armed

Services, 1970–73; Under Secretary of the Navy, 1977–79; Adviser, U.S. Delegations to Strategic Arms Limitation Talks, Helsinki and Vienna, 1969–70.

Cheryl Tina Yamamoto: Staff Member, House Select Committee on Intelligence.

Executive-Branch Officials

Stephen Ailes: Legal Staff, Office of Price Administration, 1942–46; Assistant General Counsel on Consumer Goods, Price Division, Office of Price Administration, 1945–46; Counsel, U.S. Economic Mission to Greece, 1947; Under Secretary of the Army, 1961–64; President, Association of American Railroads, 1971–77; Member, President's Foreign Intelligence Advisory Board, 1976–77; Member, Intelligence Oversight Board, 1976–77.

Jon T. Anderson: General Counsel, National Security Agency.

Kenneth C. Bass III: Staff Member, Office of Intelligence Policy and Review, Dep. of Justice.

David W. Belin: Counsel, President's Commission on the Assassination of President Kennedy; Executive Director, Commission on CIA Activities within the United States.

Seymour R. Bolten: Senior Advisor, Enforcement and Operations, Dep. of the Treasury; Intelligence Officer, CIA; Chief, CIA Review Staff for the House and Senate Select Intelligence Committees.

John A. Bross: Intelligence Officer, CIA, 1951–71.

Harold Brown: Secretary of the Air Force, 1965–69; President, California Institute of Technology, 1969–77; Secretary of Defense, 1977–81.

Zbigniew Brzezinski: National Security Advisor to President Carter, 1977–81.

Philip W. Buchen: Counsel to President Ford, 1974–77.

Admiral Arleigh A. Burke: Chief of Naval Operations, 1955–61.

Frank C. Carlucci: President and Chief Operating Officer, Sears World Trade, Inc.; Deputy Secretary of Defense; Director of the Office of Economic Opportunity; Deputy Director, Office of Management and Budget; Deputy Director of Central Intelligence.

George L. Cary: Special Assistant for Legislative Affairs, Dep. of the Army; Legislative Counsel, CIA.

Gary M. Chase: Associate General Counsel, Office of Legislative Affairs, CIA.

Leo Cherne: Adviser on Taxation and Fiscal Policy to General MacArthur, 1946; Member, President's Foreign Intelligence Advisory Board, 1973–76; Chairman, President's Foreign Intelligence Advisory Board, 1976–77; Member, Intelligence Oversight Board, 1976–77; Vice Chairman, President's Foreign Intelligence Advisory Board, 1981–83.

A. R. Cinquegranna: Deputy Counsel for Intelligence Policy, Office of Intelligence Policy and Review, Dep. of Justice.

Benjamin R. Civiletti: Assistant Attorney General, 1977–78; Deputy Attorney General, 1978–79; Attorney General, 1979–81.

Clark M. Clifford: Counsel to President Truman; Member and Chairman of President's Foreign Intelligence Advisory Board; Secretary of Defense.

Ray S. Cline: Deputy Director for Intelligence, Central Intelligence Agency; Director, Bureau of Intelligence and Research, Dep. of State; Senior Associate, Georgetown Center for Strategic and International Studies.

William A. Clinkscales, Jr.: Director, Office of Oversight, General Services Administration.

William E. Colby: Director of Central Intelligence, 1973–76.

Arnold E. Donahue: Intelligence Branch Chief, National Security Division, National Security Affairs, Office of Management and Budget.

Eleanor J. Dulles: Retired Diplomat and Educator.

Robert F. Ellsworth: Member, House of Representatives; United States Ambassador to NATO—Deputy Secretary of Defense.

John D. Erlichman: Counsel to President Nixon, 1969; Assistant to the President for Domestic Affairs, 1969–73.

Donald P. Gregg: Assistant to Vice-President Bush for National Security Affairs; Intelligence Officer, CIA.

Marilyn Haft: Deputy Counsel to Vice-President Mondale.

Samuel Halpern: Former Executive Assistant to the Deputy Director for Plans, CIA.

Bryce N. Harlow: Staff Member, House Armed Services Committee; Chief, White House Congressional Relations Staff for President Eisenhower; Counselor to President Nixon.

Richard M. Helms: Director of Central Intelligence, 1965–74; United States Ambassador to Iran, 1973–76.

James D. Hittle: Brigadier General, U.S. Marine Corps; President, Army and Navy Club.

Frederick P. Hitz: Legislative Counsel, CIA.

Lawrence R. Houston: General Counsel, CIA.

Admiral R. N. Inman: Deputy Director of Central Intelligence; Director, National Security Agency.

Spurgeon M. Keeny, Jr.: Deputy to the Director, U.S. Arms Control and Disarmament Agency.

Robert M. Kimmet: Executive Secretary and General Counsel, National Security Council; Special Assistant to President Reagan.

Axel Kleiboemer: Assistant U.S. Attorney, District of Columbia, 1967–71; Attorney Adviser, Office of the Deputy Attorney General, Dep. of Justice, 1971–73; Special Counsel, Law Enforcement Assistance Administration, 1974.

Gil Kujovich: Counsel, Intelligence Oversight Board.

Melvin R. Laird: Member, House of Representatives, 1953–68; Chairman, Republican Conference; Member, House Committee on Appropriations; Secretary of Defense, 1969–72; Domestic Advisor to President Nixon, 1973–74; Senior Counselor for National and International Affairs, Reader's Digest Association, Inc.

Anthony A. Lapham: General Counsel, CIA.

Mary C. Lawton: Counsel for Intelligence Policy, Office of Intelligence Policy and Review, Dep. of Justice.

John O. Marsh, Jr.: Secretary of the Army; Member, House of Representatives; Counselor to President Ford; Assistant Secretary of Defense for Legislative Affairs.

John M. Maury: Legislative Counsel, CIA.

Cord Meyer: Intelligence Officer, Central Intelligence Agency.

Admiral Thomas H. Moorer: U.S. Navy; Chairman, Joint Chiefs of Staff.

Emil P. Moschella: Legislative Counsel, FBI.

Admiral Daniel J. Murphy: Chief of Staff for Vice-President Bush; Deputy Under Secretary of Defense for Policy Review; Deputy to the Director of Central Intelligence for Policy Review.

David D. Newsom: Ambassador to Libya, 1965–69; Assistant Secretary of State for African Affairs, 1969–74; Ambassador to Indonesia, 1974–77; Ambassador to the Philippines, 1977–78; Undersecretary for Political Affairs, Dep. of State, 1978–81; Associate Dean and Director of the Institute for the Study of Diplomacy, Georgetown University School of Foreign Service, 1981–83.

James E. Nolan: Special Agent, FBI, 1958–83; Inspector—Deputy Assistant Director, Intelligence Division, FBI, 1980–83; Director of the Office of Foreign Missions, Dep. of State.

Walter Pforzheimer: Legislative Counsel, CIA.

Samuel R. Pierce: Secretary, Dep. of Housing and Urban Development.

Lieutenant General John S. Pustay: President, National Defense University; Deputy Assistant Chief of Staff for Intelligence, U.S. Air Force; Chief, Air Force Budget Issues Team; Assistant to the Chairman, Joint Chiefs of Staff.

Mitchell Rogovin: Special Counsel to the Director of Central Intelligence, 1975–76.

David Ryan: Special Agent, FBI, 1951–79.

Harold H. Saunders: CIA, 1959–61; Staff Member, National Security Council, 1961–74; Senior Staff Member, National Security Council, 1967–74; Deputy Assistant Secretary of State for Near Asia and South Asia, 1974–75; Director, Bureau of Intelligence and Research, Dep. of State, 1975–78; Assistant Secretary of State for Near Asia and South Asia, 1978–81; Resident Fellow, American Enterprise Institute.

Antonin Scalia: Circuit Judge, U.S. Court of Appeals, District of Columbia; Assistant Attorney General, Office of Legal Counsel, U.S. Dep. of Justice, 1974–77.

Daniel C. Schwartz: General Counsel, National Security Agency.

John H. Shenefield: Associate Attorney General, Dep. of Justice.

Gary Sick: Staff Member, National Security Council.

Deanne C. Siemer: General Counsel, Dep. of Defense.

Daniel B. Silver: General Counsel, CIA; General Counsel, National Security Agency.

Frank Snepp: Author; Former Intelligence Officer, CIA.

Stanley Sporkin: General Counsel, CIA.

Stuart L. Symington: Assistant Secretary of War for Air, 1946–47; First Secretary of the Air Force, 1947–50; Chairman, National Security Resources Board, 1950–51; Reconstruction Finance Corporation Administrator, 1951–52; Member, United States Senate, 1952–77.

Captain George Thibault: U.S. Navy; Chairman, Dep. of Military Strategy, National War College; Special Assistant to Director of Central Intelligence, 1977–81.

Lieutenant General Eugene Tighe: U.S. Air Force; Director, Defense Intelligence Agency.

Victor L. Tomseth: Director, Office of Indian, Nepalese, and Sri Lankan Affairs, Dep. of State; Political Consul, American Embassy in Tehran, 1975–81.

Louis W. Tordella: Deputy Director, National Security Agency, 1958–74.

Thomas F. Troy: Editor, *Foreign Intelligence Literary Scene*; Intelligence Officer, CIA.

Robert Turner: Counsel, President's Intelligence Oversight Board.

Admiral Stansfield Turner: Director of Central Intelligence, 1977–81.

Cyrus D. Vance: Secretary of State, 1977–80.

Raymond J. Waldmann: President, Global USA, Inc; Intelligence Consultant, American Bar Association Standing Committee on Law and National Security; Special Counsel for Intelligence to President Ford.

Peter J. Wallison: General Counsel, Dep. of Treasury; Counsel to Vice-President Nelson A. Rockefeller, 1974–77.

W. Raymond Wannall: Chairman, Board of Directors, Association of Former Intelligence Officers; Former Assistant Director, Intelligence Division, FBI.

John S. Warner: General Counsel, CIA.

Paul C. Warnke: General Counsel, Dep. of Defense; Assistant Secretary of Defense for National Security Affairs; Director, U.S. Arms Control and Disarmament Agency; Chief Negotiator for the Strategic Arms Limitation Talks for President Carter; Consultant to the State Department.

James A. Wilderotter: Associate Deputy Attorney General, Dep. of State; Associate Counsel to President Ford; General Counsel, Energy Research and Development Administration.

Robert J. Winchester: Assistant Legislative Counsel, CIA.

Judiciary

Barrington D. Parker: U.S. District Judge, District of Columbia.

Press

Benjamin C. Bradlee: Executive Editor, *Washington Post*.

Noel Epstein: Assistant Editor, Sunday Outlook section, *Washington Post*.

Seymour M. Hersh: Journalist.

Joseph Kraft: Journalist.

George Lardner: Journalist, *Washington Post*.

Anthony Lewis: Journalist, *New York Times*.

Clark Mollenhoff: Journalist.

Ike Pappas: Correspondent, CBS News.

James R. Polk: Correspondent, NBC News.

Tad Szulc: Former Latin American and East European Correspondent, *New York Times*; Journalist, Author.

Phillip Taubman: Journalist, *New York Times*.

Joseph Volz: National Security Correspondent, *New York Daily News*.

Clientele Groups

Jerry J. Berman: Legislative Counsel, American Civil Liberties Union.

Robert L. Borosage: Director, Institute for Policy Studies.

Marjorie W. Cline: Treasurer, National Intelligence Study Center.

Phillip Cox: Executive Assistant, American Security Council.

Roy Godson: Coordinator, Consortium for the Study of Intelligence; Associate Professor of Government, Georgetown University.

Morton H. Halperin: Center for National Security Studies.

Jay Peterzell: Center for National Security Studies.

Canadian Intelligence Overseers

Herbert P.G. Frazier: Counselor, Canadian Embassy to the United States.
Ray Hnattshyn: Member, House of Commons.
Claude Andre Lachance: Member, House of Commons.
Allan Lawrence: Solicitor General.
Daniel Riley: Member, Senate, Canada.
Svend Robinson: Member, House of Commons.

Index

Aaron, David, 40, 47
Aberbach, Joel, 19
Adams, Samuel, 23, 194
Addabo, Joseph P., 226, 244
Afghanistan, 96, 112, 125, 242
Agee, Philip, 64, 128, 233
Agent Identities Act, 98, 105, 227, 230, 233
Ahearn, Paul, 206
Air Force Intelligence, 3, 117
Albert, Carl, 138, 143, 152, 165, 174, 186
Alexander, Donald, 72–73
Allen, Lt. Gen. Lew, 74
Allende, Salvador, 134
American Bar Association (ABA), 115, 241
American Civil Liberties Union (ACLU), 114–15, 202, 233, 241
American Jewish Committee, 72
American Security Council, 30n, 115
Americans for Democratic Action (ADA), 30n, 72, 139, 141, 143, 147, 153, 222
Anderson, Jack, 131
Anderson, John, 203–4
Angleton, James, 26
Angola, 139, 179, 209, 210
Appropriations Committee (House), 4, 8, 9, 118, 118n, 141, 142, 143, 192, 204, 222, 225, 226, 229, 231, 235–36, 242–45
Appropriations Committee (Senate), 4, 5–7, 9, 31, 32, 85, 118n, 192
Armed Services Committee (House), 4,

7–8, 10, 107, 140, 141, 142, 143, 147, 148, 150, 151, 153, 175, 192, 204, 222, 231, 235, 236, 274
Armed Services Committee (Senate), 4, 5–7, 31, 32, 83, 85, 91, 93, 102, 106–7, 119, 132, 192, 236, 237
Army Intelligence, 3
Ashbrook, John, 222, 227, 230, 233
Aspin, Les, 141, 142, 160, 162, 164, 177, 222, 228, 229, 230, 232, 238–39, 242
assassinations, 42, 43, 47, 51–52, 58, 67, 68–71, 78, 79, 80, 171, 196, 197, 241, 262
Associated Catholic Charities, 72
Association of Former Intelligence Officers (AFIO), 104, 115, 235, 241, 242
attorney general, 78

Bach, Stanley, 191, 205, 206, 207
Bader, William, 47
Baker, Howard, 25–26, 27, 32, 34, 42, 43, 45, 51, 52, 58, 59, 63, 85, 86–87, 260
Bardot, Brigitte, 170
Baron, Frederick, 46, 58–59, 68, 70–71
Bauman, Robert, 170
Bayh, Birch, 11, 14, 88, 93, 95–97, 98, 99, 103, 107–8, 112, 121, 124, 280–81
Beilenson, Anthony, 271
Bell, Griffin, 109, 235
Bentsen, Lloyd, 88, 91, 100
Ben-Veniste, Richard, 165

Berman, Jerry, 114
Bernstein, Carl, 66, 261
Biden, Joseph, 88, 100, 113, 129
Bingham, Jonathan, 135
Blake, John, 97–98, 104
Blount, Winton M., 73–74
Boland, Edward P., 11, 101, 215, 216, 217, 219, 222, 223, 224–28, 230, 231, 232, 233, 234, 235, 236, 238, 241, 245, 247, 248, 250, 252, 257
Bolling, Richard, 168, 174, 215
Bolten, Seymour, 61, 161
Bond, James, 101, 177
Boos, John, 191, 206, 207
Boren, David L., 14, 252, 267, 268, 269, 270, 272
Boyatt, Thomas, 181, 182, 189, 194, 207
Bradlee, Ben, 114
Breslin, Jimmy, 72
Bridges, Styles, 5–6
Brooks, Jack, 264
Brown, Harold, 102, 124, 227
Brzezinski, Zbigniew, 110, 124, 239
Buchen, Philip, 26, 27, 56, 57, 184, 186
budget oversight, 91, 92, 95, 102, 105–6, 107, 116–19, 132, 191–93, 209–10, 211, 224, 226, 227, 229, 232, 233–34, 237, 242–46, 250, 252, 257, 264, 269, 271, 272, 274, 275
Bundy, McGeorge, 47, 196, 202, 203
Bureau of Narcotics and Dangerous Drugs, 74
Burlison, Bill, 222, 224, 236, 245
Bush, George, 189, 244, 272, 273
Bush, James, 231, 232
Bushong, David, 48
Byrd, Harry, 6, 106
Byrd, Robert, 52, 85, 106

Cannon, Clarence, 8
Cannon, Howard, 31, 82
Carlucci, Frank, 119, 129
Carswell, G. Harrold, 95
Carter, Jimmy, 68, 84, 96, 103, 109, 110, 111, 112, 120–21, 123, 126, 130, 132, 214, 239, 252
Cary, George L., 147–48, 174

Case, Clifford, 37, 85, 89
Casey, William, 98, 99, 108, 110, 122, 123, 130, 224, 239, 241, 256–57, 258, 264, 265, 267
Casey Accord, 123
Casper, Gerhard, 202
Castro, Fidel, 69, 70, 155
CBS, 131, 194n
Center for National Security Studies, 114–15, 241
Central Intelligence Agency (CIA), 3, 5, 6, 7, 9, 13, 25, 30, 32, 38, 44, 48, 49, 54, 57, 58, 59–61, 64, 70, 71, 72, 73, 74, 78, 79, 104, 109, 114, 117, 129, 131, 145, 147, 148, 149, 150, 151, 152, 155, 158, 161, 164, 170, 171, 172, 173, 174, 175, 176, 177, 181, 185, 186, 187, 189, 192, 193, 195, 196, 197, 200, 202, 203, 204, 208, 209, 210, 211, 214, 224, 231, 233, 238, 240, 241, 243, 245, 249, 256, 257, 262, 263, 269
Chafee, John, 89, 91, 100
Cheney, Richard, 227
Cherne, Leo, 204
Childs, Daniel, 104, 244
Chile, 30, 37, 49, 49n, 54, 76, 134, 171, 172, 174, 208
Christ, Jesus, 266
Christian Science Monitor, 173, 188
Church, Frank, 10, 14, 22, 27, 28, 30, 31, 33, 34, 35–40, 41, 42, 43, 44, 45, 46, 48, 49, 51, 52, 53, 54, 55, 56–57, 58, 59, 64, 65, 66, 67, 69–70, 71, 73, 75, 76, 81, 83, 94, 119, 156, 157, 171, 172, 175, 197, 208, 270
Church Committee, 10, 84–85, 91, 93, 95, 97, 101, 102, 107, 109, 116, 123, 124, 125, 127, 131, 146, 154, 155, 156, 160, 165, 166, 167, 168, 175, 176, 177, 179, 196, 198, 205, 211, 214, 232, 240, 249, 251, 262; assassinations study, 69–71; establishment of, 25–28; evaluation of, 80–81; final reports, 77–80; internal relations, 41–45; leadership of chairman, 35–40; public hearings, 71–77; recruitment of members, 28–35; relations

with executive branch, 55–65; relations with House, 53–55, 171–72; relations with press, 65–68, 188; relations with Senate, 49–53; staff, 45–49
Churchill, Winston, 281
Clark, Ramsey, 152
Clark, William, 129
Clifford, Clark, 2, 5
Cline, Ray, 181, 193
Cochran, Thad, 157
Codevilla, Angelo, 103, 254
Cohen, William, 100, 264, 268, 269, 270
COINTELPRO, 76, 78, 210
Colby, William, 14, 26, 27, 44, 51, 56, 57, 58, 59–61, 63, 66, 69, 149, 155, 173, 174, 178, 179, 180, 181, 186, 191, 192, 194, 200, 204
Colson, Charles, 149
Committee on Law and National Security, 115, 241, 242
Committee on Standards of Official Conduct (House), 136, 156–57, 161, 164, 166, 170–71, 206
Common Cause, 72
competitive analysis, 103
Congressional Research Service (CRS), 206, 207, 238
Contras, 100, 113, 247–48, 253, 258, 259–67, 268
Cooper, Chester, 200
Cooper, John Sherman, 37, 45
Corwin, Edwin S., 280
counterintelligence, 103, 245, 254–55, 271
covert action, 43, 69, 76, 92–93, 110, 111, 119–23, 132, 181, 183, 195, 196, 200, 202–3, 209, 210, 211, 224, 225, 230, 241, 244, 245, 246–48, 250–51, 252, 257–58, 262, 263, 264, 269, 271, 274, 275, 279
Covert Action Information Bulletin, 128, 233
Cox, Arthur, 205
Cranston, Alan, 27, 52
Cutler, Lloyd, 123
Cyprus, 181, 193, 194, 207, 210
Czechoslovakia, 210

Daley, Richard, 141
Daniel, W. C. Daniel, 257
Daniloff, Nicholas, 255
Dash, Sam, 34
Davis, Mendel J., 135
Davis, Spencer, 112
Day, Edward J., 73–74
Dayton, Elias, 1
Defense Intelligence Agency (DIA), 3, 8, 25, 38, 58, 72, 74, 78, 79, 124, 127, 150, 193, 211, 238, 249
Dellums, Ron, 136, 141, 142, 146, 152, 160, 162, 164, 169, 182–83, 198, 216, 270
Dennin, Joseph, 41, 46, 47, 55
Department of Defense (DOD), 58, 119, 132, 141, 245
Department of Energy (DOE), 3, 245
Department of Justice, 62, 203
Department of State, 3, 58, 150, 181, 183, 197, 245
Department of Treasury, 3
Dick, James, 46, 47, 81
Diem, Ngo Dinh, 69
Di Genova, Joseph, 40, 47, 48, 55, 66
director of central intelligence (DCI), 3, 5, 59, 77, 79, 80, 116, 117, 128, 130, 191, 211, 244, 246, 254, 257, 258, 263
Doar, John, 46
Dole, Robert, 31, 268
Donner, Aaron, 153, 154, 164, 167, 177, 179, 180, 181, 182, 187, 191, 206, 207
Dorsen, Norman, 172, 202
Drug Enforcement Administration, 3, 197, 198, 245
Dulles, Allen W., 5, 8, 24
Durenberger, David, 91, 100, 113, 253, 254, 255, 256–57, 268

Eagleburger, Lawrence, 181, 182
Easton, David, 15
Edwards, Don, 139, 141, 142, 152, 159, 169, 216
Egypt, 185, 186
Ehrlichman, John, 149, 150
Eisenhower, Dwight D., 70
Elliff, John, 47, 49–50, 51–52, 61, 62, 132
Ellsberg, Daniel, 130, 148, 149

Ellsworth, Robert F., 5
El Salvador, 115, 131
Epstein, Michael, 61
Ervin, Sam, 34, 49
Executive Order 11905, 79, 80, 81
Executive Order 12306, 126
Executive Order 12333, 126
Exner, Judith Campbell, 38

Fallaci, Oriani, 188
Falwell, Jerry, 266
"Family Jewels," 20, 38, 63, 149, 152,
    154, 158, 169, 176
Federal Bureau of Investigation (FBI),
    3, 25, 38, 49, 58, 61–62, 66–67, 72,
    73, 74, 75–76, 102, 109, 124, 126,
    127, 146, 166, 171, 192, 197, 198,
    199, 210, 211, 229, 245, 271
Fenn, Peter, 48
Fenno, Richard F., Jr., 8, 14–17, 19,
    118, 118n, 243, 244, 246
Ferris, Charles, 29, 215
Field, Searle, 151, 152, 153, 161,
    165, 166, 167, 191, 193, 198, 205,
    206, 207
Fisher, Roger, 202
Foley, Thomas, 259, 273
Ford, Gerald R., 9, 10, 26, 27, 51, 56,
    59, 61, 63, 69, 79, 109, 166, 180,
    184, 185, 186, 189, 194
Foreign Intelligence Surveillance Act
    (FISA), 75, 96, 101, 103, 105,
    115, 126, 133, 227, 230, 234–35,
    236, 249
Foreign Intercourse Fund, 2
Foreign Relations Committee (Senate),
    6–7, 31, 32, 85, 93, 106, 119
40 Committee, 181, 182, 183, 193, 195
Fowler, Wyche, 222, 230
Freedom of Information Act (FOIA), 98,
    105, 128, 249
Frenzel, Bill, 169
Fulbright, J. W., 6–7

"Gang of Eight," 122, 263
"Gang of Five," 147
"Gang of Six," 103
Gardner, James, 195
Garn, Jake, 85, 89, 100

Gates, Robert, 273
General Accounting Office (GAO), 23,
    77, 106, 129, 131, 192, 209, 238,
    249, 250, 279
Giaimo, Robert, 139, 140–41, 142,
    145, 151, 152, 159, 160, 162, 164,
    165, 169, 178, 198, 216, 226
Gitenstein, Mark, 61
Glennon, John, 73
Glomar Explorer, 177
Goldwater, Barry, 11, 32, 43, 44, 52,
    63, 66, 71, 89, 93, 94, 95, 96, 97–
    99, 100, 104, 112–13, 121, 122,
    123, 131, 200
Goodell, Charles, 72
Goodling, William, 222, 223
Gordon, Nathan, 71
Gore, Albert, Jr., 224, 230
Government Operations Committee
    (House), 141, 142
Government Operations Committee
    (Senate), 82, 106, 131
Graham, Daniel O., 194
Gray, L. Patrick, 149
graymail, 105, 249
Green, Theodore, 6
Greenfield, Alexander, 165
Gruening, Ernest, 72
Guatemala, 5

Haldeman, H. R., 149
Hall, Albert C., 191
Halperin, Morton, 114–15, 241
Hamilton, Lee H., 14, 222, 230, 238,
    253, 257, 258, 264, 265, 270
Harkin, Tom, 226, 247, 248
Harlow, Bryce, 173
Harrington, Michael, 134, 135, 136,
    139, 141, 142, 151, 152, 153, 159,
    164, 169, 174–75, 190, 203–4,
    216, 226
Harris, Sandra Zeune, 208
Hart, Gary, 30, 31, 34, 43, 44, 88, 91
Hart, Philip, 30, 31, 40, 43, 44, 45, 46,
    51, 75, 76
Hatfield, Mark, 85, 89
Hathaway, William, 91, 106, 116
Hayakawa, S. I., 85
Hayden, Carl, 6

Hayes, Philip, 141, 142, 145, 146, 160, 163
Haynsworth, Clement, 95
Hays, Wayne, 170
Hebert, F. Edward, 7, 134, 147, 148, 151
Helms, Richard, 7, 14, 70, 73, 149, 161, 194
Hersh, Seymour, 9, 14, 26, 56, 65, 68, 82, 151, 188, 241
Hickenlooper, Burke B., 6
Hills, Carla, 185
Hills, Rod, 184, 185
Holmes, Sven, 268
Holtzman, Elizabeth, 260–61
Hoover, J. Edgar, 72, 78, 171
Horrock, Nicholas, 36, 38
House Permanent Select Committee on Intelligence (HPSCI), 87–88, 101, 107, 118, 120, 121, 125, 211, 213, 252; budget oversight, 242–46; covert action oversight, 246–48; establishment of, 214–17; evaluation of, 250–51; internal relations, 229–31; leadership of chairman, 224–28; legislation, 248–50; 1985–1986, 257–58, 264; 1987–1989, 270–72, 273–74; recruitment of members, 217–24; relations with clientele groups, 241–42; relations with executive branch, 237–39; relations with House, 233–36; relations with press, 239–41; relations with Senate, 236–37; staff, 231–33
House Select Committee on Intelligence. See Nedzi Committee and Pike Committee
Houston, Lawrence R., 4, 9
Huddleston, Walter, 27, 30, 31, 43, 63, 75, 83, 91, 100, 113, 123, 124
Hugel, Max, 99
Hughes-Ryan Amendment, 119, 120, 121–22
Humphrey, Hubert, 30
Hunt, Howard, 149
Huston, Tom Charles, 71–72
Huston Plan, 69, 71–72, 171
Hyde, Henry, 270, 271

India, 210
INF Treaty, 269–70

Inman, Admiral B. R., 95, 99, 113, 129, 227, 244–45
Inouye, Daniel, 11, 14, 85–86, 91, 93–95, 96, 97, 98, 100, 101, 103, 112, 113, 116, 123, 126, 129, 130, 133, 253, 254, 268, 269, 270
Institute for Policy Studies, 198, 199
institutional oversight, 7, 9, 21–22, 77, 80, 84–85, 97, 98, 99, 101, 102, 118, 129, 132, 133, 150, 153, 199, 217, 227, 228, 233, 249, 250, 252, 270, 274, 277–79
intelligence analysis, 103, 115, 205, 274
Intelligence and Research (INR), 58
intelligence charters, 68, 77, 84, 91, 96, 114–15, 123–26, 214, 236
intelligence community, 3–4, 95, 97, 98, 249
Intelligence Community Staff, 104, 117, 245, 246
Intelligence Coordinating Group (ICG), 57–58
Intelligence Identities Act, 127–28, 249
intelligence oversight, 18–19, 110–11, 234, 238, 274–81
Intelligence Oversight Act of 1980, 96, 103, 105, 119–20, 121–22, 123, 125, 126–27, 235–36, 246
Intelligence Oversight Board (IOB), 79, 109
intelligence product, 91
Internal Revenue Service (IRS), 38, 69, 72–73, 78, 171, 192
International Relations Committee (House), 141, 142, 143, 222
investigative oversight, 22–24, 77, 80, 84–85, 137, 153, 199, 205, 207, 228, 232, 270, 274, 277–79
Iran, 5, 96, 125, 132, 186, 241, 252–53, 258, 259, 260, 264, 267
Iran-Contra Affair, 252–53, 258–67, 268, 270, 271, 277
Iran-Contra Committees, 253, 259–67, 268, 270
Iran rescue mission, 96, 110, 120–21, 125
Israel, 185, 193, 255, 263
Italy, 179, 210
ITT, 30, 37, 48, 74, 172, 208

Jackson, Henry, 48, 49, 88, 90, 91,
    172, 208
Jackson, Jesse, 72
Javits, Jacob, 119
Jay, John, 1
Johnson, James, 142, 143, 144, 160,
    161, 163, 164, 180, 196–97, 202,
    223, 226
Johnson, Loch, 15, 39, 40, 44, 53, 214,
    228, 231–32, 238–39, 240
Johnson, Lyndon B., 7, 26, 27, 200
joint intelligence committee, 79, 108,
    169, 203, 204, 207, 237, 277
Judiciary Committee (House), 53, 141,
    142, 143, 167, 222
Judiciary Committee (Senate), 31, 32,
    82, 85

Kaiser, Martin, 197–98
Kalb, Bernard, 186
Kalb, Marvin, 186
Karalekas, Anne, 125
Kassenbaum, Nancy, 48
Kasten, Robert, 142, 146, 153, 160,
    163, 164, 213, 216
Katzenbach, Nicholas, 47, 202–3
Keefe, William J., 18
Kefauver, Estes, 33–34, 37, 40
Kelley, Clarence, 62
Kennedy, Edward M., 131
Kennedy, John F., 26, 38, 69, 72, 77
Kennelly, Barbara, 270
KGB, 75–76, 255
Khomeini, Ayatollah, 259
King, Coretta, 72
King, Martin Luther, Jr., 75–76, 80,
    198
Kirbow, Charles, 48, 66–67
Kissinger, Henry, 26, 54, 58, 60, 136,
    164, 166, 178, 180, 181, 182, 183,
    184, 186, 189, 193, 195, 196, 197,
    201, 202, 209, 210
Knoche, E. Henry, 129
Kurds, 210

Laird, Melvin R., 173
Lardner, George, Jr., 15, 52, 67, 68,
    189
Latimer, Thomas, 231, 271

La Voy, Dianne, 232
Laxalt, Paul, 31
Leahy, Patrick, 88, 100, 113, 253, 255–
    56, 268
Legal Aid Society, 72
Lehman, William, 141, 142, 145, 155,
    160, 162, 198
Levi, Edward H., 62, 63, 81
Libya, 240
Liddy, Gordon, 149
Liebengood, Howard, 41, 60
Lindsey, John, 72
Lombard, Charles, 48
Ludlum, Robert, 101
Lugar, Richard, 89, 100
Lumumba, Patrice, 59, 69, 70
Lydon, Christopher, 35
Lynn, James, 184, 192

McClellan, John L., 27, 31
McClory, Robert, 142, 143, 145, 153,
    159, 160, 162, 163, 164, 167, 169,
    180, 186, 200, 201, 204, 208, 215–
    16, 222, 227, 230, 233, 235
McClure, James, 82–83
McCord, James, 148, 149
McCurdy, Dave, 222, 248, 252, 257,
    271, 273, 274
McFarlane, Robert, 122, 259, 264
McGovern, George, 31
McIntyre, Thomas, 31
MacLaine, Shirley, 72
McMahon, John, 129
McNamara, Robert, 141
Madigan, Michael, 33, 34, 58, 60, 66
Madison, James, 1
Mahon, George H., 8, 235, 243
mail openings, 69, 73–74
Manley, John, 17
Mansfield, Mike, 6, 25, 27, 29, 30, 31,
    32, 33, 34, 37, 40, 42, 45, 50, 82,
    85–86, 93, 94, 151, 165
Marine Corps Intelligence, 3
Marsh, John, 57, 63, 184
Marshall, Burke, 46
Mathias, Charles, 25, 27, 31, 32, 37,
    42, 43, 45, 46, 51, 52, 63, 71, 72–
    73, 89
Maury, John, 149–50, 179–80

Mazzoli, Romano L., 222, 230
Meese, Edwin, 252–53
Michel, Robert, 218, 220, 221
Milford, Dale, 139, 141, 142, 143, 144, 160, 161, 162, 163, 170, 192–93, 216
Miller, William G., 30, 31, 36–37, 39, 45–49, 51, 53, 59, 61, 62, 84–85, 102–5, 127, 165
Mineta, Norman Y., 222, 223, 241
Mondale, Walter, 30, 31, 34, 43, 44, 59, 65, 73–74, 75–76, 83, 123, 124, 214, 235
Montoya, Joseph, 72
Morgan, Robert, 30, 31, 43, 62, 63, 72
Morrow, William L., 18
Moss, John, 135
Mossadegh, Mohammed, 5
Moynihan, Daniel P., 91, 98, 100, 122, 123, 129
Murphy, Morgan, 141, 144, 146, 153, 160, 162, 181, 192–93, 198
Murphy, Robert, 204
Murtha, John, 218
Muskie, Edmund S., 25, 27, 42

National Education Association, 72
National Historical Intelligence Museum, 128
National Security Act of 1947, 3, 79, 202, 257, 264
National Security Agency (NSA), 3, 8, 25, 38, 43, 48, 54, 58, 63–64, 72, 74–75, 78, 109, 117, 124, 126, 127, 150, 171, 185, 186, 192, 227, 245, 249
National Security Council (NSC), 58, 77, 129, 181, 183, 193, 195, 210, 258
National Security Index (NSI), 30n, 115, 139, 143, 147, 153, 222
National Students Assocation, 7, 72
Navy Intelligence, 3
Nedzi, Lucien, 10, 14, 134, 135, 136, 137, 140, 141, 142, 145, 146–53, 155, 159, 161, 164, 165, 166–67, 168, 169, 173, 174, 176, 212, 216
Nedzi Committee, 10, 222, 227, 228, 232, 233, 250; abolished, 135; estab-
lishment of, 134–35; evaluation of, 211–13; internal relations, 158–59; leadership of chairman, 146–53; recruitment of members, 137–46; relations with executive branch, 173–75; relations with House, 168–69, 171; relations with press, 187–88; relations with Senate, 171; staff, 165–67
Nelson, William, 200
Newsom, David, 111
Newsweek, 247
New York Times, 9, 14, 15, 19, 26, 27, 35, 36, 37, 52, 65, 97, 113, 136, 139, 141, 152, 170, 182, 188, 190, 224, 240, 241, 247, 248, 255, 260
Nicaragua, 99, 100, 110, 113, 120, 132, 187, 224, 226, 230, 241, 247–48, 253, 258, 259, 266, 267
1973 Mideast War, 181, 185, 193, 194, 210
Nixon, Richard M., 25, 41, 56, 57, 71, 142, 167
North, Oliver, 259, 260, 261, 264, 265, 266
Nunn, Sam, 88, 100

Office of Management and Budget (OMB), 58, 184, 192, 209, 243
Ogul, Morris S., 18, 19
oil, 115
O'Neil, Michael, 215, 231, 232, 271
O'Neill, Thomas P., Jr., 107, 135, 138–39, 140, 141, 152, 165, 173, 174, 214, 215, 216, 217, 219, 225, 228, 235, 236, 259
Operation Shamrock, 63–64, 74
Osborn, Howard J., 149
Ottaway, David, 256
oversight, 12, 19, 19n

Paisley, John A., 114
Panama Canal treaties, 106, 131
Pastore, John, 27–28
Patton, Lori, 198, 199
Pauling, Linus, 72
Pearl Harbor, 2, 4, 23, 93
Pentagon Papers, 139
Permanent Subcommittee on Investigations (Senate), 72

Pforzheimer, Walter, 150, 174
Philippines, 254
Pike, Otis, 10, 14, 53, 54, 67, 138,
    140, 142, 143, 146, 147, 153–58,
    160, 161–62, 164, 167, 169, 170,
    171, 172, 175, 176, 177, 178, 179,
    180, 184, 185, 186, 187, 189, 192,
    196, 197, 198, 201, 202, 208, 212,
    216, 226
Pike Committee, 10–11, 43, 51, 57,
    78–79, 83, 125, 214, 215, 216, 222,
    220, 221, 228, 232, 233, 238, 239,
    242, 250, 261; establishment of, 135–
    37; evaluation of, 211–13; final re-
    port, 205–11; internal relations, 160–
    65; leadership of chairman, 153–58;
    public hearings, 191–205; recruit-
    ment of members, 137–46; relations
    with executive branch, 175–87; rela-
    tions with House, 168–71; relations
    with press, 187–90; relations with
    Senate, 53–55, 171–72; staff, 165,
    167–68
plausible deniability, 70, 196, 197
Poindexter, John, 260, 264
Polk, James, 2, 280
polygraphs, 49, 128
Portugal, 181, 193, 195, 210
President's Foreign Intelligence Advi-
    sory Board (PFIAB), 79
Price, Melvin, 236
Project Minaret, 74
Pueblo, 140, 153

quality of analysis, 91
Quanbeck, Alton, 47
Quayle, J. Danforth (Dan), 97
Quie, Albert, 203

Ramparts, 74
RCA, 74
Reagan, Ronald, 27n, 110, 111, 112,
    126, 132, 224, 239, 252, 253, 258,
    259, 260, 261, 262, 263, 266–67,
    270, 272
Rectanus, Earl, 204–5
Reston, James, 182
Reuters, 164

Rhodes, John, 138, 142, 186, 215, 218,
    220, 221
Richard, Eric, 56, 63, 66
Rivers, L. Mendel, 7–8
Robinson, J. Kenneth, 222, 223, 224,
    230, 233, 236, 245, 248
Rockefeller, Nelson, 10, 27, 58, 59
Rockefeller Commission, 27, 42, 56,
    58, 68–69, 79, 154, 176, 277
Roe, Robert A., 257
Rogers, William, 202
Rogovin, Mitchell, 33, 66, 71, 143,
    154, 157, 164, 175, 176, 177, 202
Roosevelt, Franklin D., 41
Rose, Charles, 230, 232
Rossiter, Clinton, 279–80
Rostow, Walt, 194
Roth, William, 100, 131
Rowe, Gary Francis, 66–67
Rules and Administration Committee
    (Senate), 82
Rules Committee (House), 141, 163, 170
Rules Committee (Senate), 6
Rumsfeld, Donald, 184, 186
Russell, Richard, 6–7, 50, 60, 277
Ryan, Leo J., 143

Safire, William, 65
SALT I, 181, 183, 200, 201, 202, 210
SALT II, 96, 100, 106, 115, 131
Saltonstall, Leverett, 6
Savimbi, Jonas, 258
Schlesinger, Arthur M., Jr., 204, 267
Schlesinger, James, 26, 63, 148, 149,
    150, 231
Schmitt, Harrison, 91
Schneider, Rene, 69
Schorr, Daniel, 136, 170, 188, 189–90,
    191, 207
Schwarz, Frederick A. O., Jr., 35, 36,
    37, 39, 41, 43, 44, 45–49, 53, 59,
    60, 62, 64, 66, 68, 75–77, 84
Schweicker, Richard, 31, 32, 43, 52, 56
Scott, Hugh, 31–33, 34, 85, 101
Scott, William, 235
Scowcroft, Brent, 184
secretary of defense (SOD), 3–4, 191,
    195, 244, 258

select committee, 18, 28, 85, 92, 138, 212, 215, 217, 253, 278
Select Committee on Ethics (Senate), 255
Senate Select Committee on Intelligence, 211, 214, 215, 224, 232, 237, 244, 246, 249, 251, 252; budget oversight, 115–19; covert action oversight, 119–23; establishment of, 82–85; evaluation of, 131–33; internal relations, 99–102; leadership of chairmen, 93–99; legislation, 123–29; 1985–1986, 253–57; 1987–1989, 267–70, 272–73; nominations and reports, 129–31; recruitment of members, 85–93; relations with clientele groups, 114–15, 241; relations with executive branch, 108–12; relations with House, 107–8, 236–37; relations with press, 112–14, 240; relations with Senate, 105–7; staff, 102–5
Senate Select Committee to Study Governmental Operations with Respect to Intelligence. *See* Church Committee
Shaba, 106
Sharer, Ralph, 131
Shultz, George, 224
Simmons, Robert, 104
Smith, Hedrick, 273
Smith, Margaret Chase, 6
Snodgrass, Chuck, 243–45
Socialist Workers Party, 198, 199, 210
Sorensen, Theodore, 47, 130
Soviet Union, 4, 73, 96, 113, 115, 131, 177, 179, 200, 201, 202, 210, 242, 248, 254–55, 256
space, 91
Spokesman Books, 191, 207
Staats, Elmer, 192
Stafford, Robert, 85
Stanton, James V., 141, 146, 152, 153, 160, 162, 164, 169, 173, 183, 188, 195, 196
Stennis, John, 6, 14, 27, 31, 83, 151
Stevenson, Adlai E., III, 91
Stokes, Louis, 236, 270, 271
Stratton, Samuel, 143, 168

Stump, Bob, 222, 230
Sultan of Brunei, 259
Symington, Stuart, 6, 27, 31

Taiwan Relations Act, 106
Taubman, Philip, 15, 113, 240
terrorism, 73
Thornburgh, Richard, 165
Thurmond, Strom, 85
Time, 113, 247
Tower, John, 32, 36, 41, 42, 43, 44, 52, 53, 58, 63, 65, 66, 70, 75, 83, 94, 253
Tower Commission, 253, 258–60, 263, 277
toxic agents, 69, 71, 171
Treen, David, 142, 143, 153, 160, 163, 200, 216
Trujillo, Rafael, 69, 70
Truman, Harry S., 2–3, 40
Turner, Stansfield, 14, 110–11, 123, 130, 214, 236, 239

Udall, Morris, 174, 234

Vance, Cyrus, 111
Vardys, V. Stanley, 18
Vietnam, 9, 37, 134, 139, 141, 193, 194, 194n, 210, 225, 248, 249, 266
Village Voice, 14, 136, 170, 183, 190, 191
Vinson, Carl, 7, 277

Wallop, Malcolm, 89, 91, 100, 116, 118–19, 128, 254
Walters, Vernon, 149
Warren, Earl, 26
Warren Commission, 26, 49
Washington, George, 1, 2
Washington Post, 15, 19, 52, 67, 71, 113, 114, 174, 182, 189, 240, 247, 256, 261, 267
Washington Times, 255
Watergate, 9, 25, 32, 57, 61, 134, 139, 148, 149, 150, 260, 262
Ways and Means Committee (House), 17
Weatherman, 109

Webster, Daniel, 280
Webster, William, 267, 273
Weicker, Lowell P., Jr., 31, 144, 165
Weinberger, Casper, 224
Weiss, Theodore, 229
Welch, Richard, 64, 82–83, 187, 189, 214, 233
Western Union, 74
Westmoreland, William, 23, 194
Wheare, K. C., 17
Whitehurst, G. William, 222, 230, 233
Whitten, Jamie L., 235–36
Wides, Burton V., 67–68
Wilderotter, James, 57, 184
Willens, Howard, 49

Wilson, Bob, 221, 222
Wilson, Edwin P., 240
Wolf, Louis, 128
Woodward, Bob, 15, 66, 113
Wright, James, Jr., 214–15, 219, 233, 235, 248, 271, 273

Young, C. W. Bill, 222, 230, 233, 236, 245, 248
Young, John, 163, 170
Young, Milton, 83

Zablocki, Clement, 222, 223
Zumwalt, Elmo R., Jr., 23, 201

Congress Oversees the United States Intelligence Community
was designed by Dariel Mayer, composed by G & S Typesetters, Inc., and printed and bound by McNaughton & Gunn, Inc. The book is set in Times Roman with Avant Garde Demi Bold used for display and printed on 50-lb Glatfelter Natural.